# INTERACTIVE DISTANCE LEARNING IN PREK-12 SETTINGS

# INTERACTIVE DISTANCE LEARNING IN PREK–12 SETTINGS
## A Handbook of Possibilities

*Jan M. Yates*

LIBRARIES
U N L I M I T E D
A Member of the Greenwood Publishing Group

Westport, Connecticut • London

LIBRARIES UNLIMITED
A Member of Greenwood Publishing Group, Inc.
88 Post Road West
Westport, CT 06881
1-800-225-5800
www.lu.com

ISBN 1-56308-820-7

# Contents

# Acknowledgments

I would like to thank the following:

- Microsoft for the use of screen snapshots. The use of Microsoft screen snapshots is provided under its copyright permissions at http://www.microsoft.com/permission/copyrgt/cop-img .htm#ScreenShot.

- Dr. Thomas MacFarland, for providing sections on evaluation (Chapter 7) and for his suggestions and support.

- Courtney and Lauren Roderick, for assisting with materials and for their support.

- April Larrabee, for assisting with proofing, manuscript preparation, technical skills, and suggestions.

# Preface

Everyday I see evidence that the economics of education and the workplace are changing. In times when the word "training" can be a deleted budget line item, I know that we have to prepare our citizenry to transition to new learning modalities. Face-to-face teaching is expensive in time, energy, and effort. Life's personal and political complications increasingly force us to do more, with less—and do it quickly, in short squeezes of time. These changes take away many of our learning options. We need to be able to learn when we have the time to access instruction. "Just-in-time" learning is a reality.

On the positive side, we have more learning opportunities, due to the daily increases and developments in technology that allow us to explore data and information to develop knowledge in new ways. Postsecondary education is applying and researching the uses of distance education with stand-alone courses and by blending distance learning aspects with traditional courses. The blending of these circumstances of time and place limitations, along with technological developments, make distance learning both a solution and a requirement for many of us. The problem is that are we are not preparing our PreK–12 teachers and students to use distance learning technologies at the rate that is necessary for them to become, and transition into, distance learners at the postsecondary and workplace levels. We need to expose teachers and students to these technologies now.

Because I work with busy PreK–12 teachers, technologists, and media specialists, I realize that many of them are savvy enough to know how to pick up on an idea or resource and implement it into the classroom. This handbook is an attempt to provide a collection of those resources and a compilation of ideas and suggestions. Though it could be a textbook or companion to a textbook, I have purposely tried to present ideas as though I were collaborating with a beginning student or colleague, in a conversational and helpful tone. It is true that many of these resources can be used by teachers who are experienced in using distance learning technologies, but my goal is to address beginning classroom teachers and veteran teachers who have not yet incorporated distance learning technologies into their classrooms.

If you are a teacher who has already incorporated interactive distance learning technologies, this handbook will help to broaden your outlook on how distance learning applications can be made. Often, we get so busy that we may miss a distance learning opportunity or overlook a basic resource that would be very helpful. This handbook attempts to pull together those basic resources that can also be useful to teachers who already incorporate distance learning. And, if you are ever approached by a colleague who comes to you and asks for help with getting started with distance learning activities, you can share this handbook until you have time to provide personalized attention.

In the two short years since I began thinking about this book, there have been tremendous improvements in PreK–12 networks. Most schools can support online connections so that at least one teacher and class can work with Internet distance learning technologies. However, this does not mean that there is an online computer in each classroom. Further, the PreK–12 networks are still going down, with no in-school technician to get things moving along again. For this reason, it is important to consider a variety of interactive distance learning technologies. Teachers and students can still work on developing skills to use in distance learning, without being online.

An additional observation during the last two years has been how learning media, and the companies that support learning media, have increasingly transitioned into Web-based delivery formats. This evolving delivery model does not require teachers to be as concerned as they were just a few years ago about the different types of equipment used to deliver distance learning. Accordingly, this handbook places a heavier emphasis on the use of Web-based interactive distance learning technologies.

During the research and development of this handbook, it was apparent that two major limitations apply to compiling text on the topic of distance learning technologies in the PreK–12 setting. The first limitation relates to the number of resources that can be included. There is an overwhelming body of literature, in a variety of formats, that applies to distance learning technologies. Even though all attempts were made to include those that were most universal to the educational profession for PreK–12 students and teachers, it is possible, and quite probable, that some were missed for this edition. However, I will continue to collect and compile further additions on this topic.

I have used references that are fairly accessible, especially those included in *Edupage*, which I recommend you begin reading for up-to-date information on distance learning and technology. (If you're in need of a French, Hungarian, Korean, or Portuguese version of *Edupage*, read about where to find it in a Learning Possibility in Chapter 6.) Some of the articles from *The Chronicle of Higher Education* were accessed online through a subscription account. If you are seeking one of these articles, you may need to make the request through a full-text database or through your librarian. Other book titles that I have referenced are readily accessible through public and university libraries or through interlibrary loan.

The second limitation, as all of you who work with online resources can verify, is that the mere existence (not to mention location) of online items can change hourly. Even though all sources were checked just before this handbook manuscript was submitted, it is inevitable that some of the Web addresses will have changed by the time that you search for the source. Knowing this, I have included as much information on each site as practical, making sure to list the title and describe the source, where possible.

Web addresses have been presented within the text, so that they are easily accessible to the reader when needed. Included with these addresses are titles. These titles will enable the reader to track down the source should the given Web address become unavailable. How? Try searching the title or URL online through a search engine. Search engines usually provide direction to the new URL. Alternatively, search for some of the keywords in the title, or try "backing down" the path of the Web address by keying in the address and then moving backward through the address (directory by directory, designated by a " / ") until you hit on a functioning site. When you enter that site, look for a logical heading that can take you into the source in a different way, or try searching that Web page for the title or related keywords. By using some of these strategies (and sharing these strategies with your students and colleagues), you will become a super sleuth in tracking down online sources. All efforts will be made to keep the accompanying Web page (http://users.adelphia.net/~idlearning) up-to-date. If you find any changes that need to be made to the sources, please e-mail me through that site.

WARNING: In every PreK–12 school district, the teacher is responsible for following school board policy. Before you visit online sites or download software, review your district's Acceptable Use Policy (AUP) on online use, especially as it relates to using software with students and downloading software on any district-owned computer. You, the teacher, are responsible for your online behavior and the online behavior of your students when they are under your supervision.

Every effort was made to include sites that are general and appropriate for PreK–12 students and teachers. However, some of these sites may have pop-up boxes or links to other sites that are not considered appropriate by your school or district. As with any medium, it is critical that you preview and evaluate each site for appropriateness before visiting it with your students or demonstrating it for your colleagues.

I have incurred no virus, worm, or other similar problems while downloading a wealth of freeware or shareware from the sites included in this handbook, but I urge you to take all precautions in checking files for problems before installing any program on your or your school's computer. Update your virus and security software before attempting the downloading of any of these programs or files.

Finally, resources and vendor information listed are not intended to be exhaustive. These listings are intended to get the reader started on investigating the materials and services available. Further research and evaluation, by telephone and by Web, will be needed before you make a final decision on which products to use with your students.

# Chapter 1

# An Introduction to the Use of Interactive Distance Learning Technologies

*"And the student said, 'When can we go online again? Do you have any more of those WebQuest things that we can use today?' and I said 'Sure, we will try some more WebQuests tomorrow.' My students are really getting a lot out of distance learning!"*

**O**ften, I have lively conversations like this with PreK–12 teachers who enjoy teaching, who are excited to get to school and see their students each morning, and who are still interested in the subjects they teach. These teachers understand their course curricula, have a handle on classroom discipline, and express a high level of satisfaction with the career they have chosen; yet they are still interested in further expanding their—and their students'—involvement in learning. To these teachers, I can suggest no better way of getting involved with exploring the many options of expanding and increasing participation in classroom learning activities than by using interactive distance learning technologies. This handbook will provide background on distance learning, professional support, and tips on how interactive distance learning technologies and activities can be brought into today's contemporary classroom.

Have you noticed that each time you open a newspaper, a magazine, turn on the television, or even listen to the radio, you see or hear WWW this or WWW that? For as much interest as the World Wide Web and the Internet have generated among educators, we must ask if the use of the Web is the only modality for distance learning. Can you possibly remember how, in the 1940s, radio was going to be the modality of learning for distance education? Or, can you recall that television, as a distance learning modality, was going to revolutionize K–12 education in the 1960s? After you have finished reading this handbook, perhaps you will agree that the use of all of today's technologies empower the teacher and the learner to use modalities that encourage learning at any time and in any place.

Separate from specific media, what are "interactive distance learning technologies" and how can a motivated educator use these to improve teaching? If this general question interests you and addresses your desire for further professional development, this handbook offers many tips that will benefit you and your students.

**Interactive distance learning technology** is an umbrella term that describes the many technologies that bring learning experiences into the classroom from outside sources. Distance learning resources can be in the form of a delayed time format (a postcard, an audiotape, a videotape, a Web page, or an e-mail message), a real-time interactive communication activity (a phone call, a two-way video presentation, on-line chats and instant messengers, or virtual learning areas), or other formats that may be in use by the time you read this handbook.

A common misconception today is that interactive distance learning activities limit you to the Internet and online utilities. Quite the opposite, interactive distance learning technologies are available in many varieties. No one doubts that the distance learning resources are many, and that you are probably interested in several of these resources, but getting started with distance learning resources may sometimes seem to be just another chore that you, a busy educator, have not found time to research and explore. Through this handbook, I will try to present distance learning opportunities to you in small snippets that can be squeezed into your busy day. First, though, let's investigate the benefits of interactive distance learning activities.

Distance learning activities and interaction can connect your classroom-based students to:

- homebound students,

- students in the classroom next door,

- the media center down the hall,

- a peer student in a similar school in another neighborhood,

- a subject expert in a community college classroom in another town,

- a military training officer on an aircraft carrier in the middle of the Pacific Ocean,

- a government resource person in Washington, D.C.,

- or, possibly, a university professor in another country.

Interactive distance learning technologies can be used in almost any spot on the globe and can incorporate many different resources.

No doubt you have followed technology developments that are described daily in all media formats, and you are aware that, beyond today's commercial and commonly accessed Internet, more research is being conducted in using even faster and more powerful online sources, such as Internet2 and high-speed communication networks. This new technology will allow the use of educational applications such as simulations, which require tremendous amounts of online bandwidth resources and speed. As an educator, you are also aware that today's research, even though it may only relate to universities and research groups, will eventually find its way into many of tomorrow's PreK–12 classroom activities. Because of our high growth rate of information and technological applications, educators understand that even though curricula may change, we must teach students how to process and learn the content in meaningful ways. In view of the growth of information, it is projected that the number of e-mail messages sent in one day will reach 35 billion by the year 2005 (*Edupage*, 13 October 2000).

Until the last decade, most PreK–12 learning activities had focused on visual presentations in print (blackboards, whiteboards, filmstrips, textbooks, overhead transparencies, etc.), in motion (filmstrip, 16mm movies, videotape, etc.), or in audio formats (record, reel-to-reel tape, cassette tape, etc.). Then, electronic presentations came into use during the 1990s, transforming educational presentations throughout the world. Educators have also witnessed a change in students, who are now using electronic formats. Some of us have watched older students and teachers struggle to learn electronic applications after their primary school years, when basic reading, writing, and mathematical skills were first introduced. These students learned about electronic applications as separate, or supplemental, activities, as opposed to students who learned and used electronic applications that were integrated into their daily, basic skills instruction. The students who used electronic applications, often as part of a game, to "learn how to learn" have assimilated these skills in such a way that the use of electronic applications is transparent to the learning process.

Students who are using technology throughout the learning process are already on track for developing cognitive skills that will be required for a lifetime of learning. Regardless of how many times a student will be expected to change jobs during a career, rapid changes (either with the technology or the job itself) will force workers to be responsible for their own training and retraining within each position. Think of the many new skills that you have learned since you entered your teaching career. For example, how did you learn word processing? How many skills (such as online searching) have you taught yourself since you earned your initial teaching certificate? How many more skills do you expect to teach yourself before the end of your educational career?

Here's an idea: Ask your colleagues to help you think of other training possibilities that will be required of you before your retirement. What are the traits that will best support this training? For example, scanning the current educational literature keeps teachers informed of trends and developments. Is this a trait that you already possess, or is it one that you wish to develop?

Fortunately, or unfortunately, depending upon your viewpoint, there is no reason to expect a decline in the rate of change in our society. Thus, educators must continue to assess not only how to provide students with the best instruction in content areas, but they must also assess how to provide students with lifelong learning skills that go beyond content, skill, and technical areas. This emphasis on teaching lifelong learning skills, or processes, supports an important transfer and construction of learning, one that is probably taking place in your school today. As schools prepare students for their future roles in society, they need to provide students with distance learning experiences because these capabilities will be expected by industry (*Edupage*, 28 August 2000). For example, computer lab technologists often teach beginning word processing students how to use introductory word processing packages. These technologists know if they stress the word processing concepts and processes (blocking, cutting and pasting, formatting, etc.) and how they apply to all word processing packages, then students will begin to realize that concepts can be transferred as they construct their own learning environments. Thus, students begin to learn how to learn in an increasingly technological environment, and colleges will be able to safely assume that students are entering with prior experience with distance learning (*Edupage*, 3 November 2000).

The question of what type of learning model to follow, as it applies to distance learning, is still being considered. For example, should distance learning software packages mimic the visual classroom metaphor (Anglin 2001)? Or, would students benefit from a transfer learning model, which may transition into a tutorial learning model, in which students receive more personalized learning experiences that promote mastery learning (Bork 2001)? In a traditional tutorial model, a student works under the guidance of a tutor and is provided access to extensive curricular materials that are collectively referred to as tutorials. Beyond making the case for moving to the tutorial learning model, Bork states that distance learning will make learning more affordable for the world's population. Echoing the concepts of individualized learning and the global aspects of evolving teaching models, Oakley and Stevens (2000) suggest that we will even be able to eventually match student learning styles with teacher learning styles, due to the increased availability of teachers through telelearning.

By increasing our awareness of the need to provide students with the opportunity to transfer and construct concepts in a technological environment, we can have an impact on our students' futures. Learning how to learn and emphasizing the teaching of strong cognitive skills will provide students with invaluable learning techniques and strategies. Interactive distance learning technologies support the teaching of this transfer and construction of learning by offering opportunities that support learning how to learn. Granted, there are still those students in the pipeline that are not very interested in interactive or self-directed learning. After all, passive listening only requires sitting back and absorbing content, letting the instructor do the work. Group work? Projects? These are not for the passive learner, but the day of passive learning, both within and outside of industry, are at a philosophical fork in the road of education. Many of us believe that students also need to develop the abilities to collaborate and problem-solve within groups (Ben-Jacob, Levin, and Ben-Jacob 2000).

Industry demands that workers be self-directed. Training may not be available for the employee that needs to learn a new skill. That employee may be directing her/his own learning. Therefore, how can we give our students a "leg up" for sound employment in a workplace that will be increasingly demanding and self-directed? You've got it—by teaching students to use interactive distance learning technologies.

Although there will always be a need for the live, face-to-face, in-person, student-teacher learning model, trends suggest that this model, as a dominant model of education, may be in decline. While many educators, currently in-service, have never taken a course presented through a distance learning model, this will not be true for the next generation (or even next year's graduating class) of teachers. Student and teacher familiarity with distance learning opportunities and technologies is increasing. Thus, it becomes a logical progression that educational institutions will increase the use of technology and distance learning models in order to decrease time and place limitations related to the face-to-face learning model. Many educators already realize the need for instruction using distance learning technologies as a way to expand current learning and to teach students to learn in the future. If you also realize this need, you may be asking, "What can I do to increase distance learning technology use in my classroom?" and "How should I begin?"

To the busy educator, this handbook is designed to provide you with the basics of interactive distance learning technologies—enough background content to keep you informed, but not too much to be overly technical. You will read about different models and implementations of distance learning and supporting technologies that promote a common understanding of these applications and their terminology. Most importantly, to the classroom teacher, this handbook provides a wide range of practical examples, tips, and sources that will help you begin to plan, coordinate, and implement interactive distance learning activities in the PreK–12 classroom. Teachers new to distance learning will explore and design distance learning experiences that will increase student interest and interaction in the classroom.

Included in this handbook are enough suggestions to whet your distance learning appetite and get you started with your own explorations and interactions. Ideas for creative ways to involve students and members of the PreK–12 learning community are provided, but you, the reader, have to supply two things: (1) an interest in finding out about interactive distance learning technologies, and (2) an openness to the idea that learning activities can be presented in many forms. You and I would probably agree that the one perfect method of instruction has not been discovered yet—however with distance learning technologies, we have a better chance of exploring multiple possibilities available to us today.

PreK–12 school administrators, curriculum coordinators, educational technologists, media specialists, and teachers who wish to expand curriculum offerings and training activities through distance learning will find this handbook to be a jumping-off point that helps educators to plan and generate effective ideas. You may even wish to share this handbook as you continue your supportive role of introducing other teachers to distance education.

Most PreK–12 students in this country are engaged in campus-based, structured learning environments. Even with the increase in home-based education, the vast majority of U.S. youth will continue to be school campus based, in a traditional, nine-month, Monday through Friday learning environment for many years to come. By no means, however, is the school campus-based classroom the only place where learning occurs, and, certainly, students learn far more than the direct recitations of content that their teacher might provide. This handbook is designed for the motivated teacher who works with these PreK–12 individuals, and who wants to bring outside resources and positive influences into the learning environment of today's youth. Many of the activities that will be suggested in this handbook are campus based, but many of the activities will also be for students as they learn outside the classroom—but under some degrees of guidance and control of their classroom teacher. With this background, let's look at the topics that will be covered in this handbook.

Chapter 2, Background of Interactive Distance Learning Technologies, covers the history, benefits, and challenges of distance learning. The chapter concludes with an operational definition of distance learning, but by the time you finish this handbook, you may have another definition of distance learning that better fits your campus and learning environment. Below are a few examples of the topics that will be covered in Chapter 2.

## History

- When you discuss the American Civil War, would it be interesting for your students to know that President Lincoln used distance learning technologies, as they were available during his era, to become a lawyer?

- Almost a century before Lincoln was president, which educational modality was used by George Washington as a youngster? Did George Washington ever attend a colonial college?

- Did interactive distance learning only begin during the past few years, with the acceptance of the Internet by the public?

- How will knowing the history of distance learning help students expand their own abilities to become independent learners?

## Benefits

- If you accept the premise that today's youth are increasingly exposed to a global, interconnected network of information, media, music, and values, how can a motivated teacher channel this exposure into a positive learning experience for students?

- What can students gain from interactive distance learning and how will this help them develop into productive citizens in a "wired" global economy?

- How many times can you, the teacher, present your subject matter in the same way, to the same students, without suffering from occupational burnout? How can new methods of subject delivery inspire you to pursue new interests and activities in your own subject area?

- Think of the number of times that you wished that you could quickly meet with a professional peer to share and communicate ideas. If you can imagine being a teacher in a high school of 3,500 students, teaching in one of many portable classrooms, away from a main building, can you think of a better way to contact a peer teacher on a rainy day than through a distance learning technology?

- Separate from self-motivation and self-actualization, can school systems benefit from, and reward, teachers who pursue new teaching technologies?

- The day of the "June Cleaver" room mother, who bakes cookies and cupcakes and helps Miss Landers, is over for most of us. Just like a teacher's, the working day of most parents is increasingly long and stressful. Can you think of how distance learning technologies can offer a variety of ways to get parents involved and into the classroom, even if their involvement is through the form of distance media?

- Along these same lines of getting parents involved, what better contribution could today's teacher make to a student's life than showing both the student and parent how to communicate with each other in a medium that is enjoyed by the student and convenient to the parent?

## Challenges

- As we pull more complex media into the classroom, we must increase time for planning and budgets for training.

- Part of the challenge that can never be forgotten, in a school that does not have a bottomless checkbook, is how can we afford to purchase technologies? What are some creative ways that will help us to overcome financial limitations?

- Assuming that you have conquered the challenges of planning and purchasing, who will install the items (hardware and software) that you need to bring technology into the classroom? Are you willing to acquire the technical expertise that you need to implement technologies, or do you have in-school support (e.g., school personnel or school volunteers) that will get you on your learning way?

- Beyond the initial demands of installing equipment and software, have you thought of who will be helping you to keep current with repairs and upgrades? You may have the capabilities of completing some repair and upgrade tasks yourself, either now or with a little training, but how can you get support with the more complex repairs and upgrades?

- Now that you have taken care of the nuts and bolts of distance learning, how are you going to decide how to implement distance learning technologies into your classroom? Who will show you how to develop an activity that matches your curriculum or state guidelines? Are there any models that you can follow to apply current learning tasks to your curriculum? Do any of the techniques that you learned in your educational methods courses still apply to today's classroom? What are the available resources that can support you in these activities?

## *Today's Definition of Distance Learning*

If the activities related to distance learning comprise a moving target, why do you need to be concerned about how anyone defines distance learning anyway? Too often in education, we allow definitions and terms to become meaningless "education-ese" that cease to hold any communicative value. Because you are taking a new, positive path in your educational career, make sure that you can explain what you are introducing and pursuing through your distance learning activities. Today's definition of distance learning must be a flexible one that reflects how you choose to implement distance learning in your classroom. Ultimately, it is your definition that will impact how you bring distance learning into the classroom. Chapter 2 will guide you through these areas of concern.

In Chapter 3, models of interactive distance learning are described as occurring in either delayed-time or real-time. If these two descriptions are new for you, simply remember that a letter mailed through the U.S. Postal Service is an example of a delayed-time communication. A thirty-minute telephone call with your friend, on the other hand, is an example of a real-time communication. An e-mail message is a delayed-time communication. However, active keying online through America Online's Instant Messenger is a real-time communication activity.

Why is this distinction important to your classroom learning activities? Delayed-time technologies and activities (audio recording, CD-ROM, correspondence, course package, electronic mail, taped television course, video recording, Web tutorial, etc.) may be easier to work into your classroom schedule, but real-time technologies and activities (audio conference, audio bridge, chatroom, electronic classroom, radio, satellite link, television, videoconference, etc.) provide a high level of spontaneity in campus-based learning. Both real-time and delayed-time modalities can have meaningful applications.

As outlined in Chapter 4, interactive distance learning settings are many and varied. For most of you, the setting will be that of a campus-based PreK–12 classroom. Whether you are teaching in a private or public school, most young students in this country still go to a traditional campus-based school. As you will learn throughout this handbook, there are many appropriate distance learning opportunities for these "traditional" students.

However, there are an increasingly large number of students who do not regularly attend a full-day, traditional classroom, whether due to parental wishes, court order, geography, or special needs. Do you see how both the independence and isolation of these students provide an opportunity for the appropriate use of distance learning modalities?

As part of the global economy and the large role of the United States in commerce and military activities, there are thousands of U.S. PreK–12 students who attend school at an international location. These students are prime candidates for distance learning modalities, whether for their own educational needs or as unique peers of their U.S., traditional, classroom-based counterparts. Imagine the opportunity of opening your students' eyes to the experiences of these students through electronic mail, digital photographs posted on a Web page, student-produced videotapes incorporated into an online travelogue, or any other of the endless opportunities available to today's technologically astute student.

Considering postsecondary students, America's colleges and universities seem to be in a frantic race as they attempt to offer courses and even entire programs through the use of distance learning technologies. For many years, Florida universities have offered a technology-based program for engineering students who are working in that field (FEEDS, Florida Engineering Education Delivery System). Similarly, Florida State University offers a preservice training program, accredited by the American Library Association, which trains media specialists. Considering the globalization of distance learning, the *United Kingdom's Open University* (http://www.open.ac.uk/frames.html), headquartered in London, England, planned to offer a baccalaureate program (based in Delaware) for U.S. students. This level of international outreach is enhanced by distance learning technologies as we work together, worldwide, to develop a strong workforce. So, for the educator who wishes to pursue in-service training, as well as the beginning student who needs preservice training, postsecondary distance learning opportunities abound!

Demonstrating their recognition of the importance of distance learning technologies and the ability to support their members, many professional organizations have created online learning opportunities for professional development. An example of a site that offers training in several skills, including e-mail use and online searching, is the American Library Association's ICONnect. Recognizing that its members have different learning levels, ICONnect "workshops" provide e-mail-delivered lessons that guide learners through activities and direct them to online sites where they can practice and develop new skills. Have you checked the Web site of your professional organization to explore the ways in which it supports professional development in distance learning?

Other individuals and groups, some for-profit and some not-for-profit, have used online environments to deliver learning opportunities. Whether you are earning a degree through "Cybercollege" or are paying to participate in noncredit, e-mail-directed learning experiences, or are training through WebCT-offered activities, you have the luxury of designing your own training plan. Sufficient learning opportunities, whether discovered through listserv, journal, or other professional recommendations, are available to you at no, or nominal, cost.

So let's say that you now have a better understanding of what distance learning technologies are, how they can be applied, who can benefit from them, and where they can be found. The big question still looms: How can I bring these interactive, distance learning technologies into my classroom? Fortunately, because I have never encountered a teacher who was at a loss for creative classroom ideas, it is inconceivable that you will be any different. As a matter of fact, because I am so convinced that it is impossible for you to not develop ideas on how to incorporate distance learning activities into your classroom, you are invited to submit all quandaries to idlearning@adelphia.net. But before you write, be sure that you have worked through the developmental processes of:

1. Consulting online resources (Have you followed a listserv on your subject to find out what other teachers are doing in your subject area? Have you located a Web page on your topic that provides Web sites and ideas?)

2. Consulting other teachers (Is there an organization in your area that focuses on technology? Have you attended any of the organization's meetings to hear how others are applying distance learning technologies? Are there state or national conferences for your subject areas? Can you attend their meetings? Have you asked your administrator for direction on how to pursue these meetings? Do you have professional development days in your district so that you can attend conferences or meetings?)

3. Consulting district personnel (What are the employees doing in your district to provide in-service training opportunities? Can you call upon them to provide suggestions for training in your subject areas?)

4. Reading professional literature (Which professional journal or magazine addresses your subject area? What are the teaching tips and suggestions provided? How can you take these tips and suggestions and expand upon them, technologically and globally?)

5. Making substitutions (i.e., think of an existing distance learning activity and substitute your subject matter, grade level, etc.).

Chapter 4 will encourage you to initiate many of these activities in your classroom.

Beyond seeking ideas of how to weave distance learning technologies into your classroom, Chapter 5, Interactive Distance Learning Technology Applications, also provides information on how to identify these applications for teachers, administrators, and staff. Yes, all segments of the school community can benefit from distance learning opportunities, both through self-actualization and through practice using the technologies themselves. However, a benefit of encouraging the entire school population to participate in distance learning opportunities is that a pervasive understanding of a distance learning curriculum develops.

Speaking of looking for ideas on how to make use of distance learning technologies, have you ever thought of consulting your educational technologist? (In some districts, the technologist may only be fourteen years old though! Some districts, such as those around Washington, D.C., are training students to be technologists. The benefits include district cost savings and the development of employable skills for the students [*Edupage*, 14 May 2001]. In Boca Raton, Florida, middle school students will soon be attending a "high-tech" middle school where they will be taking courses to prepare them for future technology jobs. In addition, their school will be located on the site where the IBM PC was created [*Palm Beach Post*, 4 January 2002].)

Chapter 6 emphasizes that support for interactive distance learning activities by the educational technologist is essential for teachers, administrative staff, students, and even parents, if the school's learning environment is to take full advantage of this teaching modality. For those of you who are fortunate enough to benefit from the proactive leadership of an educational organization that realizes that PreK–12 schools demand the services of technical experts who are sophisticated in technology training and experience, you know that the educational technologist is an integral part of the school's distance learning team. Whether providing hardware, network, software, or other technical support, the educational technologist fulfills an all-encompassing role of not only supporting the learning activity, but, in many cases, adjusting all of the "bells and whistles" to make it happen. There are many resources, such as the EDUNET listserv (send a subscribe message to info@schools.net.au or visit the link http://www.myinternet.com.au/), that support the educational technologist who is dedicated to assisting the classroom teacher, administrator, or staff person.

The educational technologist can direct you to many resources and, at the same time, make recommendations on which resource best matches yours and your students' technological level.

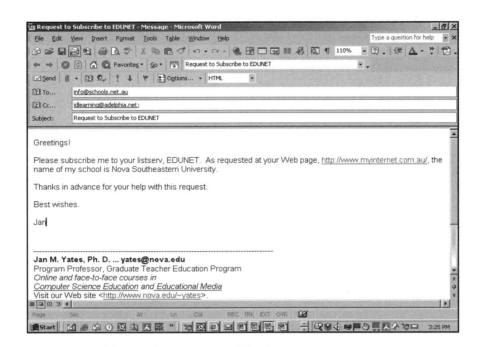

**Subscription message to EDUNET at info@schools.net.au**

In addition to the support of the educational technologist, support for interactive distance learning activities by the school library media specialist is indispensable to the teacher who wishes to plan meaningful learning experiences. *Information Power*, a major initiative of the most recently published joint standards of the American Association of School Librarians (AASL) and the Association for Educational Communication and Technology (AECT), is subtitled *Building Partnerships for Learning*. School library media specialists consider the support of learning to be a partnership within the school by partnering with classroom teachers to plan effective instruction that meets the learning needs of a diverse group of students. The role of the school library media specialist in collaborative planning lends support and encouragement to the teacher who is seeking new and creative ideas. And, because of this professional commitment to the support of the planning process, the school library media specialist is willing to provide professional guidance in the acquisition of resource materials that support excellence in curriculum development for distance learning activities.

Beyond the district personnel, educational technologists, and school library media specialists, who are the other school community members who can provide support for your distance learning activities? Your administrators, paraprofessionals, maintenance staff, state and federal educational personnel, and parents might be able to provide assistance, encouragement, and technological support.

Along with this support, assistance, and encouragement comes the expectation that distance learning activities are improving educational outcomes in the PreK–12 school environment. Yet, how do we know that these improvements are actually occurring without some form of measurement and evaluation? We do know that one of the areas that is least addressed in education is evaluation. How, you ask, can that be stated, in view of the hours that you spend inputting and averaging grades? It's true that we are very good at evaluating specific student performance, but how often do you consider the outcomes of your teaching, in general? How often do you provide content in different formats? Do you address different learning styles? And, following these varied, presentation formats, do you vary the ways you evaluate student performance? Do your evaluation methods match your delivery methods? The answer is probably, "Not very often." Up until now, you have been trying to become familiar with the technologies first. Now it is time to find effective ways to assess the value and efficiency of the distance learning activities taking place in your classroom.

With any area of instruction, establishing meaningful goals and specific objectives is critical to your classroom success. National curriculum standards and standardized testing have resulted in our trying to squeeze in more content areas into our curriculum than ever before. Because we are trying to accomplish so much more, we have to stay focused on the importance of evaluating all areas of instruction. Why is this a greater concern with distance learning technologies? Staying focused on making sure that we are evaluating the areas of instruction will keep our presentations aimed at the content that we must present to the students. Because of the expansive nature of some learning technologies, especially the World Wide Web, it is easy to get sidetracked from the learning task at hand. For example, how many of you can honestly say that you always log on to the Web, get exactly what you are looking for, and then log off? If you are like most inquisitive teachers, you probably wander over to at least one (if not, five) other sites—and, as an adult, you have self-discipline. Think of the online behavior of your students who may be even more inquisitive and prone to distraction. Therefore, using learning goals and objectives helps us to stay focused on the task at hand and guides us through well-planned instruction.

Part of this need to stay focused relates to establishing the purpose of the instruction. What will your activities accomplish? Will you be trying to develop student appreciation for the subject; will you be making a content presentation and introduction; will the activity be geared for practice or review? The purpose of instruction will determine the types of technology, resources, instructional methods, and evaluative methods used.

As discussed in Chapter 7, the issue of grades and distance learning technologies is important because traditional methods of student evaluation may not transfer easily to the new types of learning tasks. For example, you may have a very good understanding of how to evaluate the writing mechanics of a traditional, five-page term paper, but do you know how to evaluate a student-generated PowerPoint presentation that includes Web-based resource materials, and audio and video clips? Have you considered, and discussed with your colleagues, whether the traditional research methodologies are still applicable to the current presentation formats? Have your grading rubrics been updated to reflect current presentation formats? Are they sufficiently comprehensive to improve student understanding of how performances will be evaluated? Are you grading for substance or style? The whole point is are you actually grading what you think you are grading? Many times, the answer is no. These are just a few of the areas with which many of us are beginning to grapple, but this chapter will at least guide you through some of the questions that you need to ask that will lead you to your decisions.

Evaluation of interactive distance learning activities is especially critical to the continued support of technologies in the classroom. To justify costs, data can demonstrate the positive effects of distance learning activities on learning outcomes. Studies are beginning to demonstrate that distance learning activities have more positive outcomes than traditional activities for some groups. These types of studies are important to in-school administrators, school improvement teams, district personnel, school boards, state and federal legislators, parents, and, ultimately, the citizen-taxpayers who recognize the need to maximize learning potentials, while maintaining (or even reducing) budgets.

You will notice that within this handbook, Web addresses are listed after their Web page titles. Anyone who has had to scavenge for Web addresses in articles will appreciate this practice, one that I encourage you to model for your students. Great efforts have been made to gather resources that will facilitate your involvement with these challenging learning activities. Throughout are references to Internet resources that are particularly valuable, due to quality of content, stability, and broad appeal across many grade levels and disciplines. These Internet resources are also grouped in a Web page (http://users.adelphia.net/~idlearning/). If you can think of any resources that would add to this collection, please submit them to the author (idlearning@adelphia.net).

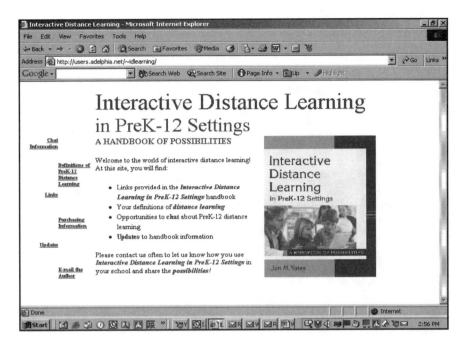

*Interactive Distance Learning in PreK-12 Settings* **Web site:**
**http://users.adelphia.net/~idlearning**

Some current vendors and service providers for distance learning technologies are listed throughout this handbook. Contact information was current as of the date this manuscript went to publication. If you didn't already know, the world of technology is moving, so changes in companies, addresses, telephone numbers, e-mail addresses, and Web addresses are frequent. If you have other vendors or service provider resources that you think would contribute to future editions of this handbook, please submit them to idlearning@adelphia.net.

Definitions of some terms are included in this narrative. You will discover that some terms have different meanings among different institutions and authors. For example, "electronic classroom" at one institution may refer to an actual room that includes different types of equipment, while another institution may use the same term to refer to a software package that supports an online classroom presentation. Just as distance learning technologies are evolving, so are the accepted definitions of many of these terms. Do not hesitate to tailor these definitions to your own unique needs.

Throughout this handbook, references are included for each chapter. Though most of these resources were gathered through online searches of the Educational Resources Information Center's (ERIC) Database, many resources are from popular educational literature to which teachers have free access. Sources were included because of their interest potential. You are encouraged to search the ERIC Database often to keep up with the current trends and changes in distance learning. If you have never taken advantage of the wealth of materials at ERIC, view the *AskERIC Site Tour* for an overview of resources (http://ericir.syr.edu /Search/Site_Tour/).

Now that you have completed the preview of the various sections of this handbook, perhaps you have a sense of the opportunities and complexities that face an educator who wants to bring interactive distance learning opportunities into the classroom. To be brief, why would someone want to go to all of this trouble of bringing interactive distance learning technologies into today's contemporary classroom, when the tried-and-true traditional methods could be continued? Student desires, collegial competition, administrator persuasion, regional accrediting association criteria requirements, parental requests, and employer demands for technologically skilled graduates mandate our collaboration and cooperation with helping students succeed in developing skills within the evolving global economy. Interactive distance learning is one strategy by which you can meet these various expectations and learning opportunities— imagine the possibilities!

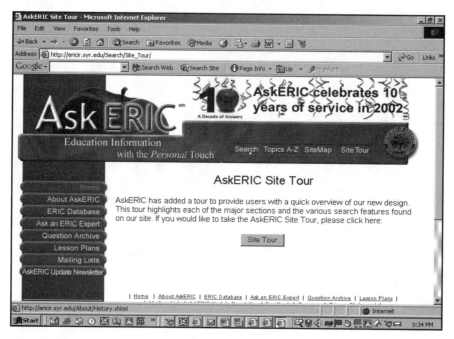

*AskERIC Site Tour* **Web site: http://ericir.syr.edu/Search/Site_Tour**

# *References*

Anglin, Gary J. "Notes on the Special Issue: Distance Education and E-Learning." *The Quarterly Review of Distance Education* 2, no. 1 (2001): 3–4.

Ben-Jacob, Marion G., David S. Levin, and Talia K. Ben-Jacob. "The Learning Environment of the 21st Century." *Educational Technology Review*, no. 13 (2000): 8–12.

Bork, Alfred. "Tutorial Learning for the New Century." *Journal of Science Education and Technology* 10, no. 1 (2001): 57–71.

"Every University Has E-Learning in Its Future," 3 November 2000, *Edupage* (owner-edupage@listserv .educause.edu) (http://www.educause.edu/pub/edupage/edupage.html).

Flannery, Mary Ellen. "District OKs Price for Ex-IBM Building." *Palm Beach Post* (4 January 2002): 3B.

Oakley, Wayne, and Ken Stevens. "TeleLearning." *Education Canada* 40, no. 2 (2000): 32–33, 42.

"Online Learning: The Competitive Edge," 28 August 2000, *Edupage* (owner-edupage@listserv.educause.edu) (http://www.educause.edu/pub/edupage/edupage.html).

"Tech-Savvy Students Offer Schools a Patch," 14 May 2001, *Edupage* (owner-edupage@listserv.educause.edu) (http://www.educause.edu/pub/edupage/edupage.html).

"Ten Billion E-Mails a Day in 2000," 13 October 2000, *Edupage* (owner-edupage@listserv.educause.edu) (http://www.educause.edu/pub/edupage/edupage.html).

# Chapter 2

# Background of Interactive Distance Learning Technologies

Incorporating distance learning technologies into classroom curricula has a fascinating background that closely chronicles changes in culture, history, knowledge, and electronic development. Throughout time, people from all areas of employment experienced and experimented with existing technologies of their day to develop new methods of working and learning that were easier, faster, and more productive. As a result, educators use these experiences and experiments to create easier, faster, more productive, and, hopefully, more enjoyable learning experiences in the classroom. Collectively, these techniques form a rich history of distance learning.

The history of distance learning is important to educators who are interested in discovering how these developments have increased interactions in today's classroom. Realizing that education is evolutionary helps us understand these technological changes in the context of today's classroom-based, teacher-directed educational model.

## Section A. History of Distance Learning

Even though we often overlook the oral tradition of transmitting knowledge from place to place, lecture and oral delivery continue to have important roles in today's education. European cultural history can offer examples of minstrels, who carried the land's news and entertainment before the days of newspapers, radios, televisions, or e-mail messages. African cultures also observed this oral tradition that was passed down by the griot, an oral historian.

## Teaching Possibility

Read the 1943 Newbery Award Winner *Adam of the Road*, by Elizabeth Janet Gray, to elementary students, or share this title with high school English Literature students prior to their reading the *Canterbury Tales*. Ask them to research the oral tradition in their own cultures. Compare the developments, noting the geographical changes and movements. How can they continue the oral tradition by carrying the "news of the day" to other students or to senior citizens?

---

Most societies can provide examples of historical figures that have made noticeable advances because of education. If you travel back in history before schools and learning were so convenient, particularly before the beginning of the Industrial Revolution in the United States, you will confirm that many historical figures did not participate in formal education processes familiar to us today. Instead, they used systems and technologies that, by today's standards, would be viewed as examples of distance learning. Did you think that distance learning was only a modern development?

## Teaching Possibility

Ask your students to select milestone dates in American history. Once these dates have been selected, ask the students "What did classrooms look like during each of these years?" Ask students to research the type of books, media centers, facilities, etc., that would have been dominant in rural and urban areas. Try to find information about the teachers of that time, which students attended school, and what their subjects were. To start, 1776 (a year of agricultural economy), 1865 (the end of the U.S. Civil War and the beginning of a heavy emphasis on the Industrial Revolution in the United States), 1957 (the launch of *Sputnik* and U.S. concern about Soviet dominance of the West and the resulting National Defense Education Act), 1969 (the year of connection of computers that would someday lead to further development and the Internet [*Palm Beach Post*, 26 September 1999, 2A]), 1976 (the introduction of the Apple Computer I by Steve Wozniak [Holzberg 1996, 30]), or, more recently, 2001 (terrorist attacks on the United States and the resulting use of information technology as part of smart bombs, media use of videophones, and cyberterrorism). After this background work has been completed, ask your students to make projections on the future of education. What do they think their schools will be like when they graduate from twelfth grade? How will schools change by the time their children and grandchildren graduate from twelfth grade?

---

Therefore, distance learning may not be quite as contemporary as you think. Distance learning probably began with the first homework assignment during which Plato may have directed Aristotle to practice his oratorical skills (Passey 2000). Actually, distance learning in America may have begun before you probably ever imagined, when Native Americans homeschooled their children in the skills needed for their society. Next, when the early Europeans and Africans came to what they called "the New World," parents and the colonial church/state governments organized home-based learning activities as a way of teaching children to read the Bible, to study other religious texts, and to cipher well enough to complete commercial transactions. Some of the few privileged male children, who lived in more urbanized areas, attended church-run Latin schools that focused on religious studies. In contrast, most females participated in studies at home. Some children in the New World were indentured to employers who provided education only to the extent that the learning served direct vocational purposes. Many rural students also studied at home, when work activities permitted, sometimes with itinerant teachers. The influence of this rural tradition continues today with a summer agricultural work schedule continuing to drive most of our school calendars, even though only a very small percentage of students work on family-owned farms during the summer when schools are dismissed.

Following colonial days, was homeschooling an American development of the 1700s, in which pioneers were forced to educate their children at home because there were not enough children in their community to populate a school? Even if there were enough students, was there enough money to provide a schoolhouse and a teacher? Abraham Lincoln, for example, kept shop near New Salem, Illinois, while he homeschooled himself by reading his law books. He taught himself the law of the land while on the Illinois frontier despite being many miles away from the closest law school.

## *Teaching Possibility*

Ask your students to choose a figure in history and research that figure's educational background. What, how, and where did she or he study? Let students compare the backgrounds of their different figures and design a time line that helps them visualize how these figures learned and attended school. Suggested figures: Louisa May Alcott, George Washington Carver, Thomas Edison, Alexander Hamilton, Abraham Lincoln, Harriet Beecher Stowe, George Washington, Madame C. J. Walker. Students might even recognize the name of Charles Schulz, of Peanuts fame, but they might not know that he was a distance learner, taking a correspondence course for artists from the Art Instruction Schools in Minneapolis (Mills 2000).

The history of distance learning, to date, traces humankind's progression from the crude processes needed to transmit and preserve knowledge to today's digital transmission and preservation of most media. As one millennium has closed and another opened, we can enjoy the transition from an age of prior limitations to an age of unlimited possibilities.

## *Teaching Possibility*

When does a millennium really begin? 2000 or 2001? 3000 or 3001? Ask your students to research the concept of calendars. How were they created? What was the intent of the creators when they established measures of time? Where will you direct your students to search for information on the concept of calendars?

## *Teaching Possibility*

Ask your students to speak with their parents, grandparents, aunts, uncles, or any available family members or friends to find out about their elementary school experiences. Instead of developing a family tree, the students will develop a "learning tree." To keep the activity positive and fun, work with students to develop a list of questions to ask such as: How old were you when you started school? What was your first-grade teacher's name? Can you remember the titles of any of the textbooks you used? What kinds of equipment and media did your teacher use? What was the most exciting thing you learned to do in first grade, besides going to recess and riding the school bus? Students will bring their information back to class to present in a way that you determine is meaningful (e.g., an assembly program; individual, oral presentations; models; database; etc.).

---

Because the creation of time lines is so important in helping students develop a better understanding of any historical event, encourage your students to categorize the events of distance learning through further research. For example, did you know that distance learning has a history of more than a century of expanding learning opportunities throughout the world? The following table presents events that may help you get started with this research.

| Distance Learning Time Line | |
|---|---|
| **Date** | **Event** |
| 1840 | Isaac Pittman offered the first courses in correspondence by using mail to teach shorthand (Smart 1987, 3). |
| 1856 | Toussaint and Langenscheidt used correspondence to teach modern languages in Berlin, Germany (Watkins and Wright 1991, 2). |
| 1862 | The Morrill Act, legislation that made educational opportunities available to citizens throughout each American state (as opposed to limiting the opportunities to only resident students), was passed. As a result, land grant institutions exist today in each state, bringing education to all residents (Smart 1987, 19). |
| 1873 | In Boston, Anna Ticknor provided education for women by creating the Society to Encourage Studies at Home (Watkins and Wright 1991, 3). |
| 1877 | The Illinois Wesleyan University first offered planned correspondence education for adult students (Watkins and Wright 1991, 4). |
| 1878 | The Chautauqua Literary and Scientific Circle used correspondence study and summer institutes to provide instruction in the liberal arts. The state of New York authorized the awarding of degrees to successful students (Watkins and Wright 1991, 32). |
| 1883 | The Correspondence University, an unsuccessful venture, was headquartered at Cornell University in New York (Watkins and Wright 1991, 3). |
| 1890 | The Blackstone School of Law was established to teach principles of law by correspondence in Chicago (Smart 1987, 23). |

| 1891 | A course in mine safety was offered through correspondence by the International Correspondence Schools of Scranton, Pennsylvania (Erdos 1967, 2). |
|---|---|
| 1892 | William Rainey Harper starts the University of Chicago, which includes correspondence education (Wedemeyer and Childs 1961, 74). |
| 1906–1916 | The University of Wisconsin enrolled 24,555 students in their Correspondence Study Department (Watkins and Wright 1991, 16). |
| 1907 | Calvert Primary School (Baltimore, Maryland) offered primary school education for children at home (MacKenzie and Christensen 1971, 35). |
| 1930 | The University of Wisconsin used an eight-station radio network to offer a "School of the Air" for rural high school students (Wedemeyer and Childs 1961, 45–46). |
| 1956 | The Ford Foundation provided a $365,000 grant to examine the use of television for correspondence study (Watkins and Wright 1991, 43). |
| 1963–1974 | Many colleges and universities (Vermont College of Norwich University, Nova University, Open University of Great Britain, Walden University) were established to specifically offer distance learning programs (Rossman and Rossman 1995, 3). |
| 1966 | The ERIC Database added "correspondence study" to its list of ERIC descriptors. (To find out when ERIC added terms, search the *ERIC Thesaurus* [http://www.ericfacility.net/extra/pub/thessearch.cfm] for a heading. The dates of additions are listed for each term.) |
| 1970 | The first distance-only program was developed by the University of the State of New York as the Regents External Degree Program, later known as Regents College (Criscito 1999, 2) and now known as Excelsior College. |
| 1972 | The Ed.D. was offered as an external degree program by Nova Southeastern University (MacFarland 1996, 5). |
| 1983 | The ERIC Database added "distance education" to its list of ERIC descriptors. |
| 1985 | Nova Southeastern University began offering a computer-based distance learning program for librarians (MacFarland 1996, 5). |
| 1986 | The Step Star Network began operations to deliver distance learning and continues to offer interactive television. |
| 1988 | The Star Schools Program was first authorized to provide grant funding for education projects that included distance learning and telecommunications. |
| 1997 | The Florida Virtual High School (now Florida Virtual School) began offering courses. |
| 1998 | The Western Governors University opened degree programs to students in a virtual university (http://www.wgu.edu/). |
| 2000 | The United States survived Y2K with minor difficulties. |
| 2001 | The United States rebuilt its telecommunications networks to support Wall Street, post 11 September 2001. |
| 2002 | The ERIC Database added "virtual classroom" to its list of ERIC descriptors. |
| 2003 | What will *you* contribute to distance learning? |

## *Teaching Possibility*

Ask students to add more contemporary items to the previous Distance Learning Time Line. Students could research the dates of origin of the Apple, the Macintosh, Windows, modems, the first e-mail message, the first listserv, the first search engine, the first universities to participate in the Internet, the creator of Netscape, the creator of Internet Explorer, the origins of AOL, the first virtual high school, etc.

---

Beyond the development of technology, why are we interested in distance learning for PreK–12 students? Teacher shortages, continued fiscal issues, and the desire to increase learning opportunities to as many students as possible drives the development of distance learning as a possible solution to many interests. In 1997, the U.S. Department of Education projected that the then 52.2 million K–12 learners would increase by 13 percent in the next ten years (by 2006) requiring an additional 6,000 schools and 2 million teachers (Giltrow 1997). Just to confirm this prediction, a search of the *National Center for Education Statistics* (http://nces.ed.gov/pubs2000/qtrlywinter/3elem/3-esq14-g.html) reinforced this by projecting that 1.7 million to 2.7 million new public school teachers will be needed by 2008 to 2009 (Hussar 1999). For those of you who are already answering the questions of "Where are we going to put them?" (because you may already teach in overcrowded classrooms), you know that alternatives are needed. An increase in instructional delivery methods is a partial solution. Through initiatives, such as the Star Schools Program, the U.S. Congress has demonstrated its desire to increase learning opportunities (Barker and Dickson 1996). Obviously, the capability to react to this predicted, increased enrollment, in a cost-effective manner, will test the planning efforts of school districts nationwide.

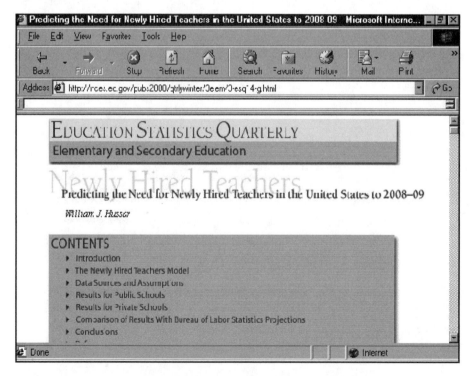

*National Center for Education Statistics* Web site:
http://nces.ed.gov/pubs2000/qtrlywinter/3elem/3-esq14-g.html

The rate of change in technology changes the history of distance learning every day. One of the best chroniclers of this distance learning history for the PreK–12 sector has been Michael Moore. A comprehensive, yet pointed, review of the literature of *The American Journal of Distance Education* is a good start for the teacher who is interested in learning from this development (Moore 1995). Background on the development of distance education through the teaching, learning, and planning processes points to the awareness (from the 1980s) of costs per student and the need for strategic planning so that purchasing mistakes could be avoided (Moore and Thompson 1990). Hanson (1997) provides a very comprehensive description of the history, multiple definitions, and theory related to distance education, noting that the definitions and theories will continue to change as the applications of distance education continue to change and evolve. Another summary of the history and theory relating to distance education appears in *Teaching and Learning at a Distance* (Simonson, Smaldino, Albright, and Zvacek 2000, 22–42).

A more recent study into the use of computers in elementary and secondary classrooms has been conducted (Becker and Anderson 1998). This study investigates how teachers are using computers, how they apply learning theory to this instruction, and how school organization supports this instruction. Results of this research can be viewed at the project Web site, *Teaching, Learning, and Computing 1998* (http://www.crito.uci.edu/tlc/html/tlc_home.html).

### Learning Possibility

Go to the *Computer Museum History Center* (http://www.computerhistory.org/timeline/index.page) and look at the time line. As long as your students were born between 1945 and 1990, you can ask them to find out what was happening in the area of computers during the year they (or their parents or grandparents) were born.

---

# Section B. Benefits of Interactive Distance Learning

Just as technology has resulted in the fast movement of goods and services throughout the world, knowledge is practically an instant commodity—compressing space and time (Edwards 1997, 53). Likewise, interactive distance learning makes education an almost instant process, offering benefits to many members of the school community. Students, teachers, administrators, paraprofessionals and staff, parents, and citizen-taxpayers all have opportunities to benefit from distance learning because of the capabilities for making content knowledge available quickly and providing almost instantaneous responses to students. Though these benefits have yet to be evaluated and quantified in a way that is communicated as "universal truth" in education, let's consider the benefits of distance learning by groups (students, teachers, administrators, paraprofessionals and staff, parents, and citizen-taxpayers).

## For Students

➤ *Interactive distance learning increases student interest in the day-to-day classroom activities.*

If you wanted to get your students interested in *America's Fund for Afghan Children* (http://www.whitehouse.gov/kids/connection/20011012.html) or anthrax (http://kidshealth.org/misc/anthrax .html), you can find current resources as close as your nearest computer.

**America's Fund for Afghan Children Web site:**
**http://www.whitehouse.gov/kids/connection/20011012.html**

As outlined in the Rand report *Fostering the Use of Educational Technology: Elements of a National Strategy*, there are many benefits to using technology in the schools (Glennan and Melmed 1996). Some schools accept that student attendance and behavior are positively impacted when technology is brought into the classroom curricula. A logical inference is that when students improve daily attendance at school, administrators and citizen-taxpayers are happy that learners are in school and productively engaged. Having students on task so that teachers can teach, and having all students engaged in learning that is not interrupted, sounds pretty ideal, doesn't it?

Many students have access to online resources that can be used for distance learning. *USA Today* (19 August 1999) reported that 60 percent of college and university students are going online every day. Similarly, it is estimated that 7 million of these students increasingly have access to high-speed online services through Ethernet connections (*Edupage*, 14 January 2000). The National Center for Education Statistics (NCES) reported (2001) that in 2000, 98 percent of all U.S. schools had online access and acceptable use policies. Additionally, 54 percent of these schools were making this online access available during, before, and after school hours. (For more information on the access ratios, types of online connections, and acceptable use policies, view the report [http://nces.ed.gov/pubsearch/pubsinfo.asp ?pubid=2001071].) While it is safe to say that most of our students and teachers can get online access through the schools, we know that the quality of access and our expectations for use may exceed what is available.

Beyond the expectations of infrastructure, how are educators supposed to manage when their students are often more familiar with the technology and have a better understanding of possibilities? Described as "creating an online community," this learning atmosphere requires input by both teacher and student in terms of setting course requirements and expectations. Using online orientation sessions is a start to defining the online behaviors (Solloway and Harris 1999). These sessions would describe the course activities, how to use the related distance learning technologies, locations of materials, assignment due dates, etc. When the student leaves a session, she or he knows what to do to be successful in the course. When some of these students return to the PreK–12 environment as teachers, let's hope that their experiences have nourished positive models that will enable them to provide productive distance learning experiences to their own PreK–12 students. However, because of their experiences as young adult learners, will their expectations exceed the capacity of the PreK–12 school infrastructure?

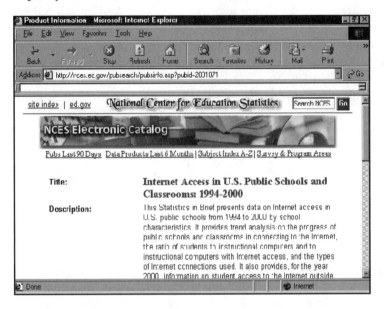

**National Center for Education Statistics (NCES)** *Internet Access in U.S. Public Schools and Classrooms 1994–2000* **Web site: http://nces.ed.gov/pubsearch/pubsinfo.asp?pubid=2001071**

It is quite possible that the "Nintendo generation," those that grew up using handheld electronic games, will have tremendous expectations for learning systems that provide immediate and rewarding learning experiences (Frand 2000). The demand will be high. The downside will be the ability of the non-Nintendo generations to catch up to the technological skills and begin to identify the learning patterns that these students have developed. For example, if the answer to why students are able to learn to use technology so quickly, and why they are able to teach the teacher, lies in the tendency for them to treat any technology as a Nintendo game, where they begin to push and turn all of the knobs and buttons as quickly as possible to try to win the game, we are still in luck! These students will become our leaders in product testing and development. But, as Frand notes, will they have the temperament to refer to the manuals and read the directions, if all else fails? If the answer is "yes," we will need to make sure that we provide instruction for them to access these support materials. If the answer is "no," we might not need the support materials because the developers might begin to create more intuitive software. Where does that leave those of us who have to read the directions?

> ➤ *Interactive distance learning expands contact with students and teachers outside the campus-based school.*

Sometimes students complain about the confining aspects of our educational system. Distance learning broadens their viewpoints about learning by allowing them to maintain contact with others in distant communities. Some students do not find outlets for learning and socialization within their campus-based school setting. And, although it may be one of our less emphasized roles as educators, we need to consider how to help students connect with society in positive and productive ways. Through interactive distance learning technologies, especially online activities such as e-mail and online chats, this can happen. The charge to educators then is to teach students how to make these connections in safe, productive, and ethical ways.

Most of us have come to the realization that traditional ways of learning (read the book, answer the questions, turn in the worksheet) do not appeal to today's student who has stepped into virtual reality through electronic games and online access. Think of how many of your students are wired to the outside world through beepers, cellular phones, pagers, and PDAs (personal digital assistants). Do their cellular phones also have wireless network capabilities? As this potential teaching modality develops, you will need to be patient as the technology evolves. You will also need to develop rules and regulations revolving around the use of this new technology within the school. (Have you thought of how you will work with students who "beam" each other during class? Will you be responsible for the safety of students who are beaming people outside of the school? Do you think that banning PDAs from school will succeed, in view of the fact that the banning of cellular phones has not been effective in most districts and that some districts have even rescinded this policy since the 11 September 2001 attacks?) The distant learning potentials with PDAs can be limitless, considering that students will be able to attend class while in the airport or in the mall.

## *Teaching Possibility*

Some say that PDA stands for personal digital assistant and some say that it stands for personal data assistant. Others refer to PDA as a personal data appliance! Which is correct? With technology, terms abound according to the whim of the industry. Don't miss this opportunity to teach your students (and fellow teachers) that there are sources they can reference that will help them with technological terms, such as *Webopedia* (http://www.webopedia.com/). Try asking students to define "HomeRF," "local loop," or "ragged" (as it applies to word processing). Ask them to further use these terms, in a database lesson, by asking them to contribute their new technology terms and definitions to a classwide database.

Do your students recognize their position in today's global economy? Do U.S. students understand the implications of an economy that has shifted to the point that fewer large corporations exist in this country today than they did in World War II? Do your students know where most consumers reside? Perceptions of our economic ranking are important to share with students (Oblinger 1998, 1). These perceptions provide a context in which students can comprehend what percentage of the global economy the United States represents. As educators, we must also consider that distance learning, worldwide, is on the increase. For example, China has plans that 5 million college students will learn online by 2005 (*Edupage*, 28 December 2001). Will this increase in distance learning impact developments of the global economy in the future?

## *Teaching Possibility*

Ask your students to use distance learning tools to determine which countries are the largest trading partners in, and with, their state of residence. What are the products that are produced in the state that are exported? An online almanac would be a good place to start this search (e.g., *World Almanac*

*Online* [http://www.worldalmanac.com/]). Let students compare using a print and electronic almanac. Which one was quickest to use? Can both be browsed?

---

➤*Interactive distance learning offers learning opportunities that are not confined to the normal seven-and-a-half-hour school day.*

Arguments are being made in many districts that the biological clock of an adolescent does not ring until breakfast (Kaufman 1999). While we could probably spend many pages debating the school day schedule, not to mention the yearly school calendar, we can show students how to spend their time outside of school hours in ways that can be beneficial to their learning. If you also consider that students are only engaged in school-based learning activities for approximately 49 hours of a 168-hour week (29 percent), students have a lot of time to expand their learning time away from school. In *A Matter of Time* (1992), 42 percent of a young adolescent's waking time was reported to be discretionary. Think of the learning opportunities that could be covered during this time!

Interactive distance learning can provide the flexibility that many students need to become self-directed and responsible learners outside the more traditional classroom. Among other convincing reasons to provide more flexible learning opportunities (Race 1994), it is this obligation that teachers have to facilitate and develop the student's ability to manage personal learning that is so compelling to today's educator.

➤*Interactive distance learning offers limitless learning opportunities.*

Teaching students to learn independently, through interactive distance learning technologies, opens possibilities during vacation time, when they need to be engaged in productive activities. Consider that many school districts are cutting back on summer school budgets to the point that going to summer school for enrichment is often a thing of the past. Distance learning can help you to teach your students to become self-directed, lifelong learners.

### Learning Possibility

Have your students keep a list in their notebooks (journals) of topics that they would like to read about when they have time. This list can form the basis of a self-directed holiday "mental excursion." You and your students can generate a log sheet that helps the student to keep track of their excursions. As you will see, distance learning can happen in many formats!

---

With distance learning opportunities that offer flexible calendars, it may be possible for students to again have enrichment learning experiences during the summer.

## For Teachers

➤*Teachers who are involved with interactive distance learning are actively engaged with curriculum development.*

Why? It takes effort to plan distance learning that occurs smoothly, but this planning is something that good teachers actually enjoy. When teachers are actively engaged with planning, administrators know that learning is going to occur. Teachers are constantly looking for ways to improve their teaching and their students' learning. In fact, one of the greatest benefits of teaching, other than the trite joke of "June, July, and August," is the improvement and change that we witness as our students learn.

Why should you be interested in teaching with distance learning technologies? Distance learning technologies allow you to bring a wealth of mediums directly into your classroom. Although distance learning may seem attractive because it generates interest and enthusiasm, due to the positive reception of most students, it does offer challenges that are directly related to time, technology, and energy (Kilian 1997). Good teaching is hard work, regardless of the technology or type of delivery. However, teaching is also a tremendously rewarding profession. Most teachers are enthusiastic and will always try something new.

## Learning Possibility

Talk to teachers who have placed existing courses into a distance learning format. Find out:

How did they do it?

Would they do it again?

Was the experience worth the time on task?

What do they suggest as their "best practices" in distance learning?

———————

Although written for the community college faculty, *TCC-J* (*Teaching in the Community Colleges Journal*) (http://naio.kcc.hawaii.edu/pub/tcc-j/) is a collection of experiences useful for secondary teachers and support personnel who wish to find out about trends in distance learning for adults.

➢ *Teaching with interactive distance learning methods keeps you up-to-date with educational trends.*

You've often heard that teaching keeps you young, right? Just as you are kept up-to-date on music and fashion, it is imperative for you to be updated on current trends within the educational sphere.

## Learning Possibility

To hear what students are listening to, go to *Amazon.com* (http://www.amazon .com), click on "music," and sample some of the top ten choices. Warning: Some of the lyrics of the songs could be on the downside of your vocabulary list, so it is a good idea to preview the songs in private before you share them with others!

———————

A great benefit of distance learning for the teacher is keeping up-to-date in the field of education. Why? Trends in distance learning usually follow technological developments. For example, on the day this paragraph was first composed, an announcement was made that a company was distributing free personal computers. The technological development of a $500 personal computer made this possible. Since then, the company has dissolved, but because distance learning encourages us to stay aware of advancements, we are always considering how these advancements may be used in our schools. (It was recently announced that a major U.S. discount chain would offer a PC for $400. Think of the potential benefits to your students if their parents get involved in online activities at home! Wouldn't it be great to e-mail your students' parents about a new concept learned that day? More outreach activities for parents are discussed in Chapter 6.)

## *Learning Possibility*

Don't let yourself or your students miss the site that describes the development of computing at *The Machine That Changed the World* (http://ei.cs.vt .edu/~history/TMTCTW.html). Make sure that students view the "bug" that Grace Hopper actually retrieved from a computer. While you are in the history mood, be sure that your students also view *Past Notable Women of Computing & Mathematics* (http://www.cs.yale.edu/homes/tap/past-women.html).

➤ *Teachers that use interactive distance learning technologies have students who are on task.*

Notice that I did not say that distance learning technologies encourage quiet classes! Most veteran teachers know that learning is not always quiet or clean, but usually occurs with some noise of excitement in the air. Because distance learning experiences can be exciting, students may seem more on task than in other traditional learning experiences.

➤ *Teachers can benefit from interactive distance learning for their own professional and personal development.*

Today, teachers can develop both professionally and personally through interactive distance learning. Whether through e-mail, CD-ROM instruction, video courses, televised courses, or Web files, learning opportunities abound! From Chisanbop to Scherenschnitte, teachers can continue their own education to the extent that they are willing to invest the time, energy, and interest.

## *Teaching Possibility*

Ask your students to research Chisanbop and find out how it works. Next, try to locate a teacher who is incorporating Chisanbop in the classroom and who would be willing to provide a live demonstration through interactive video or a videotaped session. Then, watch as your students benefit from this new knowledge! Hint: Your students' math scores will improve, and you don't have to buy a thing for the students to use!

## *Teaching Possibility*

Challenge your students to locate information on Scherenschnitte. Ask them to provide information on the origin of the word, along with a correct pronunciation. Can they find an expert on Scherenschnitte who will also provide a demonstration? Let your students attempt a Scherenschnitte project. The cost will be very low, but the intricacies will be challenging!

---

## For Administrators

➤*Administrators take pride in leading schools that are involved with interactive distance learning.*

Remember that administrators are teachers, too. They likewise have an interest in seeing students, and teachers, succeed. Teachers who are active and interested in distance learning may not require intervention from the principal due to problems related to classroom management or teacher burnout. The downside of distance education is that administrators who are leading schools may have to work hard at finding funding to support this new initiative in their school.

## *Learning Possibility*

Would you take your students to the *Oxford English Dictionary* Online (http://dictionary.oed.com/), where they could see that the word "principal" was first used in 1827 to refer to the head of a school? What other school terms would you like to search for in the *Oxford English Dictionary*, also known as the *OED*? If your district or media center does not have a subscription to the Online *OED*, there is a free "Word of the Day" feature that provides the etymology of the word, quotations using the word, and a time line for the use of the word.

---

➤*Administrators who have on-task students and teachers can spend more time on curriculum development and budgeting.*

Time saved from dealing with disciplinary or human resource problems can be devoted to areas that always seem to come last in an administrator's day. As administrators tune in to teachers and students and their unique ways of learning, they will begin to generate ideas that will support the distance learning. To support this process, consideration must be given to the principles of learning. Are the principles of distance learning different from those of traditional learning? Perhaps the better question would be whether learning principles support education, in general, and its changes (American Council on Education 1996). When developing learning initiatives within the school or district, the principal would be well advised to consider guiding principles that address learner design, learner support, organizational commitment, learning outcomes, and technology.

➤*Administrators can increase courses offered to teachers and students.*

Arguments have been made that technology has not been applied equitably throughout U.S. classrooms. Although these arguments may be defended, it is likewise true that all education is not equitable to begin with. There are districts with uneven budgets, facilities, and curriculum offerings. We know, though, that technology can be used to democratize education today, benefiting those that do not have equal access for a variety of reasons. School districts that cannot justify full-time teachers in certain subject areas, due to lack of student demand, lack of certified teachers, or remote location, can still offer a full curriculum to students through distance learning activities. With the help of a facilitator, or monitor, students in all locations can enjoy a wide variety of courses. In his article on "Jefferson's Laptop," Schneiderman (1999, 34) reinforces this use of technology as he quotes Thomas Jefferson's vision to "Educate and inform the whole mass of the people." What better way is there to support this vision today than by using distance learning technologies?

In addition to courses for students, teachers and staff are often in need of courses for certification, recertification, and everyday job survival. For example, many high school computer science teachers will be required to teach C++ and Java (object-oriented programming languages) to students taking advanced placement courses. Some school districts may be too remote from colleges or universities that offer a course that is accepted for state certification in this subject area. This is a perfect application for distance learning for the teacher who is willing to participate. Would it surprise you to know that as of December 1999, the U.S. Department of Education reported a 72 percent increase in the number of distance education programs to 1,190 programs between 1995 and 1998 (Carnvale 2000b)? (For a copy of the full report, "Distance Education at Postsecondary Education Institutions," visit *The National Center for Education Statistics* Web site [http://nces.ed.gov].) The report cites "type of institution" and "size" to be factors that affect this development, with larger public institutions being more likely to have a distance education program of some type.

## *Learning Possibility*

Select a two- or four-year college or university and visit the institution's home page. What are the distance education courses offered that are of interest to you? Even if you have completed your degree, are there any courses that you would like to take for certification or pleasure? While you are there, look at the listings for education and technology courses. Do any of these courses appeal to you? How can your search for this information help you to prepare your students for future educational needs? What can you share with them relating to the availability of distance learning courses at the postsecondary level?

## *Learning Possibility*

Contact your state board of education's office of certification. Are these requirements listed online? Is there a list of courses that are offered by community colleges or universities that are technology oriented and approved for state certification? Are any of these courses also offered through distance learning? Some community colleges and universities have partnered with PreK–12 schools to share distance learning facilities and personnel for both student instruction and professional development (Ball and Crook 1997, 21–22). Consider taking some of these distance learning courses with a group of your colleagues. How can this group learning experience ease your way into distance learning?

---

Predictions of online and independent learning will continue, based on current interest by government, industry, and military groups. Predictions indicate that as much as 96 percent of corporate training will happen online at a market price of $15 billion in 2002 (*Edupage*, 11 February 2000).

> ➤*Interactive distance learning activities promote sharing.*

Everyone is looking for ways to optimize available funds. Whether you are able to substitute an in-house field trip for an actual trip, simulate science experiments, or provide guest speakers at low to no cost, you can save money by choosing a virtual experience.

## *Learning Possibility*

Interviews of actual astronauts or laboratory experiments conducted at universities or research centers can be shown to your students through a videoconference. Ask your teachers to contact *Ask an Expert Sources* (http://www.cln.org/int_expert.html) at the Community Learning Network or Pitsco's *Ask an Expert* (http://www.askanexpert.com) to find out how to schedule a viewing of these activities.

---

## *Learning Possibility*

Many authors are overwhelmed with requests to visit schools. And even if the authors had the time to visit schools, can the schools afford the visit? Alternatives to visits could include a tele-visit through a videoconference, a commercially purchased videotape or DVD of an author's presentation, or a simple telephone call that is shared through a speakerphone for only the cost of a long-distance charge! Authors are usually happy to participate for at least fifteen to thirty minutes, but check with the author's publisher for more information. Before considering this "visit," think about what you will be accomplishing. Encourage your students to develop meaningful questions for the authors. Are they interested in finding out how the author decided to use a certain detail? Do they want to know how the book applies to the author's life?

---

Beyond classroom alternatives, materials in media centers can be supplemented through interlibrary loan activities. Here it is important to note that the Internet is not the sole source for information. Some administrators are under the misimpression that books, articles, and other media, in general, are freely available. Unfortunately, information always has a cost, even if the cost is in the form of the electricity, hardware, and the human element needed to develop and retrieve the information. The misconception that all magazines and books have been digitized, archived, and are waiting for you to access them—for free—is simply not true. Nevertheless, there are supplements for some topics online, in the form of government or commercial documents. Some supplements and some substitutes are available, but the Internet is not a replacement for all materials and media in your school.

## *Teaching Possibility*

*Virtual Library Museums Pages* (http://www.icom.org/vlmp/) will take your students to Web sites of museums and galleries throughout the world. Whether at the Betty Brinn's Children's Museum in Milwaukee, or at the Art Institute of Chicago, this site of hundreds of exhibitions will provide resources for your age groups. Also, consider that teachers living in an area that has a site that your teachers wish your students to visit may be agreeable to videotaping a site and swapping their videotapes with a videotape of a site in your area! Other field trips are available at the *Virtual Field Trips Site* (http://www .field-guides.com/).

## *Learning Possibility*

Many authors also have Web pages! Have you visited R. L. Stine's Web page at Scholastic (*Goosebumps Home Page*) (http://www.scholastic.com /goosebumps/index.htm)? Can you show your students how to find the Web page of *Harry Potter* (http://harrypotter.warnerbros.com)? Would you like to take your students to a "Wizard Challenge" to test their recall of events from the Harry Potter books (http://www.scholastic.com/harrypotter /challenge/index.htm)?

# For Paraprofessionals and Staff

➤ *Interactive distance learning technologies can help paraprofessionals support the learning process.*

Underpaid, underrated, and underrecognized, paraprofessionals and staff are very important to the success of our schools. By keeping these members of the school community informed of what is going on, and involving them in growth and personal development, they will be encouraged to learn new skills that can directly benefit the school day.

## *Learning Possibility*

New, or temporary, clerical staff may need to view training videos or access online documentation when they have questions on how to use software. For example, Microsoft offers an online tutorial for a variety of products, including FrontPage, Outlook, and PowerPoint (http://www.microsoft.com /education/default.asp?ID=Tutorials). So, if the tutorial isn't available on a particular workstation, or the staff member has additional questions, she or he has an alternative source to try to find an answer, while she or he is in a still unfamiliar workplace.

---

# For Parents

➤ *Interactive distance learning technologies can increase parent involvement.*

Educators have long been aware that increased parent participation in school activities improves the school environment. In Chapter 6, many ways will be discussed for parents to participate in their children's school day, but first we must agree to be willing to communicate outreach opportunities to parents. Although getting parents involved may not seem very sophisticated, educators must remember that many parents are not used to receiving quick feedback from schools. Teachers are sometimes difficult to contact, and parents do not always remember the teachers' schedules. Even though teachers send flyers about how to contact them, it is still difficult for parents to remember to keep this information with them at all times. Imagine the advantages to parents and teachers if they were able to communicate on a routine basis through e-mail. Chapter 6 offers guidelines for what should be communicated through e-mail and when conferences are necessary.

## *Teaching Possibility*

Schedule e-mail workshops through parent-teacher organizations! Teach parents about netiquette (yes, netiquette, not etiquette) and share teacher and administrator e-mail addresses. Encourage parents to get into the habit of e-mailing their children to open the lines of communication. (Instead of focusing on e-mail, you could teach parents to "chat" with their children. For some parents, the use of a chatroom in the afternoon at 4:00 can substitute for a phone call to find out if the child arrived home safely. This will also let parents know how much time the child is spending in chat during the afternoon! Think of how useful a chat is for parents who do not wish to share private home details with other office workers!) Parents will enjoy seeing computer labs or workstations where their children work and will appreciate your concern that they do communicate with their students. Who knows? Because of this positive, proactive contact, a parent might decide to donate computer hardware, software, or on-site training to the school!

---

## For Citizen-Taxpayers

Because school community members (students, teachers, administrators, paraprofessionals and staff, and parents) are also citizen-taxpayers, let us review some of the potential benefits of interactive distance learning.

- Interactive distance learning increases student interest in the day-to-day classroom activities.

- Interactive distance learning expands contact with students and teachers outside the campus-based school.

- Interactive distance learning offers learning opportunities that are not confined to the normal seven-and-a-half-hour school day.

- Interactive distance learning offers limitless learning opportunities.

- Teachers who are involved with interactive distance learning are actively engaged with curriculum development.

- Teaching with interactive distance learning methods keeps the teacher up-to-date with educational trends.

- Teachers involved with interactive distance learning technologies have students who are on task.

- Teachers can benefit from interactive distance learning for their own professional and personal development.

- Administrators take pride in leading schools that are involved with interactive distance learning and the positive publicity gained.

- Administrators who have on-task students and teachers can spend more time on curriculum development and budgeting.

- Administrators can increase the number of courses offered to teachers and students through interactive distance learning activities.

- Interactive distance learning technologies can help paraprofessionals and staff support the learning process.

- Interactive distance learning technologies can increase parent involvement.

So, what are the benefits of interactive distance learning technologies to citizen-taxpayers?

- Schools that can increase student interest and contacts beyond the normal school day, while offering limitless learning opportunities by up-to-date teachers who are actively engaged with curriculum development, led by administrators who are proud of the school's activities and are able to focus on improving curriculum, with the help of supporting staff members and parents, are actively engaged in coordinating all participants.

- Citizen-taxpayers gain opportunities to learn about distance learning technologies.

Whether at night or on weekends, most school districts operate community schools that provide classes for personal development, GED (General Education Diploma) tutoring, ESOL (English for Speakers of Other Languages) classes, etc. Many of these classes are offered, using some of the same technologies that are used for daytime instruction, whether in computer labs or in classrooms, using video equipment, compressed video, etc. Do not forget that, in some districts, community school funding (for adult students) is used to purchase equipment used by daytime (PreK–12) students.

> ➤ *Citizen-taxpayers are benefited by a well-prepared, entry-level workforce.*

Of the ten fastest growing occupations projected by the Bureau of Labor Statistics (http://stats.bls .gov/news.release/ecopro.t06.htm) for 2000–2010, the top five, ranked by numbers of jobs, are computer software engineers (applications), computer support specialists, computer software engineers (systems software), network and computer systems administrators, and network systems and data communications analysts. Clearly, students who have increased knowledge of technology skills are projected to have a higher employability level during the next decade over students who are not prepared for these jobs. Obvious benefits are that small businesses and corporate America will be spending less and less time training, or retraining, employees to use technology if schools treat the process of learning to use distance learning technology as a skill itself.

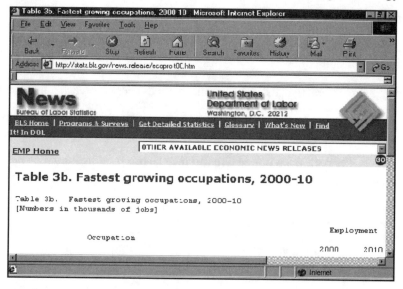

**Fastest Growing Occupations, 2000–10 (Bureau of Labor Statistics)**
Web site: http://stats.bls .gov/news.release/ecopro.t06.htm

## Teaching Possibility

Teachers can begin offering career education to students early by guiding them to the *BLS Career Information* (Bureau of Labor Statistics) for K–12 students (http://stats.bls.gov/k12/html/edu_over.htm). Information for each career includes a description of the work, the job, how to prepare for the job, future projections for this type of work, salary, and other jobs that are similar to this type of work. This and the accompanying teacher guide, also online, provide students and teachers with additional sources for more information on the jobs listed. How much money do your students want to make when they have graduated from school or college? Wouldn't it be a good idea for them to understand that if they want to make lots of money as an engineer they better start improving their math skills today so that they can be successful in required math courses?

➤ *Citizen-taxpayers gain through intangible benefits.*

No one would argue that a better-educated populace and workforce benefit society as a whole, or that our society's future depends on its children. However, those who believe insufficient resources are spent to support education will be particularly interested in Chapter 7 (Evaluation) where we will discuss how to begin to collect data that will communicate to others the importance and resulting benefits of using distance learning technology in education and the resulting benefits.

## Learning Possibility

School administrators need to find out what, if any, rewards are available at the district level for teachers who agree to teach through distance learning. Does your district have plans for recognizing the innovation of these teachers? If not, what can you, the administrator, do to reward these teachers? Remember, as we are taught in human development courses, rewards do not have to be tangible, or expensive, to be meaningful. Invite a few teachers to a focus group to discuss some of the reward possibilities that students would value. Ask your professional teacher association (union) to send a representative to this discussion. Can you identify ten teacher rewards that are meaningful and show *your* appreciation for their efforts to provide a new form of instruction to the students? Keep in mind that rewards can help to provide support and outweigh any feelings of isolation that teachers may experience as they explore these new teaching techniques (Laird 1999, B6).

---

# Section C. Challenges of Implementing Interactive Distance Learning Technologies

The media have found challenges and developments in technology to be newsworthy during the recent past as we are constantly hearing of technology in terms of computer viruses, the "Digital Divide," eroding information bases, privacy rights, the stock market, Y2K, the "bursting" of the .com bubble and the resulting loss of jobs, etc. Constraints to distance learning have included issues relating to time, place, resources, equipment, course workload, communications, policies, costs, schedules, etc. (Paulsen et al. 1991, 13) Nevertheless, the challenges to be presented in this section are teacher related. A review of the literature shows that issues such as learner perceptions and attitudes, instructor skills, media selection, cost effectiveness, policies, and quality must be considered (Moore and Thompson 1990). Our more immediate concerns relate to specific teacher issues. Some of these common challenges of implementing interactive distance learning technologies include:

- skepticism,

- lack of understanding of how technology works,

- constant changes with technology,

- lack of time to teach students to use technology,

- lack of equipment and funds to provide technology training, and

- lack of ideas on how to incorporate distance learning technology in the classroom.

Most of these challenges are school based, relating to educators' impressions of school or district support. Let's quickly explore some of these challenges and how you might address them in your school community.

# Skepticism

With all of the positive and productive outcomes that are possible through using interactive distance learning technologies, how could there be any challenges to the implementation of these technologies?

## *Teaching Possibility*

Ask students to look for "mis-predictions," such as those at *Murphy's Laws and Other Things to Keep in Mind* (http://www.compusmart.ab.ca/psc/PSC _murphy.htm). Next, help students to locate magazine articles or Web sites about new developments in technology. Ask students to share these developments with each other and to think of other technology developments that they would like to see happen. Can they distinguish between the developments that are possible and those that are *probable*? Ask students to write *probable* technology predictions for the next school year and seal these in an envelope. At the end of the year, read the predictions to find out if any came true.

Experienced educators have witnessed many designs, media, plans, etc., which were supposed to revolutionize education and streamline the learning process. Reading programs, learning systems, new math curricula, redesigning of buildings, you-name-the-catch-phrase-of-the-day. We have seen many things come and go, sat through endless in-service training sessions, and have spent millions of consulting dollars in our continuing quest to improve the education process. By this point, most educators understand that networks and software programs will not substitute for good teaching. To the contrary, we continue to learn that there is not enough well-designed software to support the learning process (Olsen 1999b). The disappointment that we have all experienced from the lack of success of these educational trends has resulted in skepticism. Representatives from universities report that their biggest challenge is still getting faculty members to work with technology (Olsen 1999a, 3). This finding points to a challenge that exists for motivating faculty to use technology, especially if there are no direct rewards for doing so.

On a negative note, some instructors want clear definition of ownership rights to materials that they develop for their classrooms. If you are keeping up with professional literature, you have seen this topic debated. Teachers want to know: "Who owns the materials that I develop?" and "Can I sell this product to a vendor?" We have to consider and monitor the vendor's role, when curriculum is purely commercially driven and learning systems are developed, independent of professional teacher input. Further, consider how commercial curriculum can impact the intellectual freedom and role of the teacher. Will these areas change with the increasing commercialism in software and learning ware? How will we make sure that there is a balance between the content and the commercial content providers? Keep in mind that when new areas of content and practices are in development, there may be no clear-cut answers to these questions. Some districts are developing policy through school boards; some are developing practice guidelines through teacher agreements. Some states are providing leadership by developing state statute and state board rule on faculty ownership of materials, which may apply to distance learning courses and materials

(*An Overview of Intellectual Property Issues Associated with Distance Learning in Florida*, 1995). To complicate these issues a bit further, what happens if you are dealing with students, intellectual property, and practices in different countries? Which set of procedures will you follow? And, of course, we have not yet factored in the issue of the vendor that hosts the learning services. Because these issues are so complex, and nonproductive, learning institutions would do well to consider ownership from a shared viewpoint, benefiting all parties (Chambers 1999, 1).

Before you let these issues get in the way of your interest in distance learning, contact administrative and faculty representatives to find out about the status of rules, policies, and laws in your district. Your state representative or state board of education may provide further sources of information. If your concern is great, be sure to keep records of development (i.e., work logs) for your products. Do you maintain Web pages on a commercial Internet Service Provider (ISP)? Are these developed during your on-duty or off-duty time? Does your district allow you to guide students to Web sites that are your personal developments? It could be that before you know the answers to these questions you will wish to develop materials on personal time with materials that you provide. If you develop materials during the course of your working day, supported by district and school funds and personnel, chances are good that the district or school would stand to gain from any commercial profits that you make.

Some veteran teachers view technology as the corporate world's newest trend for education, but without a large body of evidence that tracks learners, we cannot yet agree for certain that the skeptics are wrong. Far from being a trend, some are observing high dropout rates among online students, who may have confused convenience of access with easy content (Carnvale 2000a). Students need to be aware that the change of environment, or medium, does not necessarily mean a change of content.

## *Teaching Possibility*

Ask your students to research the person Ned Ludd or the term "Luddite." Who were the Luddites and what is the application of this term today? Use this question to introduce your students to an online dictionary of computer terms and technology, the online *Biographical Dictionary* (http://www.s9 .com/biography), or the *Encyclopaedia Britannica* Online (http://www.eb.com). Once students understand the person behind the term (Mr. Ludd) and the concept of "Luddite," take the students to The Luddites (at *Spartacus International* ) (http://www.spartacus.schoolnet.co.uk/PRIuddites.htm), a source of historical content, where they can locate more information about British and U.S. history.

To counter skepticism among educators, and to convince other teachers and administrators that distance learning technologies can benefit your students, be ready to:

- Highlight successful programs through demonstrations.

- Visit schools where distance learning technologies are being used successfully.

- Speak to parents and students who are involved in distance learning activities.

- Make teachers aware of district and state support of distance learning technology.

# Lack of Understanding of How Technology Works

There is no doubt that technology is increasingly sophisticated, complex, and often demanding to keep current with, even for the most technically trained educator. Most educators who received degrees before 1994 have never had formal teacher education training for Internet activities and have never experienced the integration of Web activities into their course curricula. Educators who received degrees before 1990 may have used DOS-based systems but were never exposed to the use of e-mail. Those who graduated before 1985 may be unfamiliar with CD-ROM technology. Graduates before 1980 may never have sat in front of a computer during their formal teacher training. Thankfully, because teachers are interested in professional development, many have participated in noncredit training activities, and many more may have taken programs of study, chiefly for the purpose of updating skills. But, for the purposes of our discussion, we have to keep in mind that technology is still not a part of the training of many teachers. Nevertheless, organizations, such as the *CEO Forum on Education and Technology* (http://ceoforum.org), have identified technology skills that should be included in teacher preparation programs. Look for these competencies to be increasingly included in in-service training activities and courses offered at the university levels.

Beyond the understanding of the mechanics of technology, there is the need to understand how technology works in terms of the curriculum. If the tendency is to think that technology, in the form of software, will replace the need for the teacher to develop and deliver curriculum, most educators realize that there will always be a role for us as the facilitator and guide for learning. To allay these concerns and help teachers understand how technology works:

- Continue to offer teachers in-service training on equipment and software.

- Make sure that training sessions are short and focused.

- Notify teachers of training opportunities through the school, the district, local organizations, the state, or professional groups.

- Offer incentives to teachers who will share their knowledge with others.

## *Learning Possibility*

Check your current state teacher certification requirements with the department of education. Can this department provide information on the titles of technology courses (and acceptable course numbers) at community colleges or universities? Are any of these courses offered through distance education? Will your state department of education accept credit for online workshops that are offered by private organizations, or teachers, much like they accept in-service training credit? Do you have any other online in-service training available, other than what is already offered by postsecondary institutions? Can some of your existing in-service training be converted to an online learning environment? Can you develop and offer an online service training opportunity to your district?

# Constant Changes in Technology

Beyond the lack of understanding or training in technology, accept the fact that technology is always changing. We used to refer to the "half-life" of computers as being a year and a half. Practically speaking, this meant that by the time that most of us had finished making the payments on one computer, it was outdated and obsolete because other computers had been designed to be more dazzling, quicker, and more efficient. Recently, I've seen reference to the "half-life" of Web pages as being three months, meaning that Web pages generally undergo a complete redesign about four times a year to keep interest and to display the most current techniques in Web page design. Admittedly, technology moves—quickly!

## *Learning Possibility*

Do a search on "Moore's Law," in relation to computers and technology. Who is/was Gordon Moore? How do you incorporate the findings of this law into planning for technology in education? Is the rate of computer storage increase outpacing Moore's Law? How can you communicate the reality of Moore's Law to administrators and citizen-taxpayers when it is time to request funding for equipment?

---

We accept that change is never ending, even if we do not like it. One of the challenges of teaching today is dealing with change in all areas. As a result, how do we teach our students to live with constant change? Some suggest that we should not even try to keep up with constant change—we should let our students teach us (Coburn, Dobbs, and Grainger 1995). However, it is believed that by teaching cognitive and problem-solving skills, students will be able to deal with change by learning how to learn, learning how to categorize, and learning many processes. Students will also learn to model attitudes, hopefully positively, which promote coping.

## *Teaching Possibility*

Do your students understand the importance of preserving data and records? (A recent television news story told of how a 1948 high school graduate lost her high school ring while swimming in the Hudson River. More than fifty years later a treasure finder found her ring with a metal detector. He contacted the same high school, and, amazingly, they had the information about this 1948 graduate in their database and they were able to return the ring to her. Do students realize the costs of saving information like this or do they take this for granted?) Go to the thrift store and pick out an old phonograph record to show to your students. Ask students if they can describe 33 1/3, 45, or 78 rpm records. Do they have the technology to play these records? Next, lead a discussion that asks students to think back to earlier computers that they or their school may have owned. Can they now access files that were created on these machines? Do they know how to convert some of these files? Just as we know it is important to preserve old documents and books, we need to consider our medium of storage over time and how we can teach students to preserve their creations indefinitely. Do they think that CD-ROM technology will exist forever? Will we always have compressed diskettes? If not, how do they think they will be able to transfer this information and migrate it to the new technologies that develop? We don't want these original electronic works that include their first compositions or early portfolios to go the way of 78 rpm records. So, think of how you can teach students to reformat and store their files so that they can be accessible in the future.

---

As technology continues to become more pervasive in our lives, computers and online services will eventually develop an appliance-type status. Through our teaching skills and strategies, we have the ability to function as change agents as we teach students and each other to deal with technological changes.

To help educators deal with changes in technology:

- Focus on the process of using programs and hardware.

- Encourage learners to become experts in one product.

- Provide incentives for the school's experts to keep others up-to-date on their products.

- Ask technology committees to scan technology literature and keep the school community informed of upcoming changes that will affect the school's technology.

- Invite outside speakers (parents, district personnel, local businesspeople) to share information on changes in the technological world.

- Model the use of distance learning technologies in as many faculty-related activities as possible. "Learning by doing" can help everyone to ease into the use of distance learning technology and can build camaraderie in the process.

- Develop an advisory committee for technological change made up of local business representatives, administrators, parents, students, and teachers. Determine a plan by which your school can incorporate change as soon as it is possible (and affordable).

## *Learning Possibility*

Can you predict change? At the turn of the millennium (whether you celebrated in 2000 or 2001), there were many future predictors who were ready to forecast how our lives would change. The *World Future Society* (http://www.wfs.org/) offers reasons on why it is important to study the future. The Society also published *The Cyber Future: 92 Ways Our Lives Will Change by the Year 2025* (Cornish 1996). Students would enjoy revisiting some of these predictions at the end of the year to discuss if any came true and which predictions are likely, or unlikely, to occur by the year 2025. Ask your students to write about how they believe these predictions will impact them by the time they graduate from high school or college. At an agreed-upon time (e.g., graduation day), mail these written predictions to the student (or student's parent). These written "time capsules" will certainly provide the future students with great memories of this activity.

---

# Lack of Time

A listserv participant, after hearing others complain about lack of time, said, "If everyone would stop complaining about how busy they are, they'd probably save a half hour a week!" No doubt, but this complaint, whether real or imagined, can quickly torpedo any school's efforts to increase the use of distance learning technology. Remember, people always find time to do things they want to do. Haven't you found this to be true?

## *Learning Possibility*

Don't let the title concern you, because the *Busy Educator's Guide to the World Wide Web* (http://www.glavac.com/) may well be one of the most comprehensive Web sites for any PreK–12 educator. Go to the site's archive and search for the July 1999 edition. Can you find reference to the "Technology Coordinator's Survival Kit" there? If not, how can you find this helpful tool on the Web?

Further, because students are so interested in technology, they will find the time, whether in or out of the school environment. Don't we have an obligation to likewise take the time to teach our students ethical uses of technology? Most schools and school districts have developed "Acceptable Use Policies," or AUPs, that restrict student activities. Nevertheless, reports of incidents of school violence and tragedy have suggested that students are still using technology in negative ways. For example, some students still use the Internet as a source for directions on creating pipe bombs (Moffett and Scharnhorst 1999). As industry groups, such as Artists Against Piracy, ask colleges to teach online ethics, which is supported by national curriculum guidelines for secondary schools through the Association for Computing Machinery (ACM), the reality seems to be that students are going to pursue illegal access to online files that include movies, music, and software (*Edupage*, 27 November 2000).

## *Learning Possibility*

Search to see if you can really find instructions for homemade explosives. How easy is this information to access? How long did it take you to find these directions? How would you react if you saw a student at one of these sites online? How could you prepare yourself to change this perceived student interest and curiosity into a learning experience? Discuss with other faculty members and administrators how to react responsibly in this situation. How can you regulate behavior with technologies that know no national borders? Provide literature and in-service learning opportunities for teachers to learn how to teach students about the ethical use of computers and technology, offering specific strategies (Johnson 1998). What are the school and district policies on this type of information? Can this information really be caught through online filters? You could let your technologist and administrator know in advance that you were searching for information on your system for testing purposes. Ask them to join you in this searching test.

## *Teaching Possibility*

Teach students about the consequences of unethical use of e-mail in the work-place. Show examples of appropriate and inappropriate e-mail examples. Do you have any examples of inappropriate e-mail? Ask your colleagues or listserv members to provide you with some examples. Explain to your students the differences between levels of appropriateness in e-mail (i.e., what is acceptable for parents and children, siblings, friends, friends' parents, teachers, etc.). Are you modeling these practices for your students? Work with students to search online to find out that workers can be fired for distributing (and even storing) e-mail messages that are not appropriate (*Edupage*, 23 August 2000).

Regardless of whether the issue of time creates stress, or whether the stress is a time-sponge, issues of "technostress" and "technophobia" have been addressed as they apply to instruction with the conclusion pointing to the possibility that teachers will appreciate the new technology as they see improvements in student satisfaction and learning (George et al. 1996, 605). "I don't have time" may be today's best euphemism for "I don't want to" or "I am not comfortable doing something new and different." Stress has also been noted in one study as ranking close to sickness as a reason for absenteeism (Brooks 1999, 8D). In one study, workers said that they spent 35 percent of the day in front of a computer (*Edupage*, 18 February 2000). Further, a 1999 Gallup survey of 771 U.S. workers showed the number of daily messages received in one day was 201, and 45 percent of those surveyed reported being interrupted at least once every ten minutes (*Palm Beach Post*, 1 October 1999, 2A).

Beyond the issues of technostress and technophobia, is it the technology and stress, or the time required to process information that is the major culprit? Since time is still one of the areas that we can control, let's address time as a real issue. Start small. Think of one area of technology that you want to learn for yourself and to share with your students. How much time do you realistically have to learn a new skill? Fifteen minutes a day or a lunch half hour? Could you squeeze in time to have someone speak to your lunch group as you eat? Can a demonstration be videotaped for you to view at home? Can you learn with your students, devoting a few minutes a day to mastering a new skill?

## *Learning Possibility*

Many multimedia software programs include step-by-step directions in paper guide and online format. Working through the process of installing your program, using the tutorial, or creating an example of a tutorial, etc., can be a class project with the teacher as the star pupil. Remember that interactive learning includes the teacher!

To increase time to work with technology:

- Consider incorporating a learning activity into your lesson plans. Why can't students practice reading with a software manual?

- Involve other teachers to help share the responsibility and added work of investigating the use of technology. Services may have to be reorganized to provide flexible, on-demand, content-specific development, support, and training, tailored to the teacher's format needs (Donovan and Macklin 1999).

- Explore the possibilities of reapportioning time in the teacher's workday in your district.

- Keep track of ways that technology can be used to save time and demonstrate these ways to teachers (send e-mail messages to parents whenever possible, use online services that will dial your telephone number with a reminder message, generate rubrics and handouts with online generators, etc.).

## *Learning Possibility*

Search for "Parkinson's Law" that is named for a British economist, C. Northcote Parkinson. How does this law apply to learner and teacher demands and expectations? Can you also find the estimate of the average U.S. workweek? Is it really forty hours per week? If our workweeks continue to expand, when will we find the time for growth and development, not to mention leisure?

## *Learning Possibility*

Everyone seems to be "infopressed" or "infostressed," but we are forgetting that technology is supposed to help solve these frustrations. For example, a computer scientist (Young 1999, A30) notes that there should be better ways to manage data electronically so that the user does not have to be "burdened by the obsolete idea of creating a name and folder for a file." Those who have many computer files, whether data, online, or document, appreciate this thought. Can you, and your students, generate more "out-of-the-box" ideas that will change the way we currently view work and technology?

## *Teaching Possibility*

Many online calendars and organizers are available to help you schedule your time, organize personal information in address books or meeting folders, etc., by providing e-mail message reminders of events, organized lists, etc. Since most of these services are free (Varhol and Varhol 1999) online, you can teach your students a "technology age" method of organizing class assignments and social opportunities. Let your students impress your administrator or other teachers by having them demonstrate how this skill can assist busy educators. Be sure that students learn about the need for security with these systems; you'll want to use a system that is more secure. Try *CalendarsNet* (http://www.calendars.net) or *Your Organiser* (http://www.yourorganiser.com.au).

---

# Lack of Equipment and Funds

An obvious answer to the lack of equipment and funds is to get more equipment through more funds. Realizing that budgets are tight, an educator always has the option of pursuing alternative funding.

## *Learning Possibility*

Speak to your school district grants office about E-rate or other distance learning funding possibilities. What grant funds are available for technology or distance education? What are the funds that are currently available within the district? What would your principal like to see the school pursue in terms of funding? Is there support for forming a committee to work on applying for funds? By the way, the *Technology Opportunities Program* (http://www .ntia.doc.gov/ntiahome/top/) offers districts substantial grant funds to close the "Digital Divide." Can your district qualify for this program?

---

## *Learning Possibility*

The term, "Digital Divide," has enjoyed much play in the press, but what does this really mean? The U.S. Department of Commerce has published *Falling Through the Net: Defining the Digital Divide* (November 1999) (http://www .ntia.doc.gov/ntiahome/digitaldivide) in an effort to identify which groups are not receiving services and information. Based on this report, who are those at risk in your school community? What are the strategies that your school can develop to make sure that these groups are fully serviced?

---

Beyond the lack of equipment in the classroom, what about the lack of equipment in some students' homes? The Commerce Department shows that the disparity between black, Hispanic, and white households on Internet access is still great (*Edupage*, 9 July 1999), but a study has suggested that the issue may be economic (*Edupage*, 20 April 2000) and not racial. Within the workplace, employees in the income bracket of $21,000 to $33,000 may not have access to the Internet, which might account for this group's higher-than-average Internet use (*Edupage*, 25 September 2001).

It is difficult to argue that distance learning technologies cannot be implemented without equipment and funding. Distance learning activities do not always have to incorporate the highest forms of technology. Barker (1989), well respected for research in distance and rural education for K–12 groups, concluded that there was no one best method or technology for distance education (5). All forms of distance learning that have telecommunication components have advantages and disadvantages (Barker 1991).

In one of the most impressive documents relating to distance education, Thomas Russell maintains a bibliography of 355 entries ranging from 1928 to the present that focused on the technological methods of presenting courses (Russell 1999). Russell has assessed that, "No matter how it is produced, how it is delivered, whether or not it is interactive, low-tech or high-tech, students learn equally well with each technology and learn as well as their on-campus, face-to-face counterparts even though students would rather be on campus with the instructor if that were a real choice" (1997, 6). The focus of this bibliography is on technology as it relates to distance education. It indicates that students learn well in distance settings, regardless of the technology used. (You can also search the *No Significant Difference Phenomenon* at http://teleeducation.nb.ca/nosignificantdifference/ for selected entries from the bibliography.)

At university settings, the argument could be made that, if learning outcomes are the same, it is advisable to use the cheapest technology that will get the job done. The same argument cannot be made for PreK–12 students, due to student reading level ranges and having fewer school years than university students. Even so, you, the PreK–12 teacher, may consider adapting the philosophy that the latest "bells-and-whistles" concept is not always the best. Another literature review addressing the topics of learner outcomes, learner perceptions, learner attributes, interaction, and distance education technology also reflected the "no significant difference" and pointed out that distance education is effective in terms of student outcomes (Maushak 1997).

Sometimes it is the lack of materials that causes educators to be their most creative and effective. If you are interested in having the students listen to a presentation by a famous Shakespearean actor, and you do not have access to videoconferencing, what are your options?

- Cancel the activity.

- Start fund-raising for equipment.

- Badger your administrator for more money.

- Complain.

- Use a telephone with a speakerphone and arrange a telephone call where the actor would read passages for students to hear.

One of these options is the most productive, because of its low expense, easy access, focus on the outcome of hearing and experiences, and, by chance, it would also give students the opportunity to practice listening skills.

To the teachers who remember school life without photocopying machines or enough textbooks for all students, you are already creative and know how to work with limited resources. Many of those same creative activities you once accomplished with paper, or limited resources, can now be accomplished with technology.

To deal with the lack of equipment and funds:

- Focus on the desired learning outcome. Are visual images always required? Can the display of one workstation be projected so that many can watch at one time?

- Search the literature. There are always examples of how teachers accomplish wonderful things on limited funds.

- Generate local, district, state, and organizational grant applications. Recycle these applications generously and submit them as a different grant request.

- Request a presentation by the educational technologist and media specialist of the types of equipment that exist in your school.

- Ask your administrator to cooperate with administrators of other local schools. What types of equipment do they have that they are willing to share, swap, or check out?

- Find out what is available from the district. If there are items that you will be using less than a half dozen times a year, borrowing equipment may be the answer.

- Keep an eye on district publications that list resources. For example, some districts or institutions have a surplus center where you can find free items to support your activities. Nova Southeastern University's Teacher Universe operates *Crayons to Computers*, a free teacher store (http://www.crayonstocomputers.org/).

- Keep a cost-saver contest going. Reward the teacher who submits the best distance learning tip. If your tips are that great, submit them for publication and earn more money for interactive distance learning technologies.

As you develop your interactive distance learning activities, you will begin to share ideas with your colleagues on inexpensive ways to implement these plans. There are many online resources (in the form of listserv communication and Web sites) that offer cost-saving ideas on using distance learning in educational settings. Don't overlook the literature as another source of ideas. Low-cost ideas are available for the searching (Fries and Monahan 1999).

## Lack of Ideas for Incorporating Interactive Distance Learning Technologies in the Classroom

Luckily for you, there are more traditional and Web-based educational publications in existence today than ever before. There is no lack of ideas on how to incorporate interactive distance learning technologies in the classroom, and you will be directed to many of these ideas in this handbook.

### *Teaching Possibility*

Revisit your teacher preparation program from years ago. Search your institution online to see if there is a description of courses available, or request a current catalog from your educational program. How has your program changed? What have been the changes in the technology or distance learning courses? What are the new competencies that are expected from graduates? Do students take courses in traditional formats, or has this delivery method changed also? What are some of the textbooks that are being used in the current courses? How are the assignments different? Do the libraries provide different materials in different formats? In "Preparing Information Professionals for the Next Century" (Small 1998), the issues of core skills, distance learning, active learning, and leadership skills are addressed for information professionals. Do these same issues apply to your area of curriculum?

To help the educator who is looking for ideas on how to use interactive distance learning technologies:

- Request a booktalk (or magazine talk) from the school library media specialist. Find out which technology publications are available in the school.

- Request training sessions from educational technologists and experienced distance learning instructors. Most teachers realize that the lack of training is a real problem when it comes to using technology in the classroom. Though this need for training may seem obvious to some, we have to keep reminding administrators and in-service trainers that one-shot training sessions are not enough.

- Ask teachers to share their professional journals and magazines. Make a list of teachers who are willing to share reading materials, and route the publications among all that are interested. (Beyond the e-book, are you ready to work with online textbooks? Could your school support this technology for its students? Can you think of a distance learning setting where the online textbook is preferable to the physical textbook? Do you want to save your students' backs and promote lighter book bags? Try the *NetLibrary* (http://www.netlibrary.com/) or *ebrary* (http://www .ebrary.com) interface. Would this be handy for the students who are reading public domain titles, such as *Hamlet*, that claim that "the dog ate the book" so the student could not finish the reading assignment? Is your school interested in helping students who have handheld devices, such as a Palm or Pocket PC, to download e-books? Will these handheld devices be available to teachers who would like to download free reference materials or e-books?)

- Monitor online listservs. In terms of current practices, with better chances for immediate response to your questions, listservs are invaluable. Listservs that are specific to PreK–12 educators and distance learning technologies are mentioned later in this handbook.

- Interview a distance learning student. This could be your child, a colleague, or a parent of a student. What did this person experience through the distance learning activity? What was liked or disliked? What was gained by this learning? Most importantly, would this person attempt another distance learning experience? Why or why not? What would have to be changed for this person to pursue another distance learning experience?

## *Learning Possibility*

Have you ever read an electronic book (e-book)? Ask your school library media specialist if e-book viewers are currently available at your school or go to *eBooknet.com* (http://eBooknet.com) for more information on the availability of the technology. Consider reading an e-book yourself (which viewer will you choose?), or invite your class to read an e-book. Benefits of this technology are the storage capacity (ten or more book contents in the space that would ordinarily provide the contents of one physical book with a push-button page-turner) (*Palm Beach Post*, 30 August 1999, 4A). You may decide to read an e-book to your class! E-book sources, such as *Online Books Page* (http://onlinebooks.library.upenn.edu/) and *Project Gutenburg* (http://promo .net/pg/), offer titles to read on your viewers (Dorman 1999). When finished, discuss the experience. Is it one that you will be likely to repeat? Are students interested in reading e-books in the future? What are the benefits and disadvantages? Would this technology improve the reading abilities of a student with physical limitations? Has the e-book been a commercial success? Even if not popular with the general population, do you expect to see an increase in the development of e-textbooks for the PreK–12 market? For the postsecondary market?

Regardless of the challenges at hand, problem solving often draws upon known models, or metaphors, to provide guidance leading to solutions. The same is true with distance learning. Because we are in agreement, for the most part, of what a traditional classroom is, we are able to communicate about learning using this metaphor. We have set practices on behaviors, participants, and the teacher and student views of what happens in a classroom (Pastor, Sanchez, and Alvarez 1991, 262). Until the distance learning model is better communicated, relying upon the existing metaphor you have about classrooms may help you to develop your own ideas on how the distance learning classroom should exist. Many have offered their own models of distance learning and design, whether verbal or virtual; however, if you do not accept these models and cannot function within them, they are meaningless. Frustrations with technology and interpersonal relations can be a reality of distance learning (Coutts 1996), but there are ways of constructively solving these problems. Nevertheless, it is important that you define the distance learning model you use in your classroom.

In your distance learning model, what happens when the network breaks down or when the teacher is absent? Just as with any other unexpected event in the classroom, a "Plan B" is needed. Along these lines, do not lose sight of the need to plan for the classroom without technological support. Whether it is a photocopying machine or a networked system that is down, the teacher with subject-matter command will have no problem continuing creative learning activities.

In this section, we have briefly discussed the challenges that prevent the implementation of interactive distance learning technologies in PreK–12 schools. The skepticism, lack of understanding of how technology works, constant changes with technology, lack of time, lack of equipment and funds, and lack of ideas on how to incorporate distance learning technology in the classroom may affect your program to varying degrees. Be aware that these challenges are affecting other instructors, both locally and globally, with further consideration being given to how to support the distance education student, how to pay for this instruction, and how to foster the communication between institutions that support distance education (Mortera-Gutierrez 1998, 2). However, regardless of your school's chief challenge, there are strategies that can be followed. Solutions can be found in literature (Pritchett 1999), online, and through your colleagues. Administrators, colleagues, parents, and students that want you to succeed with incorporating technologies into your curriculum will provide motivation. The rewards will come from seeing firsthand that interactive distance learning technologies benefit student learning outcomes.

## *Learning Possibility*

Discuss with your colleagues how they view the role of distance learning in their current classroom. Do they view this negatively, positively, or skeptically? What would encourage them to incorporate distance learning today? How do they see distance learning as changing the classroom of the future? Would anyone be interested in creating a teaching time capsule of predictions for distance learning that will be shared on the first in-service training day, five years from now?

# Section D. Today's Definition of Distance Learning in the PreK–12 School

What is distance learning? If you are reading the professional literature, you may find different definitions of distance learning based on participant involvement and location (Simonson, Smaldino, Albright, and Zvacek 2000). Among professional educators, you will find variance as to how to describe this learning model and its components. Even though these theoretical discussions within the profession deserve great respect, the chief reason for offering an operational definition in this practice-oriented handbook is not so much to encourage philosophical debate, but rather to offer guidance on commonalties of distance learning activities so that educators can communicate with each other. In *Returning to Our Roots: A Learning Society*, a joint report from the Kellogg Commission (1996) and the National Association of State Universities and Land Grant Colleges, state university leaders describe distance learning as "the linking of a teacher and students in several geographic locations via technologies that allow for interaction" (38). In 1988, distance learning meant "the live, simultaneous transmission of instruction from a teacher location at an origination site to students located in one or more distant or 'remote' sites. The instruction is considered interactive if there is two-way audio and/or two-way video transmission" (Kitchen and Kitchen 1988, 9). Lewis, Whitaker, and Julian (1995) provide a definition of distance education as "the delivery of the educational process to receivers who are not in proximity to the person or persons managing or conducting the process" (14). The United States Distance Learning Association (USDLA) defines distance learning as the acquisition of knowledge and skills through mediated information and instruction. (For this and other definitions on distance learning, link to http://www.usdla.org/html/resources/dictionary.htm#d and http://www.usdla.org.)

Regarding a definition of distance learning for PreK–12, issues related to age levels and activities will have a greater focus than they would if the definition applied only to postsecondary learners and adults. In order to arrive at this operational definition for a PreK–12 setting, consider the elements to include in the definition, along with the roles or activities for each element. These elements include:

- The learner,

- The teacher (coach, facilitator, guide, helper, leader, parent, etc.),

- The activity to be accomplished,

- The materials to support the learning activity,

- The place, and

- The time.

## The Learner

With the range of abilities present in the PreK–12 setting, remember that some students will require more guidance than others. Factor in the variety of learning styles, and it should become apparent that learners participate at a variety of ability levels. Beyond ability level, some learners will be present in the classroom, some will participate in a lab setting that requires less teacher direction than in a classroom setting, and some students will be away from the school campus where they function under a higher level of expected self-direction. For this definition, the student may be physically present with the teacher, but physical presence is not required.

## The Teacher (Coach, Facilitator, Guide, Helper, Leader, Parent)

Many educators will argue that distance learning activities do not require a teacher of any type. Although we could agree with this principle when postsecondary learners are involved, we will argue that the PreK–12 student, who is still learning process and basic subject content, continues to need some level of guidance. The student who is totally self-directed and mature is the exception, rather than the rule, in PreK–12 settings.

In our society, PreK–12 education is still directed by state mandates that address oversight and protection of our youth. Even for the exceptional student who is in the late teens or early twenties, yet enrolled in a PreK–12 environment, in loco parentis is still the expectation regarding how teachers and building-level staff engage with students. Requirements as to teacher qualifications, certifications, and general accountability measures still apply whether instruction is exclusively classroom based or whether it incorporates distance activities.

Therefore, can the student learn if the teacher is not physically present? With distance learning, the teacher becomes less directing and more guiding. Many of you have heard this educator role described as being more of the "guide by the side" than the "sage on the stage." Nevertheless, for our definition, must the teacher be present? The answer depends. If the activity is school based, an adult must be in close proximity, guiding the instruction and monitoring student behavior. If the activity is home based, a parent may or may not be physically present, but the parent must have awareness of the student's activities.

### *Learning Possibility*

What are your local and state policy procedures for home-based students? How can these students interact with school personnel via technology? What are the school services (e.g., library, gym) available to these students in real time?

## The Activity to Be Accomplished

We have district-prescribed and state-prescribed criteria for content matter in our schools. Laws, policies, and guidelines that relate to curriculum and standards drive the learning activities in most school systems. Based on these guidelines, policies, and standards, the teacher is charged with developing activities that lead to the accomplishment of these criteria. Distance learning activities can incorporate information and media that enhance student performance on various standardized tests and measures.

Are distance learning activities so different in nature from the traditional in-class learning activities? No. However, from the student's perspective, distance learning activities offer a greater opportunity to become engaged in a way that is different and fun. Must the learning activity be school based or home based? No. The learning activity, though directed by the teacher or supervised by the parent, may take place elsewhere, e.g., in a public library or at a museum, virtually or not.

## Materials to Support the Learning Activity

Never has there been a greater variety of print and electronic resources that benefit students. These learning materials are available in many media formats and in many locations. Because of this distributed access to information, students and teachers have an unparalleled degree of freedom in how, when, and where they learn.

## The Place of Learning

"If the phrase 'distance learning' sounds like an oxymoron to some ears, the answer may lie in an assumption that education takes place up close and personal" (Cunningham 1999). "Up close and personal" could certainly describe some of the learning that takes place when the learner is actively engaged with content received through a PC, whether by chat, e-mail, either within or without the confines of the classroom. However, whether learning occurs in the classroom, in the school library media center, in the school auditorium, at the county library, in an off-campus field trip, or at home, the place of learning is limited to school-sponsored or -monitored activities.

## The Time

Like place, the time of learning, for the purposes of this handbook, is limited to activities that are teacher sponsored or monitored.

## Definition of Distance Learning in the PreK–12 Classroom

For the purposes of this handbook, distance learning takes place when the teacher directs the learner in the use of selected activities and media that may or may not be in close physical proximity to each other, whether in real time or in delayed time. For example, a sixteen-year-old junior in a traditional high school, temporarily homebound for health reasons, can attend class by participating in a conference call, listening to his history teacher's lecture in real time. (A learner is not physically present in the same location as the teacher and other students; however, the teacher is directing the learner.) To continue this definition, a group of four ten-year-old elementary students can attend Japanese language class through videoconferencing with the lead teacher giving direction from a university classroom more than 500 miles away. (A teacher is not physically present in the same location with all students; however, the teacher is directing the learning.) Now, consider an online field trip to an art museum where students are able to observe separate works of art, as they listen to the guides identify each artist and provide details about the work. (An activity is taking place in a location that is physically remote from the teacher and students; however, the teacher has chosen the online source of the information and is directing the activity.) Finally, for the purpose of further placing our definition in context, a parent and seventh-grade child are at home researching the gross national product of Brazil through an online database to which the school subscribes and provides both school and remote access. (Resources are not physically present in the same location with the student; however, the teacher, in this example the parent, is working with the student to complete research.) In this example, on researching the gross national product of Brazil, resources are probably superior to those physically present in school and public libraries, because depending on which online database is being used, some sources are updated as frequently as weekly, daily, or even hourly.

# *Conclusion*

As you continue your readings on distance learning beyond this handbook, you will find multiple definitions of distance learning. You will refine your personal definition the more that you participate and study the area of distance learning. Be sure to find out how your school, district, or state defines distance learning. The American Council on Education Center for Adult Learning and Educational Credentials (1996, 10) defines distance learning as "a system and a process that connects learners with distributed learning resources," emphasizing the "separation of place and/or time between instructor and learner, among learners, and/or between learners and learning resources" and "interaction between the learner and the instructor, among learners, and/or between learners and learning resources conducted through one or more media; use of electronic media is not necessarily required." This handbook offers a definition that is not student or instructor specific, but rather "learning specific." Although place and time are related issues, they do not limit the learning activities. Again, because of the age of the learner, the student will be under some form of teacher supervision, whether the supervision is in the form of physical presence or filtering activities that are somehow controlled by technology. The key element of this definition is that the activities of the student are directed and supervised by the teacher.

A prediction for 2010: Just as multimedia has faded from the descriptions of computers and software, distance learning will fade from the educational vernacular. This format of delivery will increasingly become blended with the descriptions of everyday learning; teachers in all areas, at all levels, will be using distance learning technologies.

## Learning Possibility

Find other definitions of distance learning by searching online and print sources. Next, write your own definition of distance learning and date it for future reference. In the near future, after you have had experiences with different distance learning technologies, revisit your definition to see if it still fits the model for how you currently view distance learning. Can you articulate this definition to your peers, administrators, and parents of your students? After they have participated in distance learning activities, do your students have other viewpoints regarding this definition? Does your definition fit the test of time and the impact of change on the rapidly evolving profession of education? If you would like to share your definition of distance learning with others, e-mail this description to me (idlearning@adelphia.net), and I will collect these definitions on this handbook's Web page.

# *References*

American Council on Education Center for Adult Learning and Educational Credentials. *Guiding Principles for Distance Learning in a Learning Society.* Washington, DC: ACE Central Services, 1996.

Ball, Jennie, and Bob Crook. "Managing Change Through Distance Learning." *Community College Journal of Research and Practice* 21 (1997): 13–22.

Barker, Bruce O. *Distance Education Technologies: All That Glitters Is Not Gold* (Paper presented at the Annual Meeting of the Decisions About Technology Conference, 10 May 1989, Bismarck, ND). ERIC ED 309 894.

———. "Distance Learning Technologies in K–12 Schools: Past, Present, and Future Practice." *TechTrends* 41, no. 6 (1996): 19–22.

———. *K–12 Distance Education in the United States: Technology Strengths, Weaknesses, and Issues* (Paper presented at the Annual International Conference on Distance Learning, 10–13 April 1991, Washington, DC, 90). ERIC ED 332 687.

Becker, Hank, and Ronald Anderson. *Teaching, Learning, and Computing 1998, A National Survey of Schools and Teachers.* Irvine, CA: University of California, Center for Research on Information Technology and Organizations (CRITO), 1998. (http://www.crito.uci.edu/tlc/html/tlc_home.html) (28 March 2000).

Brooks, Nancy Rivera. "More Employees Are Missing Work Due to Stress, Feeling of Entitlement." *Palm Beach Post* (24 September 1999): 8D.

Bureau of Labor Statistics. *Employment Projections* (Table 3b. "The 10 Fastest Growing Occupations, 1998–2008"), 9 February 2000. (http://stats.bls.gov/news.release/ecopro.t06.htm) (28 March 2000).

Carnvale, Dan. "Instructor Cuts Dropout Rate by Giving Extra Attention to On-Line Students." *The Chronicle of Higher Education*, 7 January 2000a. (http://chronicle.com/free/99/12/99121601u.htm) (28 March 2000).

———. "Survey Finds 72% Rise in Number of Distance-Education Programs." *The Chronicle of Higher Education*, 7 January 2000b. (http://chronicle.com/weekly/v46/i18/18a05701.htm) (20 January 2000).

Chambers, Gail S. "Toward Shared Control of Distance Education." *The Chronicle of Higher Education*, 19 November 1999. (http://chronicle.com/weekly/v46/i13/13b00801.htm) (21 December 1999).

"Chinese Government Predicts Strong Growth in Online Education," 15 May 2001, *Edupage* (owner-edupage @listserv.educause.edu) (http://www.educause.edu/pub/edupage/edupage.html).

Coburn, Dawn, Vince Dobbs, and Sheila Grainger. "Future-Proofing the Curriculum." *Educational Leadership International* 53, no. 2 (1995): 85–87.

Connick, George P., ed. *The Distance Learner's Guide.* Upper Saddle River, NJ: Prentice-Hall, 1999.

Cornish, Edward. *The Cyber Future: 92 Ways Our Lives Will Change by the Year 2025.* Bethesda, MD: World Future Society, 1996.

Coutts, Julia. *The Effects of Distance Education Technology on Teaching and Learning*, 1996. ERIC ED 406 964.

Criscito, Pat. *Barron's Guide to Distance Learning: Degrees, Certificates, Courses.* Hauppauge, NY: Barron's Educational Series, 1999.

Cunningham, Jim, ed. "Is Distance Learning an Oxymoron?" *The Florida AAUP Newsletter* 2, no. 6 (1999): 3.

"Digital Divide: It's Money, Not Race—Study," 20 April 2000, *Edupage* (owner-edupage@listserv.educause.edu) (http://www.educause.edu/pub/edupage/edupage.html).

Donovan, Mark, and Scott Macklin. "The Catalyst Project: Supporting Faculty Uses of the Web . . . with the Web." *CAUSE/EFFECT* 22, no. 3 (1999): 18–25.

Dorman, David. "The E-Book: Pipe Dream or Potential Disaster?" *American Libraries* 30, no. 2 (1999): 36–39.

"Dow Chemical to Fire Workers for Violating Its Policy on E-Mail," 23 August 2000, *Edupage* (owner-edupage @listserv.educause.edu) (http://www.educause.edu/pub/edupage/edupage.html).

Edwards, Richard. *Changing Places? Flexibility, Lifelong Learning and a Learning Society.* London: Routledge, 1997.

Erdos, Renee F. *Teaching by Correspondence.* UNESCO Source Books on Curricula and Methods (3). London: Longmans, 1967.

Frand, Jason L. "The Information-Age Mindset: Changes in Students and Implications for Higher Education." *EDUCAUSE Review* 35, no. 5 (2000): 14–24.

Fries, Bedelia, and Brian Monahan. "Low Cost Distance Learning Strategies for Educators," 1999. ERIC ED 426 988.

George, Gerard, Randall G. Sleeth, and C. Glenn Pearce. "Technology-Assisted Instruction and Instructor Cyberphobia: Recognizing the Ways to Effect Change." *Education* 116, no. 4 (1996): 604–5.

Giltrow, David. "K–12 Enrollment Increase Requires Rethinking Distance Education Delivery." *Distance Education Report* 1, no. 8 (1997): 6.

Glennan, Thomas K., and Arthur Melmed. *Fostering the Use of Educational Technology: Elements of a National Strategy* (A Rand Report). (http://www.rand.org/publications/MR/MR682/) (4 February 2002).

Hanson, Dan. "Distance Education: Definition, History, Status, and Theory." In *Encyclopedia of Distance Education Research in Iowa*, 2d ed., edited by Beth Kumar et al. Ames, IA: Technology Research and Evaluation Group, Iowa State University, 1997.

Henderson, Brenda, L. K. Curda, and Stephen Curda. "Challenging the 'Monster Under the Bed.' " *ATEA Journal* (February–March 1999): 17–20.

Holzberg, Carol. "15 Technology Products That Changed the Classroom." *Electronic Learning* 16, no. 1 (1996): 30–31.

Hussar, William J. *Predicting the Need for Newly Hired Teachers in the United States to 2008–9* (NCES 1999-026), 1999. (http://nces.ed.gov/pubs2000/qtrlywinter/3elem/3-esq14-g.html) (26 February 2000).

Johnson, Doug. "Developing an Ethical Compass for Worlds of Learning." *MultiMedia Schools* 5, no. 5 (1998): 43–47.

Kaufman, Marc. "School May Begin Too Early for Teens." *Palm Beach Post* (26 September 1999): 2A.

Kellogg Commission. *Returning to Our Roots: A Learning Society*, 1996. (http://www.nasulgc.org/publications/Kellogg/Learn.pdf) (23 February 2000).

Kilian, Crawford. "F2F: Why Teach Online." *Educom Review* 32, no. 4 (1997): 31–34.

Kitchen, Karen, and Will Kitchen. *Two-Way Interactive Television for Distance Learning: A Primer.* Alexandria, VA: ITTE Technology Leadership Network, National School Boards Association, 1988.

Laird, Ellen. "Distance-Learning Instructors: Watch Out for the Cutting Edge." *The Chronicle of Higher Education* 45, no. 38 (28 May 1999): B6.

Lewis, Justus, Janet Whitaker, and John Julian. "Distance Education for the 21st Century: The Future of National and International Telecomputing Networks in Distance Education." In *Computer Mediated Communication and the Online Classroom. Volume Three: Distance Learning*, edited by Zane L. Berge and Mauri P. Collins, 1–30. Cresskill, NJ: Hampton, 1995.

MacFarland, Thomas. *Distance Education at Nova Southeastern University* (Research and Planning Report 96–20). Ft. Lauderdale, FL: Nova Southeastern University Press, 1996.

MacKenzie, Ossian, and Edward L. Christensen. *The Changing World of Correspondence Study: International Readings.* University Park, PA: Pennsylvania State University Press, 1971.

*A Matter of Time: Risk and Opportunity in the Nonschool Hours.* New York: Carnegie Corporation, 1992, 29.

Maushak, Nancy J. "Distance Education: A Review of the Literature." In *Encyclopedia of Distance Education Research in Iowa*, 2d ed. Ames, IA: Teacher Education Alliance of the Iowa Distance Education Alliance, Iowa's Star Schools Project, 1997.

"Message Overload Distracting, Workers Say." *Palm Beach Post* (1 October 1999): 2A.

Mills, Karen. "School Nurtures Budding Artists by Mail." *Palm Beach Post* (6 March 2000): 1D, 10D.

Moffett, Dan, and A. Scharnhorst. "Pipe Bombs Easy, Do-It-Yourself Curse That's Been Around for Years." *Palm Beach Post* (31 May 1999): 1A, 8A.

Moore, Michael G. "American Distance Education." In *Open and Distance Learning Today*, edited by Fred Lockwood. New York: Routledge, 1995.

Moore, Michael G., and Melody M. Thompson. *The Effects of Distance Learning: A Summary of the Literature.* University Park, PA: American Center for the Study of Distance Education, College of Education, Pennsylvania State University, 1990.

Mortera-Gutierrez, Fernando. *Distance Education in the Educational System of Mexico* (Paper presented at the Annual Distance Education Conference, 27–30 January 1998, Austin, TX). ERIC ED 415 426.

"No More Pencils, No More Books," 11 February 2000, *Edupage* (owner-edupage@listserv.educause.edu) (http://www.educause.edu/pub/edupage/edupage.html).

Oblinger, Diana. *Global Education in the 21st Century: Competition and Being Future Compatible.* Presentation at the Closing General Session of the 1998 Conference on Information Technology of the League for Innovation at the Miami-Dade Community College, 4 November 1998, Miami Beach, FL. (http://www.league.org/publication/keynotes /oblingers1.htm) (5 February 2000).

Olsen, Florence. "Faculty Wariness of Technology Remains a Challenge, Computing Survey Finds," 21 October 1999a, *The Chronicle of Higher Education* (http://chronicle.com/free/99/10/99102101t.htm).

———. "The Promise and Problems of a New Way of Teaching Math." *The Chronicle of Higher Education*, 8 October 1999b. (http://chronicle.com/free/v46/i07/07a03101.htm).

"Online Learning: The Competitive Edge," 28 October 2000, *Edupage* (owner-edupage@listserv.educause.edu) (http://www.educause.edu/pub/edupage/edupage.html).

*An Overview of Intellectual Property Issues Associated with Distance Learning in Florida.* The Florida Legislature Joint Committee on Information Technology Resources, 1995. ERIC ED 393 444.

Passey, Don. "Developing Teaching Strategies for Distance (Out-of-School) Learning in Primary and Secondary Schools." *Educational Media International* 37, no. 1 (2000): 45–57.

Pastor, Encarna, Gonzalo Sanchez, and Javier Alvarez. "Distributed Multimedia Environment for Distance Learning." In *Collaborative Dialogue Technologies in Distance Learning*, edited by M. Felisa Verdejo and Cerri Stefano. New York: Springer-Verlag, 1991.

Paulsen, Morten Flate, et al. "A Pedagogical Framework for CMC Programmes." In *Collaborative Dialogue Technologies in Distance Learning*, edited by M. Felisa Verdejo and Cerri Stefano. New York: Springer-Verlag, 1991.

"Pirating of Software Rampant on Campus," 27 November 2000, *Edupage* (owner-edupage@listserv.educause.edu) (http://www.educause.edu/pub/edupage/edupage.html).

Pritchett, Price. "Ground Rules for Job Success in the Information Age." *Knowledge Quest* 27, no. 3 (1999): 38–39.

"Programming Your PC No Longer Requires Advanced Skills," 28 December 2001, *Edupage* (owner-edupage @listserv.educause.edu) (http://www.educause.edu/pub/edupage/edupage.html).

Race, Phil. *The Open Learning Handbook: Promoting Quality in Designing and Delivering Flexible Learning.* East Brunswick, NJ: Nichols, 1994.

"Readers Seem to Be Flipping Past Pages of Electronic Books So Far." *Palm Beach Post* (30 August 1999): 4A.

Rossman, Mark H., and Maxine E. Rossman, eds. *Facilitating Distance Education* (New Directions for Adult and Continuing Education, no. 67). San Francisco, CA: Jossey-Bass, 1995.

Russell, Thomas L. "Explaining, Exploring, Understanding the No Significant Difference Phenomenon." *Adult Assessment Forum,* 7, no. 4 (1997): 6–9.

———. *The No Significant Difference Phenomenon: As Reported in 355 Research Reports, Summaries and Papers.* Raleigh, NC: North Carolina State University, 1999.

Schneiderman, Ben. "Jefferson's Laptop: Modern Musings on User Interfaces for Universal Creativity." *Educom Review* 34, no. 3 (1999): 34–36.

Simonson, Michael, Sharon Smaldino, Michael Albright, and Susan Zvacek. *Teaching and Learning at a Distance: Foundations of Distance Education.* Upper Saddle River, NJ: Merrill, 2000.

Small, Ruth V. "Preparing Information Professionals for the Next Century." *ERIC/IT Update* 20, no. 1 (1998): 1, 3.

Smart, Joseph E. *A Short History of the Early Years of Study by Correspondence.* Rocheport, MO: Smartco, 1987.

Solloway, Sharon G., and Edward L. Harris. "Creating Community Online: Negotiating Students' Desires and Needs in Cyberspace." *Educom Review* 34, no. 2 (1999): 8–9, 12–13.

"Surprising Data on Digital Divide," 25 September 2001, *Edupage* (owner-edupage@listserv.educause.edu) (http://www.educause.edu/pub/edupage/edupage.html).

"A Third of Workday Spent on Computer," 18 February 2000, *Edupage* (owner-edupage@listserv.educause.edu) (http://www.educause.edu/pub/edupage/edupage.html).

"U.S. Cites Race Gap in Use of Internet," 9 July 1999, *Edupage* (owner-edupage@listserv.educause.edu) (http://www.educause.edu/pub/edupage/edupage.html).

Varhol, Pamela H., and Peter D. Varhol. "Meet Me on the Web?" *Mobile Computing and Communications* 10, no. 9 (1999): 72–86.

Watkins, Barbara L., and Stephen J. Wright, eds. *The Foundations of American Distance Education: A Century of Collegiate Correspondence Study*. Dubuque, IA: Kendall/Hunt, 1991.

"The Web Began Its Spinning 30 Years Ago." *Palm Beach Post* (30 August 1999): 2A.

Wedemeyer, Charles A., and Gayle B. Childs. *New Perspectives in University Correspondence Study*. Chicago: Center for the Study of Liberal Education for Adults, 1961.

Young, Jeffrey R. "Yale Professor Aims to Bring Order to Your Computer with 'Lifestreams' Program." *The Chronicle of Higher Education* (21 May 1999): A30.

# Chapter 3

# Models of Interactive Distance Learning Activities

Interactive distance learning activities involve the use of many technologies, some of which have been in existence for years and others that are still evolving. In this chapter, descriptions of technologies that can be used for interactive distance learning activities will be provided for those educators who need simple descriptions of the modalities in order to know how to implement them.

Before we move into specific technology formats, be aware that many of these formats have commonalities; however, regardless of the format, teachers must always verify the appropriateness of the reading content for their students. In a section "Designing and Writing for Effective Print-Based Learning Materials" (Ropel 1997), thirty-four tips are presented on how to prepare print materials. Whether you are designing or evaluating study guides to accompany audio, correspondence, video, or Web learning experiences, remember that all elements must be developed with the learner in mind.

Regardless of the technology used, provisions must be made for:

1. Course materials delivery

2. Class management

3. Teacher selection

4. Participant interaction

5. Schedules

6. Technical difficulties

7. Vendor selection and support

8. Equipment compatibility

The delivery of a distance learning course can be appealing to many teachers who want a new challenge. If you are looking for a new method of teaching, or think that your current teaching methods are not working, read on to see if distance learning can help you to lead students to learn in a new way (Engler 2000).

# Section A. Delayed-Time Interactive Distance Learning Activities

The process of learning in delayed time, as opposed to real time, expands learning opportunities so that students are not bound by time or place. With delayed-time interactive distance learning activities, the learner determines when and where the learning will take place. Since delayed-time activities can be accessed according to the learner's schedule, they are particularly attractive to working students and adults who have family responsibilities. Just a reminder, as mentioned in Chapter 1, correspondence through the postal service is an example of delayed-time communication that can be used to support distance learning activities.

## Audio

Audiotape is a magnetic storage medium that can be accessed almost universally through audiocassette recorders at home, in the car, and through portable models. One of the lowest-priced mediums, audiotapes have been used for many years in education and training, and they are still widely found as a supporting technology for many distance learning activities. Today, audiotapes are usually referred to as cassette tapes.

Because of their ease of use, PreK–12 students can use audiotapes independently to listen to and record any verbal presentations. Stories, songs, musical performances, dramatic interpretations, etc., can be shared with other students in alternative locations through the use of audiocassettes. Instructors can record classroom presentations that may then be distributed to homebound students or shared with distant teachers and their students. Audiotapes support the creation of independent learning packages that present a listen-only medium, although students can also respond to the original audiotapes and record these responses on audiotape. Using audiotape for language instruction is ideal, if the goal is to focus on the spoken language. Nonreaders, whether preschool age or adult, can use this medium for education and entertainment.

In an educational setting, audiotapes can be easily paired with other print formats, such as visuals and workbooks. Adults have found audiotapes to be a convenient form for learning while performing other activities like driving or jogging. The audiotape offers the benefit of providing content that can be repeated as often as necessary.

Whether for native or foreign-language development and practice, preservation of speaker presentations, providing individualized instruction, developing listening centers, or to target specific listening skills, audiotapes can be used in any location. Remember that audiotape can be used for providing feedback to the instructor as well. If verification of practice is the objective, students can provide this evidence to the teacher on tape. If the activity relates to group work, progress can be monitored by the teacher on tape. When evaluating the ideal qualities of a medium, audiotape is a good selection (Rowntree 1994, 6).

Before using audiotape, consider these suggestions:

1.  Determine the length of your presentation to be recorded.

2.  Make sure that the audiotape's length is sufficient to record the presentation.

3.  Verify that the built-in microphone is functional. If it is not, attach a plug-in microphone for input.

4.  Reduce background noise, then push the "record" button.

5.  While recording, be sure to describe each activity sufficiently so the listener can follow along.

6. When finished with the recording, rewind and review the audiotape to make sure that the recording is audible. Do some areas need additional description that can be added to the tape, or would copies of printed materials or examples make the audiotaped message more meaningful?

7. If you would like to "cue" your recording, consult the audiocassette recorder's user manual for specific directions. This action will allow you to synchronize any accompanying printed materials with its corresponding audiotaped portion.

For presentations that are being created, commercial audiotape should be purchased through the district supply warehouse or vendor in different lengths, based on the activity. If students will be creating stories to share, a thirty-minute audiotape should be adequate. If a lesson-long presentation will be recorded, a sixty-minute audiotape should be adequate. For longer presentations, many educators choose multiple copies of sixty-minute audiotapes, avoiding ninety-minute audiotapes because of the possibility of the longer audiotape malfunctioning and causing the loss of a longer activity.

Because of the variety and quality of tape recorders, many schools wisely purchase industrial-grade tape recorders. Since these items are available in most schools, you will only need to make sure that the recorder is in good, operable condition and that the recording heads have been recently cleaned. Your media specialist will help you with this maintenance task, as well as provide guidance on ordering tapes in your school and district.

Your media specialist can also direct you to vendors that provide prerecorded audiotapes. Some vendors specialize in recorded books (audiobooks) in both abridged and unabridged formats. Others specialize in recorded courses for special populations. Products are available for a wide variety of learning levels.

It is imperative that each teacher verifies that the audio content supports the goals and objectives of the courses that the teacher has designed. Some audio course packages may be available in-state or through other educational institutions that include printed learning materials and assessments. However, be thinking in advance as to how the credit for the course will be offered and who will be the sponsoring teacher for the course.

When making purchases, check the vendor agreements for guarantees of product. Try to choose a vendor that offers a trial of the product. For direction to audio title and other vendors that provide audio products, consult:

*Bowker's Directory of Audiocassettes for Children* (New York: R. R. Bowker)

*National Information Center for Educational Media (NICEM) Audiovisual Database* (or *MediaSleuth*) (http://www.nicem.com)

School Media Associates (http://www.schoolmediaassociates.com) 1-800-451-5226

Words on Cassette (New York: R. R. Bowker) (http://www.bowker.com/bowkerweb/) 1-888-269-5372

To purchase audio titles, contact:

Audio Editions Books on Cassette (http://www.audioeditions.com) 1-800-231-4261

Audiobooks (http://www.listeninglib.com/audio/) 1-800-243-4504

Baker & Taylor (http://www.btol.com) 1-800-775-1800

Blackstone Audiobooks (Distributes unabridged audiobooks on various subjects) (http://www.blackstoneaudio.com) 1-800-729-2665

Books on Tape (http://booksontape.com) 1-800-521-7925

Follett Audiovisual (http://www.follett.com) 1-800-621-4345

The Great Courses on Tape (The Teaching Company). For noncredit college-level courses (http://www.teachco.com) 1-800-832-2412

Recording for the Blind & Dyslexic (http://www.rfbd.org) 1-800-221-4792

For more ideas on using audiotape, consult *Teaching Tips for Using Audio Cassettes* (http://www.teachervision.com/lesson-plans/lesson-4100.html). Don't forget that you can search the *ERIC Database* (http://ericir.syr.edu) (search for "teaching with audio") to locate multiple lessons plans.

Though the technology exists to record audio in CD (compact disc) format, it is still not affordable for all school levels, making audiotape a useful medium. Audiotape is an available technology that requires few skills to operate. However, as prices continue to drop, making the technology more accessible, many educators will continue to move from audiotape to the higher–sound quality CD, or place the sound presentations online. Even so, the learning principles and techniques of audiotape will still apply.

## Audio (Digital)

Though the principles are similar, digital audio in the format of either compact disc (CD) or online audio clips offers more distance learning possibilities. If using compact discs, the applications are similar to using audiotapes. The benefits, though, are that the physical medium is more durable and has a greater storage capacity. Your media specialist will be able to provide you with information on how to master CDs for your students.

Online audio clips are great to support Web learning. You can record a clip directly into your computer and upload it to a Web page. Audio clips require more memory than text. The benefits of hearing the teacher's or other students' voices to explain a specific point or express enthusiasm or personal insight allow the mode of instruction to become varied.

## CD-ROM

CD-ROM is a term that stands for Compact Disc–Read-Only Memory. This term has been used for more than twenty years, since the medium has been in existence. However, because of new technologies, the term "CD-ROM" is used here with hesitation because there are recordable forms of this medium (CD-R and CD-RW) that are still referred to as CD-ROM. Moreover, today, most software is distributed in a CD-ROM format. During the early 1990s, the term "CD-ROM" generally referred to a special type of software that tended to be multimedia in format. Today, almost all forms of software have multiple media elements and, thus, are multimedia.

The evaluation of CD-ROM for instructional purposes is important to all members of the school community. Why? We know that there is a wide variance of quality audiovisual products that includes CD-ROM.

### *Teaching Possibility*

What is the connection between Beethoven's Ninth Symphony and the physical diameter of a CD-ROM? Where is a good starting point for answering this question?

CD-ROM and software vendors are plentiful, both online and locally. The challenges when purchasing software for PreK–12 settings are few, but important. First, the question regarding returns should be asked. Some companies do not allow returns of any kind after the shrink-wrap cover has been torn. Therefore, before making a purchase, it would be wise to be accurate about all purchasing specifications including:

1.  Hardware specifications

2.  Network requirements

3.  Peripheral requirements

4.  Software support

5.  System specifications

Beyond the physical system requirements, the following considerations should be made regarding the software itself and its uses:

1.  Student grade-level requirements

2.  Student reading-level requirements

3.  Product support by vendor or producer (Is vendor support toll-free, or is there a long-distance charge? Does the vendor offer short-term, toll-free support and then only answer your questions through a "900" support line, or, worse, through paid metered service that costs you long-distance charges *and* a per-minute charge? Have you tried contacting the company via its toll-free number before you need the support?)

4.  Product support through published (CD-ROM, electronic, or paper) materials that accompany the product

Software evaluation is a skill that increasingly is being practiced by educators who desire learning experiences that are of the highest quality for their students. In addition to the issues listed, questions to guide you through the software selection process are presented in Chapter 6. Beyond your personal, professional evaluation of software, it is important to work with a vendor that understands and supports the PreK–12 environment by providing prompt service, fair pricing, and good support through toll-free telephone numbers. Some vendors, such as School Media Associates, provide value-added services that include free or reduced-price shipping, a free search system, and free order compiling.

## Correspondence

Although one of the most basic forms of interactive distance learning, correspondence (also called independent study) still has applications in today's setting. It is described as an affordable option for remote learning experiences. Even at the postsecondary level, one of the most prescriptive regional accrediting associations in the United States, the Commission on Colleges of the Southern Association of Colleges and Schools, not only recognizes the legitimacy of distance learning, but it specifically included the term "correspondence courses" when offering a list of sample distance learning modalities (*Criteria for Accreditation* 1998, 39).

What are some ways to use correspondence in distance learning? Though rarely used in the United States, newspapers have been used in African countries, along with correspondence to provide topics that "encourage participation and some two-way communication" (Jenkins 1981). Distance learning products have also been designed for African nations, such as the *Village Level Cassava Processing* field guide and tutor's manual. The tutor's manual provides background information and directs the tutor in the use of the field guides and flash cards. Production of the product was funded by the United Kingdom's Overseas Development Administration as a low-cost delivery package that teaches how to process cassava. Though the product is paper based, with no electronic materials, the product has obviously been designed with utility and cost in mind. Of course, you are probably not interested in the use of a teaching package on cassava, but think about how you can use this idea to create other learning packages. Though correspondence may seem an antiquated way of learning, remember that less than 10 percent of the world's population has online access (Nua.com 2002).

As an example of electronic correspondence, Galena, Alaska, offers homeschooling by correspondence through IDEA (Interior Distance Education of Alaska). The standards-based curriculum is focused on language arts, mathematics, science, and social studies for grades K–12. Web and videoconferencing technologies are used for home-based activities and school-based activities. Students can access the virtual library, and parents can access evaluation and curriculum forms online.

Because of distance learning, students living in rural areas are not limited in their learning potentials or content access. However, some of the issues that may impact rural students receiving courses could relate to crossing district, state, and regional guidelines. For example, if a student in Alaska wished to take a course in French, via videoconferencing, and the instructor lived in Quebec, how would administrators handle the issues of certification of the instructor? Time zones would also be a factor for a videoconference from this distance. As we continue with these types of developments, discussion in the literature and on listservs will help us share these important outcomes and solutions.

## Electronic Mail (Listserv, Keypals, or E-Pals)

For as much attention given to the World Wide Web, the dominant use of online resources, in rank order, is communication through electronic mail. One count shows that "78% of those who went online in a typical day in 2000 sent e-mail—more than double the number of those who used the Internet for any other single activity" (Boneva et al. 2001). Reports estimate that as many as 77 percent of the 100 million Internet users (reported to be 150 million users by Strauss) are using e-mail (*Edupage*, 12 November 1999). Likewise, "the number of employers watching their workers' e-mail has risen to 48 percent, up from 38 percent in 1998. Moreover, ISPs keep some record of user activity in logs that can be accessed at the behest of the FBI or a court order" (*Edupage*, 18 May 2001).

Much of this e-mail traffic is in the form of listserv messages, automatic messages that are received when the e-mail user subscribes to a listserv, much in the same way that you could subscribe to a magazine or newsletter. Listserv groups are so popular that there are listservs on almost every topic imaginable. Even as early as 1995, there were over 6,700 listserv discussion groups (May 1997, 33).

Some listservs are moderated (VanHemert 1995). A moderator, usually an unpaid volunteer, monitors and organizes the discussion list for messages to be distributed, discards messages that are unnecessary, and offers clarification when necessary.

Listservs generally offer behavior guidelines to users. These guidelines are usually sent to the subscriber at the same time that verification of the subscribing is sent out. Even though these guidelines seem tedious, please read them. Besides being good for netiquette ('Net etiquette), directions will help you avoid embarrassing listserv behavior. Though most listserv participation is free, there are some for-fee services that work like magazine subscriptions. Can you foresee the day when for-fee listserv messages will be more popular, as a way to decrease the paper publications in our lives?

## *Learning Possibility*

If you have never subscribed to an e-mail listserv, try monitoring at least one new listserv every week, for a month. (Be sure to keep the "welcome" messages that you receive when you subscribe to each listserv in an e-mail folder since they also include the *unsubscribe* directions!) At the end of the month, you will have experience with four listservs. Of the four, which do you like the best? Which listserv offered the greatest number of tips that you can use in your classroom? Based on these answers, unsubscribe from three of the listservs and keep the one subscription that was most useful. At the end of another week, reassess your satisfaction with the listserv. You may decide to go back to one of the other listservs, or you might decide to experiment with some more listserv titles. Regardless of your choice, print a copy of each subscription message and include this in a notebook so that you can easily keep track of which listservs you are monitoring, along with directions for the listserv.

For help with listservs that may not be offered in a graphical interface (i.e., you don't click on a button to subscribe), you will want to scan through an online manual of listserv commands. A thorough listserv manual (*General User's Guide to LISTSERV*) is available online (http://www.lsoft.com/manuals/1.8d /user/user.html). If you're ever interested in running your own listserv, try the listserv directions in *The Unofficial Listowner Manual* (http://www.skally .net/listowner/).

---

Electronic mail, as an asynchronous medium, has been successfully used for foreign-language study (Cummings and Sayers 1995). By using a language policy (ibid. 31) that sets the ground rules for communicating, students have been able to practice written language successfully. Even students at the first-grade level (Scott 1996, 48) can participate in e-mail projects, sharing word lists and birthday greetings with other students throughout the world. Other distance learning applications for e-mail can be successfully offered to adult students, combining listserv messages and supporting Web materials (Lippert et al. 2001). A major benefit of this method is that it is fully asynchronous and simple.

As a teaching tool, the listserv has been used to help students resolve technical problems with courses, to provide a forum for discussions (Ross 1995), and to keep students on track and monitor student progress (Dickstein and McBride 1998). The use of e-mail as a teaching tool for bibliographic instruction in libraries has proven to be effective with teaching many students simultaneously, without time constraints (Burke 1996, 40).

Because electronic mail, as a teaching and learning tool, has not been in use with PreK–12 very long, further study of its use is needed. These studies may provide insight on how to incorporate e-mail into your curriculum (Tao 1997).

Since e-mail will probably become one of the chief communication tools for your students, you want to teach them proper use and management of their e-mail boxes. This instruction will include lessons on how to handle "junk" mail or "spam," as junk mail (unsolicited e-mail) is referred to. Chances are that the students will not have great amounts of junk mail, provided they do not submit their e-mail addresses to sites indiscriminately. However, to manage these unwanted messages, one method is to filter out the sender's e-mail address, or text, after you have identified the source of undesirable e-mail. How do you do that? Most e-mail software will filter undesired messages into a designated folder (Martin 1998, 45).

Many e-mail users think the controversies over spamming are exaggerated. To test this problem in your school, ask teachers or students to monitor their e-mail accounts for a week and count the number of offending messages received. Experience shows that the easiest solution is to delete the e-mail message they receive. Responding, even with a request to not send further messages, causes some spammers to respond with more inappropriate e-mail, possibly through automated processing.

Another problem that has affected schools and businesses throughout the country are the e-mail viruses that are attached to e-mail files, as well as to other new media, such as palm-held computers and cell phones (*Edupage*, 29 December 2000). The once standard practice of scanning disks is almost moot since files can be sent online. Teaching students how to protect against these potentially damaging files is now a basic skill. Articles with e-mail handling tips are available (Eskow 1997). One treasured tip is to let your reader know whether you really need a response to an e-mail message. If you are receiving e-mail messages now, you will appreciate this tip, especially if you are tired of receiving responses that simply restate the unnecessary. Even a thank-you message can be an aggravation. A solution is to simply state "Thanks in advance for your help. No further response is necessary."

Let us say that you have taught your students how to use e-mail and are ready to contact keypals. Where do you go? There are many online services that offer connections to keypals, but one of the best interfaces for searching for the keypals is through *Classroom Connect* (http://www.classroom.com/community/findteacher/). A link to "Find a Teacher" is provided. You can search for a colleague, based on interest or place. There are many, many connections to keypals. For example, using the search engine AltaVista, a search of "keypals" on 19 February 2000 netted 2,201 sites. An update on this search using AltaVista on 11 January 2002 netted 15,537 sites. A search using the search engine AltaVista on 19 February 2000 for "collaborative problem solving projects" netted 3,051 sites. An update on this search using AltaVista on 11 January 2002 netted 38,294,926 sites. Keypals and collaborators are out there; you just need to start looking for them. Be aware that the quality sites such as Classroom Connect provide a privacy policy for its users, making sure that e-mail addresses are not distributed to vendors or visitors to the Web site. Your identity is protected, because messages of inquiry are sent through the site's server, and the recipient decides whether to respond to the request.

Another potential resource for keypals is at AOL@SCHOOL (http://school.aol.com). AOL has designed this free e-mail source for teachers, parents, and students. Age-appropriate links are included, as well as state education information. If you are interested in trying this resource with your students, call 1-888-339-0767 to request free software. What is the catch? Some may consider the use of this site and software as being too influential on students' choices for future e-mail services. Though valid, there's no assurance that some of the other currently free software sites will not one day offer ISP services, for a fee. As with all of the resources offered in this handbook, evaluate the sites and services before making up your mind. Get input from administrators and parents, and discuss whether the use of this service would be appropriate for your students and community.

If you are interested in providing keypals with language or cultural diversity, you might try *International E-Mail Classroom Connections* (IECC) (http://www.iecc.org/), a free service begun by college professors. IECC also offers virtual tours, which, at the time of this writing, take students to Europe and Japan.

You will probably need to get ready for much needed hand-holding, if you are initially teaching your students to use e-mail. The hand-holding usually comes in the form of encouragement and positive reinforcement. Do your best to be clear and unambiguous with directions for students, encouraging them to e-mail as often as possible in the beginning stages of learning (Williams and Meredith 1996, 30). Why? It is the much important activity of reinforcement that will help students to develop the confidence in using e-mail. The greater the practice, the better the execution of the e-mail activities.

## *Learning Possibility*

What is your school or district policy on "spam" and how is this policy communicated to the school community? What are teachers in your district directed to do to provide oversight on spam for student accounts? What is the connection between the British comedy group Monty Python and the use of the term "spam" in our online lexicon? Check out the history of spam at *Fight Spam on the Internet!* (http://spam.abuse.net/) Do your students know the origin of the term "spam"? Did they think it referred to food? Do you have a subscription to the *Oxford English Dictionary* (OED) that is online (http://www .oed.com)? Ask your students to search for the date that the term "spam" was first used in relation to e-mail. What other word origins and history would you like to search? When was the term "Internet" first used?

———————

Some e-mail vendors are now offering free services, such as *Hotmail* (http://www.hotmail.com), *Juno* (http://www.juno.com), or *Yahoo* (http://www.yahoo.com). A recommendation is to try these free services yourself before directing students to use them. Since the free services are not controlled by a school group, it is a good idea to request parent permissions before sending students to these sites.

As a teaching tool, e-mail can be invaluable! However, know that it may take a bit of practice to become familiar with this medium. E-mail can be very intimidating to students, and the content of an innocent face-to-face message can become anxiety-producing when the same content is sent via e-mail. What are the do's and don'ts of teaching with e-mail? Begin with these suggestions (Achterberg 1996, 306):

### *Do's for E-mail*

1. Provide students with a reasonable time frame that you will follow for responding to e-mail.

2. Respond to your e-mail at least every twenty-four hours.

3. Always respond with a greeting, by name, and let students know that you thank them for their messages.

4. Be sure that you are providing context for your response. For example, do not just respond to a message with a "Yes" or a "No." Many people receive dozens of e-mail messages a day from a variety of people. Although your e-mail message is probably important, do not depend on the receiver to remember who you are and what the previous message was. Be sure to quote the previous message as you are answering so that you receive a quicker and more meaningful response, especially if you are requesting something.

5. Respond clearly and concisely. Be sure to answer students' questions and concerns fully.

6. Reread responses to avoid ambiguity. If anything can be misunderstood, it will be misunderstood in e-mail.

7. Always include a closing. Sending e-mail without greetings and closings is bad netiquette.

## *Don'ts for E-mail*

1. Don't include any content in an e-mail message that you would not want to share with the world. E-mail does not always remain confidential, even if that was the writer's intention.

2. Especially when you are using a school account, do not e-mail anything that is of questionable content. The message may come back to haunt you because all school e-mail accounts can be reviewed at any time by your supervisor. (And don't think that just deleting a message from your e-mail box will permanently erase it. Messages can be retrieved by recovery experts, even if you have deleted them.)

3. Don't include information for an individual student when sending a group message. For example, in an e-mail message, never announce a student's grade, good or bad, or a student's failure to turn in an assignment.

4. Don't make a habit of sending "interesting" e-mail to your entire address book. Most of us already receive enough e-mail, and what is interesting to you may be an irritant to others.

5. Don't make assumptions when communicating through e-mail. Students often misinterpret assignments and deadlines. Without the face-to-face contact, you can't be sure that your students are understanding your messages, unless you are very specific with your language.

6. Don't expect any privacy with your e-mail message.

7. DON'T SHOUT. Using capital letters in e-mail messages is considered to be rude.

8. E-mail attachments can provide challenges! Be sure that your receiver knows how to open an attachment, and has the required software, before sending it.

## Learning Possibility

Research the issue of privacy with e-mail when using your school account. (Your school or district AUP is a good reference for this learning opportunity.) What is the school's, or district's, expectations on how you use your school account? Are you allowed to send personal messages through your account? Are you allowed to receive personal messages to your account? Are messages stored? Who has access to this information? When you change from one teaching job to another, do you take your computer with you? Do you transfer your files? How do you archive your e-mail for future use? How can you be sure that your e-mail is truly deleted?

Because of the time required away from work to answer e-mail messages, and the related loss of productivity, some organizations are now forbidding the reading or writing of private e-mail messages at work. In PreK–12 schools, the question can apply to all segments of the school community. Should students, teachers, and administrators be able to read and send private e-mail messages from school? If you are working to set a policy, you may wish to parallel policies on telephone usage. Can you receive a personal telephone call at school? Can your students? Eventually, this communication tool may have clear-cut policies that apply to all members of the school community. You may wish to participate in the development of such policies, working to develop an operational definition of what are appropriate uses of e-mail messages during the school day (Hamilton 1996).

Most of us enjoy using e-mail because of the quick response time and convenience of this form of communication. However, be sure to know that, as with other mediums of communication, anything that is overused becomes tedious or boring. To our benefit, most elementary, middle, and high school students will continue to enjoy using e-mail just as much as they continue to enjoy using the telephone, but be aware that the same is not always true of the adult student who feels that e-mail is just another form of work.

## Interactive Web Activities

An attempt to estimate how many Web (or Internet) users exist is, in itself, a challenge. With multiple vendors accepting customers by the second, this datum is as difficult to assess as the population! However, reports of online use are often included in standard online communiqués, such as *Edupage* (12 November 1999), which reported a *New York Times* summary that stated that "over 100 million adults in the U.S., over half of the country's adult population, use the Internet." A survey of college students showed "57 per cent of the students used the Web at least once a day, and those surveyed averaged about six hours on line every week" (Biemiller 1999, 1). The more important question for educators is "How many of our schools are connected to the Internet?" The 17 February 2000 *Palm Beach Post* reports the U.S. Department of Education's figure that 95 percent of the U.S. schools are connected. Did you know that "in 1998, 68 percent of private schools were connected to the Internet, up from 25 percent in 1995"? (This is one of the many educational references that can be found at the *National Center for Educational Statistics* [*NCES*] [http://www/nces.ed.gov].) There are so many students that access the Internet and take distance learning courses that it is difficult to keep pace with the estimates.

### *Teaching Possibility*

Take your students to the *NCES College Search* (http://nces.ed.gov/ipeds /cool/Search.asp) to search for information on U.S. two-year and four-year colleges and universities. Students can get contact information, figures on tuition, enrollment, degrees and programs offered, student population, and link to the U.S. Department of Education Student Financial Aid home page. Ask students to create a database to compare their institutions. How will they make their selections for schools? (Will they choose their schools independently, or are they likely to "follow the pack" and select the schools that their peers select?) While you are at the NCES site, can you find information on the use of technology or the Internet in PreK–12 classrooms?

Do you wish to predict this level of Internet access for the next year? "International Data estimated that in the United States approximately 2.2 million people would be registered for online courses by 2002" (*Edupage*, 10 September 1999). Beyond the growth of users, the Web had approximately 800 million pages (Kiernan 1999, 1) as of September 1999. In the file, *Distance Learning*, NCES (http://www .nces.ed.gov/fastfacts/display.asp?id=80) shows that the Star Schools Program already offers distance learning to 1.6 million students.

Why is this access becoming more attractive? You know that PC (personal computer) prices have decreased, along with the price of online access. Whereas in 1995 (Reed 1995, 11), online access through service providers, such as America Online, cost around $10 with a limit at five or less hours, today (2002) unlimited access is available for about $25 monthly. Now with the uncertainties about the monthly online bill taken care of, the World Wide Web is educationally viable. There is no argument that access to online resources will benefit students and teachers as never before. The Internet has fostered the stretching of learning and lessons in ways never imagined by teachers twenty years ago in classrooms worldwide (Bayram 1999).

For those of you who are new to the Internet, you may not know that we used to access online materials through the UNIX operating system. Files were housed at gopher sites and access was text based. Some of you may even remember when the use of local bulletin board systems was popular, and many government and university offices offered bulletin board access. The World Wide Web was the 1989 creation of Tim Berners-Lee (http://www.w3.org/People/Berners-Lee/), a software engineer (Wilson 1997, 7D). Even before we accessed the World Wide Web with a graphical browser, many of us used lynx. A nongraphical (text) browser, lynx is fast, easy to read, and less distracting than most graphical browsers. Some of you may still be able to use lynx today. Mosaic was the first graphical browser used to access the World Wide Web, preceding the Netscape and Internet Explorer browsers. In the spirit of Mosaic, viewed as the original graphical browser, which was shared freely, we also have *Opera* (http://www.opera .com/), which touts itself as being "the fastest browser on earth."

## Learning Possibility

Ask your ISP if you have lynx (or UNIX) access for text-based Web access. Lead your students through a lynx activity. For example, at the command line, key "lynx http:// " and the address of the site you are trying to access. (If the site does not offer text access, you will not be able to view the text.) Try to elicit from students the differences they see between lynx and other browsers. Are there students who prefer this type of browser? If so, you may have identified students that need fewer distractions in their learning environments. (Would these same students prefer the Google search engine to the Excite search engine?)

----

When you are accessing World Wide Web pages, be attentive to the concepts of instructional design. Observe content over style. Is the Web page desirable? Does it promote student learning outcomes? Think about how schools may be accountable, under federal government guidelines, if they use the Web as a more dominant form for instruction and enrichment. Follow the spirit, as well as the letter, of the Americans with Disabilities Act (ADA). Remember, a graphics-rich Web page can be limiting for some students because of visual, spatial, or cognitive limitations, not to mention computing requirements. Many educational designers are becoming more attuned to the importance of layout, format, and visual mapping and how these issues contribute to, or distract from, learning (Horn 1999, 24). Try to offer your students a choice of presentations in both textual and graphical formats. The multitude of image-editing programs available today, with higher-end software that offers features that support the development of Web graphics, will help those that want to develop online products, in addition to accessing those already available.

## Learning Possibility

You surely have a digital camera in your school or media center, but have you used it to take a digital picture? If not, practice using the digital camera. Ask your students to help read and "cipher" the directions. Many of your students may already have experience using a digital camera and may be able to speed up this learning opportunity for you. While you are exploring the use of the digital camera, find out if you have district policies and procedures that address students' images online. What are the releases that have to be signed for this? Do you have copies of the releases? If so, read these agreements and be familiar with the process of obtaining a release, in the event that you would like to post pictures online to share with students in another school that may be keypals to your students.

---

Regardless of the distance learning format used, if there is a possibility that the students will post Web materials, they must learn to post responsibly and understand the importance of the U.S. Copyright Law in protecting ownership rights. For the school, who will be responsible for monitoring what students place online? Obviously, the teacher must be aware of the copyright policies as they apply to classroom activities and make students aware that there are regulations on what can be copied and distributed (McCollum 1999). If students are developing materials for the school to post, the school needs to contract with the student (or, if the student is underage, the student's parents) to set the agreement (Becker 2001).

A related issue that has affected more colleges and universities, but which is increasingly becoming a concern for high schools, is the pirating of student compositions and term papers. Some instructors are trying to address this problem through screening software offered by sites, such as *Plagiarism.org* (http://www.plagiarism.org), that will search a database of electronic copies of works that have been submitted by instructors. Students' compositions are compared to text in the database.

## Teaching and Learning Possibility

Did it ever occur to you that students do not really understand what plagiarism is? Have you taught students what it means to plagiarize? We often tell students to "write the information in your own words," but we often neglect to provide practice on how to do that. We also often neglect to tell students that it is acceptable to quote or acknowledge another writer's work, but that they must remember to also reference the work. Be sure you have defined and discussed plagiarism with students. Be sure that they understand what it is and why they should not do it.

---

Do you want to risk showing students where to locate term papers on the Internet? Why not? Do you think that students don't know where to find term papers for sale? Let them understand that you know where to go to locate term papers, too. Take students to *Academic Term Papers* (http://www.academictermpapers.com) or *RealPapers.com* (http://www.realpapers.com/) and review some of the papers available. Demonstrate for the students how easy it is for a teacher to recognize that the writing is not original. Show the students how you can detect a plagiarized paper by using clues, such as those suggested at *Plagiarized.com* (http://www.plagiarized.com/index.shtml) or by using software that is offered at sites such as *PlagiServe* (http://www.plagiserve.com/).

Finally, do not forget to tell students what the consequences are for plagiarism. What are your school's rules? What types of punishments should the students expect? How will you inform parents about plagiarism and how can parents work with you to ensure that their students are submitting original work?

Students enjoy Web activities because they are "hands-on" and allow students to move at their own rates. For the student who needs to be actively involved in learning, the Web offers good options for today's classroom. Just what can you do on the Web? The answer is limitless. From accessing all types of information to using online test reviews (Florida students can practice their *Florida Comprehensive Assessment Test* [FCAT] online [http://www.firn.edu/doe/sas/fcat.htm] and teachers can review test results by district) at any time and any place, possibilities with the Web are limitless, as long as you have the bandwidth and computer memory storage needed.

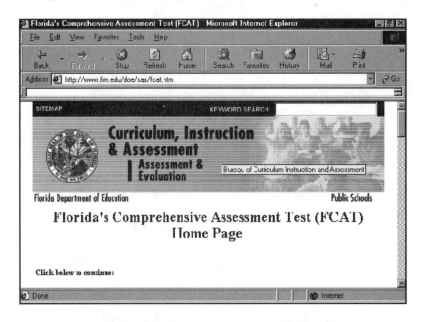

*Florida Comprehensive Assessment Test* **(FCAT) home page:
http://www.firn.edu/doe/sas/fcat.htm**

The daily increasing Web capabilities give creative teachers ways of delivering instruction in constantly evolving ways. Recorded lectures, which are uploaded, compressed, and linked to a presentation software slide, can now be placed online by converting the slide to a Web page that is loaded onto the school's Web site. By working with your educational technologist to guide you in the process of placing lectures on a Web server, you are expanding students' links to the classroom.

Because it is so easy for students to get tangled in the Web, teachers will wish to provide a structured Web learning experience for most classroom applications. Today, this structured format is popularly called the "WebQuest." A WebQuest is a directed learning experience, composed by teachers, that takes students to preselected sites that present or demonstrate content that relates to the learning experience. WebQuests minimize the frustration of students and teachers who often find themselves wandering aimlessly online when they cannot locate a site. WebQuests can be used with students of almost any age, provided that they can use a mouse to navigate the Web. Do students have to read to use WebQuests? This depends on how you are structuring your WebQuest. If students recognize numbers, or letters, or have been told how to progress through the screen page using pictures or colors, they might be able to access picture-only sites or sites that provide audio or video clips. With some attention to the instructional design, WebQuests can be used with students who have limited reading skills.

Predesigned WebQuests can be located online through the San Diego State University's Education Technology Department *WebQuest Page*, developed by Dr. Bernie Dodge (http://edweb.sdsu.edu/webquest/). WebQuests are classified based on the Taskonomy that includes categories ranging from retelling and compilation to analyzing, judgment, and scientific. For teachers who are beginning to develop WebQuests, be sure to evaluate each WebQuest with a rubric prior to using it with students (Summerville 2000). A

WebQuest rubric is also available online (http://webquest.sdsu.edu/webquestrubric.html) at the *WebQuest Page* (http://edweb.sdsu.edu/webquest/webquest.html).

## *Learning Possibility*

To experience a WebQuest, access *Teaching Tools for Tomorrow* (http://library .thinkquest.org/T0211380/) and work through the steps of the WebQuest. When you have completed this, think about your experience. What did you learn? Did you enjoy the WebQuest experience? Was it a sequential learn-ing experience? Would you restructure anything in this WebQuest? If you were designing a WebQuest for your colleagues for an in-service training activity, how would you approach the task? How would you organize it? Do you think that most of your teachers are sequential in learning preference?

---

WebQuests have also been developed that are in the form of presentation slides. At the Web site *Educational Applications of the Internet or Surfing Less, Learning More* (http://facstaff.buffalostate.edu /beaverjf/internet/), presentations are targeted for teacher populations. A wonderful format to promote independent learning, WebQuests have many applications for teachers, from in-service training, to district meetings, to online courses. In one study, teachers who received online training through WebCT and e-mail were evaluated based on the WebQuests they produced. No significant difference in quality was evident between WebQuests produced by two classes of students, one class being face-to-face and the other class being online (Sujo de Montes and Gonzales 2000).

One class of graduate education students was enrolled in a course (Evaluation of Information Technologies) during which they created a virtual community in the form of an evaluation center. Stu-dents developed projects and experienced teamwork as they used information technologies to evaluate Web pages of their virtual community. Though no conclusions were drawn as to whether using the simu-lation was a good way to teach the students how to teach their students about technology, the simulation did result in the students changing their virtual environment as they interacted with it (Hinn, Leander, and Bruce 2001). What does this tell us? Students can adapt to online environments, and they will change those environments to make them more responsive to their learning needs.

When considering taking your courses to the Web, there is much planning to do. You will have to consider where students will be when they access the materials and how they will get online connec-tions. Who will provide the technical support to the students? Will you be the teacher on call, or will stu-dents get support from other staff members in the school? Will there be certain software packages and services that will be supported? If so, do your students know which packages are supported? If you are even considering teaching with the Web, you probably have some idea of how to post materials on the Web, either through HTML (HyperText Markup Language); a Web editor, such as FrontPage; or through your word processing package. Many schools also offer course management packages, such as Web Course in a Box (WCB) or WebCT. If you are deciding how to deliver instruction with the Web, be sure to search the literature for benefits and advantages of either path (Kaplan 1998).

Web developments that are targeted for PreK–12 students are occurring in many states. For example, students involved in a distance learning project in Washington participated in an introductory geology course through the "Virtual UW (University of Washington) in the High School." The medium of contact is teleconferencing (*Edupage*, 2 May 2001), but students may be taking field trips to the university to provide context for the learning environment. For more information on this and other K–20 initiatives in Washington, go to *Teaching & Learning Tools for K–20* (http://depts.washington.edu/edtecdev/k20/k20.pdf).

## *Learning Possibility*

I bet you are familiar with HTML (HyperText Markup Language), but do you know about XML (eXtensible Markup Language)? *Access XML: A Language to Manage the World Wide Web* (http://ericir.syr.edu/ithome/digests/EDO-IR-1999-10.html) and learn how XML will enable you to search Web pages through "metatags" that the user establishes, allowing the search engines to search both the tags and the content. By the way, here is another example of how distance learning technologies evolve quickly to respond to the users needs, in this case being the capacity to better search existing documents.

In considering Web developments, think about how you are going to take care of issues such as personalized learning. Will students be able to work collaboratively online? How often will information be updated at your Web site? What will you list at your course page? How often will students be expected to interact with the instructor? Districts, course management vendors, and teachers are answering these and many other questions (Boettcher 1998, Hallett and Cummings 1997, Huffington et al. 1997, Serwatka 1999). You may want to put full course content online, or, as is the case for most PreK–12 teachers, you may only wish to have an online component that is offered for enrichment. The beauty of offering instruction online is that you are able to invite guests that you probably would never dream of inviting. But with the use of online chat, you can invite authors, experts, etc., into your classroom. By preparing students ahead of time to be aware of the guest's writing style or intensity, you have an opportunity to expose your students to facets of the delivery that go beyond just content (Cotlar and Shimabukuro 1995).

Remember, even though many students are online, many others do not have access. However, because of the support of the U.S. Department of Education's Learn Anytime Anywhere Program for universities, the focus on this format continues (Carnvale 2000b, 1). For more information on the distance learning initiatives at the *Distance Learning Resource Network*, access http://www.dlrn.org/. Its "for K–12 students" link will take you to a listing of online courses and virtual schools, many of which are also noted in this handbook. Among the many links to online journals is the *Electronic School* (http://www.electronic-school.com/). One of its articles is "The School Board of Tomorrow" (2001). Read it to find out if we are going to have virtual school board meetings!

Ever spawning new related technologies, Watson is a personal information system that is being evaluated as a go-between for the PC and the Web. While the instructor is keying information into the word processor, *Watson* (http://infolab.nwu.edu/watson) is searching the Web for materials to support the topic.

Even though there are multitudes of online resources on the Web, many beginning students and teachers like the convenience of having an instructional booklet (e.g., *Education on the Internet* or *The Busy Educator's Guide to the World Wide Web*). Printed versions of handbooks and guides are often all it takes to get the more print-oriented learner involved with Web activities. Certainly you will want to offer a precourse information and training session to get students in the swing of the format and to allow them to interact with the instructor and other students before they begin (Carnvale 2000a, 1).

"Practice makes perfect" certainly applies to the Web format. Therefore, encourage students to develop their online communications skills during the course. Training sessions can include existing online tutorials at the *Toronto Public Library Virtual Reference Library* (http://vrl.tpl.toronto.on.ca/internet/01net_f.html). You will see the further development of professional resources that combine specifics of developing online lessons with Web page support (Leu and Leu 1999).

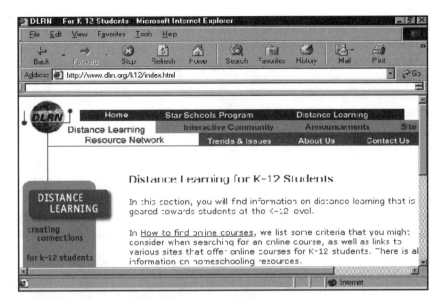

**Distance Learning for K–12 Students Web site:**
**http://www.dlin.org/k12/index.html**

*LearningWebs: Curriculum Journeys on the Internet* (Keating, Wiles, and Piazza 2002) is a compilation of Web "journeys" developed by classroom teachers that can be adapted to multiple grade levels. The Web journeys provide useful models for creating journeys for your own students from more than 1,000 sites and are listed by topic, from aardvark to zebra. Whether your students are learning about elephants or literary criticism, the links provided are plenty but not so many as to be intimidating.

With the continued development of Internet2 lines, allowing audio and video to travel at faster rates without shaky movements, interactive Web activities will improve.

## *Teaching Possibility*

Though you and your students may not have the money to travel, in person, you can jointly visit the *National Museum of Science and Industry* (London) Web site and view the many exhibits. During winter 2002, one exhibit was "Cosmic Globes," a collection of pictures of celestial globes dating back to the 1500s. Before traveling to the museum, review the current exhibits. Do they apply to your current curriculum? If you are a media specialist or a lab instructor, do any of the topics apply to other subject-area teachers that might be interested in collaborating on an applied lesson?

## Video

Videotape is still widely used and has a well-supported base. Like audiotape, videotape is an inexpensive medium to use for distance learning activities. In this context, the use of video is an educational activity that directly supports class goals and objectives. However, not to mix the medium with the purpose, videotape must be used appropriately. Whether for distance learning or live instruction, copyright limitations still apply to videotape. Further, for institutions that wish to distribute educational opportunities in a broadcasted activity, be it through the Internet, videoconferencing network, or satellite delivery, some copyright questions are still unanswered (Gasaway 1999). What seems to be clear is that you cannot use videotapes or other recording formats that might have a licensing right. Also, if copyrighted materials are used to create sessions to be presented at a later time, the "Fair Use Guidelines" apply (Becker 2001).

Be sure that you are familiar with your school or district viewing and copyright policies on videotape. Further resources are available through the *United States Copyright Office* (http://loc.gov/copyright). Check the links on "Copyright Basics" and "Distance Education." You can also try the *Crash Course in Copyright* (http://www.utsystem.edu/ogc/intellectualproperty/cprtindx.htm), available through the University of Texas, or the *Copyright* Web site (http://www.benedict.com/), a comprehensive site that addresses copyright for both print and nonprint sources. The "Report on Copyright and Digital Distance Education" (25 May 1999), as required by the Digital Millennium Copyright Act of 1998, offers issues to be further considered and debated that directly impact distance learning (http://www.copyright.gov/reports/studies /dmca/dmca_study.html).

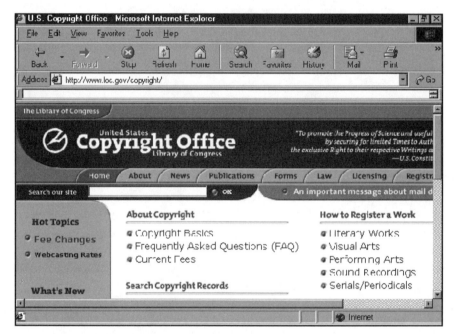

**United States Copyright Office Web site:**
**http://www.loc.gov/copyright/**

## *Teaching Possibility*

For a product that accompanies a video package, access *The Machine That Changed the World* (http://ei.cs.vt.edu/~history/TMTCTW.html). After viewing and discussing the presentation, send your students to the scavenger hunt! How can you duplicate this activity for other content areas online?

Like other technologies, videotape continues to evolve with one of the most recent developments being a personal video recorder (Srinivasan 2000, 17B). These personal video recorder systems, offered through companies such as *TiVo* (http://www.tivo.com) and *ReplayTV* (http://www.replaytv.com), require a receiver box to use with televisions. With services provided through additional monthly fees, programs are searched through servers run by the companies, downloaded, and saved on a hard drive that is included in the personal video recorder system. Users can preselect programs so that customized viewing is easier. Applications for school settings would allow a media specialist or technologist to search for programs that have been requested for teacher use, as allowed by "Fair Use" of the U.S. Copyright Law.

Like the audiotape and CD change that is taking place, many videotapes are being replaced by digital video discs (DVDs). DVD players are now on the market for less than $200, and the DVDs are increasing in availability. For the teacher who is using this medium with students, increased video quality and the ability to search through the disc make this an attractive medium.

On a larger scale, some commercial producers are digitizing videotape. CNN (Cable News Network) is in the process of converting twenty-one years of videotapes and expects to take five to seven years to complete the project (*Edupage*, 23 April 2001). Soon though, this searchable database will be for sale. Imagine the teaching possibilities that will be available with this resource!

For listings of videocassettes to use for instruction, consult the *Bowker's Directory of Videocassettes for Children* (1998).

## Course Packages

Course packages offer flexibility in course delivery, much the same as prepackaged curriculum relieves the classroom teacher from researching and developing original curriculum. The development of course packages requires a great deal of research and time. Some course packages are available in print format, such as *Safe Blood and Blood Products*, issued by the *World Health Organization* (http://www.who.int /home-page/). As described in the trainer's manual, structured materials are often needed to "provide a comprehensive and in-depth training programme that would normally only be available in a specialist training institution" (1993, 2). Consistency, economy of scale, and geographic limitations are among the many reasons to offer course packages. Print course packages may already be used in your classroom. This type of package can be created for homebound students or vacationing students. You may have already implemented this in your class without thinking that it was also a type of distance learning.

### *Teaching Possibility*

Do you often wish for more meaningful course information for health or world studies? Ask students to access the World Health Organization's *Weekly Epidemiological Record* (http://www.who.int/wer/) to review current health concerns. What is the most current week's topic of concern? Can students estimate how many people are affected by this health concern? Have students pinpoint the location of the health concern on a world map and then estimate the distance to the place in miles from your school.

Many textbooks are now supplemented by course packages, often placed on a Web page that includes downloadable video, lesson plans, and even PowerPoint slides. You may see these Web pages referred to as "companion Web sites." Companion Web sites are available to schools that have adopted the textbooks and are very useful when there are multiple teachers, at multiple locations, that need copies of these course supplements. How do you find out if there are companion Web sites for your textbooks? First, check the text itself. Read through the forward, preface, or introduction. Usually, there will be a mention of the companion Web site there. If it is not mentioned there, next look for resources for this text online at the publisher's Web site. If this fails, try calling the toll-free publisher's number. A representative will put you in touch with the publisher's division for this title and will let you know about the availability of additional materials. You can also contact the authors of your textbooks to see if they have made materials available at another Web site. If all of these options fail, you can check with your professional listserv to find out if there are other instructors that use the same text who have created materials that they are willing to share with teachers in your district. Perhaps the teachers in your district can partner with the teachers in another district to identify materials that are needed, create them, and post them online. What might these materials be? Handouts, worksheets, PowerPoint slides, overhead transparency content, sample test questions, reading lists, Web link list, etc.—the possibilities of the materials that you can create and share are endless! (After you have created these materials and provided access to them, think about presenting them to your colleagues at your professional conference and share them with others who are also interested in contributing materials to your collection.)

## *Learning Possibility*

In case you have never created your own PowerPoint presentation, a Library of Congress tutorial (*Games Kids Play* [http://learning.loc.gov/learn/educators /workshop/pizazz/index.html]) explains how to use this software package to create a presentation and then save the presentation as a HTML file that can be posted online. Do you have a few minutes to experiment with this? What is a lesson that you teach very well, which would be enhanced by the creation of a PowerPoint presentation? Better yet, what is a complex concept that you teach that you can illustrate better in a visual presentation, such as PowerPoint? Is there an opportunity where everyone in the group will not be able to attend, such as Open House Night? Could you post your presentation online for parents to view at a different time?

*Games Kids Play* **Web site:**
**http://learning.loc.gov/learn/educators/workshop/pizazz/index.html**

Another type of course package is being marketed to college and high school advanced placement and dual enrollment instructors to support the media aspects of course delivery. These materials can be modified to support the instructor's particular course goals and objectives. Some courses are also available to individual students, such as homeschool students; however, be sure to check on the type of credit to be offered for the course, if it is not to be delivered by a certified in-house instructor. For examples of this type of support, look at *Vcampus* (http://www.vcampus.com/corpweb/index/index.cfm).

In addition to these adjunct types of materials, more focus has been given to electronic courseware that is used as an independent learning tool or as a support for in-class instruction. Many of these programs, offered by companies such as Compass or Plato, are already successfully used in schools. Some of these packages can be delivered directly to students through online access. When implementing courseware systems, make sure that evaluation occurs through a team of students, parents, teachers, and administrators. This will promote coordination of the software with classroom curriculum. Plan to also study, evaluate, and track student performance, based on the use of the courseware. Though well intentioned, this type of purchase without teacher and parent input, or student piloting, is counterproductive. Nevertheless, due to online delivery of some of these packages, there are many applications for unique learning situations, such as:

1.   Homebound students (for short-term illnesses or for long-term injuries)

2.   Homeschooled students

3.   Specialized content delivery

4.   Vacationing students

The *Education Program for Gifted Youth* (*EPGY*) (http://www-epgy.stanford.edu/) is offered through Stanford University, as the implementation of a National Science Foundation research project that began in 1985 (Gilbert-Macmillan 2000). The project has fostered the development and offering of multimedia courses to K–12 gifted students in the areas of computer programming, English, mathematics, music, physics, and political science. Some summer residential courses are also offered. EPGY software is used to deliver multimedia courses that also include an audio component. The opportunities that this project offers to districts with small populations in gifted or specialized courses are great for students who need self-paced courses.

For additional offerings of K–12 distance learning courses, look at the Distance Learning Resources Network's *How to Find Online K–12 Courses* (http://www.dlrn.org/k12/how.html). Included at this site is also a listing of criteria (http://taste.merlot.org/eval.html) to use to evaluate distance learning course offerings. Another method of evaluation could include the application of the Web-based learning materials criteria used at the *Merlot Project* (http://www.merlot.org).

## *Learning Possibility*

Have you stopped to evaluate your use of technology in the classroom? Try the *Self-Evaluation Rubrics for Advanced Teacher Computer Use* (http://www .ed.gov/pubs/EdTechGuide/appc-7.html) to see how you score.

Here are a few of the courseware vendors that offer course packages in a variety of delivery formats at different grade levels:

A+dvanced Learning System, A+nywhere Learning System—AMERICAN EDUCATION CORPORATION (http://www.amered.com/) 1-800-342-7587 (1-800-34-APLUS)

ClassWorks Gold—NetDay Compass (http://www.netdaycompass.org) (This site also offers a free newsletter.) For information, e-mail compass@netday.org.

Lightspan Achieve Now—Lightspan Inc. (http://www.lightspan.com) 1-888-425-5543

NovaNet and SuccessMaker—NCS Learn (http://www.ncslearn.com/successmaker/) 1-888-627-5327

PassKey: A Prescriptive Learning System—McGraw-Hill Learning Technologies (http://www.passkeylearning.com) (1-800-598-4077)

The PLATO Solution—PLATO Learning Inc. (http://www.plato.com) 1-880-447-5286

Tomorrow's Promise—Compass Learning (http://www.compasslearning.com) 1-800-422-4339

Of course, at this point, it may be too late to introduce the idea that there is disagreement as to whether young children should use computers. However, this issue has been identified as a need for further study by the American Academy of Pediatrics and the National Association for the Education of Young Children (*Edupage*, 15 December 2000). Balance of instruction among different modalities, in addition to monitoring your professional organizations' research, would be a good strategy to follow until there is consensus among the professions. For more information on this area go to *Learning in the Real World* Web site (http://www.realworld.org/morereading.html). Research is in process.

## Taped Television Courses

Taped television courses, also referred to as "course in a box," have been used since the advent of the videotape format. Some of these courses are also offered in a DVD (digital video disc) format. Organizing this type of instruction, whether on tape or DVD, can be improved if the teacher will:

1. Provide learners with advance organizers (summary sheets, visuals, vocabulary lists, etc.) of what will be presented.

2. Provide a note-taking structure or guided questions that will keep students attentive during the presentation.

3. Develop a process for pausing the presentation for questions.

4. Offer to review notes that students have taken during the instruction. Students can e-mail these notes to the teacher, if they are participating at a distance.

5. Follow up with activities that address presentation content.

6. Provide feedback for student questions and activities.

7. Collect materials in the media center or online that will supplement the television presentation and develop a process for distributing these with the other materials.

## Summary

Delayed-time interactive distance learning activities offer a great deal of flexibility, because students are not time- or place-bound. This flexibility is an added convenience if students are also separated from other learning participants by time zone. When students are participating in delayed-time learning experiences, issues such as disrupted cable, online, or satellite connectivity do not stop the learning process. Based on the "No Significant Difference" bibliography compiled by Thomas Russell, the quality of the learning should not differ from real-time learning experiences.

What might be the reasons for selecting delayed-time learning? Student preference for one type of learning must be considered; for example, a student just may not like using audio media, or the student may like a sequential course organization that requires the use of many printed materials. This type of learner must also be self-directed and able to function independently of a scheduled meeting time.

If you are interested in pursuing additional delayed-time interactive distance learning activities, become familiar with the *Asynchronous Learning Networks* (http://www.aln.org/). This group of educators publishes an online journal (*The Journal of Asynchronous Learning Networks*) and is working on a research project to evaluate the effectiveness of asynchronous learning. More readings on learning theories and tutorials on evaluative methods are available at this site.

# Section B. Real-Time Interactive Distance Learning Activities

Real-time distance learning activities present an element of interactivity that encourages automatic feedback and response among the "live" participants. If you accept the general principle that interactivity is better, because you believe that students learn more when they can see each other, listen to each other, hear feedback, and provide responses, you will want to consider whether you actually apply opportunities for interactivity as you develop courses and materials. (A study of more than 400 Web sites found that most of the Web sites only offer low levels of interactivity [Mioduser et al. 2000] and that most of that interactivity is e-mail based.) Regarding the interactive versus noninteractive debate, this handbook assumes that students are in the presence of an adult, with whom interaction is possible. For most of these applications, students can be together in a PreK–12 classroom, so the students are interacting with each other on one side of the learning medium, even if they are not interacting, in real time, with the learners on the other side of the medium.

Putting the debate between real-time and delayed-time instruction aside in the interest of sharing a variety of distant learning modalities, Section B presents real-time activities for which the learners and teachers must work together at the same time but, possibly, in different locations.

## Audioconference

The audioconference (also referred to as audiobridge) is an easy-to-use medium that requires little training. It can be used locally, regionally, or even internationally. Audioconference has been used successfully for PreK–12 author and guest speaker visits in the classroom. Audioconferencing has also been used for the training of adult educators by putting teachers in touch with each other to save driving time (Coburn, Dobbs, and Grainger 1995, 87). For example, in one audiobridge, where participants were located in Florida, the audio quality was very low due to a raging snowstorm in the Rockies, where the host company and its technicians were located. Some students who called into the audiobridge received a message to the effect of "We're sorry you are experiencing delays entering your call. We have limited staff due to the severe snowstorms we are experiencing." Students called to ask where was the snow in Florida!

Regardless of audio quality, audioconferencing may become a more popular delivery method, because students participate from the convenience and safety of their homes. And the equipment required by students—the telephone—is already in most students' homes. The piece that is missing is the audiobridge equipment, which is supplied by companies that have the technology to connect multiple telephone lines, joining the instructor and many students, on one call. The costs for audioconferences are determined by the vendor's charges, which are usually a per-minute rate that may be negotiated, due to your volume of calls. (Do not overlook the audioconferencing that may be available through your current phone service that can connect three or four callers together, without having to use an audioconferencing vendor.)

An audioconference allows multiple students—from a few to dozens—to dial into class sessions, controlled by an operator that sets up the connections between participants, in real time. The students can hear and speak to each other and the instructor (often called the moderator), but they cannot see each other. Even though audioconferencing calls can include as many as fifty lines, depending on the vendor's equipment, you will want to base your decision on class size by the level of interaction you want to promote with students.

## Learning Possibility

Have students ask grandparents and great-grandparents if they remember telephone "party line" conversations, in the days before individual telephone connections were available to each house. Can they compare these party line conversations to conference calls or chats?

During an audioconference, students and teacher use the telephone to meet for a scheduled time. Calls are scheduled through the audioconference vendor that receives calls, provides a roll call, and monitors class participation, letting the instructor know when students are leaving class early. The audioconference vendor's operator provides assistance by muting lines that are causing static or too much background noise.

The audioconference can provide student-teacher interaction and student-student interaction. It originates from wherever the teacher and a telephone are located. Receiving students must have a telephone connection. If multiple students are trying to listen to a call through a speakerphone, acoustics can be poor, making the audio sound cut off by the speech-activated speakers. Because there is usually no visual aspect to the audioconference delivery, participants can either react to the content they hear or to the content that has been previously provided by mail, fax, e-mail, etc.

If your school has an automated calling system for outreach, you can use it to support some of the distance learning functions, such as assignment delivery and clarification. Some schools have voice mail for all teachers, which can also allow teachers to leave assignments and students to phone in with quick answers to assignments or tests. Though not as popular as some other distance learning systems, telephones can be used creatively and inexpensively (Young 2000), especially for language and foreign-language disciplines that have speech components (Bruning et al. 1997).

What are the benefits of the audioconference? In addition to the simplicity of the equipment, and convenience and safety factors, the audio focus can minimize personality issues that sometimes develop between students and teachers, due to personal characteristics. This medium would also support instruction for the visually impaired. (You might think that students with hearing disabilities cannot participate in audioconferencing. Agreed, the technology requires more than a simple telephone, but with the development of wireless pages that can be used to send messages by fax, e-mail, and telephone, it is possible to include these students in this technology.)

Audioconference instructors can be more successful if they:

1. Welcome students to class, by name.

2. Use humor and vocalization to create a friendly, relaxed environment.

3. Request participation and responses.

4. Describe what cannot be seen.

5. Clarify information and ask for feedback.

6. Provide advance organizer materials so that the students know what to bring to class and what they are expected to have covered before class begins.

7. Incorporate group work to build camaraderie among the students. (Most audioconference vendors can group phone lines together and then return all participants to the group call. Teachers need to provide specific group work guidelines so that students can stay on task without the teacher being present during the call. The teacher can jump from one call to another, with the help of the audioconference operator.)

8. Summarize what has occurred during the audioconference and provide direction on what the students need to do next.

Although audioconferencing has not received a great deal of support by educators, partially due to its perception as being the "least-desirable" technology for rural education (Barker 1994, 128), remember that this technology does have desirable qualities. Audioconferencing can be a technology of choice due to the availability of telephones and the low learning curve for participants (Schmidt, Sullivan, and Hardy 1997). Remember, audioconferencing, as with other distance learning technologies, does not have to be used alone. It can be coupled with other distance learning technologies.

Check with your local telephone service provider to see if these services are already available through your existing services. Search for other vendors online, or try:

AT&T (http://www.att.com/conferencing/)

Premier Conferencing (http://www.atsgroup.com/default.asp) 1-800-234-2546

WorldCom (http://www.worldcom.com/) 1-800-465-7187

Audioconferencing generally assumes that the technology to be used is the telephone, but since the PC and Web services have become more versatile you might consider using online access in place of the telephone. How? By using an online telephone for free. You must have a sound card, speakers, and a microphone as part of your configuration, but you can register with online services, such as *Dialpad.com* (http://dialpad.com). Privacy policies are listed at these services, but before you encourage students and minors to register, please review policies.

## Chatroom

If you have had to pry your son or daughter away from the monitor, you probably have a chatroom or instant messaging service in your home. Chatrooms allow all participants to view your messages, while instant messaging only allows the person you are messaging with to view the conversation. Some online sites are now offering chatrooms with voice capabilities, using the computer's sound card and microphone, such as Voice Chat.

Chat has received some negative attention in the press, due to the practice of some adults assuming other identities in order to meet people online, often for illegal activities. The meeting becomes a problem when the students are encouraged to provide personal information that allows the adult to contact them. Remember that because this handbook follows a definition of distance learning in which the student is under adult supervision, this negative pursuit should not happen. As has been suggested by parent and protection agencies, students should not be left alone with chatroom or instant messaging systems for long periods of time. If the student does not want the adult to view what is being written, chances are good that the communication is not about school or learning.

How can you take a popular desire by students to communicate with each other and change it into a learning possibility? Let's imagine that you are working on a unit on careers. You can take students to the *Monster Career Center* (http://community.monster.com/chats/) where there are moderated chats about work. Also, most software packages, such as *ClassLeader* (http://www.classleader.com), *WebCT* (http://www.webct.com) or *Embanet* (http://www.embanet.com), offer chat capabilities. If you are conducting a course, you can ask students to attend a chatroom where they will participate in discussions that you direct. Parents, likewise, may enjoy attending an "Open House" online, especially if the *live* Open House occurs during normal work hours. *FirstClass* (http://www.education.softarc.com) supports communication tools that can be used for instruction, in addition to district e-mail and conferencing.

Are you interested in using a free online site for teaching courses or workshops? Try the Internet Classroom Assistant (ICA) at *Nicenet* (http://www.nicenet.org/). You can post discussion topics, send e-mail to participants, and post Web sites for each other. What is the benefit of the ICA? You are using a no-fee site to meet and share information online, without the inconvenience of making sure that everyone has clearance or accounts to access the information.

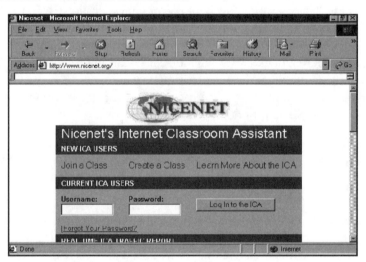

**Internet Classroom Assistant (ICA) at *Nicenet* Web site: http://www.nicenet.org/**

## *Learning Possibility*

The *Turing Game* (http://www.cc.gatech.edu/elc/turing/) is a chatroom that was developed for online research. In this chatroom, the goal is to communicate in a way so that no one can guess your identity, i.e., gender, religion, ethnicity, etc. Visit the Turing Game to learn how to encourage meaningful communication in a chatroom.

Some chat services are available for a fee. For example, *Tutornet* (http://www.tutornet.com) provides courses and tutoring to students in science and math.

Chatrooms are not only for student use. Teachers and parents can also benefit from information and support that they receive through chatrooms. Imagine how you can reassure parents and encourage participation in a weekly or monthly chat session.

What are the benefits of chatrooms, a form of computer conferencing? A training benefit suggests that computer conferencing "allows people to learn from each other, while they work" (Gundry 1991, 167). Further benefits include (175):

1. Collaboration

2. Openness

3. Informal setting

4. Democratic environment with no position authority

5. Lack of hierarchy

6. Self-responsibility

7. Self-judgment

Students that might have been hesitant to participate in live classroom sessions might be more inclined to participate in chat sessions, since they are not as liable to be as shy behind a keyboard! And for the students who are overactive during a live class, the chatroom can calm these tendencies. The best feature of the chatroom could arguably be its ability to promote simultaneous reading and writing activities, forcing the student to focus on the written word as well as comprehension skills. Because chatrooms offer a sense of openness, where ideas and opinions can be freely shared, students enjoy a freer sense of expression than they might in other learning environments. Can you imagine how you can use chatrooms to help your students develop communication skills that allow them to interact positively and constructively in all situations?

Be sure to have a discussion with your students about the importance of selecting chatrooms. Help them learn which chatrooms are safe to enter and how to protect their personal privacy while in the chatroom. Involve parents in this activity, suggesting that parents participate in chatroom activities with their students and that parents provide consent, through a signed form, based on the local school or district policy.

Be aware of the potential for disjointed, unfocused chat sessions that develop with large groups. Students and teachers must also recognize that it may take a while for them to adapt to this type of conversation flow. However, the opportunities offered for brainstorming, decision making, discussions, and one-on-one advising make chats beneficial for small group and individual activities. Instructors need to also present guidelines to help keep the chatters on task. For example, when using chat for a class or parent meeting, state that you (the teacher) will be providing some information in the beginning followed by the opportunity for each member to add comments and questions to the conversation. Follow-up messages or transcripts (provided by most of the online learning courseware, such as WebCT) of the chat sessions serve as good summaries of the learning activities. Be sure to keep notes on effective chat sessions as your experience with this form of communication increases.

To get started with chatting in a class-based system, contact some of the vendors listed below about their products:

BlackBoard CourseInfo (http://www.blackboard.com/) 1-800-424-9299

ClassLeader (http://www.classleader.com) 1-954-568-1980

FirstClass (Softarc) (http://www.softarc.com/) 1-888-588-3444

Lotus LearningSpace (http://www.lotus.com/products/learnspace.nsf/wdocs/homepage) 1-800-346-6409, 1-617-577-8500

WBT Top Class (http://www.wbtsystems.com/) 1-781-684-8270

WebCT (http://www.webct.com/) 1-877-932-2863

## Electronic Classroom

Today, there are many different formats, varieties, and descriptions of the electronic classroom. Some electronic classrooms refer to a physical classroom that includes equipment, such as video projectors, online connections, and instructor workstations. Other online electronic classrooms combine Web links, conferencing or chats, and the transmission of video, audio, and text. In some implementations, the electronic classroom is only intended for use by the particular classroom or school.

One version of the electronic classroom incorporates infrared technology and laptop computers, allowing students to access a schoolwide network without the limitation of wired connections (Flanagan 2000). Students and teachers can take the laptops home or move them from class to class. Because of this movement, no hard drives are included in this laptop design. Flash memory is the storage medium. The machines are loaded with teacher tools, curriculum information, and Web links that have been preselected to support the curriculum. The vendor, *NetSchools* (http://www.netschools.com), reports increases of parental involvement, test scores, attendance, teacher use of technology, and student motivation with declines of absenteeism.

Be sure to request sources of information to confirm vendor claims. Ask for actual teacher and administrator references. Reliable vendors provide documentation of their claims and facilitate the communication between satisfied customer and prospective customer.

Many colleges and universities are creating their own online electronic classroom environment, using commercially developed packages to create student and teacher tools, such as calendars, chatrooms, and quizzes. As we progress through educational developments in technology, exploring where one institution's turf begins and another one ends, we should consider the important element of cooperation and collaboration for educators. Why? The sharing of resources probably involves policies that regulate behavior and the collection and use of information. Agreements and standards that protect participants by delineating their roles and responsibilities will keep misunderstandings to a minimum (Bernbom, Lipincott, and Eaton 1999).

When discussing electronic classrooms, you will probably see reference to online packages, such as those offered by BlackBoard, Embanet, or WebCT. The online environment provides the context for students to participate in communications. Teachers must be certain to establish specific rules on expected behaviors and activities, in addition to monitoring any classrooms that are not under the direct control of the teacher.

For adult learners, online learning opportunities continue to develop through public, private, and online institutions. Groups such as *e-education* (http://www.e-education.com/) work cooperatively with other institutions to offer specific degrees, courses, and certificates, along with providing the opportunity to build courses at their Web site. *BlackBoard* (http://www.blackboard.com) offers courses developed by K–12 schools, colleges, and universities.

## Radio

Radio was going to be the great medium for distance learning in the 1920s, but for a variety of scheduling conflicts and power transmission limitations, the numbers never grew in the United States. In contrast, in Britain and Canada during the 1920s and 1930s, radio was used more extensively for study

(Jenkins 1981). One of the reasons for a lack of growth of radio as an instructional medium related to the limitation of location. Because of the wide distribution needed, the radio stations that could profit most had the poorest radio reception, especially at night. Many countries, such as Australia and Thailand, have used radio formats for instruction (Brande 1993, 229). For remote learners and educators, whether limited by travel in a highly populated, urban area or in an area that is impassable because of the lack of roads or bad weather, radio offers an option.

## *Learning Possibility*

Access an online radio station, such as *KCDU-FM* (http://www.cd93.com) or *KLAQ-FM* (http://www.klaq.com/). What are the technology skills that your students need to know before accessing these sites?

Radio technology, though not exploited, is a technology that could be used for more learners. With the advent of Web versions of radio, such as Webcasts, radio delivery is increasing in popularity. Due to the advancements in online abilities to download or stream audio over the Internet, students can hear recorded, or live, radio presentations in seconds. Why would students be interested in listing to radio presentations? If the class is related to social studies and there is interest in a current news event that is not shown during the evening news, or the recording is interesting for historical purposes, this format can provide meaning to your instruction. Even if it is not designed to be a formal learning experience, teachers can use Webcasts when they apply to class content. *National Public Radio* (http://www.npr.org/) offers a listing of schedule presentations and archives of shows that brings up-to-date information into the classroom.

## *Teaching Possibility*

Do your curriculum standards include "comparison and contrast" in your subject area? If so, access *RTE* (Radio Ireland, written in Irish Gaelic) (http://www .rte.ie/) and select a program to play for your students. Your students might be interested in listening to Irish pop or traditional music, the news from a European perspective, or a Gaelic language lesson. (Help your students locate the home of the rock group U2.) Ask students how they perceive the content and format of these radio presentations to be different from what we hear in the United States. Help them to establish criteria that help them compare the content and format. Can they apply these same criteria to other radio stations broadcasts, such as the BBC (British Broadcasting Company)?

In order to play radio broadcasts from the Internet, you will need to download the audio file and then use an audio player to listen to the file. If you are going to listen to streaming audio for *live* presentations, you will need to download a player, such as RealNetwork's *RealAudio* (http://www.real.com), the Microsoft Windows *Media Player* (http://www.microsoft.com/windows/windowsmedia), or the Apple *QuickTime Player* (http://www.apple.com/quicktime). Download the appropriate player and install it on your computer. Next, visit a site that routinely offers live broadcasts, such as *British Broadcasting Corporation (BBC)* (http://www.bbc.co.uk/), *National Public Radio (NPR)* (http://www.npr.org), or *Yahoo! Broadcast* (http://broadcast.yahoo.com/home.html).

## Satellite Link

Distance learning through satellite is complex, complicated, and "arguably the most expensive" (Piskurich 1997, 19) form of distance learning today. However, technology prices have decreased for satellite technology, and for those districts that have already invested funding in the satellite format, the opportunity to provide interactive, live instruction is great. When first implemented, satellite television programs offered tremendous distance learning opportunities for students and teachers in schools that were small or geographically distant (Barker 1998). Remember, today's students have watched evening reporters present real-time news from Afghanistan, using satellite videophones. As a result, they already have an appreciation for how satellite delivery provides instantaneous connections.

The *Star Schools Project* (http://www.ed.gov/prog_info/StarSchools/) granted $100 million funding (Barker and Dickson 1996) in the early 1990s to schools and projects, such as *SERC* (http://www.serc.org) and TI-IN (now *Starnet* [http://www.starnet.org], offering instruction for K–12 throughout many states), that were interested in partnering and developing distance learning opportunities. The carryover benefit has been that these initial projects have led to continued support for groups that need distance learning support.

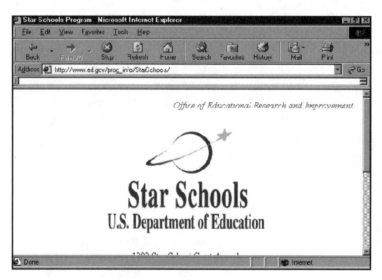

**Star Schools Project** Web site:
**http://www.ed.gov/prog_info/StarSchools/**

The key to satellite projects seems to be organizing the delivery and getting those in the linked audience to interact with the broadcasters. Checklists will help with the organization of the delivery (Barker and Dickson 1996, 22), and experience will help with increasing the interaction. Most states offer some form of satellite and television programming coordination, such as *PeachStar Education Services* (http://www.gpb.org/peachstar) (1-888-501-8960). *Televentures* (http://www.televentures.org/) is a free service that can be accessed through Texas PBS stations and satellite. The *Annenberg/CPB Learner.org Channel* (http://www.learner.org) carries K–12 programming on math, science, and other subjects that are free to those with satellite capabilities or to those educational stations that will download programming. Free licenses are available for off-air recording, rebroadcasting, and/or duplication. For more information, call 1-800-228-8030. Programming is also available through C-band satellite from the *Prince William Network* (http://www.pwnet.org). Topics such as science, music, dance, and teacher development are available, along with online teacher guides.

Because of new federal regulations, new services through the DISH Network, a direct-broadcast satellite television service, allow the broadcasting of some university channels (McCollum 2000). The direct-broadcasting satellites, using equipment similar to the home versions, require the purchase of a satellite system and, usually, the payment of a monthly service fee, unless there are provisions in your area for the waiving of the fee. The benefit for PreK–12 schools is the use of programs that are suitable for students, for enrichment and dual enrollment, and for teacher training, in-service training, or graduate-level courses (Jaeger 1997). For the receiver price, many schools can have access to more than 500 channels, several of which are university based, such as Northern Arizona University's *Universityhouse* (http://www .universityhouse.nau.edu). *UCTV* (*University of California Television*) (http://www.uctv.tv), also available through *StarNet*, has offered programming on a wide variety of interests, including medicine and art.

Satellite connections were used to install Internet connections in Alaska, supported by a NTIA/TIIAP (National Telecommunications and Information Administration/Telecommunications and Information Infrastructure Assistance Program, now known as TOP or Technology Opportunities Program) grant. (Find more information online about funding sources through the *National Telecommunications and Information Administration* [http://www.ntia.doc.gov/].) An entire community benefited from access to an online wealth of knowledge, the ability to publish documents, and the ability to communicate worldwide (Odasz 1999).

Satellite television is very similar to the television delivery of any other program, allowing large groups of students from a number of remote locations to see the teacher. The video portion of satellite delivery is usually one-way (students only see the teacher), and the audio delivery is usually two-way, with students and the teacher having verbal interaction. A facilitator can monitor the student verbal interaction. This technology can be supplemented with faxed delivery of materials and tests or videotapes of prerecorded or commercial presentations. Delivery of satellite instruction generally follows a fixed schedule, determined by the vendor or originating teacher, so the receiving site must be sure that time zone changes, class schedules, or breaks do not conflict with the schedule. Limitations related to the satellite format tend to be that of delivery and coordination. Geographic distance and multiple groups of participants do not increase the costs of delivery by the sender. Videoconferencing by satellite requires an outside antenna, a network control center, outdoor unit, indoor unit, a codec, and a system controller (PC). Because the technology includes physical components, such as the receiving dish, users have to be aware of physical limitations that can exist (Ku band). For example, unless physically protected, snow and ice on the dish can cause reception problems. Relating to coordination, contact names and numbers need to be made available to teachers and facilitators, in case materials need to be faxed or if a student requests direct contact with the instructor. Receiving teachers have to ensure that fax lines are secure and that communications go to the intended recipients.

Teachers have to be aware of strategies to use to keep sessions lively and interactive, especially for students who may have problems keeping on task. Through instructor-developed materials, questioning techniques, the use of a variety of media, and discussions, this is possible.

An example of a system that incorporates satellite delivery is the Utah Education Network, *UENSS* (*Utah Education Network Satellite System*) (http://www.uen.org/ednet/html/uenss.html), an interactive satellite system that uses one-way video and two-way audio to provide interactive courses. The system also provides two-way interactive video through *EdNet* (http://www.uen.org/ednet/). Satellite courses are also available through *StarNet* (http://www.starnet.org/) (1-888-828-7352), which also offers Web courses to students and teachers. (*StarNet* is part of the United Star Distance Learning Consortium [http://www.usdlc.org/].)

The *Public Broadcasting Services* (*PBS*) (http://www.pbs.org/) (1-800-257-2578) provides courses through its Adult Learning Service (ALS). From time to time, events such as course previews are offered at no charge. For example, during spring 2002, a free, interactive event, "Exploring Society," was being offered to promote a distance learning course in sociology. Even though you and your high school students would not be taking part in the course itself, it would be a wonderful learning activity for your students to view this introductory presentation, both in terms of the content and in presentation. Stay aware of other future offerings through the *PBS Adult Learning Service* (http://www.pbs.org/als/). Some courses are also offered for college credit, both through satellite link and through videocassette.

## Television

As with radio, television was going to solve many instructional issues. Again, due to issues such as scheduling, reception, and equipment, television did not become a primary instructional tool in the classroom.

The delivery of interactive television requires scheduling coordination and cooperation between many groups, including local schools, school districts, and state offices that, in many cases, include distance learning offices (Kitchen and Kitchen 1988, 11). The use of television in real time demands that both the teacher and the learner accommodate the medium. This time-bound and place-bound medium is not convenient for all classrooms and learners.

National groups (such as Public Broadcasting Services and Mind Extension University), regional groups (such as the Tennessee cooperative), universities (such as Barry University using WXEL), and PreK–12 school systems work with consortia in their areas to determine which delayed-time courses are needed and how they are to be scheduled. If you are using programs based on PBS (Public Broadcasting Services), you already have a well-established base of support. The *PBS Teacher Source* (http://www.pbs .org/teachersource/) not only offers over a thousand lesson and activity plans designed to support its television programming, it also offers a correlation of these plans to curriculum standards within U.S. states and districts.

The *Iowa Communications Network* (*ICN*) (http://www.icn.state.ia.us/), which began as part of the Star Schools grants, designed a system that allows students to have two-way audio and visual capacity through fiber-optic cable connections that are being upgraded from T1 lines to DS3 (digital signal level 3 is equivalent to approximately the capacity of 28 T1 lines) with the teacher and learners at other sites (Fees and Downs 1995). Each student has a microphone that provides direct contact with the teacher. Some instructors also include an online component with e-mail and Web activities. Costs for providing an interactive television classroom are negotiated by the ICN, which also coordinates the scheduling of the courses. The ICN has been used for instruction ranging from harp lessons to chemistry, with "foreign" travel and advanced placement courses, along with teacher in-service training and administrator conferences that were convenient and saved time and money (Sorensen, Maushak, and Lozada 1996).

A follow-up study of the Star Schools Project reported that teachers saw greater achievement among students when using technology (Maushak and Chen 2000). Students participating in interactive television settings have shown a preference for eye contact with the instructor, use of the microphone by all students, sufficient feedback from the instructor on assignments, and visits by the instructor, along with the opportunity to do small group activities with other site participants (Baker 1999). Whether using television interactively, or in delayed mode, a built-in benefit seems to be that most students enjoy watching television and will tune in to the medium.

## Videoconference (Compressed and Desktop Video)

Videoconferencing is a good application for students who are inaccessible to each other in real time and place. Beyond issues of time and place, videoconferencing can bridge certain situations where a simulated presence is more desirable.

Imagine being able to view those "once-in-a-lifetime" events! With distance learning technologies, such as videoconferencing, that is a possibility. Using a Webcam, the University of Wisconsin was able to let the world watch the blooming of the "corpse flower" (*Edupage*, 18 June 2001). Viewing eclipses is another example of this type of event. Some of these can be viewed at the *Eclipse Home Page* (http://sunearth.gsfc.nasa.gov/eclipse/eclipse.html).

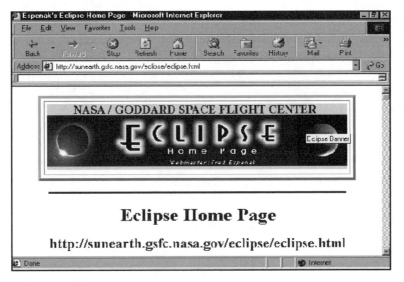

***Eclipse Home Page* Web site:**
**http://sunearth.gsfc.nasa.gov/eclipse/eclipse.html**

Another eclipse project managed by astronomy instructors and students is *ProfJohn.com* (http://www.profjohn.com/), where you can view a total solar eclipse that occurred in Zambia, Africa, on 21 June 2001. This particular project was broadcast by a community college instructor (Dr. John Berryman) and students in the field, while students and colleagues at home in Florida (Palm Beach Community College) viewed the eclipse.

Another live Webcam site for eclipses is at *High Moon* (http://eclipse.span.ch/liveshow.htm). (The home page is *High Moon* [http://eclipse.span.ch/total.htm].) Pictures of past eclipses can be viewed, and future eclipses will be shown in 2002 (Mexico) and 2003 (Antartica and Iceland).

Videoconferencing is the ability to transmit audio and video, one-way or two-way, through cable, DSL, fiber optics, satellite, high-speed Ethernet over the Internet, and satellite. Cable and fiber optics may not be available to those in remote locations, thus limiting the receiving audiences. The use of compressed video requires several technicians and is expensive at present, but initial costs of setting up a two-way video system can be supported through grant money or a local partnership that includes businesses that can also use the technology. Desktop video (and audio) is evolving in the form of streaming media and has great potential, but it is still resource intensive, due to the limitations that many students still have through copper wire, both at home and in the classroom.

Because technological developments are happening every day, a wide variety of videoconference options should be considered by asking local vendors to offer proposals to support your learning. At the time of this writing, videoconferencing systems designed to use with groups cost in the neighborhood of $8,000 to $10,000, not including educational discounts. Setups for individual workstation use can be purchased for less than $800. The videoconferencing classroom should include the conferencing system, a faculty workstation that includes a computer for Internet connection, a visual presenter that will show images or objects in 3-D, a telephone, a fax machine, at least two cameras (one for showing the teacher and one for showing the participants), three monitors (one for showing the participants at a distance, one for the teacher to monitor the actual presentation, and one for the participants to view themselves), and wireless microphones.

What else is needed to support a videoconferencing classroom? A lot of planning and support is required to deliver an effective distance learning course that is interactive and effective. Beyond the initial costs of the equipment, personal support is required for both students and teachers. For those of us who have offered a presentation through videoconferencing, we know that coordination of time, materials, and technology makes this type of delivery demanding, yet rewarding.

Boone (2001) makes good arguments for also using two cameras at each site, in addition to a speakerphone. This additional equipment will allow the instruction to continue, in the event that a camera or the audio link fails. After all, with videoconferencing, if either the delivery or receiving site has a video or audio failure, class is over. At the very least, if there is failure of both video and audio, at least the class can continue with the use of the speakerphone. Boone's discussion of the use of videoconferencing for teacher training also points to the importance of fostering interaction between the two sites, which can occur during or after the class through group work. The point of teaching teachers, by modeling, to use more group work is well taken.

Materials, including textbooks, handouts, course syllabi, assignments, and tests, must be distributed efficiently. As well, some type of communication link, whether through mail or e-mail, needs to be established for students and teachers. Teachers must be willing to work with the technology to ensure that content is presented logically and that students interact as much as possible, within the limitations of the technology.

An early pilot project that taught students and teachers to use computer-mediated communications for sending data, text, sound, and video to the desktop demonstrated interest and cooperation between K–12 gifted students and higher-education groups that wanted to promote these technologies for distance and independent learners (Stammen and Richardson 1992). Interest has continued since this pilot, resulting in increasing demand for videoconferencing. Today, instructors are using streaming media for online course development and research (Mortensen, Schlieve, and Young 2000). Additionally, streaming video has been used to provide distance learning students with taped presentations of a live classroom session (Smith 2000). Though the distance students viewed the presentations in delayed time, they used e-mail and discussion sessions to interact with the live students.

A comparison of available video training costs and technologies noted advantages, disadvantages, and predicted trends (Redding and Fletcher 1994, 78). Trends continue to show that videoconferencing saves costs, both time and expenses, by reducing travel time and related "down" time (when other work would not be accomplished because the participants would be away traveling). Industry has also realized this cost savings by comparing costs of training workers with face-to-face programs ($1,800 per worker) to training with Web-based courses ($120 per worker) (*Edupage*, 4 May 2001).

Videoconferences increase the number of participants, because travel costs are not an issue. This feature makes videoconferencing a viable alternative for teachers who participate in after-school courses or in-service training. Two-way audio/video has been used successfully to offer science and mathematics education courses (Boone, Bennett, and Ovando 1995). In this study, the teachers (in the role of students) wanted to see and hear everything. As a result, the use of multipoint connections was important to the participants. In addition, because there can be connection failures, backup plans were suggested. This experience, like others, indicated that since the group is focused on the medium during a videoconference, it seems logical that the learning will likewise be more focused.

Some of the better-known videoconferencing for teacher training has occurred through NASA (Petersen 2000). Whether training teachers to use online sources or having students interact with scientists and astronauts, the most successful presentations have involved a lot of activity and dialogue between the participants. If you cannot afford to take your students to the NASA John H. Glenn Research Center in Cleveland, Ohio, then look at the many educational activities online (http://www.grc.nasa.gov/doc/educatn.htm).

Making good use of some of these existing NASA materials, a group of teachers and scientists developed interactive, inquiry-based materials through the *CERES (Center for Educational Resources) Project* at Montana State University (http://btc.montana.edu/ceres/). The lesson plans, including handouts, are posted online and even provide an indication of how long it will take to present the lesson. Longer

"Spacequests" guide the students through a problem-solving activity. Materials are available for K–12 students. Teacher certification courses in space science are also available, in coordination with this project. A benefit of this project was the resulting quality curriculum that was developed by content experts who teamed with teachers to emphasize the active inquiry model of learning using authentic NASA data (Slater et al. 2001). Be sure to visit this well-designed and highly organized Web site, both as a source of materials you can use now and as a model upon which you may develop a similar project.

According to a recent study (Towler, Miller, and Kumari 2000), teachers have also used video-conferencing for technology training to promote collaborative teaching skills. This study suggested that teachers who are going to help other teachers learn to use technology should be open to the technology in the beginning.

One drawback to the videoconference, especially at the desktop, is that many students do not like losing their anonymity when they are at home. Another weakness of videoconferencing is that it does not promote the presentation of abstract concepts and ideas. Videoconferencing is very useful if there is a visual component, but without visual aids, it becomes like the traditional lecture hall. Also, do not overlook background sources of noise, which can be distracting when videoconferencing with two-way audio.

An online *Video Conferencing Cookbook* (http://www.vide.gatech.edu/cookbook2.0/) provides basic introductory information that addresses the issue of open systems and specifications that are needed for two-way communication systems. Vendors, such as *Pacific Bell* (http://www.pacbell.com), *Polycom* (http://www.polycom.com), and *VTEL* (http://www.vtel.com), also provide descriptions of system speci-fications and other resources for teachers who wish to begin distance learning opportunities, such as Pacific Bell's *Videoconferencing for Learning* (http://www.kn.pacbell.com/wired/vidconf/). Presentation skills, directories, and links for videoconferencing are quickly available at this site.

Why is the use of videoconferencing rewarding? Without videoconferencing, it is possible that many students could not participate in a course, due to lack of instructors or geographic distance from the course. With training for both students as participants and teachers as delivery people, videoconferencing is a very good educational solution. Forster and Washington (2000) offer a positive, yet realistic, model of organization for videoconferenced courses. Though based on the delivery of a graduate program, many of the same concerns and solutions apply to the PreK–12 environment.

## *Tips for Videoconferencing*

### Instructor tips to avoid distraction:

1. Arrange materials needed during the videoconference nearby so that they are easily accessible.

2. Test all equipment prior to start time to ensure that students can see all participants at each site.

3. Arrange seating for the class. A U-shape arrangement is generally the best.

4. Use the area behind the instructor to display information about the class.

5. Maintain camera eye contact. Inform the students if and why you are moving away from camera range.

6. Speak in short segments (ten to fifteen lecture minutes).

7. Articulate everything that you are doing. Do not assume that students will be able to see what you are doing.

8. Vary activities and pacing (lecture, directed discussion, open discussion, panel discussion, panel presentation, interview, viewing, reading, writing, online activity, etc.).

9. Vary speakers.

10. Vary speaking voices.

11. Be specific with questions. Identify the person that you wish to answer a question and that person's location.

12. Review frequently.

## Visual tips:

1. Vary focal points. Switch from viewing the instructor to viewing different students and places in the room.

2. Use nonmoving images.

3. Plain paper is better to use than textured paper. Pastel shades are suggested.

4. Dark markers (other than black) are suggested. Felt-tip markers with sharp tips provide fine-line markings.

5. Print! Letters need to be between one-and-a-half and two inches high.

6. Prepare visuals by the same rules of thumb used to prepare overhead transparencies. Limit concepts and words on each transparency.

7. Avoid fancy fonts.

8. Display signs that offer directions. For instance, create a sign that informs others if you are experiencing technical difficulties or one that announces the class commencement time.

9. Before using audiovisual materials, be sure to test the receiving view.

10. Do not use copyrighted videotapes for broadcasting without first verifying that you have broadcast rights.

11. Provide a list of the visuals to be used for the video operator.

## Tips to involve all audiences:

1. Teach with no students at the originating site (preferred for first-time teachers).

2. Make equal eye contact, verbal contact, etc.

3. Vary contact equally among students.

4. If using demonstrations, labs, or other types of hands-on activities, be sure to do each activity equally at each site.

5. Make use of predelivered activity sheets.

6. Provide a nearby fax machine for receiving groups to fax in questions or receive additional materials.

7. Avoid making students feel self-conscious by forcing them to participate in verbal activities between sending and receiving sites; however, encourage students to participate through incentives (participation points).

8.  Keep students informed of their activities.

9.  Maintain a log of student interactions so that you can work to involve those who are not participating as much.

10. Allow students to designate which students will speak, answer, participate, etc. You can also provide students with a set process for taking turns (Nayman 1999). Videoconferencing does not accommodate the old raise-your-hand method of student recognition as well as face-to-face teaching.

11. Remember to never provide student contact information beyond class members, and then only do so with student and parent permission.

## Room management at remote sites:

1.  Be sure that students have a list of all participants' names at each site.

2.  Encourage the instructor to prepare a handout that includes course introductory material, the syllabus, and a potential activity that is interactive for the first opening session and for facilitator interaction.

3.  Schedules of exact video start and end times should be provided to all receiving participants. Make reservations far in advance to avoid all conflicts.

4.  All students should have all course materials at the beginning of the first session. Prepare a list of all support materials needed for each session.

5.  A site facilitator should be appointed to introduce students to each other and to any support personnel. Students should have names and telephone numbers of an additional contact in the event of a technical breakdown.

6.  The facilitator should take attendance and get the group started in the first activity.

7.  Assign receiving students a partner for joint activities.

8.  Facilitators should choose a student to interact with the instructor, or an order can be established and followed among students.

9.  Set prearranged break times to be observed for all groups, taking into account any time zone differences.

## Instructor evaluation activities:

1.  All sites should have the same assignment, test requirements, and due dates.

2.  Exceptions to instructor directions should be discussed privately between the teacher and the student by telephone, or messages can be sent through e-mail.

3.  No references of any type should be made about an individual student's progress (or lack thereof) during the videoconference.

4.  Instructors should prepare a chart that identifies participants at each location, along with descriptive information about each site.

5.  Make use of "dead" time before the class begins to display required information (description of activities, etc.).

Additional videoconferencing guidelines for presenters, developed for NASA presentations, address the need to keep students' attention through varying the presentation techniques, engaging the students in a dialogue, and encouraging questions.

If you are interested in using videoconferencing, the first thing to do is find out what equipment you have available on your campus, or in your district, that supports videoconferencing. Next, speak with teachers that have used this modality. Ask to observe the instruction.

A general listing of videoconference vendors follows:

First Virtual Communications (http://www.fvc.com/) (1-800-241-7463)

General DataComm (http://www.gdc.com/) (1-800-523-1737)

OK-STEP (http://www.sel.sony.com/SEL/rmeg) (1-800-686-7669)

Polycom (http://www.polycom.com/home.asp) (1-800-POLYCOM)

Qwest (http://www.qwest.com/) (1-877-490-6342)

VTEL (http://www.vtel.com/) (1-800-299-8835)

The California Community College's *TIPS* (*Telecommunications Infrastructure Project Statewide*) (http://www.tipsnews.org/misc/about.html) offers resources that include articles of teaching tips and Web sites to support the videoconferencing teaching process. Some districts may use videoconferencing for specific presentations, not ongoing instruction. Some of these videoconferences require fees, and thus, it is important to consider why you would want to receive the conferences. When making videoconference selections, in addition to content consider:

1. Rationale

2. Audience

3. Goals and objectives

4. Presenters

5. Support for content and cost

If the videoconference will be a large group event, designate a coordinator who will work with media experts and content experts to make sure that reception and group discussions are provided.

By this point, you probably have realized the importance of implementing distance learning experiences in your classroom. At different times throughout the process of implementing distance learning technologies, there has been an unfounded fear that teachers would be replaced by the technology (Ruth 1997). To the contrary, good teaching is still needed—now more than ever. Just as the U.S. Postal Service (http://www.usps.com) is beginning to use the Internet to offer new services that improve on the value of the old postal services, distance learning technologies will supplement, not supplant, existing learning structures.

A recent implementation of technology in education is the *Digital Dakota Network* (http://cts .state.sd.us/status.htm) in South Dakota. The network connects all public schools through high-speed telecommunications lines so that they can share classes through videoconferencing or access online resources. Qwest and equipment companies, such as VTEL, have supported this effort. Whether for point-to-point or multipoint meetings, interviews, staff development (Hyman 1999), or instruction, videoconferencing offers more alternatives. These alternatives will continue to develop with changes in the technologies.

## *Learning Possibility*

Conduct an audit of what you need to bring videoconferencing technology into the classroom. To do this, plan a visit to a neighboring school that already offers videoconferencing. Notice the configuration of the technology. Is a separate room designated for use for this technology? What is the hardware needed and where was this purchased? Is there a district or a state bid price that you can use to get less-expensive equipment? What are the policies on how this medium is used in your district? Do these policies change when you are using videoconferencing for out-of-district distance learning activities? Are you allowed to use this equipment for videoconferencing with students in another state or country? (If working out of your time zone, be sure to help your students calculate the time difference. Can they do this by map? Or do they prefer using some of the online time zone calculators?)

---

# *Conclusion*

There is no lack of media for interactive distance learning, and no lack of resources that will offer tutorials, guides, and basic introductory information for new technologies. New technologies are ever evolving, and educators will find a way to use these technologies. How will the technology develop? There is no way to predict what the creative imagination can develop! Remember the robot maid "Rosie" on the Jetsons cartoon shows? Now, meet "Dawn" or "Mabel," in the form of a chatterbot that hangs out in a MUD (a Multi-User Domain), waiting to speak to you. Chatterbots, a Web-based communication that incorporates elements of artificial intelligence, hold great promise for teachers whose students need practice with predictable language. These chatterbots may eventually be useful for the average classroom with support materials and lesson plan suggestions.

Models and examples of interactive distance learning probably exist for your application, but it will require some research on your part to identify literature that describes them. However, this research is an important part of the distance learning process and it should not be overlooked. Also, as part of this distance learning design process, because of the constant changes with technology and the increase of experience, we must be open to input by all members of the school community in the hopes of improving the learning model. A blending of the Instructional Design Model (IDM), with the instructor having responsibility for course design and delivery, and the Constructivist Model, involving all participants through the design process, will probably ensure greater success of the course (Ravitz 1997).

A caution for the teacher who enthusiastically accepts all technology as positive for the classroom: Be sure to evaluate the technology for the learning outcomes and skills produced. For example, some students and instructors, who despise taking notes, have embraced technologies, from the lowly photocopy to sophisticated systems and computer files that have done away with this need. Exceptional Student Education (ESE) teachers can recognize the benefits of this system for their students, and for the adult student who already knows how to take notes, this may be a technological advance. But for the beginning student who is developing the cognitive skills needed to encode and structure information through note taking, further developing eye-hand and fine-motor coordination, this may not be such a positive. Therefore, thoroughly evaluate the role that the technology will have in the class. "Distance learning's future will see the convergence of a mix of technologies to deliver instructional content as well as to promote interaction between students and teachers" (Barker and Dickson 1996, 22), if the educator is focusing on the student needs, and not the convenience or cost of systems.

To be realistic, distance learning is not the solution for all learning needs. Some students, due to learner characteristics caused by physical, intellectual, or emotional factors, may not be suited to distance learning. Let us also remember that some students just do not like learning in any way other than with a teacher and other students physically present. The latter student will become increasingly rare, simply because students will be forced to function in a partially distance learning world. Consider your distance learning atmosphere holistically, where quality governance, planning, teaching, materials, and learning converge.

Today, though, for the beginning distance learning educator, it is often difficult to know where to go to look for materials that are current and easy to understand. One such resource is *Distance.Educator.com* (http://www.distance-educator.com/). In addition to having a Web site that is frequently updated with new materials, this source is searchable. There are also listservs that provide support for distance learning that include DEOS-L (The Distance Education Online Symposium; send list commands to listserv@lists .psu.edu), DEOS-R (Distance Education Online Research; send list commands to listserv@cmuvm.csv .cmich.edu), and DEOSNEWS (The Distance Education Online Symposium; send list commands to listserv@lists.psu.edu. The *DEOS-L archive* is online [http://www.ed.psu.edu/ACSDE/deos/deos.asp] at the *American Center for the Study of Distance Education* [http://www.ed.psu.edu/ACSDE/]). Though DEOS-L participants tend to be from the postsecondary environment, many of the ideas apply to PreK–12. Consider monitoring one of these listservs to decide whether the level of content will be useful to you. You can also subscribe to the DEOS-L listserv by Web at http://lists.psu.edu/cgi-bin/wa?SUBED1=deos-l&A=1.

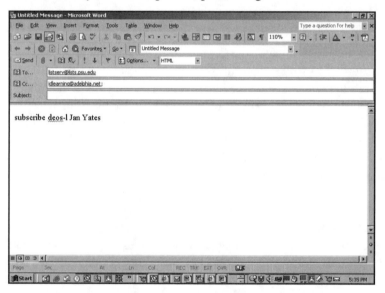

**Subscription Message to DEOS-L at listserv@lists.psu.edu**

Finally, do not forget that online presentations are becoming more and more accessible and attractive as sources of professional development. For example, the National Education Association's presentation of *Tech: Making the Grade* shows how teachers nationwide have implemented technology in the classroom, along with providing the specifications for the learning configuration (http://www.makingthegrade .org/experience.html). Educational support, whether it centers on distance learning, technology, or traditional applications, requires us to first think of our often overlooked purpose in education, as defined by state, district, or school statements of purpose. However, most educators are not simply content to accept the status quo when it comes to teaching, and we almost always are in the process of refining our personal educational philosophies. If this describes you, you will be interested in an online hyperbook, *Engines for*

*Education* (Shank and Cleary 1994) (http://www.ils.northwestern.edu/research/tech_rep_58.pdf) that addresses the issue of how students learn. In the arena of distance learning, the "how" of learning may dramatically influence the type of distance learning technology used with students. This hyperbook's authors believe that the student's involvement in learning is valued and that the development of learning technologies that support this involvement should be encouraged.

At this point, you still may not feel ready to begin interactive distance learning activities, due to lack of assurance about being able to successfully use computer application software. If this is the case, be sure to start accessing some of the many links to online courses and tutorials that are provided. If you would feel more confident with a printed text in hand, *Integrating Computer Technology into the Classroom* (Morrison and Lowther 2002) provides a thorough discussion of the use of application software in K–12 classrooms. With ideas ranging from the design and planning to the evaluation of a lesson, along with a database of lesson plan ideas and a companion Web site (http://cwx.prenhall.com/bookbind/pubbooks /chet_morrison_integratin_2/), this text may be helpful in providing beginning development support.

Again, the vendor sources are intended to get you started with your evaluations of distance learning technologies. Their listings are not provided as endorsements but rather as a convenience to the reader. For listings of other distance learning technology vendors, try the *e-learning Buyer's Guide* (http://www.mediabrains.com/client/ELearning/BG1/search.asp).

# *References*

Achterberg, Cheryl. "Tips for Teaching a Course by E-Mail." *Journal of Nutrition Education* 28, no. 6 (1996): 303–7.

"Back to School," 10 September 1999, *Edupage* (owner-edupage@listserv.educause.edu) (http://www.educause .edu/pub/edupage/edupage.html).

Bainbridge, Zoe, Karen Wellings, and Andrew Westby. *Distance Learning Package: Village Level Cassava Processing*. Greenwich, England: Natural Resources Institute, 1997.

Baker, Molly Herman. "Distance Teaching with Interactive Television: Strategies That Promote Interaction with Remote-Site Students." In *Encyclopedia of Distance Education Research in Iowa*, 2d ed., edited by Beth Kumar, Nancy J. Maushak, Michael Simonson, and Kristen Egeland Wright. Ames, IA: Technology Research and Evaluation Group, College of Education, Iowa State University, 1999.

Barker, Bruce O. "Satellite TV programs for Rural and Small Schools." *Rural Educator* 10, no. 1 (1998): 1–4.

Barker, Bruce O., and Michael W. Dickson. "Distance Learning Technologies in K–12 Schools: Past, Present, and Future Practice." *TechTrends* 46, no. 2 (1996): 19–22.

Bayram, Servet. "Internet Learning Initiatives: How Well Do Turkish Virtual Classrooms Work?" *T.H.E. Journal* 26, no. 10 (1999): 65–68.

Becker, Gary. "Copyright and Distance Education." *TechTrends* 45, no. 1 (2001): 4–6.

Bernbom, Gerry, Joan Lipincott, and Fynnette Eaton. "Working Together: New Collaborations Among Information Professionals." *CAUSE/EFFECT* 22, no. 2 (1999): 6–9.

Biemiller, Lawrence. "Highlights of a Student-Marketing Survey Reveal That the Net Is 'In.'" *The Chronicle of Higher Education*, 8 September 1999. (http://chronicle.com/daily/99/09/99090801t.htm) (10 October 1999).

Boettcher, Judith V. "Taking Off with Distance Learning: Are We There Yet?" *Syllabus* 12, no. 4 (1998): 22–26, 53.

Boneva, Bonka, et al. *Using E-Mail for Personal Relationships: The Difference Gender Makes*, 2001. (http://www .pewinternet.org/papers/paperspdf/CMU_Boneva_Gender.pdf). (A working paper of the Pew Internet & American Life Project [http://www.pewinternet.org/papers/]) (11 January 2002).

Boone, William J. "Qualitative Evaluation of Utilizing Dynamic Quad Screen Technology for Elementary and Middle School Teacher Preparation." *Journal of Technology and Teacher Education* 9, no. 1 (2001): 129–45.

Boone, William J., Christine Bennett, and Carlos Ovando. "Teachers' Attitudes Towards Distance Learning Technology in a Science/Society Global Issues Course." *Journal of Computers in Mathematics and Science Teaching* 14, no. 3 (1995): 305–3.

*Bowker's Directory of Videocassettes for Children.* New York: R. R. Bowker, 1998.

Brande, Lieve van den. *Flexible and Distance Learning.* New York: Wiley, 1993.

Bruning, Roger, Melodee Landis, Elizabeth Hoffman, and Kristin Grosskopf. "Perspectives on an Interactive Satellite-Based Japanese Language Course." In *K–12 Distance Education: Learning, Instruction, and Teacher Training*, edited by Michael G. Moore and Margaret A. Koble. University Park, PA: American Center for the Study of Distance Education, College of Education, Pennsylvania State University, 1997.

Burke, John J. "Using E-Mail to Teach: Expanding the Reach of BI." *Research Strategies* 14, no. 1 (1996): 36–43.

Carnvale, Dan. "A 'Boot Camp' Proves Helpful to New Online Students." *The Chronicle of Higher Education*, 20 January 2000. (http://chronicle.com/free/2000/01/2000012001u.htm) (27 January 2000).

———. "U.S. Backs the Development of Dozens of Internet-Based Courses." *The Chronicle of Higher Education*, 28 January 2000. (http://chronicle.com/weekly/v46/i21/21a04602.htm) (12 February 2000).

"CNN Video Archives to Become Digital Database," 23 April 2001, *Edupage* (owner-edupage@listserv .educause.edu) (http://www.educause.edu/pub/edupage/edupage.html).

Coburn, Dawn, Vince Dobbs, and Sheila Grainger. "Future-Proofing the Curriculum." *Educational Leadership International* 53, no. 2 (1995): 85–87.

Cotlar, Morton, and James N. Shimabukuro. "Stimulating Learning with Electronic Guest Lecturing." In *Computer Mediated Communication and the Online Classroom, Volume Three: Distance Learning*, edited by Zane L. Berge and Mauri P. Collins. Cresskill, NJ: Hampton, 1995.

*Criteria for Accreditation.* Decatur, GA: Commission on Colleges of the Southern Association of Colleges and Schools, 1998.

Cummings, Jim, and Dennis Sayers. *Brave New Schools: Challenging Cultural Illiteracy Through Global Learning Networks.* New York: St. Martin's Press, 1995.

Davis-Tanous, Jennifer R. *XML: A Language to Manage the World Wide Web.* ERIC Digest (EDO-IR-1999-10). Syracuse, NY: ERIC Information and Technology Clearinghouse, 1999. (http://www.ericit.org/digests/EDO-IR -1999-10.shtml) (28 October 2002).

Dickstein, Ruth, and Kari Boyd McBride. "Listserv Lemmings and Fly-Brarians on the Wall: A Librarian-Instructor Team Taming the Cyberbeast in the Large Classroom." *College & Research Librarians* 59, no. 1 (1998): 10–17.

"E-Mail Catches Up to Snail Mail," 18 May 2001, *Edupage* (owner-edupage@listserv.educause.edu) (http://www .educause.edu/pub/edupage/edupage.html).

Engler, Natalie. "Distance Learning in the Digital Age." In *The Digital Classroom: How Technology Is Changing the Way We Teach and Learn*, edited by David T. Gordon. Cambridge, MA: Harvard Education Letter, 2000.

Eskow, Dennis. "Beat Information Overload." *PC World* 15, no. 2 (1997): 148–62.

Flanagan, William P. "A Small School Reaches Worldwide." *Mobile Computing & Communications* 11, no. 3 (2000): 90–92.

Forster, Michael, and Earlie Washington. "A Model for Developing and Managing Distance Education Programs Using Interactive Video Technology." *Journal of Social Work Education* 36, no. (2000): 147–58.

Gasaway, Laura N. "Distance Learning and Copyright: Is a Solution in Sight?" *CAUSE/EFFECT* 22, no. 3 (1999): 6–8, 25.

Gilbert-Macmillan, Kathleen. "Computer-Based Distance Learning for Gifted Students: The EPGY Experience." *Understanding Our Gifted* 12, no. 3 (2000): 17–20.

Gundry, John. "Understanding Collaborative Learning in Networked Organizations." In *Collaborative Learning Through Computer Conferencing: The Najaden Papers*, edited by Anthony Kaye. New York: Springer-Verlag, 1991.

Hallett, Karen, and Jack Cummings. "The Virtual Classroom as Authentic Experience: Collaborative, Problem-Based Learning in a WWW Environment." In *Competition Connection Collaboration* (Report of the Annual Conference on Distance Teaching and Learning, 6–8 August 1997, Madison, WI). ERIC ED 413 870.

Hamilton, Malcolm C. "The Trouble with E-Mail." *CUPA Journal* 47, no. 2 (1996): 1–5.

Hinn, D. Michelle, Kevin Leander, and Bertram C. Bruce. "Case Studies of a Virtual School." *Journal of Adolescent & Adult Literacy* 45, no. 2 (2001): 156–63.

Huffington, Dale, et al. *Designing and Developing Courses for Internet and World Wide Web Delivery* (Presentation at the 13th annual conference on Distance Teaching and Learning, 6–8 August 1997, Madison, WI), 439–50.

Hyman, Linda Woods. "Videoconferencing: The Quiet Revolution." *Knowledge Quest* 28, no. 2 (1999): 49–50.

"Internet Users Now Exceed 100 Million," 12 November 1999, *Edupage* (owner-edupage@listserv.educause.edu) (http://www.educause.edu/pub/edupage/edupage.html).

Jaeger, Michael. "Science Teacher Education at a Glance." In *K–12 Distance Education: Learning, Instruction, and Teacher Training*, edited by Michael G. Moore and Margaret A. Koble. University Park, PA: American Center for the Study of Distance Education, College of Education, Pennsylvania State University, 1997.

Jenkins, Janet. *Materials for Learning: How to Teach Adults at a Distance*. Boston: Routledge & Kegan Paul, 1981.

Kaplan, Howard. "Building Your Own Web Course: The Case for Off-the-Shelf Component Software." *CAUSE/EFFECT* 21, no. 4 (1998): 44–46, 52. (http://www.educause.edu/ir/library/html/cem9849.html) (3 February 2000).

Kiernan, Vincent. "As Goes Kevin Bacon, So Go the Web, Researchers Report." *The Chronicle of Higher Education*, 9 September 1999. (http://chronicle.com/free/99/09/99090901t.htm) (2 March 2000).

Kitchen, Karen, and Will Kitchen. *Two-Way Interactive Television for Distance Learning: A Primer*. Alexandria, VA: ITTE Technology Leadership Network, National School Boards Association, 1988.

Leu, Donald J., and Deborah Diadiun Leu. *Teaching with the Internet: Lessons from the Classroom*. Norwood, MA: Christopher-Gordon, 1999. (This professional title also has an online support site [http://web.syr.edu/~djleu/sites.html].)

Lippert, Robert M., Rama Radhakrishna, Owen Plank, and Charles C. Mitchell. "Using Different Evaluation Tools to Assess a Regional Internet Inservice Training." *International Journal of Instructional Media* 28, no. 3 (2001): 237–48.

Martin, James A. "You've Got Junk Mail." *PC World* 16, no. 4 (1998): 45–46.

Maushak, Nancy J., and Kuo-Tsai Chen. "Learners and the Learning Environment: Impact of Technology Use in K–12 Schools in Iowa." *The Quarterly Review of Distance Education* 1, no. 3 (2000): 215–24.

May, Andrew D. "Automatic Classification of E-Mail Messages by Message Type." *Journal of the American Society for Information Science* 48, no. 1 (1997): 32–39.

Mayman, Ira. "Lessons from a Videoconferenced Course." *CAUSE/EFFECT* 22, no. 3 (1999): 45–47.

McCollum, Kelly. "How Forcefully Should Universities Enforce Copyright Law on Audio Files?" *The Chronicle of Higher Education*, 19 November 1999. (http://chronicle.com/free/v46/i13/13a05901.htm) (1 December 1999).

———. "Under New Federal Rules, Satellite Broadcaster Offers University Programming." *The Chronicle of Higher Education*, 13 January 2000. (http://chronicle.com/free/2000/01/2000011301t.htm) (20 February 2000).

Mioduser, David, Rafi Nachmias, Orly Lahav, and Avigail Oren. "Web-Based Learning Environments: Current Pedagogical and Technological State." *Journal of Research on Computing in Education* 33, no. 1 (2000): 55–76.

Morrison, Gary R., and Deborah L. Lowther. *Integrating Computer Technology into the Classroom*, 2d ed. Upper Saddle River, NJ: Merrill, 2002.

Mortensen, Mark, Paul Schlieve, and Jon Young. "Delivering Instruction via Streaming Media." *TechTrends* 44, no. 2 (2000): 36–41.

"News, Trends, and Resources: Watson Makes Online Research Elementary." *Syllabus* 13, no. 5 (1999): 12.

Nua.com. "How Many Online?" February 2002. (http://www.nua.ie/surveys/how_many_online/index.html) (29 June 2002).

Odasz, Frank. "On the Frontier of Online Learning, in Galena, Alaska." *Multimedia Schools* 6, no. 2 (1999): 42–45.

Petersen, Ruth. " 'Real World' Connections Through Videoconferencing—We're Closer than You Think!" *TechTrends* 44, no. 6 (2000): 5–11.

Piskurich, George M. "Reconsidering the Promise of Satellites as a Distance Learning Technology." *Performance Improvement* 36, no. 2 (1997): 19–23.

Presley, Bruce, Beth Brown, and Elaine Malfas. *The Lawrenceville Press Guide to the Internet*. Pennington, NJ: Lawrenceville Press, 1997.

Ravitz, Jason. *An ISD Model for Building Online Communities: Furthering the Dialogue*, 1997. ERIC ED 409 863.

Redding, G. A., and J. D. Fletcher. "Technical and Administrative Issues in Distributed Training Technology." In *Learning Without Boundaries: Technology to Support Distance/Distributed Learning*, edited by Robert J. Seidel and Paul R. Chatelier. New York: Plenum Press, 1994.

Reed, Jodi. "Learning and the Internet: A Gentle Introduction for K–12 Educator, Part 1." *The Distance Educator* 1, no. 1 (1995): 2, 8–11.

Rees, Fred J., and Dennis A. Downs. "Interactive Television and Distance Learning." *Music Educators Journal* 82, no. 2 (1995): 21–25.

"Research on Educational Technology," 15 December 2000, *Edupage* (owner-edupage@listserv.educause.edu) (http://www.educause.edu/pub/edupage/edupage.html).

Ropel, Timothy. "Preparing Print-Based Distance Learning Materials in the Age of the Web: 34 Tips for Effective Typography, Page Design, and Structured Content." In *Competition Connection Collaboration* (Report of the Annual Conference on Distance Teaching and Learning, 6–8 August 1997, Madison, WI). ERIC ED 413 870.

Ross, Tweed W. *LISTSERVs as a Method to Enhance Instruction: Our First Year Experience*, 1995. ERIC ED 387 863.

Rowntree, Derek. *Teaching with Audio in Open and Distance Learning: An Audio-Print Package for Teachers and Trainers*. London: Kogan Page, 1994.

Ruth, Stephen. "Getting Real About Technology-Based Learning: The Medium Is Not the Message." *Educom Review* 32, no. 5 (1997): 32–37.

*Safe Blood and Blood Products*. (WHO/GPA/CNP/93.2 E.) Geneva, Switzerland: World Health Organization, 1993.

Schmidt, Kathy J., Michael J. Sullivan, and Darcy Walsh Hardy. "Teaching Migrant Students Algebra by Audio-conference." In *K–12 Distance Education: Learning, Instruction, and Teacher Training*, edited by Michael G. Moore and Margaret A. Koble. University Park, PA: American Center for the Study of Distance Education, College of Education, Pennsylvania State University, 1997.

Scott, Jane. "Creating Your Own Internet Projects with E-Mail." *School Library Media Activities Monthly* 12, no. 9 (1996): 43, 48.

Serwatka, Judy Ann. "Internet Distance Learning: How Do I Put My Course on the Web?" *T.H.E. Journal* 26, no. 10 (1999): 71–74.

Shank, Roger, and Chip Cleary. *"Engines for Education,"* 1994. (http://www.ils/northwestern.edu/research/tech _rep_58.pdf) (23 November 1999).

Slater, Timothy F., Brian Beaudrie, David M. Cadtiz, Donna Governor, Elizabeth E. Roettger, Stephanie Stevenson, and George Tuthill. "A Systemic Approach to Improving K–12 Astronomy Education Using NASA's Internet Resources." *The Journal of Computers in Mathematics and Science Teaching* 20, no. 2 (2001): 163–78.

Smith, Sean. "Teacher Education." *Journal of Special Education Technology* 15, no. 4 (2000): 40–43.

Sorensen, Chris, Nancy Maushak, and Marcia Lozada. *Iowa Distance Education Alliance Evaluation Report.* Ames, IA: Research Institute for Studies in Education, College of Education, Iowa State University, 1996.

Srinivasan, Kalpana. "High-Tech Video Recorders Refocus TV Habits." *Palm Beach Post* (29 January 2000): 17B.

Stammen, Ronald M., and Jolene Richardson. *Desktop Video: Multi-Media on the NeXT Computer* (Paper presented at the International Rural and Small Schools Conference, 30 March–1 April 1992, Grand Forks, ND). ERIC ED 348 964.

Strauss, Howard. "The Future of the Web, Intelligent Devices, and Education." *Educom Review* 34, no. 4 (1999): 16–19, 52.

Stull, Andrew T., and Randall J. Ryder. *Education on the Internet: A Student's Guide.* Upper Saddle River, NJ: Merrill, 1999.

Sujo de Montes, Laura E., and Carmen L. Gonzales. "Been There, Done That: Reaching Teachers Through Distance Education." *Journal of Technology and Teacher Education* 8, no. 4 (2000): 351–71.

Summerville, Jennifer. "WebQuests: An Aspect of Technology Integration for Training Preservice Teachers." *TechTrends* 44, no. 2 (2000): 31–35.

Tao, Liqing. *Online Strategies Used in Reading Email Messages,* 1997. ERIC ED 407 656.

Towler, Annette J., Leslie Miller, and D. Siva Kumari. "A Case Study of Project OWLink: Teachers' Reflections." *Teacher Education Quarterly* 27, no. 1 (2000): 29–38.

"UW Drops in on Small-Town Students," 2 May 2001, *Edupage* (owner-edupage@listserv.educause.edu) (http:// www.educause.edu/pub/edupage/edupage.html).

VanHemert, Shannon L. "PUBYAC: Yacking It Up on the Internet." *Youth Services in Libraries* 9 (1995): 79–85.

"Virtual Classroom Is the Future," 4 May 2001, *Edupage* (owner-edupage@listserv.educause.edu) (http://www .educause.edu/pub/edupage/edupage.html).

"Viruses Await: PDA, Cellphones Are Vulnerable," 29 December 2000, *Edupage* (owner-edupage@listserv .educause.edu) (http://www.educause.edu/pub/edupage/edupage.html).

Visual Language: "Conveying Information in Instruction and on the Web." *Syllabus* 12, no. 9 (1999): 24, 26, 60.

Williams, Hilda Lee, and Eunice M. Meredith. "On-Line Communication Patterns of Novice Internet Users." *Computers in the Schools* 12, no. 3 (1996): 21–31.

Wilson, Warren. "Web's Creator Amazed but Critical." *Palm Beach Post* (2 September 1997): 7D.

Young, Jeffrey R. "The Lowly Telephone Is Central to Some Distance-Education Courses." *The Chronicle of Higher Education* 46, no. 36 (12 May 2000): A46.

# Chapter 4

## Interactive Distance Learning Settings

Interactive distance learning settings can be found wherever learners and educators are connected. Even though the level of sophistication of the connections may vary, the settings must provide for communication between all participants, whether learner, educator, or facilitator.

The distance learning model provided in this handbook acknowledges traditional, as well as legal, responsibilities of school personnel. In this distance learning model, students are under the constant supervision of the teacher or other adult (such as the media specialist, technologist, administrator, staff member, volunteer, or parent) who serves in a facilitator role. As a result, this distance learning model describes distance learning settings for PreK–12 students, not for adults.

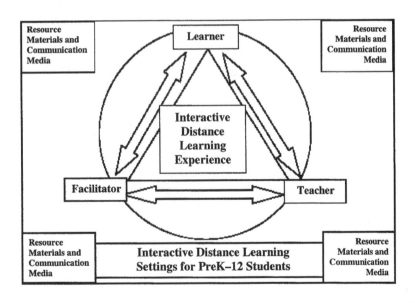

**Distance Learning Model**

### Teaching Possibility

Did you know that "cyberstalking" is difficult to prevent? Even though there are laws against cyberstalking, which is often accomplished through chatrooms and e-mail, this crime is continuing (*Edupage*, 16 June 2000). Is it because some of our most trusted members of society (in all areas, including education, law enforcement, medicine, and religion) have participated in cyberstalking that we must be especially vigilant with our supervision and instruction? Be sure to teach your students how to protect themselves against cyberstalking by knowing the proper use of the Internet. You could use the U.S. Department of Justice's *The Internet: Know Before You Go into Cyberspace!* Web site (http://www .cybercrime.gov/rules/kidinternet.htm) to make sure that students understand the "rules of the road," along with some of its roadblocks, such as cyberstalking.

---

Some schools require online "driver licenses" before allowing students online access at school. Can you include some cyberstalking questions in your online driver's test? *Online Safety: A Primer for Parents and Children* (http://www.juvenilenet.org/jjtap/archives/primer/index.html) would be a good document to review as you are planning this lesson.

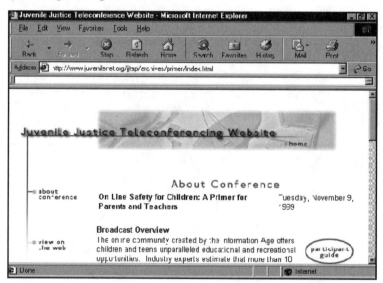

*Online Safety: A Primer for Parents and Children* **Web site:**
**http://www.juvenilenet.org/jjtap/archives/primer/index.html**

## Section A. Public Schools

As you recall from Chapter 2, interactive distance learning started in the United States, on a broad scale, through the independent sector of education with groups, such as Anna Ticknor's Society to Encourage Studies at Home, in Boston in 1873, and the Chautauqua Literary and Scientific Circle in New York, in 1878. It was not until a generation later, in 1907 in Baltimore, Maryland, that the Calvert Primary School offered instruction for children at home. Although the Morrill Act of 1862, also known as the Land Grant College Act, and the county extension service (as an offshoot of the Morrill Act) provided educational opportunities for large numbers of rural residents physically distant from land grant colleges, large-scale acceptance of distance learning did not develop until the 1990s when computing machinery gave the individual user control of the learning experience.

This chapter will address settings for distance learning, but bear in mind that due to rapid changes in the field of distance learning these settings are evolving. The items to be discussed today might very easily be moot tomorrow.

Let's begin with some important issues to consider. How do you determine if distance learning services are available in your local district or state level? Here are suggestions for locating these resources:

1.  Does your school have an educational technologist, learning specialist, or media specialist? If so, ask one of these professionals to refer you to a distance learning coordinator in your district.

2.  If there are no professional support personnel in your school, ask your principal for a reference to a district distance learning coordinator.

3.  If you have a district contact, be sure to follow through with a telephone call or e-mail message inquiry to find out more about the available distance learning opportunities.

4.  After you have exhausted your local school contacts, look to your own professional organizations for support. Is there a local chapter of your professional group in your district, at the state level, or at the national level? If so, follow through with a telephone call or e-mail message to inquire about the distant learning opportunities that exist.

5.  If you do not have a district contact, begin to locate a state contact. Start with the general information number for your state department of education and ask who coordinates these activities. It could be that the distance learning initiative is not very active in your state yet, but that is doubtful. You might get transferred to a few offices, but be sure to use phrases and terms such as "distance learning," "e-learning," "Star Schools Program," "satellite instruction," "instructional television," or "videoconferencing."

6.  If you do not have a district or state contact who is active in your area, contact a local community college or university and ask someone in the department of education for a reference to a distance learning group.

7.  Consult conference postings that list presentations to find out the names of some of the presenters on distance learning. These presenters can guide you to the right contacts.

8.  Barring the unlikely possibility of still not contacting a distant learning person, start contacting your state chapters for computer users, educational technologists, or media specialists. If there are distant learning activities that are available, one of these groups will know about them.

## *Learning Possibility*

For an impressive collection of distance learning links, go to *Degree.net* (http://degree.net), a site operated by Dr. John Bear, a noted distance learning resource person, to get an idea of the tremendous number of resources available for a variety of learning levels.

## Learning Possibility

If you would like to start following a news group that focuses on distance learning, go to *Deja.com* (http://deja.com) and key in "alt.education.distance" in the search box. Be sure to bookmark this selection if you would like to follow the information regularly. If you are new to the online world, know that news group messages can be searched through *Deja.com* by name. So, in other words, be sure that the words you key in the news group messages are the words you would like to have associated with your name for posterity! It should go without saying, that whatever you put in electrons should be suitable for reading by your boss, your significant other, your students' parents, etc. Get the idea? Private e-mail has a way of getting around, so use good judgment. If you haven't already taught this to your students, start now.

---

Public school systems, with the support of state departments of education and business, have been forging ahead with distance learning initiatives for quite a few years. Perhaps one of the oldest, if not the oldest, distance learning efforts in the United States is through the Division of Independent Study, a division of the *North Dakota Department of Public Instruction* (http://www.dis.dpi.state.nd.us/). Begun in 1935, the division offers courses for students in grades 5–12, ranging from elementary science to high school Russian. The North Central Association of Colleges and Schools regionally accredits these courses, in print and online formats.

Students who need to complete coursework quicker than the normal school calendar—homeschooled students, homebound students, and students who need to travel or work and cannot meet the normal school day schedule—can participate in a virtual online school. A survey conducted in 2000 claimed that 1.7 million homeschooled students used online courses, chatrooms, and e-mail (*Edupage*, 17 July 2000). The state of Florida's *Virtual School* (http://www.flvs.net/) has been in operation since its first offering of programming courses and an SAT preparatory course in 1996 (Johnston, Start, and Young 1998). Since then, course offerings have expanded to include courses that meet general requirements, advanced placement courses, computer science courses, and even Latin.

Other virtual high schools exist throughout the country. Maryland's *Virtual High School of Science and Mathematics* (http://mvhs1.mbhs.edu/mvhs.html) got its start in 1995 through a National Science Foundation Grant. As reported in the *Palm Beach Post* (9 October 1997), the *Virtual High School* in Massachusetts started in 1997 (http://www.govhs.org) as a collaborative effort whereby each school that contributed one teacher and one course could enroll twenty students. The result has been a consortium with hundreds of students enrolled throughout the country. Reports show that participation in the Virtual High School Project, begun with a U.S. Department of Education grant (Carr and Young 1999), continues to increase. Its most successful students tend to be those that "are focused, self-directed, independent, motivated, and comfortable expressing themselves in writing" (Engler 2000, 55). Participants and teachers are encouraged to interact with each other to increase the likelihood of student success during these Net courses.

*Choice 2000* (http://www.choice2000.org/), a charter school based out of Riverside, California, is fully online for secondary students (Barker 2000). In addition to being unique as a charter school, Choice 2000 encourages a social climate by offering time- and place-bound extracurricular activities, such as dances, in addition to online gatherings. (A review, by case study, of *Virtual High Schools* is available at http://www.vhs.ucsc.edu/vhs/casestudies.htm.)

For adults who still need a high school diploma, there is the *Mindquest Online High School* (http://www.mindquest.org/), operated by the Bloomington, Minnesota Public Schools. *CLASS.COM* (http://www.class.com/) grew from a project of the Division of Continuing Studies Independent Study High School at the University of Nebraska, Lincoln, and it offers distance learning. CLASS.COM is contracted with the state of Kentucky to develop its distance learning courses. *CyberSchool* (http://www.cyberschool .k12.or.us/), accredited by the Northwest Association of Schools and Colleges, provides online learning for the state of Oregon. In a vendor-type model, *APEX Online Learning* (http://www.apex.netu.com) develops and offers advanced placement courses. Outside the United States, Ontario has its *Virtual High School* (http://www.virtualhighschool.com/), offering high school courses beginning with ninth grade.

Some districts are offering videoconferencing to multiple schools in their own district. In addition to those listed in Chapter 3 as offering videoconferencing applications, an example of such a district is the *Guilford County Schools* in North Carolina (http://www.guilford.k12.nc.us/). This district has developed its own online learning technology center, complete with district course materials and WebQuests for both students (K–12) and parents. The distance courses are offered in video, online, and educational television formats.

## Campus Based

There is no doubt that interactive distance learning activities have the potential to enhance and enliven the day-to-day classroom curriculum. These activities provide access to resources that cannot be conveniently or economically available in a physical, traditional on-campus environment. For some curriculum areas, such as science, distance education technologies, such as videoconferencing, have been found to increase the class participation and learning outcomes because of the lab element (Boone 1996). On the other hand, for other subject areas, such as mathematics, which require instructor monitoring while students are working through calculations, videoconferencing or computer lab classrooms connected through fiber optics may require that monitoring be done by facilitators or the students themselves, and then reported back to the distance teacher (Zbiek and Foletta 1995). The point is that the need for informal assessment, just as the element of selection of a distance learning modality, varies from subject to subject.

## Distance Learning for Students with Special Needs

Interactive distance learning activities can provide alternatives for students with special needs who are not campus based. For whatever reason that these students may not be on campus, interactive distance learning activities can be viewed as substitutes, or supplements, to campus-based learning.

The equipment and settings of distance learning classes are challenges for special needs students. For example, it is very difficult for students with hearing impairments to use the Internet, due to their inability to hear audio cues. Special needs students may need to have screen font sizes adjusted or have furniture rearranged in a videoconferencing setting. As with other classrooms, distance learning classrooms must have adjustable tables and seating that can accommodate students who are using wheelchairs, walkers, crutches, etc.

The applications of distance learning for students who are homebound, or place-bound, are many. Students with visual impairments can participate in audiobridges, videoconferences with two-way audio, or use Web materials with audio links. Students with hearing impairments will benefit from the visual presentations online, and can also participate in videoconferences; however, an interpreter will be needed to sign for the student.

Many special education teachers have participated in distance learning opportunities. In a Web course that taught Braille code skills, teachers learned to use "Perky Duck" (http://www.duxburysystems .com), a freeware program that translates text to Braille (Koenig and Robinson 2001). Results of this learning experience pointed to the need for a preassessment activity that would ensure that students could send and receive e-mail and e-mail attachments correctly. Teachers also commented that this program should include more student interaction on the course bulletin board and a video that demonstrates how to use the software package. The need for additional interaction among students was noted in an evaluation of a course for teachers of visually impaired students using interactive videoconferencing (Cooper and Keefe 2001). Whether the preference for more interaction is common overall, or whether it is common for special education teachers that teach in isolation for much of each day who were in this course, students were still positive about the course and its availability through the *Texas School for the Blind and Visually Impaired* (http://www.tsbvi.edu/pds/index.htm).

## *Learning Possibility*

Access *Bobby* (Think of the British police!) (http://www.cast.org/bobby/), an online software program designed to point out accessibility problems for Web pages. (Does *Bobby* like tables?) Think of three Web sites that have similarities, e.g., three school pages, three search engines, or three library catalogs. As you review these pages, using *Bobby*, consider whether the Web page layout accommodates users with limited vision. Do the colors limit users that are colorblind? How would educators use assistive devices with these Web pages? (To find out, check with your district Exceptional Student Education [ESE] coordinator.)

---

## *Learning Possibility*

Section 508 of the Rehabilitation Act of 1973 requires that federal agencies, and higher education institutions that receive federal funds, make electronic documents, including Web sites, accessible to people with disabilities. This ruling impacts the development, and even purchasing, of technology used after August 2000. How do you rate, in view of Section 508? You can read about this ruling at the *Section 508* Web site (http://www.section508.gov/) or at the *Office for Civil Rights at the U.S. Department of Health and Human Services* (http://www.os.dhhs.gov/ocr/504.html). If you still have questions on compliance, call the U.S. Department of Health and Human Services Office for Civil Rights (1-800-368-1019). Also check with state schools for additional access information, such as the *Texas School for the Blind and Visually Impaired* (http://www.tsbvi.edu/pds/index.htm).

---

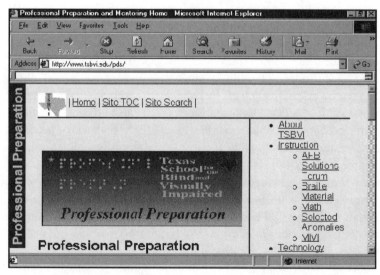

*Texas School for the Blind and Visually Impaired, Professional Preparation* Web site: http://www.tsbvi.edu/pds/index.htm

# Section B. American-Sponsored International Schools

There are many opportunities for distance learning participation with the thousands of students in dozens of international schools that are sponsored by the United States through the *Department of State* (http://www.state.gov/www/about_state/schools/wide.html). Many of these schools are operated through the Department of Defense; however, independent schools established by corporations and religious groups also exist in foreign settings.

For the U.S.-based student, connection to these fellow citizens in foreign locations can provide conduits to multicultural activities as never emphasized before. And for the remote citizens, connection to American students allows them to share their many experiences while feeling connected to what is going on in their home country. To organize distance learning opportunities with these students, begin by contacting a principal of a school in an area that has curriculum applications for your students. Or, you might be able to contact students that attend school in your city's "sister city." (First, you need to introduce your students to the concept of "sister city" and help them research the names of sister cities for your local areas at *Sister Cities International* [http://www.sister-cities.org/].)

# Section C. Colleges and Universities

Responding to both internal and external requests through state and federal agencies, the role of postsecondary institutions has been that of leadership and facilitation. Most universities have provided in-service training to local area schools, while some have offered further service through online courses for both graduate and in-service credit.

## Learning Possibility

An example of this type of partnership between a state department of education, a state university, and school districts has been the offering of online Web-based technology courses and in-service training from Sunlink at the University of Central Florida (http://www.sunlink.ucf.edu/) and Florida's Instructional Technology Resource Center (http://www.itrc.ucf.edu/). What are the in-service training possibilities that are available through these groups?

The state of Kentucky in the form of the Commonwealth's Virtual University provides students with a directory service to listings of distance learning courses, along with a virtual library and toll-free support center (Young 1999a). Similarly, the University of North Carolina at Chapel Hill School of Education has created *Learn NC* (http://www.learnnc.org/) that provides Web sources and training, along with online classroom space (Learning Space) for K–12 educators (Walbert 2000). *Learn NC* also provides a lesson plan database that includes shared plans that are categorized by topic.

Throughout the United States, colleges and universities are rapidly developing distance learning opportunities for as many markets as possible. Distance learning programs have been developed in areas for which previous instruction was only in a traditional format. This move to develop distance learning has put new demands on teachers who now must provide more than subject matter expertise. Teachers must now be able to transmit their knowledge through other communication modalities. The related obstacles become time and money (Keegan 1994). Like PreK–12 teachers, postsecondary instructors have had growing pains while learning to use distance learning technologies.

Because telecommunications services continue to become faster, more powerful, and more sophisticated, such as the online services offered through the Internet2 and desktop videoconferencing, instructors have more distance learning options within the classroom. Instructors can now team-teach and serve multiple classrooms on multiple campuses, much like PreK–12 schools are doing through their virtual school projects (Olsen 1999). Even though this arrangement requires considerable cooperation between institutions and instructors, the opportunities to offer instruction in programs for which there are no full-time instructors available are limitless. There are currently a limited number of institutions that participate in the Internet2, but with the *Internet2 K20 Initiative* (http://www.internet2.edu/k20/), opportunities will increase for the PreK–12 sector.

Of course, faster Internet connections benefit the students and instructors who are campus based, but we still need to consider the true distance teachers and students who are using standard telephone lines and modems. With the increase of cable modems and fiber optics, connection speed will increase, but do not assume that these connections will be available for all, especially those living in rural areas. (Despite the benefits of the fast services through cable today, how will cable connections impact continued development of the Internet? If online access continues to be through a cable subscriber service, how likely is it that companies will direct us only to select services that they provide and control [Chester 2001]? Is there a possibility that services that were once available at no charge will be captured and available only through a for-fee service?)

Some businesses and schools are ready to take advantage of faster Internet service. With promises for newer fiber-optic technology, lines are estimated to handle 100 terabits of data per second (20 billion one-page e-mails) (*Edupage*, 6 July 2001). In addition to the development of speedier Internet service to the school, students will also have access to faster service at home. ISPs and direct broadcast satellite services are showing that they can conquer the "last mile" link to most homes by connecting mini satellite dishes to systems that offer DSL-speed connections (*Edupage*, 7 February 2001).

While colleges and universities have worked to develop instruction for a variety of media, electronic mail has remained the most common distance learning medium. When asking distance learning programs about their practices, one study found that 93 percent of the programs polled were using e-mail for correspondence (The Primary Research Group 1999, 57). In 1999, "there was more e-mail than actual postal mail in the United States" (Hundt 1999, 15). Whether this concept concerns or delights, it indicates that the visions of institutions must change to reflect technology-induced changes. An example of a change to expect is the way in which educational institutions increasingly see themselves as businesses who are in competition with other learning institutions. This business orientation may result in more responsive colleges and universities, but it could also result in profit-focused institutions, to the detriment of students and faculty. This type of business focus is demonstrated by the problems that have occurred with the MIT Media Lab, its sponsors, and faculty, due to present and potential conflicts of interest that demand ethical solutions if the lab is going to continue to receive funding from corporations (*Edupage*, 13 November 2000). Along with the developments of technology and the areas of conflict, distance learning will force institutions to revisit their missions and goals and reconsider the needs of the customer base and the need of the developers and academicians to benefit from their products.

Probably one of the most debated issues related to distance learning, at the postsecondary level, is ownership. Who owns the course materials that are developed for distance learning? Some institutions have determined that ownership will be by the institution, usually providing compensation to the developer. Others have not. In a report by a faculty group at the University of Illinois (1999), the recommendation was that the ownership be retained by the creator with the rationale that "Quality is best assured when ownership of developed materials remains in the hands of faculty members" (3).

One current implementation of technology that further thwarts this philosophy is the practice of companies hiring students to take notes that are posted online (Blumenstyk 1999a). When the perpetrator of this shared information is not, in this case, the institution, how do instructors go about protecting their property? Who owns a lecture, demonstration, bulletin board, or test? As an indication of the complexity of this issue, the ownership question was even being reported as an issue of faculty resistance and debate in 1995 (Parrott). Clearly, it is a question that has been with us for a few years and is not going to be resolved easily. Efforts to provide fair guidelines for distance educators, students, and copyright holders have been made through the TEACH (Technology, Education, and Copyright Harmonization) Act (Gasaway 2001), which would allow, among other provisions, additional types of works to be used in distance learning, along with the opportunity for educators to create digitized materials from print or analog versions.

Regarding ownership and copyright, some institutions are still awaiting state or federal court decisions. The problem is that many of the talented individuals who can build technology-based distance learning infrastructures may leave education to pursue employment in nonprofit industries (Magner 1999). Some online users believe in the freedom of the distance learning environment where academia shares. Think of the many online documents and e-texts that you have viewed, most of which are freely shared. You may even be able to think of documents or Web pages that, once available through the developer's generosity, are now sponsored by commercial groups, with the developer maintaining control and input rights. In the spirit of Internet sharing, a group of botanists, supported by a grant, has decided to make available a free database of the scientific names of every flowering plant in existence, in addition to a citation of the document that records the discovery of the plant. The rationale for the cost of this use is that it will be accessible those who cannot afford to subscribe to the database, including scholars in developing and developed countries (Kiernan 1999). In a time when successful entrepreneurs are envied, this professional altruism is to be admired.

Not without its problems, postsecondary institutions have grappled with students who do not yet know how to learn independently by sometimes offering one-credit orientation courses or seminars (Young 1999b). In these courses, expectations of the student are discussed and clarified. For some reason, students who are willing to accept feedback that takes days to weeks to receive, in traditional classes, demand a quicker response rate in online classes. Why? Is it that the students are demanding the quick turnaround, that the instructors feel pressured to respond quicker, or that the turnaround rate has not been defined and expectations are not delineated? Regardless of where the communication problem lies, issues such as response time can affect retention rates in online courses.

Another issue related to instruction in the distance world is the level of control an instructor has over evaluations and how this information is reported. Students can post almost anything on the Web and still enjoy the protection of free speech outside of the classroom (*Edupage*, 20 September 2000). If the content is libelous about the instructor, what can the instructor do? What should the instructor expect the institution to do to maintain a sense of professional dignity?

Class size for distance learning courses has also caused some concern. If class management of large traditional courses is a challenge, how do you deliver basic services to distance classes? While some instructors anticipate large classes with large workloads, predicted to be as high as 1,000 students in a few years (Carnvale 1999), some institutions have not experienced the predicted growth (Carr 2000). Overall, college enrollment in the United States is increasing by 1.5 percent annual growth with distance learning being viewed as a cost-effective means of offering levels of service and instruction to more students (McClenney 1998). When discussing growth and costs of distance learning, it sometimes seems like we are in a Catch-22. In order to increase growth, we must provide for the costs of distance learning. In order to provide for the costs of distance learning, we must experience growth in student enrollment. If a segment of the traditional population moves to a distance format, overcrowding and construction costs could, theoretically, be decreased. Of course, you can also argue that you can replace the distance group, former traditional students, with a new block of traditional students.

Regardless of the growth rates, good teaching and management practices must occur in distance learning. Class schedules must be developed and communicated early so that students and instructors can plan ahead. Teachers must be hired in time to prepare and update materials. Textbooks and other materials must be declared so that bookstores, traditional and electronic, can order them in time for delivery to the student. In-service training for distance learning instructors on issues such as management, student orientation, and positive affect online is still needed. *Edupage* (1 September 1999) reported a survey from the University of California that showed "67 percent of professors are regularly stressed by keeping up with emerging technology," compared to the 62 percent that reported being stressed by teaching loads. In the same survey, about a third of the instructors indicated that they use technology and online services for research and class presentations.

## *Learning Possibility*

Is there widespread acceptance of distance learning and supporting technologies in your school? Do a quick show of hands (at your faculty meeting) to count how many teachers used the Internet in the last week for research. Ask also how many used a form of technology for a class presentation. Do your results show a great use of technology in your school? Finally, how many teachers used interactive distance learning technologies in your school last week?

What do we need to do to get teachers prepared to use technology in instruction? Is part of the problem the delivery of the training? If teachers deliver instruction only through a distance learning modality, it seems that the same modality should be used to provide in-service training. Are these opportunities readily available at times other than the traditional nine-to-five workday?

The issue of service providers affects postsecondary institutions. Because of the costs of providing online services, some colleges have signed up with Web sites that act as portal sites (Blumenstyk 1999b). Students can access these sites, pay for class, read announcements, and look at assignments. However, just as with free online accounts, blinking and scrolling advertisements are at these sites. With college students, unless some are minors who are dual enrolled, the issue of advertising is not as much of a concern as with PreK–12 students. Would your local school board policy allow free Web access and delivery for teachers if this meant that advertisements not reviewed and selected by the school board would be allowed at a portal site?

These new developments have brought about the identification of new educational career areas. Programs to provide training in these areas have been developed and have come into the forefront. Just as some PreK–12 schools have called upon the resources of outside vendors to deliver distance learning, some postsecondary institutions have turned to vendors, such as *eCollege* (http://ecollege.com), to support and provide course development services. For institutions that cannot seem to move beyond the ownership question, vendor-offered instruction may be the answer. Whether the vendor is being asked to provide development support or teach the actual course instruction, institutions will have to ask some difficult questions. What will be the changes to the mission and focus of education if commercial vendors have a large role in design of courses? Will these changes be positive?

For institutions that are sensitive to issues of regional accreditation, vendors bring some new concerns. For example, if the vendor is hiring the online instructor, who is responsible for evaluating the instructor's credentials: the vendor or the institution that is awarding the credit? If there is a dispute between the student and the instructor hired by the vendor, who is responsible for mediating and resolving the dispute? If the vendor has hired an instructor who commits acts of moral turpitude, who is responsible for damages? These are just a few of the issues that can impact a learning institution, whether PreK–12 or postsecondary. Policies and contracts must be evaluated carefully with the rights and protection of the student in mind.

Aside from the evaluation of teachers, how will the student learning outcomes be evaluated if a vendor delivers the course? Will students continue to take traditional tests, or will tests be posted and submitted online? If a distance learning modality such as videoconferencing is used, a proctor is usually available to the online course. Who hires the proctor? Who determines who is on the other side of the screen in a test-taking situation? Is the answer covered by a student code of conduct, or will the teacher individualize questions so that answers must be student-specific? Does the teacher also need to worry about the source of other assignments, in terms of originality? How will we address the issue of plagiarism in PreK–12 and postsecondary levels? What will we do if we see a pattern that indicates that the distance student scores higher than the traditional student? Would this indicate that the teaching methods are actually superior in a distance class, or that the independent learner selects the best learning environment based on self-understanding?

## *Learning Possibility*

Speak to your colleagues that have taken online courses. (If you cannot find anyone who has done so, it is time that you try one yourself. You can begin with a course that is simple to access, such as *ICONnect* [http://www.ala .org/ICONN/onlineco.html]. Free courses are being offered on searching the Web, integrating technology into the curriculum, etc. Subscribe through e-mail and complete the whole course. Do all of the assignments. Give the experience a fair evaluation.) Was the course motivating? Was it inspiring? What was the focus—the development of the student or learning outcomes? What aspects of this course would your colleagues, or you, like to model? What would you change if you were delivering a similar course?

Further related to the issue of accreditation, what are the standards that are being applied to distance learning? For example, one regional accrediting association may make unannounced visits to ensure that courses are being offered. Another might require visits to all branch campuses of an institution. New regulations issued by the U.S. Department of Education no longer require these surprise, or branch, visits (McMurtrie 1999). Some critics believe that these regulations are too lenient and that they do not allow for a true evaluation, based on traditional evaluation methods, of a distance learning institution. The accreditation of Jones International University, an online-only institution, has provided the impetus to discuss where we are going with more electronic classrooms and distance learning infrastructures (Perley and Tanguay 1999). Because educational accreditation is a peer-review process, this allows the open forum for many evaluation issues to be considered with equal input from all institutional members. The continued development of guidelines for distance learning will be interesting to watch. We will have to consider issues such as observing and evaluating instruction online and deciding what methods evaluators will use to measure the quality of services (e.g., learning resources, health, and advisement).

Distance learning also has economic implications. We have already seen the growth of online bookstores, such as *Barnes and Noble* (http://www.barnesandnoble.com) and *Follett* (http://efollett.com), that have marketed to college students. Financial aid can be requested on the Web at *Free Application for Federal Student Aid* (*FAFSA*) (http://www.fafsa.ed.gov/). Electronic signatures, personal identification numbers (PINs), and smart cards are moving e-commerce along. Will these services be available to all students? How will local taxpayers and businesses support, or hinder, local and district purchasing with electronic commerce sites that do not bring revenues into the local economy?

Just as the institutions offering the instruction will be creative in providing the services, the accrediting bodies will be equally creative in evaluating them. In addition, there is the *Distance Education and Training Council (DETC)* (http://www.detc.org) and other professional accrediting bodies that evaluate programs.

## Learning Possibility

What is the name of your regional accrediting association? Can you locate this association's Web page? What are the association's criteria that apply to distance learning? To PreK–12? To postsecondary institutions? Do these criteria address the infrastructure of distance learning or the equivalency of distance learning outcomes? Look for policy and procedures, in addition to accreditation criteria and principles on distance learning.

---

Concord Law School, an online-only law school, was opened in California through the Kaplan Education Center, which also offers review services for the Law School Admissions Test (LSAT). Since Concord is not accredited by the American Bar Association (ABA), students can only practice in states, such as California, that do not require ABA accreditation (Mangan 1999). To continue to address accreditation issues when you attend an online-only school, where are you located and which state department of education governs your activities? Your home state? The institution's home state? Who will be responsible for regional accreditation if the institution has an international presence?

Fortunately for college and university personnel, professional organizations provide support and leadership, as well as a forum for discussion and debate, on distance learning. The *American Association of Community Colleges* (http://www.aacc.nche.edu) and the *League for Innovation in the Community College* (http://www.league.org) provide conferences, publications, and research leadership for community college issues.

An example of support at postsecondary institutions is the development of *A Teacher's Guide to Distance Learning* (http://fcit.coedu.usf.edu/distance/) at the University of South Florida (Barron 1999). In a very attractive e-book format, this online guide would be perfect to recommend to the teacher or administrator who wanted a quick, but comprehensive, overview of distance learning. *The Florida Center for Instructional Technology* (http://fcit.coedu.usf.edu/), funded by the state of Florida and located in Tampa at the University of South Florida, sponsors workshops for PreK–12 teachers and develops resources that support Florida teachers.

Universities, such as the University of Wisconsin, provide professional support through Web site development and collection of information on distance learning. Their *K–12 and Distance Education Clearinghouse* link (http://www.uwex.edu/disted/k12.html) provides a good starting point for teachers who want an overview of definitions, research, and publications.

In years past, changes in a discipline's body of knowledge would be documented at the postsecondary level, where it would filter into the college curriculum, impact educators in training, and eventually move into the PreK–12 schools. Those who plan a future in PreK–12 would be wise to observe the distance learning influence in postsecondary institutions. Even though some services to children cannot be replaced in distance learning today, such as direct reading instruction or guidance services, PreK–12 learning may evolve from today's offerings into a more online-supported format. Predictions of some things to come in PreK–12 learning can be seen at today's postsecondary levels. If you link to the *Electronic Campus of the Southern Regional Education Board* (http://www.electroniccampus.org/), you can view a movie about their campus. While you are there, observe how many institutions cooperate to offer courses at the Electronic Campus. What would it take for PreK–12 institutions to do the same thing, on an intra- and interstate basis? How would this be different from some of the virtual school models that are already in place?

# *Section D. Professional Organizations*

Professional organizations have been at the forefront of the development of the practices that we refer to as distance learning. By encouraging workshops, speaker presentations, publications, and the sharing of ideas at conference sessions, organizations have provided direction, through their agendas, as a reflection of current trends in education.

Because of the electronic nature of professional organizations that support distance learning, much of the information you need is online. Even if you are unable to attend a conference, due to cost or distance, many of the professional organizations, such as the *National Educational Computing Conference* (*NECC*) (http://www.neccsite.org), are offering copies of their lectures through the *International Society for Technology in Education* (*ISTE*) (http://www.iste.org) online bookstore under "Teacher Education." The lectures are usually available in print or CD-ROM format. ISTE also provides quality Web items under its "Teacher Resources" section.

The *Association for Educational Communications and Technology* (*AECT*) (http://www.aect.org) is unique in the sense that it has been able to attract members and participants from a wide range of interests, from preschool to postsecondary educators. Members benefit from this organization's sense of cooperative and collaborative professional development. If you teach in the areas of computer science, educational media, or educational technology, you will benefit from membership in this group. If you are a PreK–12 support person, you will also benefit from the many conference presentations on managing and networking services offered by AECT.

Almost all professional organizations that support conferences, such as the *Florida Educational Technology Corporation* (*FETC*) (http://www.fetc.org), provide information at a Web site. It is interesting, from a historical viewpoint, to review some of the proceedings to see the decline and fall of certain technologies, based on the number of presentations during a year.

The *American Center for the Study of Distance Education* (*ACSDE*) (http://www.ed.psu.edu /ACSDE/), located at the College of Education at Pennsylvania State University, has supported distance learning through its publications, symposia, and conferences, as well as through its online discussion group, *DEOS-L* (Distance Education Online Symposium-Listserv), and *DEOSNEWS*, an electronic journal. *The American Journal of Distance Education*, edited by Michael Moore, has provided an invaluable resource for the presentation of distance learning practices and theory. The *Distance Education Online Symposium* (*DEOS*) provides an online archive (http://www.ed.psu.edu/acsde/deos/deosnews/deosarchives.asp) with thought-provoking articles and research, such as "Good Teaching Is Good Teaching: An Emerging Set of Guiding Principles and Practices for the Design and Development of Distance Education" (Ragan 1998). For readings on distance learning in K–12, contact the ACSDE to order *K–12 Distance Education, Learning Instruction, and Teacher Training* (Moore and Koble 1997).

Another organization with a broad perspective is the *International Council for Educational Media* (*ICEM*) (http://www.icem-cime.com/), which includes institutional members from forty countries. The purpose of the group is to encourage the exchange of information related to educational media and its use for training. Conference participants include producers and trainers, as well as teachers.

Professional organizations, such as the American Library Association, show support for distance learning by providing professional development activities, such as through the previously mentioned ICONnect. Beyond online initiatives, professional organizations realize the importance of implementing instruction that supports standards (Zbiek and Foletta 1995). Oftentimes this implementation requires technology upgrades to classroom infrastructures that promote the cooperative learning between multiple school sites and populations.

## Section E. Independent Online Training Groups

Sometimes it is difficult to identify the origins of distance learning groups. How to locate, as well as evaluate, online learning opportunities, whether for commercial groups and clearinghouses, is an important skill for the distance learning educator. *Diversity University* (http://www.du.org) provides direction to online courses on technology and online support groups such as the *On-Line Educators Resource Group* (*OERG*) (http://www.du.org/duSvcs/OERG/), which also supports OERG-L, a mailing list to support the work of OERG (OERG-L@wvnvm.wvnet.edu).

Independent or commercial groups, such as *Cybercollege* (http://www.cybercollege.com/), *Learning Tree* (http://www.learningtree.com/), or *Kovac's Consulting* (http://www.kovacs.com), provide workshops that would be appropriate for teachers for in-service training or personal development. Beyond the online offerings of courses, online tutorial and independent learning sites, such as *Homework Central at bigchalk* (http://www.bigchalk.com), offer study skills, games, and projects to students who are self-directed learners.

How will you make decisions about using independent online training groups? Contact the groups and ask for recommendations from other PreK–12 schools. Check your professional journals for reviews and descriptions of services. Quality services will be happy to provide you with brochures for evaluation and share contacts that can give good recommendations.

## Conclusion

Because of the need not to duplicate services, there will continue to be efforts made toward partnering of distance learning offerings. In addition, the partnering of research through public and private sectors (in projects such as *LemonLink*, a Technology Innovation Challenge Grant [http://www.lgsd.k12 .ca.us/lemonlink/] supported by the U.S. Department of Education) will eventually help districts to get all of their students connected and crossing the Digital Divide.

## References

Barker, Bruce O. "Anytime, Anyplace Learning." *Forum for Applied Research and Public Policy* 15, no. 1 (2000): 88–92.

Barron, Ann. *A Teacher's Guide to Distance Learning*. Tampa, FL: Florida Center for Instructional Technology, College of Education, University of South Florida, 1999. (http://fcit.coedu.usf.edu/distance/) (26 February 2000).

Blumenstyk, Goldie. "Colleges Get Free Web Pages, But with a Catch: Advertising." *The Chronicle of Higher Education*, 3 September 1999a. (http://chronicle.com/weekly/v46/i02/02a04501.htm) (3 September 1999).

———. "Colleges Object as Companies Put Course Notes on Web Sites." *The Chronicle of Higher Education*, 17 September 1999b. (http://chronicle.com/weekly/v46/i04/04a04102.htm) (17 September 1999).

Boone, William J. "Advanced Distance Education Technology and Hands-On Science." *Journal of Science Education and Technology* 5, no. 1 (1996): 33–46.

Carnvale, Dan. "On-Line Courses of 1,000 Students Will Become Common, Industry Group Says." *The Chronicle of Higher Education*, 2 December 1999. (http://chronicle.com/free/99/12/99120201u.htm) (10 December 1999).

Carr, Sarah. "Enrollment Growth Remains Slow at Western Governors U." *The Chronicle of Higher Education*, 14 January 2000. (http://chronicle.com/weekly/v46i19/19a04901.htm) (20 January 2000).

Carr, Sarah, and Jeffrey R. Young. "As Distance-Learning Boom Spreads, Colleges Help Set Up Virtual High Schools." *The Chronicle of Higher Education*, 22 October 1999. (http://chronicle.com/weekly/v46i09/09a05501.htm) (26 October 1999).

"Censored Students Post Their Exposes Online," 20 September 2000, *Edupage* (owner-edupage@listserv.educause.edu) (http://www.educause.edu/pub/edupage/edupage.html).

Chester, Jeffrey A. "Web Behind Walls." *Technology Review* 104, no. 5 (2001): 94–95.

Cooper, Holly, and Charlotte Hendrick Keefe. "Preparation of Teachers of Visually Impaired Students via Distance Education: Perceptions of Teachers." *Journal of Visual Impairment & Blindness* 95, no. 9 (2001): 563–66.

Engler, Natalie. "Distance Learning in the Digital Age." In *The Digital Classroom: How Technology Is Changing the Way We Teach and Learn*, edited by David T. Gordon, 51–59. Cambridge, MA: Harvard Education Letter, 2000.

"Feds Find Dangerous Cyberstalking Hard to Prevent," 16 June 2000, *Edupage* (owner-edupage@listserv.educause.edu) (http://www.educause.edu/pub/edupage/edupage.html).

Gasaway, Laura N. "Balancing Copyright Concerns: The TEACH Act of 2001." *Educause* 36, no. 6 (2001): 82–83.

"Home Schooling's Net Effect," 17 July 2000, *Edupage* (owner-edupage@listserv.educause.edu) (http://www.educause.edu/pub/edupage/edupage.html).

Hundt, Reed. "The Telecom Act, the Internet, and Higher Education." *Educom Review* 34, no. 6 (1999): 14–18, 48–51.

Keegan, Desmond. *Otto Peters on Distance Education: The Industrialization of Teaching and Learning*. New York: Routledge, 1994.

Kiernan, Vincent. "Botanists Turn to Database to Resolve Issues of Plant Taxonomy." *The Chronicle of Higher Education*, 23 September 1999. (http://chronicle.com/free/99/09/99092301.htm) (28 September 1999).

Koenig, Alan J., and Margaret C. Robinson. "Online Instruction in Braille Code Skills for Preservice Teachers." *Journal of Visual Impairment & Blindness* 95, no. 9 (2001): 543–57.

Magner, Denise K. "Journal Articles Are a Poor Basis for Judging Engineering and Computing Professors, Report Says." *The Chronicle of Higher Education*, 14 September 1999. (http://chronicle.com/free/99/09/99091404n.htm) (14 September 1999).

Mangan, Katherine S. "Justice Ginsburg Raises Questions About Internet-Only Law School." *The Chronicle of Higher Education*, 13 September 1999. (http://chronicle.com/free/99/09/99091302t.htm) (20 September 1999).

McClenney, Kay M. "Community Colleges Perched at the Millennium: Perspectives on Innovation, Transformation, and Tomorrow." *Leadership Abstracts* 11, no. 8 (August 1998). (http://www.league.org/publication/abstracts/leadership/labs0898.htm) (19 January 2000).

McMurtrie, Beth. "With an Eye Toward Pliancy, Education Department Publishes New Accreditation Rules." *The Chronicle of Higher Education*, 21 October 1999. (http://chronicle.com/free/99/10/99102102n.htm) (26 October 1999).

"M.I.T. Media Lab at 15: Big Ideas, Big Money," 13 November 2000, *Edupage* (owner-edupage@listserv.educause.edu) (http://www.educause.edu/pub/edupage/edupage.html).

Moore, Michael, and Margaret Koble. *K–12 Distance Education, Learning Instruction, and Teacher Training* (Readings in Distance Education, no. 5). University Park, PA: American Center for the Study of Distance Education, College of Education, Pennsylvania State University, 1997.

Olsen, Florence. "Using the Internet, 2 Colleges Share Professors." *The Chronicle of Higher Education*, 17 September 1999. (http://chronicle.com/weekly/v46/i04/04a03801.htm) (20 September 1999).

Parrott, Sarah. *Future Learning: Distance Education in Community Colleges*. ERIC Digest. Los Angeles: ERIC Clearinghouse for Community Colleges, 1995. ERIC ED 385 311. (http://www.ed.gov/databases/ERIC_Digests /ed385311.html) (2 February 2002).

Perley, James, and Denise Marie Tanguay. "Accrediting On-Line Institutions Diminishes Higher Education." *The Chronicle of Higher Education*, 29 October 1999. (http://chronicle.com/weekly/v46/i10/10b00401.htm) (29 October 1999).

Primary Research Group. *The Survey Distance Learning Programs in Higher Education*. New York: Author, 1999.

Ragan, Lawrence C. "Good Teaching Is Good Teaching: An Emerging Set of Guiding Principles and Practices for the Design and Development of Distance Education." *DEOSNEWS* 8, no. 12 (1998). (http://www.ed.psu.edu/acsde /deos/deosnews/deosnews8_12.asp) (30 January 2002).

"Scientists Raise Fiber-Optic Limits," 6 July 2001, *Edupage* (owner-edupage@listserv.educause.edu) (http://www .educause.edu/pub/edupage/edupage.html).

"Speedy Internet Providers Struggle with 'Last Mile,' " 7 February 2001, *Edupage* (owner-edupage@listserv .educause.edu) (http://www.educause.edu/pub/edupage/edupage.html).

University of Illinois. *Teaching at an Internet Distance: The Pedagogy of Online Teaching and Learning*. Urbana-Champaign, IL: Author, 1999. (http://www.vpaa.uillinois.edu/tid/report/tid_report.html#summary) (8 February 2001).

Walbert, David J. "The LEARN NC Model: Overcoming Obstacles to Technology Integration." *TechTrends* 44, no. 2 (2000): 15–17.

Young, Jeffrey R. "At Iowa, An Experimental On-Line Course for 19,000 Students Runs into Problems." *The Chronicle of Higher Education*, 16 November 1999a. (http://chronicle.com/free/99/11/99111601t.htm) (16 November 1999).

———. "Kentucky's Virtual University Aims to Help Students and Institutions." *The Chronicle of Higher Education*, 13 August 1999b. (http://chronicle.com/free/99/08/99081301t.htm) (20 August 1999).

Zbiek, Rose Mary, and Gina M. Foletta. "Achieving Standards in a Fiber Optic Mathematics Classroom." *Learning and Leading with Technology* 22, no. 8 (1995): 26, 28–29.

## Chapter 5

# Interactive Distance Learning Technology Applications

*Yes, Mrs. Smith, we are studying glaciers. Yes, we did see a penguin today. Your son is telling the truth—he did ask an astrobiologist how life survives on glaciers!*

Imagine having this conversation with a doubting parent who thinks her son is stretching the truth! Elementary and middle school students and teachers are using distance learning technologies, such as videoconference and chat, to observe and work with scientists to answer questions in Alaska and Antarctica. Using a well-defined curriculum, the *Jason Project* (http://www.jason.org), an interdisciplinary curriculum that is standards based, actually engages students and teachers in real-time and delayed-time science activities that follow a team approach to distance learning.

## *Teaching Possibility*

Go to the *Jason Project* (http://www.jason.org) and review the curriculum, in view of your school's curriculum for science, assuming you are in an elementary or middle school. Could your school access the Jason Project? Has someone else in your district purchased a license that your class could share? If not, what are the possibilities that you could get grant or parent-teacher organization funds to participate in this project? If you cannot directly participate, can you use the *Jason* broadcasts on the *National Geographic Channel* (http://www.nationalgeographic.com/channel/) for your students? Could you contact another scientist or university professor that would be willing to chat or e-mail your students on topics that are similar to those that the Jason Project has already visited?

So far, we have looked at the background, benefits, challenges, and formats of interactive distance learning applications. This chapter will provide ideas for integrating interactive distance learning applications into actual learning environments for a variety of age and content areas. Before we begin looking at examples for interactive distance learning activities, be aware that there are multiple Web sites available with lesson plans. Planning is essential to distance learning activities. "Effective teaching at a distance is more the result of preparation than innovation" (Willis 1992). We have noted many of these planning ideas throughout this handbook, but for the busy teacher there is a Web tool to search lesson plan sites throughout the Internet. This tool is *The Gateway to Educational Materials* (*GEM*) (http://www.thegateway.org/), which allows topic searching by keyword, Boolean operators, subject, and grade level. This interface presents the description and location of the activity, and it links you right into the lesson plan at that location. GEM represents a consortium of educational institutions interested in sharing collections of lesson plans and educational materials found on the Internet sites of over 100 various federal, state, university, nonprofit, and commercial organizations. GEM operates as the gateway to the resources. Sponsored by the U.S. Department of Education and the *ERIC Clearinghouse on Information and Technology* (http://www .ericit.org/), GEM is a growing consortium. Why don't you visit GEM right now and search for a lesson plan or activity that you could use with your students?

# Section A. Applications for Students

PreK–12 students will be most enthusiastic about using interactive distance learning activities for no other reason than the novelty of doing new things. Bill Gates is attributed with naming the group of children born after 1994 "Generation I," those who have always had the Internet. His prediction was that these Generation I students, who will be starting college around 2012, will live "in a world where everything is online, and that will be taken for granted" (McCollum 1999). Based on the current interactive distance learning technologies that are readily available, this section will provide specific examples that can actually be implemented in your classroom and that will, hopefully, encourage you to either expand upon ideas presented here or to develop your own classroom activities. Each section includes suggestions on where to locate and/or discuss more lesson plan ideas for interactive distance education learning activities. If you are a parent using this handbook, or if you are a teacher that works with parents to extend learning to the home environment, remember that the interactive distance learning applications can be accomplished very well at home with parents. Whether you are following up on your child's schoolwork, homeschooling your child, or working on home learning activities, most of these suggestions provide opportunities for both of you to expand on joint interests.

Internet access, used for distance learning, has a challenge to overcome in some districts in the form of filtering. Filtering, depending on your point of view, is either a method of restricting certain Internet Web sites or a method of protecting students from certain Internet Web sites, sometimes sites with sexual or extremist content. There are many issues that impact the question of filtering including how to handle requests from parents to filter sites, how to help teachers become completely familiar with the content and links of sites, and how to encourage teachers and media specialists to preview sites for maturity-appropriate content before taking students to sites. Some educators argue that, overall, the school is accountable for knowing what students access and how they use information. Some groups also argue that students should not be constantly monitored, but that educators have the responsibility to teach students about what should or should not be accessed. As we found out with the Child Online Protection Act and the Children's Internet Protection Act, there are many issues to be weighed, such as the access rights of adults to information, before we agree that filtering information is the best way to protect children from inappropriate materials (*Freedom to Read Foundation News* 1999).

Beyond the pros and cons of filtering, further complications come from the type of filtering software to use and the responsibility for customizing the software so that meaningful restriction is accomplished. Beaver College, located in Pennsylvania, decided to change its name to Arcadia University, due to the filtering process that directed potential students away from applying to the college (*CNN.Com* 2000). Seasoned teachers know that natural curiosity causes students to look for examples of profanity and nudity, but determining how to address this issue with the online explosion of access and volume of content with questionable terms is the problem.

Regardless of your personal opinion on restriction of sites, and related issues of intellectual freedom, reality will require you to follow school board policy (if it exists) that addresses access. As a result, the first step is to find out if your district requires that certain Internet sites be restricted. If a policy is unavailable or has yet to be developed, speak with your administrator and educational technologist on the status of a policy for the school. If software is to be used, how will the software be selected? There are many Internet filters, such as *CyberPatrol* (http://www.cyberpatrol.com/), *NetNanny* (http://www.netnanny.com), *SurfWatch* (http://www.surfwatch.com), or *X-Stop* *(8e6)* (http://www.xstop.com). Documentation for some filter software specifies that the product is for monitoring, not filtering, online activity. Professional statements, such as those offered by the American Association of School Librarians (*Statement on Library Use of Filtering Software* [http://www.ala.org/alaorg/oif/filt_stm.html]), ERIC (*AskERIC Response on Internet Filtering in Schools* (http://ericir.syr.edu/cgi-bin/printresponses.cgi/Virtual/Qa/archives/Educational_Technology /Internet/filtering.html), or *IP Filtering Options & Objectives* (http://www.more.net/technical/netserv /tcpip/ipfiltering.html), are good starting points for reviewing information that will help you to develop a personal response to these issues and for locating resources to share with your colleagues. The American Library Association's Web site on *Filters and Filtering* (http://www.ala.org/alaorg/oif/filtersandfiltering.html) provides additional links to many sources that will be useful when considering a filtering policy. Anticipate that filtering will continue to be a hot topic for years to come.

Courses are developing at a tremendous rate. For example, *Florida Virtual School* (http://www.flvs .net/) started offering a few courses to about 250 students in 1997. Currently, it offers a complete secondary curriculum, including honors and advanced placement courses. The original intent of the Florida Virtual School was to develop a way to alleviate overcrowded schools, supplement courses in rural areas, and offer alternatives to students that were on a fast track to graduation. Plans are in the works to use some of these courses for adult education students (Colavecchio 2002).

Kentucky also has its virtual school, the *Kentucky Virtual High School* (http://www.kvhs.org/), that offers advanced placement courses, courses in the content areas of English, language arts, health, science, and mathematics, as well as professional development courses for teachers. Using eClassroom and eCollege software to deliver courses, students in grades 9 through 12 can take a course for $275 per semester. The state of Utah operates the *Electronic High School* (http://ehs.uen.org). It is probable that most states will develop, if they are not already in the process of developing, a virtual school to service their students.

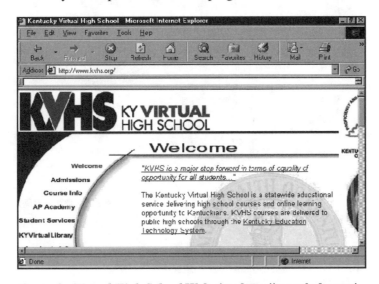

*Kentucky Virtual High School* **Web site: http://www.kvhs.org/**

Though there might be a charge, distance learning programming is also available through *PBS* (http://www.pbs.org), the *Massachusetts Corporation for Educational Telecommunications* (http://www .mcet.edu), and *SERC* (http://www.serc.org/).

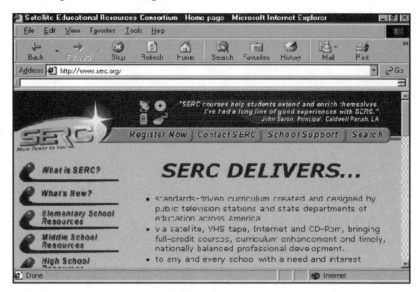

**SERC Web site: http://www.serc.org/**

A site that can fit so many categories for PreK–12 distance learning is the *American Memory Historical Collection* (http://memory.loc.gov/). With visuals and time lines that can be used with elementary students, and pathfinders that are good for middle and high school students, you can find a variety of sources to use in history and social studies courses.

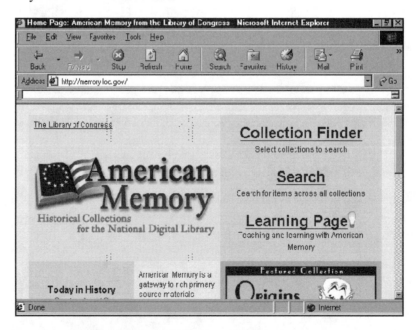

**American Memory Historical Collection Web site:**
**http://memory.loc.gov/**

# Grades PreK–2

PreK–2 students are so much fun to teach because they bring an openness to learning in almost every content area. These grades give the teacher an opportunity to explore quality Web sites and delivery methods that are well designed and that avoid ambiguity. Many of the ideas provided offer PreK–2 students the chance to explore learning technologies independently, capturing their natural tendency to want to power their own learning. Early childhood and elementary teachers will want to visit the *ERIC Clearinghouse on Elementary and Early Childhood Education* (http://ericeece.org/) for lesson plans and tips that apply to these age groups.

## *Delayed-Time Interactive Distance Learning Activities*

**Format:** Audiotape/Audio CD

**Subject:** Music

**Idea:** Do you believe in the "Mozart" effect? Do you think that listening to music will help students to overcome learning challenges? Prepare audiotapes or CDs with noncopyrighted classical music to send home with your students. Ask parents to listen to the music with their children and discuss how they feel while listening to the music or create drawings, etc. Teachers might want to create more focused activities based on their curriculum. How can you track the Mozart effect on your students throughout the year? (Many classical music stations broadcast on the Web. Can you locate an online station for your area?)

**Vendor:** None required.

**Web site:** *The Mozart Effect* (http://www.mozarteffect.com)

———————————

**Format:** CD-ROM

**Subject:** Language Arts—Writing (Graphic Enhanced E-Mail)

**Idea:** Teachers can visit a variety of Web sites that offer free clip art, such as the Discovery School's Clip Art Gallery, and select appropriate clip art based on seasonal or subject activities. Check the copyright guidelines at each site, and, if allowed, copy the appropriate clip art to CD-ROM to discuss with students for appropriate use in e-mail or other student-created documents. This activity can also offer the opportunity for teachers to begin to teach students about copyright guidelines and how they apply to this activity.

**Vendor:** None required.

**Web site:** *Awesome Clip Art for Kids* (Part of EduHound.com) (http://www.awesomeclipartforkids.com/)

> *Discovery School's Clip Art Gallery* (http://school.discovery.com/clipart/)

> *TeachNet.Com* (http://www.teachnet.com/how-to/clipart/school/)

———————————

**Format:** Correspondence

**Subject:** Character Education—Neighborhoods and Brotherhood Acts of Kindness and Justice

**Idea:** Discuss the importance of "random acts of kindness" and good deeds with students. Brainstorm with students to generate ideas on what possible good deeds would be, and then ask students to draw pictures or write letters to a group (e.g., nursing home residents) that show how they would like to do a good deed for someone else. Schools that complete 1,000 or more acts of kindness will receive special recognition by the current year's challenge competition. Whether the reward recognition is continuing or not, students can still feel a sense of achievement by participating in a community activity.

**Vendor:** None required.

**Web site:** *DoSomething.org* (http://www.dosomething.org)

---

**Format:** Electronic Mail

**Subject:** Character Education—Sharing

**Idea:** Although keying may be difficult for younger students, they can always share and communicate through pictures. What would students like to communicate? With whom would they like to communicate? Whether with keypals or parents or grandparents, introduce the concepts of sharing information through electronic mail. Check out the media center's digital camera (or ask the principal about purchasing an inexpensive camera) and show the students how to use the camera to take group pictures, individual pictures, etc. (as time permits) that they want to send to a group. If your digital camera accepts floppy disks, you can keep a record of the pictures that you take of your students throughout the year. If your digital camera has a USB connection (did you know that USB stands for Unified Serial Bus and this refers to the small rectangular connection that you attach to your computer?), you can save your pictures on your hard drive or on a floppy disk. If you do not have someone to show you how to use your camera, most camera manufacturers have Web sites with directions. Some companies also offer lesson plans on how to incorporate picture taking into the curriculum, e.g., *Kodak* (http://www.kodak.com/US/en/digital/edu/lessonPlans/).

**Vendor:** None required.

**Web site:** *Kodak* (http://www.kodak.com/US/en/digital/dlc/plus/chapter5/index.shtml)

*Sony* (http://www.ita.sel.sony.com/support/dvimag/mavica/)

---

**Format:** Interactive Web Activities

**Subject:** Computer Literacy/Educational Games

**Idea:** When you look at the TVOntario site for kids, you will see a very pleasing screen that will beckon students to practice their "mousing" skills. Sounds and visual effects will keep students alert and responsive. Students that need practice with independent reading will be encouraged by the large bold print.

**Vendor:** None required.

**Web site:** *TVO Kids.com* (http://www.tvokids.com)

---

**Format:** Videotape

**Subject:** Language Arts—Viewing (V-Pals)

**Idea:** If you can have e-pals (and keypals), why not v-pals (video pals) that create video-tapes that you share with other students in distance communities? For example, rural students and urban students would enjoy seeing each other's school sites, or learn about how they travel to school. A student in southern California or Texas would be amazed at how students in the Rockies of Colorado or the far reaches of Maine travel to school in the winter. Teachers, even though they do not yet have high-speed online access, can use an activity of this type to begin to communicate with teachers and classrooms in distance sites to broaden the students' understanding of varying geographical and cultural issues. Added benefits include working with students to create simple videotapes, the development of a videotape library for the classroom (children enjoy watching other children!), and the ability to do delayed-time activities that include responding to the videotape with discussions, role-playing, writing about what they observed, etc. Where can you find out about teachers that might be willing to work with you on this type of project? Start with an e-pal teacher list and e-mail the request to develop v-pals. (In the meantime, ask your media specialist to help you and your students learn to use the video camera in your school.)

**Vendor:** None required.

**Web site:** *ePALS.com* (http://www.epals.com/) (Older students can communicate in a variety of languages.)

---

**Format:** Course Packages (Online Tutorial)

**Subject:** Mathematics

**Idea:** Since using fingers to count and add seems to be natural for students, why not take them to a "real" tutorial that will help them to learn to use Chisenbop? You and your students can learn to add, subtract, multiply, and divide. Do you think there might be any benefits to lifelong learning skills by counting with your fingers?

**Creator:** Andy Harris, Indiana University/Purdue University, Indianapolis

**Web site:** (http://klingon.cs.iupui.edu/~aharris/chis/chis.html)

---

**Format:** Taped Television Courses

**Subject:** Language Arts—Viewing

**Idea:** Do your students like popular characters, such as Arthur or Clifford? You can find out when *Clifford* airs at the *PBS Kids* site (http://pbskids.org/in_your_town/index.html?nola=CBDG& program=clifford). Many of the *Clifford* shows can be used as part of units on the community, character education, or even drawing still-life pictures (e.g., Babysitter Blues, episode 128a). Remember that copyright laws apply! (Go to *Nolo-Law for All* [http://www.nolo.com /lawcenter/ency/] and search for "Grading Teachers on Copyright Law—Videotaping for the Classroom" before selecting videotapes for your instruction. Use videotaped programs as part of your *planned* curriculum.)

**Vendor:** None required.

**Web site:** *PBS/PBS Kids* (http://www.pbs.org)/(http://pbskids.org)

---

## *Real-Time Interactive Distance Learning Activities*

**Format:** Audioconference

**Subject:** Social Studies—Community (Jobs)

**Idea:** How many different jobs are represented by parents of your students? After listing these jobs with your students, you may have compiled a listing of dozens of jobs. Sometimes parents may be able to come to your school to speak about, and demonstrate, their jobs. Sometimes due to busy work schedules and distance, they cannot. With audioconferencing, you can invite almost every parent into your classroom to speak with the students about their jobs. Work with your students to compile lists of questions and "assign" these questions to individual students. Whether a parent is out of town on business (or stranded by traffic), you have a good chance of increasing parent participation and student interest in jobs. (If this is successful, you could expand your scope of topics, e.g., what did you enjoy studying in school, hobbies, etc.)

**Vendor:** Local telephone service.

**Web site:** None required, but seek out your local state employment office or visit the *USA Jobs* (Office of Personnel Management) (http://www.usajobs.opm.gov/) for more ideas on the types of jobs that you would like your students to learn more about. There is also a *Studentjobs.gov* link (http://www.studentjobs.gov/) that will interest older students.

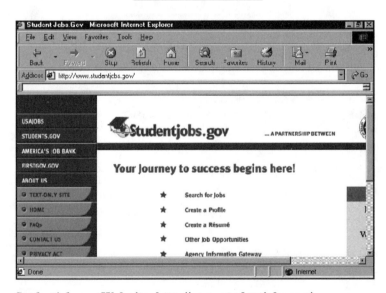

*Studentjobs.gov* **Web site: http://www.studentjobs.gov/**

**Format:** Chatroom

**Subject:** Student Well-Being—Mom and Dad (Grandma and Grandpa)

**Idea:** Sometimes PreK–2 students (or their teachers) need to be able to connect during the school day. Whether parents have restricted phone access at work, due to policies or concrete barriers to cellular phones, or whether teachers do not have access to outside lines, alternative communication may be a good idea. Or, you might just want to encourage visual access between your students and their parents (or grandparents). For example, if a student creates an outstanding picture (or has just learned to read or pulls the first tooth!), you can use a simple

Web camera and access to an instant messenger service, such as Yahoo, to connect to a parent with similar access to communicate the great event! By the same token, a Web camera view might help those parents who are not really sure about the seriousness of a child's illness when they are trying to decide whether to leave work to pick up the child.

**Vendor:** Web cameras are available at a variety of online and computer stores.

**Web site:** *AOL Instant Messenger* (http://www.aol.com)

*Yahoo Messenger* (http://www.yahoo.com)

---

**Format:** Electronic Classroom

**Subject:** Language Arts—Spelling

**Idea:** Have you discovered electronic flash cards? Create flash cards to help students review spelling words. Use a theme, such as rhyming words, in your flash cards. Electronic flash cards can be developed at *SchoolNotes.com*, a free service of the Copernicus Education Gateway. In addition to creating flash cards for your students, you can post weekly lessons, reviews, notes for parents, etc. In addition to being free, *SchoolNotes.com* allows access to materials through the Web without passwords and does not require any formatting or programming skills on the part of the teacher!

**Vendor:** None required.

**Web site:** *SchoolNotes.com* (http://www.schoolnotes.com)

---

**Format:** Radio

**Subject:** Computer Literacy

**Idea:** Go to *Radio Disney* and navigate the site map. This activity can combine helping students learn to use Web information to lead them to radio information and schedules. Under "Activities," students can practice beginning computer literacy skills by "mousing" around to identify Disney characters and learn more about safe online behavior, creating calendars, printing, etc. This is a site that you can also recommend that your parents visit with their students. Even if there is not a *Radio Disney* station close to you, there are downloads of screen savers and pictures that you can use to motivate your students!

**Vendor:** None required.

**Web site:** *Radio Disney* (http://psc.disney.go.com/radiodisney/index.html)

---

**Format:** Satellite Link

**Subject:** Language Arts—Writing

**Idea:** Use the largest distance learning provider for elementary grades, TEAMS, to help your students learn to create stories and write in the content areas, using *Teaching Writing, Kindergarten—Grade 1*. Programming is available on a wide variety of content areas and support topics. (If you want to update your online skills, use *Gayle's Electronic Classroom* at *TEAMS* [http://teams.lacoe.edu/documentation/classrooms/gayle/gayle.html].) Speak with your principal or district distance learning coordinator to find out if you are already capable of receiving digital satellite programming through TEAMS. (TEAMS also offers programs through public broadcasting, cable, and electronic classrooms.)

**Vendor:** Satellite service provider.

**Web site:** *TEAMS Distance Learning* (http://teams.lacoe.edu/)

---

**Format:** Television

**Subject:** Critical Thinking—Forming Opinions

**Idea:** It is a growing trend for local and national newscasts to encourage interaction with their viewing public through opinion polls and surveys that require telephone or e-mail responses. This type of interaction is important to help students understand how they develop and voice their opinions. Kids' networks, such as Nickelodeon, offer opinion questions that may relate to school life. If you want students to respond to local or national events, select a radio or television Web site to see if they have an opinion input. Help your students learn how to give voice to their ideas!

**Vendor:** None required.

**Web site:** *Nickelodeon* (Nick.com) (http://www.nick.com/)

---

**Format:** Videoconference

**Subject:** Character Education—Kidcast for Peace

**Idea:** You are probably already familiar with some Web events that are annual. One example is the award-winning *Kidcast for Peace*. Make plans now to participate in next year's *Kidcast for Peace* by downloading and learning to use CU-SeeMe shareware that will allow your students to see the group from Hawaii via computer. (Check to see that you have a computer with video input capability, a video camera or Webcam, and online access.) The *Kidcast for Peace* Web site will provide you with a full description of the activities that you will want to do with your students before participating in the Web cast.

**Vendor:** Internet Service Provider connection.

**Web site:** *Kidcast for Peace* (http://creativity.net/kidcast2.html)

*Rocketcharged.com CU-SeeMe Cool Site* (http://www.rocketcharged.com/cu-seeme/download.htm)

---

# Grades 3–4

Students in grades 3 through 4 tend to be excited by most new learning experiences. Take advantage of this natural interest with project-type activities that incorporate a variety of learning mediums. A collection of projects like this has been compiled in *Technology Connections for Grades 3–5* (Heller 1998). The projects can easily be adapted to curriculum standards on social studies, literacy skills, literature, mathematics, and science. In addition to the *ERIC Clearinghouse on Elementary and Early Childhood Education* (http://www.ericeece.org), the *Clearinghouse on Information and Technology* (http://www.ericit.org/) will provide many ideas to help you strengthen your technology activities.

### *Delayed-Time Interactive Distance Learning Activities*

**Format:** Audio

**Subject:** Music—Instruments and Musical Traditions

**Idea:** Introduce students to the use of musical instruments in many cultures. For example, the use of drums in different cultures, as part of music and communications, can be heard in a short clip of an interview of Nina Jaffe, the author of *Patakin* (published by Cricket Books). Teachers will want to listen to this clip (http://teacher.scholastic.com/professional/music/) or other similar clips prior to sharing information from this book. A follow-up activity might include encouraging students to create their own drumming songs that they record on audiotape or CD to share with other students and their parents. (Other audio clips of music are included at this Scholastic site.)

**Vendor:** None required.

**Web site:** *Scholastic Music Curriculum* (http://teacher.scholastic.com/professional/music/) Additional resources are available for a variety of grade levels at *Teacher Radio* (http://teacher.scholastic.com/teacherradio/index.htm).

---

**Format:** CD-ROM

**Subject:** Computer Literacy

**Idea:** Teach students how to compile their class materials in weekly folders to take home and share with their parents or to show parents during Open House. Audio, graphic, video, etc., files of each week's work can also be saved in monthly files on a read-writable CD-ROM. This activity will provide you with an opportunity to teach students about the types and variance in file sizes.

**Vendor:** None required.

**Web site:** The Web site of the company that provides your school's word processing package probably has online tutorials that you can show your students, if they have problems with saving file formats.

---

**Format:** Correspondence

**Subject:** Language Arts—Writing

**Idea:** If your students are in scouts, they might want to earn a badge that relates to correspondence or communication. You can speak with your local troop leader to find out the exact requirements, or ask the students to share their scouting manual. Activities that might contribute to the badge include writing a letter, writing a news story, and interviewing a person and writing the dialogue. How does this constitute distance learning? Ask your students to communicate by letter with a person (perhaps their e-pal) who can provide information on the topic. (Remember, for some students, letter writing is an unknown skill.)

**Vendor:** None required.

**Web site:** *Boy Scouts of America* (http://www.scouting.org/)

*Girl Scouts of America* (http://www.girlscouts.org/)

---

**Format:** Electronic Mail

**Subject:** Language Arts—Writing

**Idea:** The "art" (or skill) of keying electronic mail (e-mail) is one that your students may be more comfortable with than their teachers! Nevertheless, students are not born with knowledge of all of the elements of e-mailing. If you work with students to connect with keypals in other states or countries, you will provide them with a motivation to develop their writing skills. (Suggestion: Before connecting students with keypals, discuss this activity with your principal. Speak about how you will communicate this activity with parents. Design a letter that you will send to parents and share this with your principal, prior to sending it home. Some school districts and parents may not wish to encourage keypals and communication with unknown students. However, if you do a good job of communicating to parents that the students communicate under the supervision of you and the distance teacher, you will probably have few objections.) Check your curriculum guidelines for existing e-mail and letter-writing objectives. A teacher guide and suggestions for safe e-mailing are provided at *ePALS.com*. Another service that facilitates e-pal communication is IECC (Intercultural E-Mail Classroom Connections), which was founded by teachers.

**Vendor:** None required.

**Web site:** *ePALS.com* (http://www.epals.com/)

               *IECC* (http://www.iecc.org/)

---

**Format:** Interactive Web Activities

**Subject:** American History—Thanksgiving

**Idea:** Teachers can lead students through the many documents (primary sources) and pictures at the *Library of Congress* that explain how Thanksgiving evolved as a celebration. The "Thanksgiving Timeline" can be explored, by year, as determined by the teacher. Students could access certain years, independently, and summarize and explain to other students why those years were significant in the evolution of this holiday.

**Vendor:** None required.

**Web site:** *Library of Congress* (http://memory.loc.gov/ammem/ndlpedu/features/thanks /thanks.html)

---

**Format:** Videotape

**Subject:** Field Trip Video Collection

**Idea:** Though it is true that you can find online field trips of many locations and topics, students like viewing field trips through the eyes of other students. Work with some of your e-mail teacher contacts to locate teachers who are interested in collaborating on videotape projects. After you contact this teacher (the hard part), collaborate and develop ideas for projects that will benefit both groups. For example, if you and the collaborating teacher are studying plants, you can ask each other to work with the students to create a videotape of the plants in your local area (or school yard). This type of project will give you the opportunity to integrate a variety of subject and skill areas, e.g., organizing, outline, developing story boards, writing dialogue, framing pictures, and editing videotape. (Ask your media specialist to show you how to use the videocamera and edit videotape.) Remember that this type of project is for beginners who are developing video skills.

**Vendor:** Check for the online Web site of your videocamera vendor. Manuals and teacher materials may be available.

**Web site:** *Panasonic* (http://www.panasonic.com/)

*Sony* (http://www.sony.com)

---

**Format:** Course Packages

**Subject:** Mathematics

**Idea:** Electronic course packages are being developed for elementary use, such as the *TEAMS Electronic Classrooms*. Designed to be used in conjunction with the TEAMS satellite broadcasts, the course packages offer lesson plans and interactive Web activities for a variety of mathematics (and other subject) areas.

**Vendor:** None required.

**Web site:** *TEAMS Electronic Classrooms* (http://teams.lacoe.edu/documentation/classrooms/classrooms.html)

---

**Format:** Taped Television Courses

**Subject:** Mathematics

**Idea:** PBS has created a variety of lesson plans to correspond with many of its television offerings. Look at your local PBS station's programming and see which lesson plan topics are offered. If you have access to taped courses through your district's instructional television service, you can search for the series under your instructional topic. For example, if you want to locate a special lesson on measurement for grades 3 through 5, you will find that many series (Life by the Numbers, Newton's Apple, PBS Mathline, PBS Winter Games Cyberschool, and Zoom) have programs (and lesson plans) that relate to these topics.

**Vendor:** None required.

**Web site:** *PBS Teacher Source, Measurement, Grades 3–5* (http://www.pbs.org/teachersource/math/3-5_measurement.shtm)

(Look for other instructional topic ideas and related programs at the *PBS Teacher Source* [http://www.pbs.org/teachersource/].)

---

**Format:** Interactive Web Activities

**Subject:** Children Through the Ages

**Idea:** Do your students understand that children throughout history have not always enjoyed the benefits of children today? Take your students to an interactive site where they can learn about how students of the Victorian days learned, worked, and played. Opportunities for learning are plentiful, e.g., students can read a log entry of what happened in a school in 1879 and 1881. Can you extend this learning by asking students to find out about other events that occurred during 1879 and 1881?

**Vendor:** None required.

**Web site:** *Children in Victorian Britain* (http://www.bbc.co.uk/schools/victorians/) at the *BBC Education in Scotland Site* (http://www.bbc.co.uk/scotland/education/)

---

## Real-Time Interactive Distance Learning Activities

**Format:** Audioconference

**Subject:** Science

**Idea:** There is a good chance that your local extension agent will be happy to participate in a learning activity with your students via audioconference that can be achieved easily with a telephone with a speaker! Extension agents can speak on a wide variety of topics, such as plants, insects, animals, etc., in the local area. They will also be happy to share with your class printed materials or online materials. Call the extension agent's office in your area to discuss some of the topics that would apply to the curriculum. Ask students to keep a list of unanswered questions that they have about the topic as you are studying it. You can share this list with the extension agent as a start for the audioconference. (Perhaps you would like your students to e-mail these questions to the agent!) This type of activity can be extended to a variety of topics and guests. If you are studying a topic that would not be covered by your local extension agent (e.g., if the plant or animal is not in your area), ask your local agent for help with locating the appropriate agent or agent's Web site. Here is an example: If you live outside of Florida, but your students want to learn more about hermit crabs, you could locate a southern Florida extension agent's Web page (http://www.co.broward.fl.us/agriculture/english/marine/Hermitcrabs_files/frame.htm) and learn a lot about these crustaceans. (In addition to your county extension agent, you may have a local FFA [Future Farmers of America] organization that can offer speakers for your class. The FFA has groups throughout the nation and the world.)

**Vendor:** None required.

**Web site:** Can you locate the Web site of your local extension agent?

> *FFA* (http://ffa.org/)

---

**Format:** Audio

**Subject:** Missing School

**Idea:** There may be times that a student cannot attend an important event, such as the presentation of a group project or speaker. Some students may be homebound, due to weather or illness. One possibility for making sure that a student does not miss the special event is to use audiotape (or CD) to record the event for the student and mail (or e-mail) the recording to the student. (Could a student also use a speakerphone to participate?)

**Vendor:** None required.

**Web site:** For more ideas on how to make a distance student feel like part of the class group, read *Reach Homebound Students Through Technology* (http://www.infotoday.com /MMSchools/mar00/hillman.htm).

---

**Format:** Chatroom

**Subject:** Telecommunications and Computer Literacy

**Idea:** Elementary grades offer the right opportunity to begin to teach students (and parents and teachers) about safe chatting and how to find safe chats. Explain that "moderated" chats are monitored for appropriate topics and responses. Get involved in role-playing and demonstrate safe and unsafe topics to students and parents. Are there any district guidelines for chatting during the school day? Are there any district guidelines to share with parents who want to learn more about safe chatting?

**Vendor:** None required.

**Web site:** *McAfee's Ten Tips for Safe Online Chatting* (for parents) (http://kids.mcafee .com/forgrownups/safechatting.asp)

 *Yahooligans Directory* (lists of moderated chats) (http://www.yahooligans.com /Arts_and_Entertainment/Chat/)

---

**Format:** Electronic Classroom

**Subject:** Language Arts, Mathematics, Science, Social Studies

**Idea**: For younger students, games offer interesting strategies for review and reinforcement. Try some Web learning games!

**Vendor:** None required.

**Web site:** *Online Learning Fun II* (http://childparenting.about.com/library/weekly/aa032098.htm)

---

**Format:** Radio

**Subject:** World Events

**Idea:** What are the learning skills that you can reinforce by asking your students to listen to radio programs? Did you know that quality radio existed for elementary students? At the beginning of the school year, check the *Kids Internet Radio* site to see what is planned for the upcoming year. Programs, such as the Earth Day Radio Show, will be repeated. (Internet access is required for listening to the Kids Internet Radio program.) *New York Kids* is another radio program that can be accessed online. Be sure to check your local radio stations to see if a radio program for kids is available.

**Vendor:** None required.

**Web site:** *Kids Internet Radio* (http://www.kir.org/listen.htm)

 *New York Kids* (http://www.nykids.org/)

---

**Format:** Satellite Link

**Subject:** Varies

**Idea:** How can you incorporate satellite programming into your curriculum? Read a "success" story about how teachers and students in grades 5 and 6 used satellite programming to teach students about oceans.

**Vendor:** *T-Star Online* (http://www.t-star.org) (Operated by the Texas Education Agency).

**Web site:** *T-Star Schools* (Keane Independent School District) (http://www.t-star.org/keane.html)

---

**Format:** Television

**Subject:** Space Science

**Idea:** If you are a teacher who attended school during the 1960s, you can probably remember going to an auditorium with other students to watch the astronauts on television. We have certainly come a great distance, technologically, so that today's students can view NASA Television (NTV) through local or cable television providers, or even on the Web. In addition to current viewing of the astronauts in space and the control rooms, you can select from a wide variety of archived programs at *NASA TV Educational Programs.* Is space not your strongest subject? You can find teaching materials already prepared for you under "Educational Services." (A simple activity to get you started is to ask students to keep a log of their observances of the astronauts, noting the time and day that they observe. Ask the students to compare their notes. This practice with journaling can help students become motivated note takers.)

**Vendor:** Television service or Internet Service Provider connection.

**Web site:** *NASA Television* (http://www.nasa.gov/ntv/)

> *NASA TV Educational Programs* (http://spacelink.msfc.nasa.gov/NASA.News/ NASA.Television.Schedules/Education.Schedule/NASA.TV.Educational.Programs /.index.html)

---

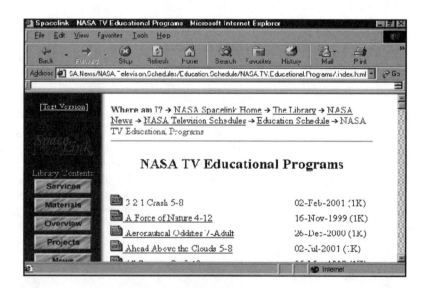

***NASA TV Educational Programs* Web site:**
**http://spacelink.msfc.nasa.gov/NASA.News/NASA.Television.Schedules**
**/Education.Schedule/NASA.TV.Educational.Programs/.index.html**

**Format:** Videoconference

**Subject:** Language Arts

**Idea:** Nothing encourages practice like a little competition, and a spelling bee (via videoconference) is a wonderful opportunity to do this. Contact some of your peer teachers in your feeder pattern or other part of your district (or state) and schedule some practice spelling bees. If you want to generate more participation, ask parents or principals to be the moderators.

**Vendor:** Check with your local newspaper to see if it sponsors a spelling bee.

**Web site:** *Merriam-Webster's Spelling Bee Hive* (http://www.m-w.com/promos/spell/)

> *National Spelling Bee* (http://www.infoplease.com/ipa/A0862710.html)

> *Scripps Howard National Spelling Bee* (http://www.spellingbee.com/)

---

# Grades 5–6

Most of your middle school students are already on the Web, chatting with friends and communicating. Students in grades 5 through 8 are ready to do online research or function as independent learners with other types of distance learning modalities. They will benefit from a variety of distance learning activities that keep them engaged with each other. Cooperative group work can provide this age group with the connection that they need with each other while they are constructing projects. Teachers in grades 5 through 12 will want to look at the many ERIC Clearinghouses online sites (http://www.eric.ed.gov/sites/barak.html#ir) for the one that applies to the subject area taught (e.g., Reading, English, and Communication; Science, Mathematics, and Environmental Education; etc.).

## *Delayed-Time Interactive Distance Learning Activities*

**Format:** Audiotape

**Subject:** Science—Animals—Birds

**Idea:** Can your students identify birds by their "songs" and sounds? Ask students to tape the sounds of birds in their backyard or neighborhood. What do they know about these birds, i.e., where do they winter, what do they eat, what are their nesting patterns? Can you help students to develop their listening skills by learning to identify a bird by its song?

**Vendor:** None required.

**Web site:** *Native Songbirds in Color and Sound* (http://www.naturesound.com/birds/birds.html)

> *North American Bird Sounds* (http://www.naturesongs.com/birds.html)

---

**Format:** CD-ROM

**Subject:** Computer Literacy—Ethics—Downloading

**Idea:** You've heard the media reports about problems with downloading MP3 (music) files, but what do students really know about the legal downloading of files, such as MP3s and graphics? After you have acquainted yourself with information on ethical downloading, along with your district's policy on downloading, visit some sites that offer free downloads. Show your students some of the sites that offer free downloads and teach them how to actually download files. (Search for "free clip art for kids"+safe or "free music for kids"+safe. Also try searching for downloadable+kids+free. Be sure to review the sites before you search them with your students.) Show students how to create "gifts" of a saved screensaver that can be downloaded to diskette.

**Vendor:** None required.

**Web site:** *Education World "Tools for Teaching Cyber Ethics"* (http://www.educationworld .com/a_tech/tech055.shtml)

> *Free Clip Art for Kids at The Kidz Page* (http://www.thekidzpage.com/freekidsclipart/)
>
> *Kids Domain Clip Art* (http://www.kidsdomain.com/clip/)
>
> *Kids Domain Musical Downloads* (http://www.kidsdomain.com/down/pc/_music-index.html)
>
> *Web Clipz Clip Art for Kids* (http://www.webclipz.com/kids.htm)

---

**Format:** Correspondence

**Subject:** Language Arts—Writing/Reading—Newspaper/Social Studies—Letters to the Editor

**Idea:** Introduce students to the concept of "letters to the editor." Start reading letters to the editor from your local newspapers to teach students that the ability to voice opinions, without fear, is an important element in our democratic society. Is there an issue that is important to students that they would like to voice in a newspaper, e.g., is there a special type of community park that they would enjoy?

**Vendor:** Your local newspaper publisher.

**Web site:** Varies

---

**Format:** Electronic Mail

**Subject:** Language Arts—Letter Writing/Social Studies—Government

**Idea:** While you are teaching students to voice opinions, help them learn who their local, state, and national representatives are and how to e-mail messages to representatives and senators. (Do you know how to help students find out who their representatives are?) Does your text-book (or teacher's guide) include a section on writing letters to congresspeople? If not, ask students to research the process in the media center. (Sections in some almanacs, encyclopedias, etiquette handbooks, or letter-writing manuals will describe the protocols to follow.)

**Vendor:** None required.

**Web site:** *CongressLink* (http://www.congresslink.org/)

> *Contacting the Congress* (http://www.visi.com/juan/congress/)
>
> *"Write Your Representative Service" at the U.S. House of Representatives* (http://www.house.gov/writerep/)
>
> *Writing Your Senator* (http://4h.unl.edu/citizenship/unicameral/writesenator.htm)

---

**Format:** Interactive Web Activities

**Subject:** Social Studies—Westward Expansion

**Idea:** Opening your students' eyes to the world of the pioneers will be a very rewarding teaching experience for you if you use a resource such as "Free Land" at the Frontier House Project. A quiz (Do You Have What It Takes to Be a Pioneer?), video clips, documents, and pictures help to provide students with an inkling of what it was like to move west during the 1880s. Teachers can also look for online WebQuests in social studies.

**Vendor:** None required.

**Web site:** *PBS Frontier House* (http://www.pbs.org/wnet/frontierhouse/resources/lessons.html)

*WebQuests from Blue Web'n* (http://enternet.lth1.k12.il.us/pac_ms.htm)

---

**Format:** Videotape

**Subject:** Health—Nutrition

**Idea:** Introduce your students to the concepts of nutrition, food servings or portions, food groups, etc. Help them understand that their nutritional needs will change as they age and where they can locate information on how to eat. Do your students understand that your cafeteria manager has special knowledge about nutrition and sizes of health portions of food? Arrange an in-school field trip to the cafeteria, or ask the cafeteria manager to visit your classroom. After students have a better understanding of what we accept as healthy food, ask students to create a videotape about the food items that a healthy person purchases. (Students could bring examples of these foods to school, or locate pictures to tape. Perhaps the cafeteria manager would allow students to videotape cafeteria foods. A local food store manager may also give students permission to videotape in the store.)

**Vendor:** None required.

**Web site:** *Food Guide Pyramid from the National Agriculture Library of the U.S. Department of Agriculture* (http://www.nal.usda.gov:8001/py/pmap.htm)

*"Kids and Nutrition" at FoodFit.com* (http://www.foodfit.com/healthy/archive /healthyNutriSmarts_aug09.asp)

---

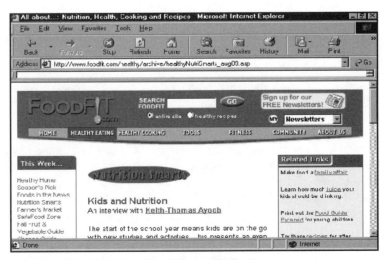

***"Kids and Nutrition" at FoodFit.com* Web site:**
**(http://www.foodfit.com/healthy/archive/healthyNutriSmarts_aug09.asp)**

**Format:** Course Packages

**Subject:** Student Presentations

**Idea:** *The best way to learn something is to teach it.* Do you believe this adage? Think about working with your students to develop your own course package that will explain a difficult concept. For example, some students in this age group have problems converting decimals to percentages and vice versa. If so, this is a topic that you can use to work with your students to develop a course package in a format that you enjoy. Some students enjoy using HyperStudio, PowerPoint presentations, Viewlet Builder, or some other package that is available in your district. (Could games be used in your course package? If so, ask students to locate online math games or games for the topic that you want to develop. Students would benefit by using games to review the concepts and by creating games for which they must know the right answers!)

**Vendor:** None required.

**Web site:** *AAA Math* (http://www.aaamath.com/grade5.html) (You will be amazed at the number of math sites that are available. Just search for "math games" and your grade level.)

---

**Format:** Taped Television Courses

**Subject:** History

**Idea:** *The History Channel Classroom* actually encourages teachers to videotape its programs and use them for up to a year, recognizing that teachers have challenging schedules. This program is commercial-free and copyright cleared for a year from taping. Study guides and teacher manuals are also available online. (You may decide that you want to combine a bit of history and entertainment when you guide students to the History Channel's "Modern Marvels" games of "bluewater race," "jungle excursion," and "racecar rally" [http://www.historychannel.com /boystoys/]. Students might also enjoy searching the History Channel's calendar for events that occurred on their birthdays! Students can complete mini-research projects on one of these topics for extra birthday credits.)

**Vendor:** None required.

**Web site:** *The History Channel Classroom* (http://www.historychannel.com/classroom/index.html)

---

## Real-Time Interactive Distance Learning Activities

**Format:** Audioconference

**Subject:** Social Studies—Political Representatives

**Idea:** It is true that your elected officials are very busy people, but the audioconference may make it possible for your students to speak with their mayor or other representative. The keys to providing a good experience will be advance scheduling, development of questions or areas of interest (the more focused, the better), and the follow-up with the person to speak right before the event (to remind them of the date and time) and after. (Ask the speaker, in advance, if she or he would be agreeable to your audiotaping or videotaping the experience so that you can review it later with your students.) Be sure to practice the interaction with the students and set a protocol for participation. Try to rehearse questions (and follow-up questions) with your students. Remember to send thank-you notes after the event.

**Vendor:** Local telephone service.

**Web site:** Search the Internet for your local government's Web site.

---

**Format:** Chatroom

**Subject:** Social Studies/Civics

**Idea:** If you are studying the workings of the U.S. or other country's government, a chat about the content with other students (outside the classroom) would offer a broader perspective on how others view government. *Civics Online* is a site that offers content chats for students and teachers, along with many resources to expand the discussions and interest. Contact information on other teachers that may be willing to participate in a cooperative learning experience is available. (*Civics Online* also offers the "civics link" of the day.)

**Vendor:** None required.

**Web site:** *Civics Online* (http://civics-online.org/)

---

**Format:** Electronic Classroom

**Subject:** Science—Solar System

**Idea:** If you are looking for motivating materials that will show your students detailed graphics (and content) on the solar system, look at the materials at *Views of the Solar System* (http://www.solarviews.com) or *Space Weather* (http://www.sel.noaa.gov/info/School.html). Directions for teacher-led projects, such as how to create a model of a comet, are here. (Caveat: Before you send students to this or any other Web site, always be sure to first visit and evaluate the site yourself. Why? You will want to evaluate for difficulty of reading levels, pop-up boxes, content of side bars, etc.)

**Vendor:** None required.

**Web site:** *Space Weather* (http://www.sel.noaa.gov/info/School.html) (Other materials are available at the National Oceanographic and Atmospheric Administration Site under "Education" [http://www.sel.noaa.gov/info/].)

        *Views of the Solar System* (http://www.solarviews.com/ss.html)

---

**Format:** Radio

**Subject:** World Events—Ideas from a Distance

**Idea:** It's not too early to help students become aware of a variety of viewpoints, and this can be accomplished through radio. Ask students to listen to the news focus on a single day. If you are working with students to study foreign languages or if you have multilingual students, they will enjoy listening to the other languages. If you are teaching students about primary sources of information, don't forget to point out the lifelong benefits of seeking news that is produced where it actually occurs. If incorporating radio into your writing curriculum appeals to you, look at the *Rural Voices, Country Schools Project* at the National Writing Project. (If your school does not have a "rural" voice, could you adapt this project to apply to your particular school?)

**Vendor:** None required.

**Web site:** *British Broadcasting Corporation* (BBC) (http://www.bbc.co.uk/learning/)

        *Canadian Broadcasting* (4 Kids) (http://www.cbc4kids.ca/)

        *Radio Kids* (http://www.radiokids.com.ar/) (Argentina)

        *Rural Voices, Country Schools Project* (http://writingproject.org/Programs/rvcs/)

---

**Format:** Satellite Link

**Subject:** Foreign Language—Spanish (Grades 5–6)

**Idea:** Elementary Spanish instruction is available to students in the form of satellite viewing (or a videotape program) through Northern Arizona University's Universityhouse programming. Viewing is available through the DishNetwork, and videotapes and workbooks are available for a fee. (Remember, distance learning is accessible, but this access is not always free.) By the way, programming for grades 7–8 is in progress at the Universityhouse.

**Vendor:** NAUHS (Universityhouse).

**Web site:** *Universityhouse* (http://universityhouse.nau.edu/)

---

**Format:** Television

**Subject:** Social Studies—Watching History

**Idea:** The concept of television news without commentators telling us what we should observe and think about occurrences may be a new one for students this age. If you agree, and if your students are inclined toward "virtual television," think of asking them to view an occurrence (such as a presidential speech) or House or Senate activity. Let them keep viewing logs of what they see and discuss how their impressions differ from those of other students. (They will be surprised at what they may have missed.)

**Vendor:** C-SPAN.

**Web site:** *C-SPAN* (http://www.cspan.org/) (Check for program listings and schedules.)

*C-SPAN/Video and Audio* (http://www.cspan.org/watch/) (Did you know that you can watch and listen to C-SPAN online?)

---

**Format:** Videoconference

**Subject:** Community Events

**Idea:** How much do your students understand about the local community and the work of citizens to create a positive environment for all? Participation in the "classroom conference," CyberFair (an annual event), gives you the opportunity for your students to learn about local leaders or events and then communicate this knowledge to other students throughout the world. Other types of events are also available that students in grades K–12 can participate in.

**Vendor:** None required.

**Web site:** *Global Schoolhouse* (http://www.gsh.org/cf/)

---

# Grades 7–8

## *Delayed-Time Interactive Distance Learning Activities*

**Format:** Audiotape

**Subject:** Language Arts/Social Studies (Oral History)

**Idea:** Middle or junior high students have the basic skills required to begin story circles through interviewing, transcribing interviews, and developing presentations (or plays) based on the stories they gather. Story circles can follow family or social history, cultural developments, etc. Start students with the collection of stories on audiotape that they share with the class. (You might want to begin the circle by reading a discovery story to your students.) Watch as the students learn about others, as well as themselves.

**Vendor:** None required.

**Web site:** *Story Circles International, Inc.* (http://callingpaul.com/SCI_home.htm)

---

**Format:** CD-ROM

**Subject:** Computer Applications; Mathematics—Statistics

**Idea:** Are you interested in a computer applications or math project that will interest students who like baseball? Allow students to visit the Major League Baseball Web site and check out the batting averages. These data could be categorized by team, player, league, or other categories that you and your students select and use as the basis for creating a spreadsheet and a database. Ask students to convert these documents into graphical representations that can be imported into a PowerPoint presentation. (You can include this project with participating in the Math and Baseball Videoconference at the *National Baseball Hall of Fame*. This project is also available to elementary and high school students.)

**Vendor:** None required.

**Web site:** *Major League Baseball* (http://mlb.mlb.com/NASApp/mlb/mlb/homepage/mlb_homepage.jsp)

> *National Baseball Hall of Fame Math and Baseball* (http://www.projectview.org/MathandBaseball/MaBHome.htm)

---

**Format:** Correspondence

**Subject:** Language Arts

**Idea:** Students at this level should be familiar with the concept of quotations. What is a quotation? Why are some quotations more notable than others? Why does our society value certain quotations? After an introductory lesson on quotations and the demonstration of printed quotation dictionaries that you borrow from your school library media center, take your students to *BrainyQuote*. Practice searching the site for quotations by topic and speaker. Ask each student to select one quotation that is meaningful. After you have discussed with your students why they believe the quotations are meaningful (spoken by a significant figure in history, politics, etc.), ask each student to write a letter to someone that they think will benefit from the quotation. For example, a student might select a quotation on education that she or he wants to share with a child in the future.

**Vendor:** None required.

**Web site:** *BrainyQuote* (http://www.brainyquote.com)

---

**Format:** Electronic Mail

**Subject:** Social Studies

**Idea:** Ask students to take a sample Immigration and Naturalization Services exam of 100 questions. Can they pass the test?

**Vendor:** None required.

**Web site:** *Immigration and Naturalization Services* (http://www.ins.usdoj.gov/graphics /services/natz/)

> *Sample exam* (http://www.ins.usdoj.gov/graphics/services/natz/100q.pdf)

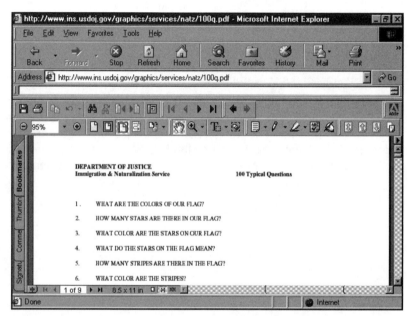

**Sample Immigration and Naturalization Services Exam Web site:**
**http://www.ins.usdoj.gov/graphics/services/natz/100q.pdf**

**Format:** Interactive Web Activities

**Subject:** Foreign Languages

**Idea:** Connect to *Translate Free* and ask students to use some of the translation services to check the accuracy of the translations that they write. *Babblefish.com* is another translation service, and it also includes currency conversions.

**Vendor:** None required.

**Web site:** *Babblefish.com* (http://www.babblefish.com/babblefish/bfish_lang.htm)

> *Translate Free* (http://www.translate-free.com)

> (Have you taught your students how to key in special characters, such as vowels with accents and characters? Your word processing package, such as Microsoft Word, probably offers these features under "symbols." You can also go to the *Microsoft Home Page* [http:// www.microsoft.com] and search for "international keyboard" to get directions for your version of Microsoft Word.)

**Format:** Video

**Subject:** U.S. Government—Touring the U.S. Capitol

**Idea:** How much would it cost you to take your students to the U.S. Capitol? If the price of "free" appeals to you, you can take your students right now—for the cost of an online connection. *The U.S. Capitol Virtual Tour* includes a 360-degree video view, printed narration that you and your students can read, and links to items of particular interest with information on the background. See the Old Supreme Court Chamber, Senate Chamber, President's Room, etc., without worrying about your students breaking a vase or getting left behind.

**Vendor:** None required.

**Web site:** *The U.S. Capitol Virtual Tour* (http://www.senate.gov/vtour/index.html)

---

**Format:** Course Packages

**Subject:** Earth Science—Ecosystems

**Idea:** Course packages come in many formats, including online packages. The Missouri Botanical Garden (MBG) has created *MBGNet* and features three segments: biomes of the world, freshwater ecosystems, and marine water ecosystems. This site combines bright colors, clear pictures, and lots of content into an instructional site that guides students along with on-target questions that are connected to the content.

**Vendor:** None required.

**Web site:** *MBGNet* (http://mbgnet.mobot.org/)

---

**Format:** Taped Television Courses

**Subject:** Latin American Studies

**Idea:** Are there experts in your local area or at your local university that provide access to quality instructional programs? *The Center for Latin American Studies* offers video loans of presentations about Latin American geography, economics, culture, etc.

**Vendor:** None required.

**Web site:** *The Center for Latin American Studies* (http://las.arizona.edu/outreach.html)

---

### *Real-Time Interactive Distance Learning Activities*

**Format:** Audioconference

**Subject:** Health

**Idea:** What do your students need to know about drug use, and abuse, in your local area? Where can they find help and support for themselves or their friends? Contact your local public health officials and request an audioconference (by speakerphone) on drug usage. Prior to the conference, work with students to develop their questions to provide to the speaker.

**Vendor:** None required.

**Web site:** Search for your local public health Web site.

*Drug Abuse Resistance Education* (http://www.dare-america.com/)

---

**Format:** Audio

**Subject:** Sports Events

**Idea:** Many students participate in sports during and after the school day. Encourage all of your students to learn about sports opportunities by preparing an audio diary (and taking pictures) of sporting events, players, coaches, teams, etc., that they can use to develop a classroom or whole school presentation on sports. This information can be captured as a stand-alone presentation or as a Web site to encourage existing and new students and parents to get more involved in physical activities.

**Vendor:** None required.

**Web site:** Ask students to search for a Web site on their favorite sport or locate an online article on a sport that they can use for research on their audio diary.

---

**Format:** Chatroom/Instant Messenger

**Subject:** Homework

**Idea:** Assign homework buddies to your students as their primary contacts for questions and help with homework after school. (Send parents a request for students to download software for an instant messenging service, such as AOL or Yahoo. A benefit to point out to them is that using chat may keep a telephone line clear for telephone calls. And, who knows? The student may see the teacher online offering help sometimes.) Are there any incentives you can offer to homework buddies?

**Vendor:** Your choice of vendors that provide instant messenging software.

**Web site:** *Yahooligans Parents' Guide* (http://www.yahooligans.com/parents /createfamilypledge.html)

---

**Format:** Electronic Classroom

**Subject:** State History

**Idea:** Try to locate recent, visual information on state history, e.g., the *Golden Crescent* (http://www .cr.nps.gov/goldcres/) provides sources on both Florida and Georgia. Provided through the National Park Service, you can check to find out if there are locations that can be viewed by your classes.

**Vendor:** None required.

**Web site:** *National Park Service ParkNet* (http://www.nps.gov/)

---

*National Park Service ParkNet* **Web site: http://www.nps.gov/**

**Format:** Radio

**Subject:** Consumer Events—Canvassing Radio Stations

**Idea:** For a project that students will enjoy, ask students to list and research their favorite radio stations. Why do they enjoy the radio stations? What are the programs or contests that they like the most? How can they contact their radio stations through telephone or e-mail? What are the programs that they would like added to the radio stations? Which radio station offers the most school news? As a follow-up, students may wish to interview one of the local radio personalities or ask one to visit the class in person or by speakerphone.

**Vendor:** Local radio channel.

**Web site:** Ask students to locate the Web site of their preferred radio channel. Are there educational materials located at this site?

---

**Format:** Satellite Link

**Subject:** Satellite Locations

**Idea:** Students that participate in conferences that are transmitted through satellite links will be interested in knowing what the satellites look like and how they move in their areas. NASA's *J-Pass* site will provide you with the software to view current locations of satellites.

**Vendor:** None required.

**Web site:** *J-Pass Satellite Passes* (http://liftoff.msfc.nasa.gov/RealTime/JPass/)

---

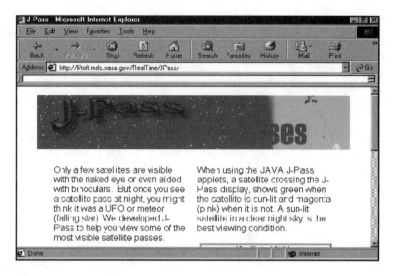

**J-Pass Satellite Passes** Web site:
**http://liftoff.msfc.nasa.gov/RealTime/JPass/**

**Format:** Television

**Subject:** Social Studies—Weekly Events in Pictures

**Idea:** Many television broadcasters offer added resources, such as *KYW*'s "Photo Essays" link, that feature outstanding pictures (through CBS) that depict events that are local, regional, national, and international. Pictures are available for past-week events also. To get students started, watch live television news with them and discuss the events that are most significant. Then, assign viewing times to students and ask them to keep a log of the news events that they believe are the most significant, along with their reactions to the news events. During the following week, look at a picture review or a television Web site of your choice, to find which news events, selected by the students, were captured in the "Photo Essays." (Do your students know how television call letters are assigned? Is there another television station that begins with the letter "K" that is located east of the Mississippi River?)

**Vendor:** None required.

**Web site:** News channel of your choice, e.g., *KYW* in Philadelphia, Pennsylvania (http://kyw .com/news/#)

---

**Format:** Videoconference

**Subject:** Science—Freshwater Animals

**Idea:** If you are missing a Leopard Gecko, Madagascar Hissing Cockroach, or Tomato Frog from your local lab packet, you can schedule a videoconference with top scientists (and their animal friends) at the Tennessee Aquarium. Be prepared to pay a fee for the videoconference, but think of the money you will save on transportation for this field trip!

**Vendor:** Tennessee Aquarium.

**Web site:** *Tennessee Aquarium Projects and Events* (http://learn.tnaqua.org/learn/projects _and_events.asp)

---

# Grades 9–12

High school students are ready for the variety of content areas that can be delivered to them through distance learning. They need to become involved in deciding the topics that they want, and need, to learn to help them become independent lifelong learners. Whether functioning within a class group or pursuing courses independently, high school students can enjoy the freedom that distance learning provides, while still having a guide to direct them when they need help.

## *Delayed-Time Interactive Distance Learning Activities*

**Format:** Audio

**Subject:** All

**Idea:** Under the guise of asking students to develop "testimonial" tapes to share with middle and junior high school students that offer course suggestions and guidance, ask groups of students to prepare positive audiotapes that advertise your course. What are the benefits? Students will use a storyboard to organize the presentation, noting audio clips, interviews, sound effects, etc. These audio tapings can be digitized and included on a class or school Web page.

**Vendor:** Audio recorder of your choice.

**Web site:** There are many sites that offer assistance for digitizing audio. Start your search with your district's technology support page or your vendor's home page.

---

**Format:** CD-ROM

**Subject:** College Preparation

**Idea:** Are all of your students aware of the resources available on CD-ROM to help them with preparation for taking standardized tests for college admission? Be sure to refer them to the school or public library, bookstore, or Web sites to find out how to get copies of course preparation software, sample questions, and sample exams.

**Vendor:** Varies.

**Web site:** *ACT Assessment* (http://www.act.org/aap/)

> *SAT: Taking the Tests/College Board* (Educational Testing Service) (http://www.collegeboard.com/testing/0,1136,3-0-0-0,00.html)

---

**Format:** Correspondence Supported by Web Resources

**Subject:** Civil War

**Idea:** Expand on the use of primary sources with American History students. View digitized copies of documents at *The Valley of the Shadow: Two Communities in the American Civil War.* (Another source of primary sources on the Civil War is available at *Documenting the American South* at the University of North Carolina at Chapel Hill.) After demonstrating the importance of correspondence as primary sources, ask students to capture their opinions and experiences relating to the War on Terrorism and Afghanistan Conflict in a hand-written letter.

**Vendor:** None required.

**Web site:** *The Valley of the Shadow: Two Communities in the American Civil War* (http://valley.vcdh.virginia.edu/)

*Documenting the American South* (http://docsouth.unc.edu)

---

**Format:** Electronic Mail

**Subject:** All

**Idea:** Many service organizations would like to provide ways for all of their members to participate in service projects. Using e-mail to allow students to tutor other students is a great way to do this! Start by reviewing the types of tutoring you want students to do, i.e., homework review, math assistance, etc. Train your students to use e-mail to tutor, to answer questions, or perhaps even to review assignments and papers. Part of your tutoring training may be teaching the tutors to locate information and answers online through sites that they have researched and collected in a Web page listing. (Note: There are many commercial tutoring resources online. Be sure that students know if they are not to contact commercial resources. However, know that you can refer parents to these types of resources if their students require additional tutoring online.)

**Vendor:** None required.

**Web site:** *Free Learning* (http://www.freelearning.com) (Provides links to a variety of subject sources)

*Virtual Volunteering Project* (http://www.serviceleader.org/vv/direct/)

---

**Format:** Interactive Web Activities

**Subject:** Biology

**Idea:** Students can connect to either site to dissect a frog online. Other interactive projects are available at the *Center for Technology and Teacher Education* (University of Virginia's Curry School of Education) (http://www.teacherlink.org/siteindex.html). Benefits of Web simulations, such as this, include convenience, safety, and savings. Absent students can still experience the "fun" of dissection. All that is missing is the fragrance of freshly dissected frog and formaldehyde!

**Vendor:** None required.

**Web site:** *Frog Guts* (http://www.froguts.com) or *Interactive Frog Dissection* (http://frog.edschool.virginia.edu)

---

**Format:** Interactive Web Activities

**Subject:** Consumer Awareness

**Idea:** Yes, there are two entries for this category—on purpose. Students at the high school level may be vulnerable to "too good" offers online, such as "inside information on scholarships." Of course, these offers are made for a fee, and many students (and their parents) are hoodwinked into purchasing these services. Be sure that you let students know that there are all kinds of scams online and what they can do about them.

**Vendor:** None required.

**Web site:** *Scholarship Scams* (http://www.ftc.gov/bcp/conline/edcams/scholarship/)

---

**Format:** Videotape and Web Materials

**Subject:** Science

**Idea:** Imagine having an interactive periodical table chart available that also includes the history and sources of the elements, or being able to chart through a virtual telescope, or taking a deep-sea tour! These and other activities will help you to bring "living science" to your students. The newspaper-type format presents science events in a very appealing way.

**Vendor:** None required.

**Web site:** *Living Science* (A partnership of school districts, a community college, a university, and state and federal agencies, funded by a U.S. Department of Education Grant) (http://www.living-science.org/)

---

**Format:** Course Packages

**Subject:** Varies

**Idea:** Whether students choose to attend a virtual school in the home state, or whether students need to attend a virtual school in another state (to get the course they are seeking), students and parents will benefit from knowing that there are many choices.

**Vendor:** Varies.

**Web site:** *Distance Learning Resources Network* (Virtual Schools List) (http://www.dlrn.org/virtual.html)

---

**Format:** Taped Television Courses

**Subject:** Collaboration

**Idea:** Is it necessary to always have to use the resources of a commercial provider? You know that there are teachers in your district and state who do a super job of presenting a variety of topics. Can these presentations be taped and shared in your district and state? What are the topics of greatest need? Could you qualify for a grant project that will support this development? If not, there are resources that are available for a price, such as the programs through the *Public Broadcasting Services Videodatabase*. (Ask your media specialist for other video sources that your school can use.)

**Vendor:** None required.

**Web site:** Search your district and state education Web sites to find the availability of taped television courses that have been created by local educators.

*Public Broadcasting Services Videodatabase* (http://pbsvideodb.pbs.org)

---

### Real-Time Interactive Distance Learning Activities

**Format:** Audioconference (Speakerphone)

**Subject:** College Admissions

**Idea:** Ninth-grade students would benefit from hearing the admissions counselor at a university or local community college speak about how to start preparing for college admissions. Students (and parents) can prepare their questions and submit them in advance to the admissions counselor.

**Vendor:** None required.

**Web site:** *Peterson's* (http://www.petersons.com/)

---

**Format:** Chatroom

**Subject:** All

**Idea:** Tutoring—Whether using in conjunction with delayed-time e-mail or not, the use of a chatroom to tutor students is a highly productive way to encourage students to combine a pleasurable activity (chatting!) with a service activity! Try using free services such as *Yahoo Messenger, ICQ,* or *AOL Instant Messenger* (*AIM*).

**Vendor:** None required.

**Web site:** *AOL Instant Messenger* (http://www.aim.com/index.adp)

   *ICQ* (http://web.icq.com/)

   *Yahoo Messenger* (http://messenger.yahoo.com)

---

**Format:** Electronic Classroom

**Subject:** Mathematics

**Idea:** Tutoring—In addition to using e-mail and chat, there is a wealth of online tutors that are beneficial to your students

**Vendor:** None required.

**Web site:** A variety of online mathematics tutoring sites is found at *Online Tutoring* (http://www.back2college.com/library/tutor.htm).

---

**Format:** Radio

**Subject:** World Events

**Idea:** High school students will benefit from the presentation of in-depth interviews on current, global topics at the *Voice of America* (*VOA*). *VOA* notes on its Web page that the reporting aims for a balanced view. Does it succeed? Ask your students to compare interviews and coverage of radio programming at *VOA*, National Public Radio, BBC Radio, or other stations that are of interest to your students.

**Vendor:** None required.

**Web site:** *Voice of America/News Now* (http://www.voanews.com/newsnow/)

---

**Format:** Satellite Link

**Subject:** Varies

**Idea:** *Satellite Educational Resources Consortium* (*SERC*) combines the resources of state departments of education and public television stations. These courses, which include higher-level science and mathematics and foreign languages, are available for a fee by satellite services. (Check for courses for other levels, along with professional development and special programming opportunities.)

**Vendor:** SERC.

**Web site:** *SERC* (http://www.serc.org)

---

**Format:** Television

**Subject:** Psychology/Sociology—Evaluating Television Advertisements

**Idea:** The role of advertising and customer motivation are important for high school students who are getting ready to make major purchasing decisions. Do they know how to evaluate these advertisements? Ask students to keep a log of advertisements that they see for thirty minutes each day. Divide students into groups to compare and categorize the advertisements that they see. What do they believe are the messages behind these advertisements? The next phase of this evaluation can be in the form of Web advertisements (of companies selected by the teacher) from other countries. What are the similarities in the advertisements? Are there cultural differences?

**Vendor:** None required.

**Web site:** Search the Internet for foreign companies' Web sites for comparison.

---

**Format:** Videoconference

**Subject:** Science Fair Projects

**Idea:** How often do you regret that the time and energy put into science fair projects only stays within your own school? A videoconference would be one way for students to share their projects with students in other schools (while also presenting them to your class or a larger school group). You and other collaborating science teachers in other schools may wish to ask students to share their projects based on category, future research potential, etc.

**Vendor:** Videoconferencing service provider of your district.

**Web site:** *The WWW Virtual Library: Science Fairs* (http://physics1.usc.edu/~gould /ScienceFairs/)

---

# Extracurricular Activities and Programs

It doesn't take much experience in education to know that an important aspect of the secondary school's academic day is the socialization of students. If you ask a student what the most important times of the day are, "lunch" might be the popular answer. Lunch is *the* social hour, the time when students interact. This interaction might be carried over to some forms of distance learning. For any parent who has a student with online access to chatrooms, you know how hard it is to drag a teenager away from the screen when there are online friends on the other side of the screen. Whether some of the more traditional interactions of students, such as class parties, pep rallies, homecoming games, and prom and club activities, can be translated to the distance format remains to be seen; however, this need is being realized as an important aspect of building school support and spirit. Without the development of this interaction, and a resulting identity with the institution, other areas, such as development, donations, and foundations, stand to lose in the future. Therefore, you may think about how to solidify this element of spirit and how to define it in an online space. If you do not develop an online alma mater, what will replace it? Online video game contents and T-shirts are among some suggestions for the university levels that can be applied to the high school level (Young 2000b, 1).

## *Teaching Possibility*

Speak to your students about "what" makes them bond with other students. Ask them how they maintain contact with each other during extended breaks. How would they suggest this development of "community" if they were geographically distant from each other and did not have the ability to be with each other, physically, during a school day? Do they think that they would enjoy going to college or working if they were geographically distant from other students or workers? If the answer is no, brainstorm with your students to think of strategies that they could follow that would make working in physical (not electronic) isolation more bearable.

## *Extracurricular Activities*

Some noncampus-based and campus-based activities that can be achieved through distance learning modalities include:

- Alternative education
- Club activities
- Dual enrollment
- Intramural activities
- Language activities
- Military groups (training online)
- Online field trips
- Research

## *Teaching Possibility*

Have students go to the writing lab to practice foreign-language skills. If you are teaching French or Spanish, the new versions of Microsoft packages include spell checkers for these languages. If you are working with other languages, you can still download spelling and grammar checkers through Microsoft. Using the spelling and grammar checkers for the language you are teaching, ask students to key in passages of the language text to test the spell checker. Next, have students key in passages that they have previously translated to check *their* spelling. What are the challenges of using a foreign language spell checker? Are these students familiar with using online search tools in their language of study?

---

Keep reading for some extracurricular ideas!

## *Delayed-Time Interactive Distance Learning Activities*

**Format:** Audiotape

**Subject:** Club or Practice Activities

**Idea:** Tape the chorus practice or band practice or club meeting so absent, sick, or homebound students will not miss what was covered. The taping will also help with the recording of minutes, if this is required for a meeting.

**Vendor:** None required.

**Web site:** Does your group have a Web site? If so, digitize your recording and put it online for everyone to access. (Remind students that they are being recorded.)

---

**Format:** CD-ROM

**Subject:** Electronic Publishing

**Idea:** Paper publications can get very expensive for clubs that do not have large treasuries. Think about publishing the documents on CD-ROM for distribution. Don't forget that in addition to CD-ROM yearbooks (that include more than the printed version), you can create CD-ROMs of literary books, etc.

**Vendor:** CD-ROM writers of your choice.

**Web site:** Many Web resources that apply to publications are available in areas such as layout, font choice, etc.

---

**Format:** Correspondence

**Subject:** Penpals

**Idea:** Service organizations can sponsor penpal activities that focus on a particular age, country, or topic. If distance students need to acquire language skills or wish to sponsor a class of disadvantaged students that can use assistance with writing skills, this is a great activity. Remind your students that students may exist in their district or state that will benefit from having a penpal. What is the related distance learning experience? Get the activity started (post messages about your organization online) and stand back and watch your students' perspectives expand.

**Vendor:** None required.

**Web site:** *TeacherNet* (http://teachernet/projects/penpals/)

---

**Format:** Electronic Mail

**Subject:** Club Announcements

**Idea:** In addition to making announcements on the public-announcement systems or morning news, thing about e-mailing meeting announcements. If a goal is to increase parent participation in this extracurricular activity, include them in the announcements—at least to remind them that their student might need a ride home in the afternoon.

**Vendor:** None required.

**Web site:** None required.

---

**Format:** Interactive Web Activities

**Subject:** Web Résumés

**Idea:** While students are in the whirl of an active social life, they need to remember to keep a running Web résumé page of their extracurricular activities for college applications.

**Vendor:** None required.

**Web site:** There are many Web sites with résumé suggestions.

---

**Format:** Videotape

**Subject:** Varies

**Idea:** There are many learning areas that will interest students for which there are instructional videotapes available through your school library media center, district instructional television office, or the public library. Topics such as songwriting, dinosaurs, chess, travel, etc., are available in video format. Ask your media specialist for help with locating these materials.

**Vendor:** None required.

**Web site:** Search your district's instructional television site or your public library's Web page to locate videos of interest for your extracurricular students.

---

**Format:** Course Packages

**Subject:** Speed Reading

**Idea:** A noncredit learning activity, such as speed reading, can benefit many of your students. Some resources may already be available in your district. Other resources (that include manuals and videotapes) may be purchased inexpensively.

**Vendor:** Varies.

**Web site:** *Speed Reading 4 Kids* (http://www.speedreading4kids.com/)

---

**Format:** Taped Television Courses

**Subject:** History Topics

**Idea:** How many of you recall never getting past World War I in a history course? It is very difficult for history teachers to cover all of the historical periods to the satisfaction of some students. For these students, club activities that focus on specific events or royalty, using taped television courses, offer the chance for students to work with a teacher on noncredit history activities. Many history teachers would not need the support of taped courses, but students could check these out and view them at home before meeting with the group or club to discuss the event. Extension activities in the form of independent research would be enjoyed by many of the more serious history students.

**Vendor:** Discovery, the History Channel, or PBS offer series for purchase if they are not available locally.

**Web site:** Search your district's instructional television site or your public library's Web page to locate videos of interest for your extracurricular students.

---

## *Real-Time Interactive Distance Learning Activities*

**Format:** Audioconference (Conference Call)

**Subject:** Project Work

**Idea:** With competing schedules of family members, jobs, sports, etc., it is often very difficult for students to meet to go over group projects or practice skits. Start encouraging students to use conference calls so that they will have a great choice of meeting times. Remind them that they may need to e-mail drafts or other documents in advance so that everyone can see what is being discussed.

**Vendor:** Telephone service with conference call service.

**Web site:** None required.

---

**Format:** Chatroom

**Subject:** Math Club

**Idea:** Encourage students to increase their math skills (and complete homework!) with some productive chatting at the Math Forum's High School Student Center. Students, parents, and teachers can chat about many levels of math, K–12.

**Vendor:** None required.

**Web site:** *Math Forum* (http://mathforum.org/students/high/)

*Math Forum's High School Chat Areas, Mailing Lists, and Newsgroups* (http://mathforum.org/students/high/chat.html)

---

**Format:** Electronic Classroom

**Subject:** ThinkQuest (Annual)

**Idea:** Though some may not see this activity as a "formal" electronic classroom, many believe that participation in *ThinkQuest*, which offers many programs throughout the world, is actually better than attending an established classroom—from a constructivist's viewpoint. If your students participate in *ThinkQuest USA* as an extracurricular activity of the Honor Society or Media Club, they will be collaborating, researching, and developing Web materials.

**Vendor:** None required.

**Web site:** *ThinkQuest* (http://www.thinkquest.org/)

---

**Format:** Radio

**Subject:** Radio Production

**Idea:** Does your school have its own radio station? Could it develop a low-broadcast community station or offer Web-based radio? Could this radio station be used to provide credit and noncredit courses to homebound students?

**Vendor:** None required.

**Web site:** *WHJE Radio* (http://www.whje.com)

---

**Format:** Satellite Link

**Subject:** Environment Club

**Idea:** Though this is really a delayed-time activity (except for the fact that the Web pages are frequently updated), club members will be able to actually view satellite images from around the world that show environmental changes. Each satellite image includes a well-researched narrative with links to other sources. There are many categories that include city, desert, disasters, wildlife, etc. Some of the images include Chernobyl and the Great Salt Lake. Would your students be interested in developing a similar site that describes local environmental changes? Since this site is directed by the U.S. Geological Services, students might also be interested in arranging an audioconference (by speakerphone) with some of the expert geologists.

**Vendor:** None required.

**Web site:** *USGS* (U.S. Geological Services)

**Earthshots:** *Satellite Images of Environmental Change* (http://earthshots.usgs.gov/)

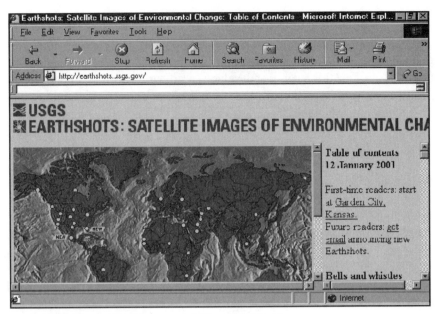

*Satellite Images of Environmental Change* Web site:
http://earthshots.usgs.gov/

**Format:** Television

**Subject:** School Television

**Idea:** Your school probably has a television program that is closed-circuit, but can you also offer programming through your local community television? Would students enjoy developing monthly (weekly or daily) programming for younger students promoting school activities (request community help in fund-raising), broadcasting school performances (plays, recitals, etc.), or interviewing officials on tax money spent for kids' interests, etc.? Many of the local communities may also have educational television that is independent of larger broadcasting areas.

**Vendor:** Your local community television station.

**Web site:** *Boca Raton Educational Television* (http://www.bretonline.tv/)

---

**Format:** Videoconference

**Subject:** Local and Regional Meetings

**Idea:** Does your school have videoconferencing equipment available for after-school use? Can you use the equipment to meet with other club chapters (to organize regional or state meetings) or share speakers at meetings?

**Vendor:** Your local videoconferencing services.

**Web site:** None required.

## Rural

The use of distance learning for the rural setting has been in practice for many decades, with the state of North Dakota being one of the first states that developed a structured process for delivering correspondence courses. Issues relating to rural education are simple. It is not practical to transport students hundreds of miles. Student populations are often too low to justify the costs of facilities and personnel, and if you could entice personnel to live in remote areas, chances are not likely that they will be available for a wide range of subjects and grade levels. In a survey of 311 schools, with 42 percent responding, 50 percent of the responding schools indicated that they were using distance learning in their K–12 curriculum with satellite programs being most commonly used, followed by cable television delivery (Barker and Hall 1994). Many learning technologies are applicable for rural settings, all with advantages and disadvantages (Barker 1991).

Distance learning has been used to provide teacher training in rural locations via satellite for career education (Brolin, Cook, and O'Keefe 1994) and to provide instruction in soil science in the Netherlands through study-units that focused on printed materials and workbooks that were complemented by interactive videodiscs (Lansu, Ivens, and Hummel 1994). Recently, the TICKET (Technology Integration Certification for K–12 Educators and Teachers) Program was implemented in Pennsylvania to provide teachers with technology training. In cooperation with Pennsylvania State University, teachers had the opportunity to learn to use basic computer application programs, use the Internet in the classroom, design Internet materials, and design multimedia learning packages. The need for time to plan and organize the instruction is noted, along with the importance of providing a cohort to support all learners (Kochery 2000). Similarly, a course on Internet Applications in Science Education was offered to middle and high school teachers using WebCT. The use of online discussions was reported as a drawback, due to students not posting responses in time for group discussions to occur; however, for these teachers who could not attend face-to-face classes, they were able to learn to implement Internet resources into the classroom (Baron and McKay 2001). A separate chart for rural distance learning ideas will not be provided, since many of the other ideas can be adapted. However, this category is included as a reminder that there is a continuum for PreK–12 rural students, from those who cannot stay at school in the afternoon, due to lack of transportation, to those who cannot travel to and from school daily. The *ERIC Clearinghouse on Rural Education and Small Schools* (http://www.ael.org/eric/) offers a Web site that you will want to visit to monitor developments in distance learning for rural schools.

## Students with Special Needs

Built-in school support for students with special needs in Exceptional Student Education (ESE) programs exists in the position of the school library media specialist. Because the media specialist supports the philosophy that a wide range of media facilitates learning with a variety of learning styles, and has been trained to develop learning packages in many mediums that support many learning styles, ESE teachers will find a productive ally in the media specialist. Many online resources—Web pages and listservs—exist for teachers and parents of students with learning disabilities, or learning *differences* (Young 1999). The media specialist can help the ESE teacher to locate these resources.

### *Learning Possibility*

You may have heard of Dr. Mel Levine's work on learning theory that recognizes a variety of areas that impacts students, including language, memory, attention, etc., and contributes to many learning patterns. At his Web site, *All Kinds of Minds* (http://www.allkindsofminds.org/), Dr. Levine practices what he professes (some students need to listen to learn, some need to read to learn, etc.) by providing both audio clips and written transcripts. Do you think that the teacher's ability to address a variety of student learning needs can be met through distance learning?

---

Many distance learning opportunities can be adapted for the ESE student. For example, video-taped instruction has been used for C++ courses that also served students with hearing impairments. Sign language, graphics, closed captioning, and cartoon animation enhance these courses (Mallory 1997). Ideas to assist with adapting these learning opportunities can be found at EASI. *EASI* (*Equal Access to Software and Information*) (http://www.rit.edu/~easi/) provides special educators with information and online training on the types of assistive devices used by persons with disabilities. The site includes an archive of Webcasts on topics such as "K–12 Asssistive Technology." If you need help with devices or advice on adapting Web pages, this is a good place to start. The *ERIC Clearinghouse on Disabilities and Gifted Education* (http://ericec.org) is a good starting point for exceptional educators. Note the link on accessibility of Web sites.

# *Section B. Applications for Teachers*

Interactive distance learning activities can help teachers to work productively by bringing learning and teaching opportunities into the classroom or into the home. There are so many areas of study that teachers would like to take advantage of, but they may not have the time to drive to them, or they may have a conflicting schedule, due to their home responsibilities. The teacher activities presented are ideas on how to help teachers get the training and learning opportunities that they want, and need, in convenient ways.

## *Teacher Activities*

The many activities for which interactive distance education technologies offer potential formats include:

- District meetings
- In-service training (acquired, commercial, and district)
- For-credit courses
- Certification (credential changes)
- Graduate programs
- Noncredit courses (independent learning)
- Outreach (parent conferences, parent visits to class for presentations by students)
- Professional activities and meetings
- Support activities (subjects, sponsored activities)

### *Delayed-Time Interactive Distance Learning Activities*

**Format:** Audiotape/CD

**Subject:** Virtual Conference

**Idea:** Most teacher conferences provide audiotapes or audio CDs for a fee. Sometimes the conferences will post audio files online, following conference presentations. If you know of a particular conference (or conference presentation) that you cannot attend (due to finances or other reasons), check the conference Web site to see if a set of audiotapes or audio CDs are available for your school or e-mail the contact to request purchasing information on the conference recordings.

**Vendor:** NECC (National Educational Computing Conference).

**Web site:** NECC (http://neccsite.org/)

---

**Format:** CD-ROM

**Subject:** Computer Applications Training

**Idea:** Many software packages include a tutorial with the package, or a link to a tutorial at a Web site. Other companies make training materials available on a separate CD-ROM for downloading. Search online software catalogs or take a visit to your local computer store to see what types of packages are available for purchase by your school. Some organizations, such as the For Sea Institute of Marine Science, offer CD-ROM training packages that include curriculum and training.

**Vendor:** Various software producers.

**Web site:** *For Sea* (http://www.forsea.org/forseacd.html)

---

**Format:** Correspondence

**Subject:** Recertification Courses

**Idea:** You may not be one of those students who enjoy electronic learning, but you still need to recertify, and the closest university may be over a hundred miles away. There are accredited courses available through correspondence. Contact your local college or university or search for correspondence courses online. (Make sure that the schools are accredited by their regional accreditation association.)

**Vendor:** Various colleges and universities.

**Web site:** *Middle Tennessee State University Correspondence Courses* (http://www.mtsu .edu/~corres/)

*University of Georgia* (http://www.classics.uga.edu/corres.html)

---

**Format:** Electronic Mail

**Subject:** E-Mail Newsletters

**Idea:** E-mail newsletters, delivered directly to your e-mailbox, relieve you of having to search for (or remember to link to) online sources. These newsletters also help you to make sure that you are receiving fresh, up-to-date information. Try a newsletter like *TeAch-nology* that offers ideas on incorporating technology into your curriculum. *Edupage* offers up-to-date developments in technology news. (How will you make sure that your students can distinguish between "marketing" spelling and correct spelling? For example, would your students know that "TeAch-nology" is intended to be a combination of the words "teach" and "technology" and would they know that "TeAch" is not the capitalization that they should follow for "teach" on their spelling tests?)

**Vendor:** None required.

**Web site:** *Edupage* (http://www.educause.edu/pub/edupage/edupage.html)

*TeAch-nology* (http://www.teach-nology.com/)

---

**Format:** Interactive Web Activities

**Subject:** Grading Rubrics

**Idea:** Start checking the many online lesson plan sites to see if there is also a rubric generator at that site. As a companion to lesson plan development, you can also retrieve or customize rubrics that will apply to your lesson and help students develop a better understanding of how they are to create their assignments, based on how you will evaluate the assignment.

**Vendor:** None required.

**Web site:** *Lesson Plan Search* (http://www.lessonplansearch.com/Rubrics/)

*Rubistar* (http://rubistar.4teachers.org/)

*The Rubric Processor* (http://insys.ed.psu.edu/~lin/Rubric/H_rubric.htm)

*TeAch-nology* (http://teachers.teach-nology.com/web_tools/rubrics/)

---

**Format:** Videotape

**Subject:** Using Instructional Video

**Idea:** Who are the teachers that use instructional video in your school? Remember that video needs to be used as an integral part of your curriculum to be effective. If there are teachers who are using video effectively in the classroom, consider asking them if they will consent to be videotaped to share ideas on presentations. Read the *National Teacher Training Institute*'s article "Why Use Video in the Classroom?" and view other suggestions on incorporating video into your presentations.

**Vendor:** None required.

**Web site:** *National Teacher Training Institute—Video Strategies* (http://www.thirteen.org /edonline/ntti/resources/video1.html)

---

**Format:** Course Packages

**Subject:** Language Study

**Idea:** "Teaching Spanish to Speakers of Spanish" is a "course package on the Web" in the sense that if you are interested in learning about the pedagogy of teaching language to native speakers, this site is a model. Including a lengthy bibliography that includes articles, listserv groups, ERIC Digests, Web sites, etc., this site combines a variety of resources and presents the topic in a well-organized way.

**Vendor:** None required.

**Web site:** *Teaching Spanish to Speakers of Spanish* (http://www.cal.org/ericcll/faqs/rgos /sns.html) from the ERIC Clearinghouse on Languages and Linguistics

---

**Format:** Taped Television Courses

**Subject:** Educational Topics

**Idea:** The *Annenberg/CPB (Center for Public Broadcasting) Channel* offers television by broadband and satellite and offers the programming to teachers, which includes liberal taping and viewing rights. Programs are available for students and for professional development. Search the *Annenberg/CPB Channel* for the topics and levels of your choice. You will be surprised at the number of programs available.

**Vendor:** None required.

**Web site:** *Annenberg/CPB Channel* (http://www.learner.org/channel/channel.html)

---

## Real-Time Interactive Distance Learning Activities

**Format:** Audioconference

**Subject:** Mentoring First-Year Teachers

**Idea:** A very convenient way to help first-year teachers is through an audioconference, if you work at another location. By audioconferencing, first-year teachers at a variety of locations could call a common number, where they gather with a mentor and share events and strategies. (While you're mentoring, send first-year teachers to their own lesson plan site at *TeacherVision.com* [http://www.teachervision.com/lesson-plans/lesson-6494.html?rn].)

**Vendor:** Audioconferencing vendor used by your district, e.g., Premier Conferencing (http:// www.atsgroup.com/).

**Web site:** *Qualities of Effective Technology Mentors* (http://www.techlearning.com/content /outlook/pdq/2002/6-11.html)

---

**Format:** Chatroom

**Subject:** Teacher Communication

**Idea:** There are more teacher chats than you can imagine! How can you find them? You can link to *Topica* and search for the teacher category of your choice.

**Vendor:** None required.

**Web site:** *Topica* (http://www.liszt.com/dir/?cid=4)

---

**Format:** Electronic Classroom

**Subject:** Teacher Training—Picture Book Read-Alouds, Digital Language Experience Approach

**Idea:** *Reading Online* is an online journal offered by the International Reading Association. In the Reading Online's "Electronic Classroom," teachers can select from well-structured lectures that include Web links and bibliographies. Recent postings in the "Electronic Classroom" include "Picture Book Read-Alouds" (remember, you're never too old for read-alouds!) and "Digital Language Experience Approach." Some other article reprints are also offered. Look at the archive section of "Electronic Classroom" for some classes you may have missed, e.g., "Information Overload: Threat or Opportunity."

**Vendor:** None required.

**Web site:** *The Electronic Classroom* (at *Reading Online*) (http://www.readingonline.org /electronic/elec_index.asp)

---

**Format:** Electronic Classroom

**Subject:** Definition of Electronic Classroom

**Idea:** For the purposes of this handbook, an "electronic classroom" is an online class. However, in many schools and districts, this term may be used to refer to a *physical* classroom that has a variety of technology for teaching. For example, an electronic classroom in one school may include a computer with a video projector and online access. In another school or district, an electronic classroom may be defined as a room that includes a videoconferencing system with multiple monitors, cameras, speakers, etc. How does your district define "electronic classroom" and will this definition impact how you will develop an equivalent for your school? (If you would like to read comparisons of Web-based teaching software for electronic classrooms, articles are available online.)

**Vendor:** None required.

**Web site:** *Comparison of Web-Based Course Environments* (Edutech) (http://www.edutech .ch/edutech/tools/comparison_e.asp)

---

**Format:** Radio

**Subject:** Educational Topics

**Idea:** Does your local school district provide any radio programming about your school system? If you don't know, check with your local Public Broadcasting Station. In Boston, Massachusetts, for example, *WGBH* ("Eye on Education") interviews students and faculty on local educational issues and needs. You can search at other radio Web sites that archive broadcasts (e.g., *National Public Radio*) and search under the keyword "Education." You should find either written or taped transcripts of the broadcasts.

**Vendor:** None required.

**Web site:** *National Public Radio* (http://www.npr.org)

WGBH (Boston) (http://www.eyeoneducation.tv/students/)

---

**Format:** Satellite Link

**Subject:** Teacher Education and Training

**Idea:** You may already have a gold mine of teacher education and training opportunities available for teachers! The DISH Network offers programming to several channels that offer teacher (and student) education television (CCN, HITN, NAUHS, PAEC, PBS-U, and WNET). *PAEC* (Panhandle Area Educational Consortium) produces the Florida Educational Channel and provides programming on current topics of interest, e.g., brain research. PAEC also offers "Tuesday Teacher Training," a program that gathers noted professionals on current educational topics. (Some of these recorded programs can be streamed to your desktop.) Check with your district to find out if these programs can be accepted for in-service training credits. (Some districts in Alabama, Georgia, and Florida are eligible to participate in training activities that range from face-to-face to Web-based delivery. Search the *Florida Learns Database* at http://www. paec.org.) Are there other educational television services provided by your district or state?

**Vendor:** Dish Network (http://www.dishnetwork.com).

**Web site:** *Florida Educational Channel* (http://www.floridalearns.org)

> *PAEC* (*Panhandle Area Educational Consortium*) (http://www.paec.org) (877-USE-PAEC)

> *Tuesday Teacher Training* at *PAEC* (http://www.paec.org/ttt/may2002/video.htm)

---

**Format:** Television

**Subject:** "Heads Up!"

**Idea:** Using the U.S. Department of Education's televised series, Head Start teachers (and parents) can view courses that can be taken for credit toward an associate degree.

**Vendor:** None required.

**Web site:** *U.S. Department of Education* (http://www.heads-up.org) (1-800-GET-HUTV)

---

**Format:** Videoconference

**Subject:** Locating Participants for Videoconferencing

**Idea:** Let's say that you have the equipment for a videoconference, the idea for the topic, and even an idea about where the participants need to be located. For example, if you are developing a videoconference on rain forests, you might want to collaborate with a class that is located in a tropical rain forest area. Where do you go next? *The Global Schoolhouse* has a site for "Classroom Conferencing" that offers sites for conferencing, projects in process, and resources.

**Vendor:** None required.

**Web site:** *Global Schoolhouse/Classroom Conferencing* (http://www.gsh.org/cu/index.html)

---

# Section C. Applications for Administrators

If you think that teachers are busy, they are! If you think that administrators are not busy, think again! Administrators have to provide leadership for the entire school population. They are responsible for everything from the drip of a faucet to the fight on the field. Administrators also miss many learning and training opportunities because of their schedules. Distance learning opportunities offer administrators the chance to attend meetings and training sessions, while still being accessible at school where they are needed. The *ERIC Clearinghouse on Educational Management* (http://eric.uoregon.edu) is a resource that administrators need to monitor for issues such as school finance, law, safety, etc.

## Administrator Activities

Activities that support PreK–12 administrators vary widely, due to the responsibilities of the administrators for whole school activities and curricular development. These areas include but are not limited to:

- District meetings
- In-service training (acquired, commercial, and district)
- For-credit courses for certification or graduate programs
- Noncredit courses (independent learning)
- Outreach (to parents, PTA/PTO)
- Professional activities and meetings
- Support activities

### Delayed-Time Interactive Distance Learning Activities

**Format:** Audio Messenging

**Subject:** Communication with Home

**Idea:** You may remember some of the earlier telephone "robots" that some administrators used to telephone announcements. The newer automated systems can help you to let parents know about conferences, Open House, lunch menus, etc. For students whose parents speak a language other than English, automatic communication systems can record a spoken message in any language and dial out to the home and even leave a message on an answering machine.

**Vendor:** *School Messenger* (http://www.schoolmessenger.com/)

       *U.S. Netcom* (http://www.usnetcomcorp.com/)

---

**Format:** CD-ROM/DVD

**Subject:** The School Sleuth—The Merrow Report

**Idea:** If you haven't read the *Merrow Report,* you might prefer viewing "School Sleuth: The Case of an Excellent School."

**Vendor:** Learning Matters (877-2Merrow, toll free).

**Web site:** *The School Sleuth* (http://www.pbs.org/merrow/tv/sleuth/index.html?)

---

**Format:** Correspondence

**Subject:** Communicating with Congress

**Idea:** If your students know how to write letters to Congress, shouldn't you? (And this is bound to be an educational experience!) What are the topics that you think should be communicated to your congressional representatives?

**Vendor:** None required.

**Web site:** *National Association of Elementary School Principals* (Communicating with Elected Officials) (http://capwiz.com/naesp/issues/basics/?style=comm)

---

**Format:** Electronic Mail

**Subject:** Legalities of E-Mail

**Idea:** What are the legal issues surrounding e-mail that apply to your students, teachers, staff, parents, and to yourself? Are you familiar with your district's e-mail policies for each of these groups? Have you informed each group of their responsibilities? Does your district have a separate policy for retaining school-based e-mail? If so, how long must you retain these messages? Are you required to retain all messages to and from students and parents?

**Vendor:** None required.

**Web site:** Search your district's Web site for policies that pertain to e-mail.

---

**Format:** Interactive Web Activities

**Subject:** Your School's Web Site

**Idea:** Your school may already have a Web site that is very effective, but how do you know if it is effective? For example, can parents easily locate the e-mail address or telephone number of a teacher? Are key instructional areas, such as the media center and computer lab, described on the Web page? Can parents locate the principal's e-mail address so that they can leave a message? Do all of your links work? Is the information up-to-date? Do you link to a map generator that will create a map that will help visitors find the way to your school? If you are not sure, try navigating your Web site. Ask parents, students, and other teachers to navigate the site with you so that you can learn more about their search patterns and the links that they are trying to locate—but can't. (*Administrative Uses of the Internet* [http://backpack.ipsd.org/ipa/] will lead administrators to other sources for technology planning, funding, etc.)

**Vendor:** None required.

**Web site:** Individual schools have created many Web site rubrics for evaluating instructional sites. Search for "quality" and "school Web sites." Even if you have a Web page, look at the following link for some review tips to make sure that your page is logical and navigable: *Creating School Web Pages* (http://www.eduscapes.com/tap/topic61.htm).

---

**Format:** Video

**Subject:** Welcome to Our School

**Idea:** How many times have you wanted a brief, but lively, way to introduce others to your school? When videocameras first came into schools, most schools created a videotape of school life, but many of those are now dated and dusty. Does your school have an up-to-date video that shows what a great school you have? Can you modify this video so that you can include it on your school's Web site? Does your district offer video support to assist your school with production of a school video?

**Vendor:** Supplier of your videocamera.

**Web site:** Check your district's Web site for video support information.

---

**Format:** Course Packages

**Subject:** Professional Development for Administrators

**Idea:** The National Middle School Association offers courses for professional development for teachers and administrators. These for-fee courses are in the format of Webcasts and online course activities. (Look under "Professional Development.")

**Vendor:** National Middle School Association.

**Web site:** *National Middle School Association* (http://www.nmsa.org/)

---

**Format:** Taped Television Courses

**Subject:** Critical Issues in School Reform

**Idea:** View this taped television course with your faculty, parents, and staff to begin to make meaningful changes in your school.

**Vendor:** Annenberg/Center for Public Broadcasting.

**Web site:** *Annenberg/Center for Public Broadcasting* (http://www.learner.org/resources /resource.html?uid=109&sj=EDUC)

---

## *Real-Time Interactive Distance Learning Activities*

**Format:** Audioconference

**Subject:** Parent Communication

**Idea:** How can an administrator make a better contribution to the school's atmosphere than by communicating regularly with parents? Offer a weekly audioconference with parents on what is going on at school. (If attendance at the school's advisory committee meetings is sparse, or if weather discourages evening meetings, consider moving these meetings to audioconferencing.)

**Vendor:** Audioconferencing service of your district.

**Web site:** Check the Web site of your audioconference provider for tips on how to conduct an effective audioconference.

---

**Format:** Audio

**Subject:** Directed Messages to Parents

**Idea:** Though your students may have an uneven level of technology in their homes, most parents have a telephone. Use your school's automatic dialer ("robot") to call and leave directed messages, e.g., calling the parents of a specific class to praise students for improved test scores. (Principals may wish to use the automatic dialer to call teachers about their first day of school and the in-service training schedule for that day.)

**Vendor:** Automatic dialer provider for your district.

**Web site:** Check the Web site of your automatic dialer for support materials.

---

**Format:** Chatroom

**Subject:** Educational Leadership

**Idea:** If you are a principal who feels isolated, join one of the administrators' chatrooms, such as the *Administrator ChatBoard* or *K12ADMIN*. (If you want to subscribe to *K12ADMIN*, send an e-mail message to listserv@listserv.syr.edu that states "subscribe *K12ADMIN*" and you will receive directions on how to use the chat information.) Did you know that you can search the saved messages from listservs (known as "archives")? Link to the *K12ADMIN Archives* at ERIC to search for your topic of interest.

**Vendor:** None required.

**Web site:** *Administrator ChatBoard* (http://administrators.net/)

> *ERIC K12ADMIN Archives* (http://ericir.syr.edu/Virtual/Listserv_Archives/K12ADMIN
> -List.shtml)

---

**Format:** Electronic Classroom

**Subject:** School Development

**Idea:** What are the online training opportunities available to staff members? Does your district or state offer staff training opportunities? Did you know that the U.S. Department of Education supports ten groups through the *Regional Technology Education Consortia*, including *NEIR\*TEC* (*NorthEast and the Islands Regional Technology in Education Consortium*) and *SEIR\*TEC* (*SouthEast Initiatives Regional Technology in Education Consortium*). The Consortia are sources of information on training opportunities for staff. Go to your area consortium to find out which training programs are available to your school staff. Start with the R\*TEC link below.

**Vendor:** None required.

**Web site:** *R\*TEC* (Regional Technology Education Consortia) (http://www.rtec.org/)

> *NEIR\*TEC* (http://www.neirtec.org/)

> *SEIR\*TEC* (http://www.seirtec.org/pd.html)

---

**Format:** Electronic Classroom

**Subject:** Teacher Development

**Idea:** Are you generating ideas on how to implement technology in your school? Do you think that some of your teachers are hesitant to make the changes? Are you confused about whether to spend the budget on an in-house electronic class curriculum? Find resources to lead you to decisions on these and other technology issues.

**Vendor:** None required.

**Web site:** *Electronic School Online* (http://www.electronic-school.com/0398f2.html)

---

**Format:** Radio

**Subject:** Variety of K–12 Teacher Topics

**Idea:** Whether you are interested in "Teacher Talk" or "Everyday Science," *Teacher Radio* offers daily Web radio on a variety of topics that range from professional development, to classroom curriculum, to (at the time of this writing) ideas on teaching mathematics.

**Vendor:** None required.

**Web site:** *Teacher Radio* at *Scholastic* (http://teacher.scholastic.com/professional/music/)

---

**Format:** Satellite Link

**Subject:** Expanding Course Offerings

**Idea:** Imagine that you have college-bound students who want to take courses in Latin and there is no certified Latin teacher available. *KET* (Kentucky Educational Television) offers a solution through satellite television throughout the East and Midwest. Other difficult-to-cover areas include German, physics, etc.

**Vendor:** KET (Kentucky Educational Television).

**Web site:** *KET* (http://www.dl.ket.org)

---

**Format:** Television

**Subject:** Current Events Affecting Education

**Idea:** *MiddleWeb* offers many resources that relate to a variety of topics that impact middle schools, and it also provides links to news shows and documentaries that are of interest to middle school teachers and students. (Links to newspaper articles and Web sites that impact middle schools are also provided.)

**Vendor:** None required.

**Web site:** *MiddleWeb* (Exploring Middle School Reform) (http://www.middleweb.com/)

---

**Format:** Videoconference

**Subject:** Videoconference as an Educational Technology

**Idea:** How in the world can you monitor and keep up with ideas on videoconferences? Monitor the "ed1vidconf" listserv. (If you would like to view an archived videoconference on Virtual High Schools, login to *ULiveandLearn.com* [http://208.185/32.25/launcher.cgi?] and view the "ABCs of the Virtual High School.")

**Vendor:** None required.

**Web site:** *Collaboration Collage* (ed1vidconf) (http://www.kn.pacbell.com/wired/vidconf /ed1vidconf.html)

---

# Section D. Applications for Paraprofessionals and Staff

Staff members are often overlooked members of the school community who also need learning and training opportunities. Where can we find training for them, and how can we deliver it? How can we also use distance learning technologies to increase staff effectiveness, while at the same time increasing support for teachers and administrators?

## Paraprofessional and Staff Activities

Because wise district administrators provide learning opportunities for staff, whether for developing new skill sets or earning continuing education units (CEUs), staff activities can be as varied and effective as desired. Like teachers and administrators, potential development for staff can be in the form of:

- District meetings
- In-service training
- For-credit courses (certification or diploma-earning programs)
- Noncredit courses
- Paraprofessional activities and meetings
- Support activities

## Delayed-Time Interactive Distance Learning Activities

**Format:** Audiotape

**Subject:** Various Educational Topics

**Idea:** To cut down on the boredom of a day where the paraprofessional is completing clerical tasks, think of listening to audiotaped books on educational topics. If these are not readily available through your school or public library, look for tapes that are motivational or tapes of books that your students may be reading.

**Vendor:** School library media center or public library.

**Web site:** Check your public library's Web site for tape availability.

---

**Format:** CD-ROM

**Subject:** Varies

**Idea:** Many textbooks are available with either CD-ROM or Web companion sites. Ask your teacher to see any available CD-ROM with classroom materials that you might use to help create bulletin boards, displays, handouts, etc.

**Vendor:** The vendor would be the publisher of the particular textbook.

**Web site:** Search online to find the Web site of the publisher. Most textbooks also list these sites in the introduction to the book or in the teacher's guide.

---

**Format:** Correspondence

**Subject:** Education Courses

**Idea:** Would paraprofessionals in your school consider taking correspondence courses that are self-paced and available through printed correspondence? Some of these opportunities still exist. Check with your local and state colleges and universities. Whatever courses you select, always be sure to verify that these courses are approved and will count toward certification for your state department of certification.

**Vendor:** Colorado Consortium for Independent Study.

**Web site:** *Colorado Consortium for Independent Study* (http://www.colorado.edu/ccis/)

---

**Format:** Electronic Mail

**Subject:** Paraprofessional Use of E-Mail

**Idea:** Do you have a school e-mail account? If so, are you aware of the appropriate use of your e-mail account while on the school campus? Using your e-mail account to contact the paraprofessional of your grade at another school to collaborate on the development of materials for your classes is a wonderful use of your school e-mail account.

**Vendor:** Your school's e-mail provider.

**Web site:** Search the Internet for a Web site for your school's e-mail provider. If you are using a Web-based e-mail service, such as MSN (Hotmail) or Yahoo, each provider has its own online guide for using e-mail.

> *TechTutorials* (http://www.techtutorials.com/Applications/Email/Outlook/)
> (For assistance with setting up Microsoft Outlook)

---

**Format:** Interactive Web Activities

**Subject:** Locating Resources

**Idea:** There are many resources available to help paraprofessionals do their jobs. From support materials for textbooks, to directions, to creating new art projects, paraprofessionals will find an incredible amount of information online.

**Vendor:** None required.

**Web site:** *Educational Support Personnel: Working Together to Improve Schools* (http://www.nea.org/esp/resource/improve.htm)

---

**Format:** Videotape

**Subject:** The Whole Child: A Caregiver's Guide to the First Five Years

**Idea:** The importance of caring for children is stressed in this videotape series.

**Vendor:** Annenberg/CPB (Center for Public Broadcasting).

**Web site:** *Annenberg/CPB (Center for Public Broadcasting)* (http://www.learner.org/resources resource.html?uid=59&sj=EDUC)

---

**Format:** Course Packages

**Subject:** Varies

**Idea:** Have you ever had the desire to take a course on a computer application, such as Excel, FrontPage, or PhotoShop, but you just did not have the time to go to the course? There are increasing opportunities online through groups such as *LVS Online Classes* that offer a variety of inexpensive courses and free tutorials on producing a Web page and using telnet and WinZip, etc., for the busy professional that just wants to try to conquer a small part of the technological world.

**Vendor:** None required.

**Web site:** *LVS Online Classes* (http://www.lvsonline.com/)

---

**Format:** Taped Television Courses

**Subject:** Paraprofessional Training

**Idea:** Conduct an audit of the taped television courses that are available to your district. Are there sufficient courses available? Provide a listing of the courses that you have located to your principal and discuss your desire to participate in training through taped television courses. Your principal will probably ask you to provide information on the availability of other course tapes or topics that you would like to have developed so that he or she can make a purchasing request through district resources. For example, districts that have large numbers of non-English-speaking students often create or purchase language tapes to teach paraprofessionals sufficient language to help these students and their parents with day-to-day school operations. Also check with your instructional television office to find out if past courses are available on videotape, whether created in your district or another school district.

**Vendor:** Varies.

**Web site:** *Multilingual Books Video Courses* (http://www.multilingualbooks.com/video-courses.html)

---

## *Real-Time Interactive Distance Learning Activities*

**Format:** Audioconference

**Subject:** Developing Classroom Materials

**Idea:** Do you have an idea that you would like to share with paraprofessionals on how to develop classroom materials? An audioconference is a quick and inexpensive way to keep paraprofessionals in contact with each other in districts. Audioconferencing is also an inexpensive, but almost universally accessible, tool for staff training.

**Vendor:** Audioconferencing provider of your district.

**Web site:** Check the Web site of your audioconferencing service provider for tips on providing, and participating in, audioconferences.

---

**Format:** Chatroom

**Subject:** Staff and Paraprofessional Chats

**Idea:** If you are a school staff member or paraeducator (paraprofessional), you might not be surprised to learn that it is a challenge to locate chats to support the very important work that you do in a PreK–12 school. One is available through the National Education Association (NEA), and it is called *ESP List.* (ESP stands for Educational Support Personnel.) You might also think about starting your own chat. It can be easy to do, but it requires a bit of time. Link to Topica, register, and start learning how to create your own chatroom—for free! Here is a suggestion: Since there are few, if any, functioning chatrooms for staff and paraeducators, consider keeping your topics broad enough so that members from other districts and states can participate.

**Vendor:** None required.

**Web site:** *NEA's ESP List* (http://www.nea.org/esp/converse/esplist.htm)

   *Topica* (http://www.liszt.com/create/index2.html)

---

**Format:** Electronic Classroom

**Subject:** Staff Development

**Idea:** Software vendors often offer online tutorials that provide varying levels of training. These tutorials are great for helping the beginner or advanced user with time-saving tips and suggestions.

**Vendor:** None required.

**Web site:** *Microsoft Education Tutorials* (http://www.microsoft.com/education/?ID=Tutorials)

---

**Format:** Radio

**Subject:** Locating Radio Programming

**Idea:** We've already mentioned the use of *National Public Radio* (*NPR* ) as a source of information on educational updates, but NPR provides programming on a wide variety of subject areas that can be useful in your school's curriculum, including folk songs, holidays, history, etc. Searching for radio broadcasts is something that the classroom paraprofessional can do to support the classroom teacher. The paraprofessional might also monitor some of the age-appropriate online radio stations that offer programming that students enjoy.

**Vendor:** None required.

**Web site:** *National Public Radio* (NPR) (http://www.npr.org)

---

**Format:** Satellite Link

**Subject:** Satellite Town Meetings (Education News Parents Can Use)

**Idea:** A variety of topics is covered in the U.S. Department of Education's *Satellite Town Meetings* and *Education News Parents Can Use.* Whether you choose to receive your programming through satellite link (or through Webcasts), there are many topics that are of interest to school staff members. "After-School and Summer Programs: Helping Kids Get Smart and Stay Safe" is an example of a topic that will be of interest to many of your schools.

**Vendor:** Satellite television provider or Internet Service Provider.

**Web site:** *Education News Parents Can Use* (http://ed.gov/offices/OIIA/television/index.html)

---

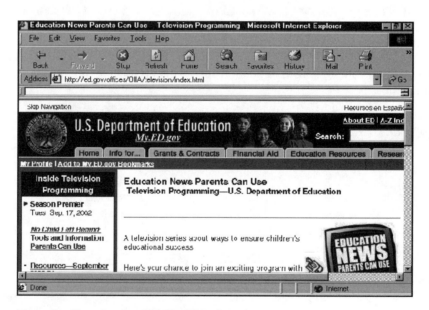

*Education News Parents Can Use* **Web site:**
**http://ed.gov/offices/OIIA/television/index.html**

---

**Format:** Television

**Subject:** School Board Policy

**Idea:** Many times, paraprofessionals are asked to implement (or enforce) school board policies without actually having the needed background for understanding the policies. What are the local district's policies that pertain to your school's use of television? Are there only certain types of television viewing (such as instructional television) that are permitted?

**Vendor:** None required.

**Web site:** Is your district's school board policy provided online?

_____

**Format:** Videoconference

**Subject:** Professional Development for Paraprofessionals

**Idea:** Videoconferencing (whether for a group of paraprofessionals who are viewing a Web-based videoconference or using videoconferencing software) offers tremendous potential for short training segments, whether within the district or within the state. Is there a particular area of training that paraprofessionals need in your school? District, state, or university personnel will probably be positive about helping you to define, plan, and implement a training session that will benefit many. Do you need a model for this type of project? Try your local university's community education service or *Educational Outreach at the University of South Florida (USF)*.

**Vendor:** Your local videoconferencing service provider.

**Web site:** *Educational Outreach at USF* (http://www.outreach.usf.edu/)

_____

# *Conclusion*

Distance learning technologies are becoming more plentiful and user-friendly. Public acceptance of technology is so great that school districts and state boards of education, along with the support of the U.S. Department of Education, are providing more funding opportunities for classrooms than ever before. The limit today, it seems, is not the technology or the support funding, but our imaginations. How do we envision students learning with new technologies and how can we facilitate this process to encourage students to go beyond our traditional learning bounds? If we have not ourselves experienced the power of distance learning technologies within our own curricula, how will we be able to convince students of the opportunities? The key may lie in the creativity of not only the student or the teacher, but in the creativity of the educational system and the support of all members of the school community (Intrator 1999).

Regardless of the distance learning technology used, teachers will wish to use a variety of components so that their students become more experienced with different learning modalities. Additionally, teachers will want to vary the nature of instruction and assignment, again to provide variety, keeping ever aware of ways to develop higher-order thinking skill among students. One method of developing the skills of organization, synthesis, analysis, and evaluation is through projects (Henry 1994, 49). By leading students through the process of developing projects, students will gain competencies including self-direction, inventiveness, problem-solving skills, integrative skills, decision-making skills, and interpersonal communication skills (Henry 1994, 49). Through projects, teachers encourage students to develop independent learning skills required for lifelong learning.

Management of distance learning activities will become an area of focus for educators who are monitoring the development of courses and the technologies that impact them. How can you contribute to this effort?

1. Keep notes on the practices that you are following to make your distance learning experiences the best you can.

2. Meet with other distance learning teachers to share ideas and resources.

3.   Offer to cooperate in course and curriculum development models that can be used throughout your district.

4.   Jointly monitor technology and media issues, their developments, costs, and budgeting impact.

5.   Evaluate your efforts regularly. Communicate these evaluations to your administrators and school board members.

6.   Contribute to your professional literature. Submit articles on your best practices and consider compiling handbooks for publication. Know that these publications will always need to be updated due to the development of the technology, but consider sharing these publications online.

Recognize that you do not have to totally redesign your curriculum to adapt it to the distance or online environment. If this were the case, it would take many of us a long time before we could ever offer distance learning activities. Ideas on converting existing courses involve planning, transferring existing materials into new formats, learning to use the supporting technologies, and evaluating the experience (Carlson 1999). Harrison (1999) provides a summary that includes the stages of analyzing, designing, developing, testing and improving, implementing, and evaluating. Most importantly, realize that the first distance learning experiences are not going to be flawless. This is definitely a "learning-by-doing" process. Distance courses evolve and develop in concert with the growth and development of the instructor's skills and understanding of distance learning skills and concepts.

Regardless of the medium, regardless of the level of interactivity, keep the contact interpersonal (Young 2000a). Students, whether PreK–12 or adult, distance or not, want to know that the teacher is in tune with their learning. Teachers can ensure this by directly communicating class processes and expectations. For example, because of class sizes and e-mail volume, teachers may not be able to respond to all students within twenty-four hours. Although this is highly recommended, students will accept other response time frames, if these response times are clearly communicated by the teacher at the beginning of the class. Look for these types of tips in the literature, such as an early manual, *Managing Distance Education Courses* (Houdek 1990), that is organized into chapters on recruitment (of instructors), orientation, supporting the course development process, supporting teaching at a distance, and evaluation. Perhaps you will develop and publish your distance learning successes in a manual for all of us to share!

# *References*

Barker, Bruce O. "Technological Delivery Systems and Applications for K–12 Instruction in Rural Schools." In *Rural Education: Issues and Practice*, edited by Alan J. DeYoung. New York: Garland Publishing, 1991.

Barker, Bruce O., and Robert F. Hall. "Distance Education in Rural Schools: Technologies and Practice." *Journal of Research in Rural Education* 10, no. 2 (1994): 126–28.

Baron, Joshua D., and Mercedes M. McKay. "Designing and Delivering an Online Course for K–12 Educators." *T.H.E. Journal* 28, no. 9 (2001): 68–75.

"Beaver College Changes Oft-Derided Name to Arcadia University," 20 November 2000, *CNN.Com*. (http://www.cnn.com/2000/US/11/20/embarrassingbeaver.ap/).

Brolin, Donn E., Iva Dean Cook, and Stephen O'Keefe. "Going the Distance with Life Centered Career Education." *Rural Special Education Quarterly* 13, no. 1 (1994): 64–67.

Carlson, Rosemary. "Migrating Your Course to the Online Environment." *Syllabus* 13, no. 2 (1999): 20–24.

Colavecchio, Shannon. "Virtual School May Be Option for Adult Education." *Palm Beach Post* (8 January 2002): 1B.

"Enforcement of COPA Barred for Now, Government Appeals." *Freedom to Read Foundation News* 23, no. 4/24, no. 1 (1999). (http://www.ftrf.org/vol23no4vol24no1.html#3).

Harrison, Nigel. *How to Design Self-Directed and Distance Learning: A Guide for Creators of Web-Based Training, Computer-Based Training, and Self-Study Materials.* New York: McGraw-Hill, 1999.

Heller, Norma. *Technology Connections for Grades 3–5: Research Projects and Activities.* Englewood, CO: Libraries Unlimited, 1998.

Henry, Jane. *Teaching Through Projects.* London: Kogan Page, 1994.

Intrator, Sam M. "Leonardo at the Keyboard: Encouraging Creative Thought Through Networked Computers." *Knowledge Quest* 28, no. 2 (1999): 41–42.

Kochery, Timothy S. "Providing Inservice Teachers with a 'TICKET' to Digital Delivery Systems." *TechTrends* 44, no. 4 (2000): 21–25.

Lansu, Angelique L. E., Wilfried P. M. F. Ivens, and Hans G. K. Hummel. "Distance Education in Soil Science: Reaching the Nontraditional Student." In *Soil Science Education: Philosophy and Perspectives*, edited by Phillippe Baveye, Walter J. Farmer, and Terry J. Logan. Madison, WI: Soil Science Society of America, 1994.

Mallory, James R. "Developing Accessible Distance Learning Instruction for Special Needs Students in Education and Industry." In *Competition Connection Collaboration* (Report of the Annual Conference on Distance Teaching and Learning, 6–8 August 1997, Madison, WI). ERIC ED 413 870.

McCollum, Kelly. "Bill Gates Looks Ahead to the Era of 'Generation I.'" *The Chronicle of Higher Education*, 29 October 1999. (http://chronicle.com/free/99/10/99102902t.htm) (5 March 2000).

Willis, Barry. *Strategies for Teaching at a Distance.* ERIC Digest. Syracuse, NY: ERIC Clearinghouse on Information Resources, 1992. ERIC ED 351 008. (http://ericir.syr.edu/plweb-cgi/fastweb?getdoc+ericdb2+ericdb+931129+0+wAAA+%28Willis,Barry%29%26AND%26%28073%29%26%3Apublication_type) (10 January 2002).

Young, Jeffrey R. "Advice for the Online Instructor: Keep It Interpersonal." *The Chronicle of Higher Education*, 11 January 2000a. (http://chronicle.com/free/2000/01/2000011101u.htm) (28 January 2000).

———. "Virtual Universities Dream of Fight Songs and Tournaments—Online, of Course." *The Chronicle of Higher Education*, 24 January 2000b. (http://chronicle.com/free/2000/01/2000012401u.htm) (28 January 2000).

Young, Terrance E., Jr. "But What About Me? Making Education Work for Students with Learning Differences." *Knowledge Quest* 27, no. 5 (1999): 50–52.

## Chapter 6

# Support for Interactive Distance Learning Activities

The National Center for Education Statistics completed a study (1999) on *Teachers' Feelings of Preparedness* (http://www.nces.ed.gov/pubsearch/pubsinfo.asp?pubid=2000003) and found that the majority surveyed (80 percent) did not feel prepared to integrate technology into the classroom. If you were to take an informal survey of teachers in your school, do you think that results would be similar? The Milken Exchange (now known as the *Milken Family Foundation* [http://www.mff.org/edtech/]) and the *International Society for Technology in Education* (ISTE [http://www.iste.org]) completed a joint project (1999) that evaluated teacher response on a study and likewise found that teachers felt ill prepared for integrating technology into the classroom curriculum. This feeling of lack of preparation is especially an issue among many female teachers. A study conducted by the University of California (*Edupage*, 1 January 2001) stated that, among freshman females, only 23.2 percent thought their computer skills were above average as compared to 46.4 percent of the males. This estimation of computer skills seems to be reflected in the low number of females that pursue studies in computer science and information technology (*Edupage*, 12 April 2000) that was found in a study report issued by the *American Association of University Women* (http://www.aauw.org/2000/techsavvy.html).

However, even though some teachers feel that they do not have the ability to integrate technology into the curriculum, they must begin to rely upon local school expertise to support the development of these skills and activities. Some claim that during the first decade of the new millennium, the United States will need over 2.2 million new teachers, but if the claim that "less than half of the nation's teacher preparation institutions require students to design and deliver instruction using technology" is accurate, teachers will not be ready to show students how to use technology (CEO Forum 2000, 1). Also, remember that this finding does not even account for the need for technology training among current teachers.

Sometimes, however, we all need that extra push to get us to explore the technology support that is available. One of the ways that students mention receiving this push has been the use of e-mail for the distribution of daily notices, such as absentee lists or announcements. The use of school Web pages in media centers has also been an incentive for some teachers to get online and use technology.

Like any other learning activity, interactive distance learning requires full support of the school community to be successful. Much of this support is already present in your school, in the form of personnel, equipment, materials, the school community, and community businesses. This chapter presents an overall description of how this support can be optimized and organized to support learning. If you do not know the name of a distance learning contact for your school or district, keep reading for ideas on how to identify a resource to help you (or refer back to Chapter 4, Section A. Public Schools).

If you are new to your school, or just new to interactive distance learning, the first task will be to identify the personnel who can help you get started with your distance learning activities. Start with your principal. Ask if a faculty or staff member has been charged with leading or supporting distance learning activities. If you discover that an in-house employee is responsible for leading distance learning activities, your search for support will be a bit easier. If, on the other hand, your school does not have a personnel member who is charged with this activity, find out the name of a district personnel member who is. Obviously, if your principal cannot think of a district-level person who is responsible for distance learning, then this activity is not at the forefront of district priorities. It could be that a staff member at another school has the lead responsibility, and you can contact that person with your questions. This staff responsibility should be determined by contacting the curriculum support person for your district. (Ask who has attended the statewide conferences for technology or distance learning, or if any distance learning reports have to be filed with state offices. This may lead you to your support person.) For those who live within easy travel distance from Orlando, Florida, the *Florida Educational Technology Conference* (http://www.fetc.org) offers a wide variety of presentations, group sessions, and vendor displays on current topics relating to technology applications in education. As with other conferences and publications, distance learning sessions are on the rise!

If no single staff member with distance learning responsibilities can be identified, consider becoming that support person in your school or district. Begin by finding out if other teachers, including educational technologists, media specialists, and administrators, have an interest in exploring distance learning opportunities. Contact your state department of education to get the name of the distance learning specialist. Speak with this specialist and ask for the names, dates, and places of statewide conferences and meetings on distance learning. Also, ask if there are state-sponsored resources online, such as chatrooms and listservs, that provide a meeting place for others with interests similar to yours. Try top-down searching, starting with national-level organizations, such as the American Association for School Librarians (AASL), Association for Educational Communications and Technology (AECT), or listserv groups, such as *EdTech*.

## *Learning Possibility*

For current subscription directions to *EdTech*, access the listserv's subscription Web page (http://h-net2.msu.edu/~edweb/list.html). Sign on to the list and monitor activities for a while. Observe the variety of topics that are discussed each day. For back issues of *EdTech*, you can visit the list's archive site at *AskERIC* (http://askeric.org/plweb-cgi/fastweb?searchform+listservs). Also, don't overlook Usenet news groups, such as *alt.education.distance*, which can lead you to district or state contacts. The alt.education.distance news group receives regular postings from recognized experts in the field. (As with all news groups that you join, read the messages without responding for a week or two before you post your own comments or queries so that you get a sense of appropriate topics and so that you don't begin a discussion of a topic that was just recently completed. Searching through the last month of the news group's past messages is the best way to get up to speed on what the members' current areas of interest are.) This news group often offers as many as fifty messages per day, so be prepared for heavy traffic. Additionally, *alt.education.distance* is an unmoderated news group. This means that everything that is submitted by subscribers is posted to the group, without any screening by a moderator. Until you are more familiar with this news group, or any other news group, assume that you are reading messages written by adults, for adults. As you read either of these services, prepare a folder for saving many of the great ideas that you will read to help you as you develop your interactive distance learning environment.

## *Learning Possibility*

Another type of online information about distance learning and technology is the electronic newsletter. (Think of this as a one-way listserv that is delivered to your e-mailbox at regular intervals.) *Edupage* is a thrice-weekly update that highlights current trends in computing, information technology, and related areas, such as interactive distance learning. *Edupage* tends to be geared for the postsecondary audience and market, but because of its condensed nature and reference only to high-quality media, it is still a useful resource for any educator interested in distance learning. *Edupage* is translated into multiple languages, including Estonian, French, Greek, Hungarian, Korean, Portuguese, and Spanish (http://www.educause.edu/pub/edupage/edupage .html), reflecting a broad international interest in technology. Many foreign-language educators will find *Edupage* to be a valuable resource for current information of interest to many students.

There is a lot of support for the distance education teacher in the form of e-mail, Usenet news groups, and listservs. This information comes in messages in an easy-to-use e-mailbox that can be downloaded and reviewed offline, when it is convenient, in delayed time.

# *Section A. By the Educational Technologist*

The job description of the educational technologist may be constantly evolving in your school or district. The role of the educational technologist was commonly designated to provide technical assistance to teachers and media specialists who were overwhelmed with schoolwide responsibilities for networking. Thus, the role of the educational technologist may range from being the school's sole network administrator, to having full teaching responsibilities in a lab setting, in addition to being the school's network manager and chief troubleshooter for all computer problems.

Some states and districts have not yet defined the position of educational technologist, or the certification requirements for that position. As a result, this position in your district may not be filled. Because the position of the educational technologist may not even be present in your particular school or district, or is yet to be defined and implemented, much of the content in this section may apply to the school library media specialist or a special teacher on assignment.

## *Learning Possibility*

Can you find the teacher certification requirements for your state? If so, can you determine if "educational technology" is a certified area? Which degree(s) is required? Is only technical expertise required, or are foundations courses in education included in the recommended course list? Is this position compensated similarly (more or less) to that of instructional positions? In your district, does the educational technologist also provide technician services?

When thinking about positions for educational technologists, consider that currently students that graduate with a B.S. in computer science can immediately enter industry positions paying $30,000 and more, often with stock options. Though a degree in computer science may not be required for the position of educational technologist in your district, do you think that the position of educational technologist is compensated so that schools can compete with high-paying jobs in the computer industry? Quite simply, PreK–12 computing has become too pervasive and too sophisticated to allow it to be an add-on responsibility for one or two teachers or media specialists who enjoy working with technology, whether as a supplemented or noncompensated activity.

## *Learning Possibility*

Use commonly accepted definitions of educational technology provided through professional organizations, such as the Association for Educational Communications and Technology (AECT), or by federal offices, such as the Educational Resources Information Clearinghouse (ERIC). The ERIC Clearinghouse on Information and Technology sets definitions for this field in a digest, *The Field of Educational Technology: Update 1995—A Dozen Frequently Asked Questions* (1995). ERIC Digests provide definitions, information about the professional activities, organizations, preparations, publications, requirements, etc. All digests are quickly available online and indexed in the *ERIC Database* (http://ericir.syr.edu) and at the *U.S. Department of Education* Web site (http://www.ed.gov/databases/ERIC_Digests/index/) or through the ERIC toll-free number (800-464-9107). For further updating, the *Clearinghouse on Information Technology* (http://www.ericit.org/) provides a listserv archive for *EdTech*, a listserv for educational technology (http://www.ericit.org /edtechdiscussion.shtml). Take advantage of this resource! (All ERIC Clearinghouses are linked at the *U.S. Department of Education* Web site [http://www.eric.ed.gov/].)

---

# How to Offer and Organize Support

As the educational technologist, you have the responsibility of communicating your role in supporting other teachers in your school, as defined by your district and your supervisor. Based on how your role is defined, you must:

1. Communicate to your school's staff members exactly what you can do to help them with distance learning activities. Create brochures, posters, signs, and Web sites describing the services you offer to staff members. Ask to speak at faculty, parent-teacher, and school improvement meetings about your role and level of service.

2. Establish a support or advisory committee that assists you with developing services and further communicating your role throughout the school.

3. Provide in-service training opportunities where you:

   • Demonstrate the use of software products that have distance learning applications.

   • Explain how and where online connections can be made at school and home.

## *Learning Possibility*

What better way is there for students (in this case, teachers) to learn than by viewing the modeling of the desired outcome? If the outcome is the ability to conceptualize, organize, and execute a demonstrative PowerPoint presentation, you might develop your presentation materials so that they can be delivered both live and by the Web. Examples of Web presentations that could be used for student or teacher training can be found at *NetSquirrel.com* (http://www.netsquirrel.com/classroom/) or at *Merlot* (http://www.merlot.org). (Search by topic to locate the presentations that you would like to use. Don't forget that the Merlot resources have been developed, and contributed, by in-service teachers.)

Did you also know that the Massachusetts Institute of Technology (MIT) is promoting the sharing of course materials (including notes, reading lists, syllabi, etc.) through its OpenCourseWare (OCW) Project? What does this mean to you? If you are involved in curriculum development projects, for example, you could take advantage of reviewing the bibliographies of a variety of courses (e.g., *Children's Culture* [http://www.media.mit.edu/groups/gn/children_culture /bibliography.html]). Or, if you have aspiring students who would like to know what to expect from a college course, they can also review these materials. During the next few years, it is estimated that materials for hundreds of MIT courses will be added to this online project.

Wouldn't it be wonderful if the PreK–12 schools of the United States collaborated in a similar project, by placing quality learning materials online? This idea goes beyond just sharing lesson plans. What about adding handouts, video presentations, multimedia projects, audio clips, etc., in one place, organized by curriculum topic and by grade? Could you start the project by posting materials used just in your school? Could this be extended to other schools in your feeder pattern, in your district, or in your state? Imagine the possibilities!

---

## *Learning Possibility*

Teachers often hear the term "network," but they do not understand exactly what the term means. If you don't understand your school's network, ask your technologist to show you or to create a schematic of your network. If you are creating a schematic, use handouts, such as the ERIC Digest on "Local Area Networks for K–12 Schools" (Lederman 1995). Share this information with your teachers by using these visuals to point out functions and related terms at each junction of the network. Ask the teachers to take notes and be able to explain how the network impacts their classrooms. What are the benefits of having teachers use visuals to communicate about their network? We are always hearing that the network is "down." What does that mean to a nonnetworking teacher? Help the teacher understand where the problem might be and how he or she might contribute to the health of the network. For example, if teachers are aware that wiring is a problem, they can teach their students why it is important to avoid touching the wiring. If you are fortunate enough to have a wireless network, how can teachers arrange their rooms so that connections are more predictable?

4. Provide outreach training opportunities for parents where you:
   - Explain how to set up a home workstation.
   - Demonstrate online services.

5. Sponsor a student , teacher, or parent organization for distance learning activities. Find out how students are using online resources to get a better understanding of the skills that need to be taught and developed.

6. Provide hardware and networking support.

What are the physical resources needed to facilitate distance learning? As with the role of the educational technologist, this is a moving target, depending on the level and frequency of distance learning activities in your school. However, consider making hardware and networking support transparent in this process by allowing for as much flexibility as possible. This can be accomplished by configuring equipment so that individual, small group, and large group distance learning activities can occur throughout the school. Ideally, each teacher needs online access in each classroom for at least one workstation, but consider the following:

1. Is there a place where a small group of students (three or four) can work on a project online?

2. Is a lab available to accommodate your largest classroom with simultaneous online access?

3. Where can a classroom have access to a speakerphone with a long-distance connection?

4. Where can a classroom have access to long-distance service and online access?

5. Where can a classroom have access to a satellite downlink and online access?

6. What are the types of furniture that are needed to support these kinds of configurations? Consideration must be given to:
   - **Size.** What are the differences in chair and table sizes for students at different grade levels? What are the considerations for furniture sizes for students with different abilities? Be sure to consult teachers for input on chair and table heights. Consider the need for flexibility in furniture size for future purchases.
   - **Portability.** Will distance learning systems and setups have to travel within the school? To portable classrooms? What size casters will be needed to move to different locations? Are power strips built into traveling systems? Are there fire code specifications for power strips in different locations? Some districts have developed "labs on wheels," using vans and buses that take technology to multiple sites.
   - **Configurations.** Will students be working individually, in pairs, in small groups, in large groups?
   - **Security.** Are safety straps included with the systems? Are power strips out of the way of little fingers and objects? Can equipment be locked down? Does the design of the moving system prevent materials from sliding off? How can sharp corners be protected? Are cart bases wide enough to keep from tipping? Are connections welded, or otherwise reinforced, to support heavy equipment? PLEASE: Verify your district safety guidelines for student transportation of equipment. Most districts forbid having students transport heavy equipment, such as televisions and monitors.

The question becomes, can the school be flexible and accommodate:

1. Classes of various sizes?

2. Connections of varying numbers and types?

3. Different equipment types?

The educational technologist might have the lead responsibility for not only accommodating current requests, but also for anticipating future computer and equipment and access needs. Many schools have met this need by designating certain classrooms as multimedia classrooms that can be reconfigured to include the latest components.

Affordable wireless technology will make access and labs less of an issue as the technology develops so that we can provide students and teachers with laptops that can access networks from a variety of settings on the school campus. The increase of the wireless technology, along with personal, portable computers and PDAs, also holds the promise for increased connectivity in the workplace and throughout society as we are able to access information and services (*Edupage*, 7 July 2001).

Staying on top of developments, such as Internet access, seems to be a full-time job, but the educational technologist has to be a quick study in many advances. For example, ADSL (asynchronous digital subscriber loop), popularly called DSL (digital subscriber line), is the telephone company equivalent to cable modems. DSL offers dedicated online access, currently at rates of 1.5 million bits per second. In other words, online images reach you in a fraction of the time that they currently take with a dial-up modem. DSL shares existing telephone lines and still offers you the capability of being able to be online and on the telephone at the same time. Some companies are including Internet Service Provider (ISP) access with the DSL service, along with free promotional modems. You know that information on these services can be searched online, but how will you become informed of the next technological development?

The educational technologist might have teaching responsibilities in the classroom or lab, such as teaching students to use applications software. In this case, the technologist also needs lab tools that provide teacher control of computers. If the technologist is expected to have teaching and curricular responsibilities, it is critical to locate and implement existing district curriculum guidelines for technology instruction. If you do not have clear direction for your curricular responsibilities, here are suggestions for you to follow:

1. Ask your principal to identify district personnel with responsibility for technology curriculum.

2. Participate in district curriculum development activities.

3. Find out how technology instruction is being implemented in similar (and feeder) schools in your district.

4. Review national technology standards for consistency and support with district standards. The National Educational Technology Standards (NETS) evolved through a cooperative effort between Apple Computer, International Society for Technology in Education (ISTE), the Milken Exchange on Education Technology, National Aeronautics and Space Administration (NASA), and the U.S. Department of Education. Supported by professional organizations, such as the National Council for Accreditation of Teacher Education (NCATE), the NETS gives direction for teacher competencies and encourages the preparation of students to become independent learners that can work with a variety of media and formats to process information and solve problems, while collaborating and cooperating with other learners in ethical ways. With lifelong implications for functioning in a technological world, the NETS frameworks are divided by grade level (PreK–2, 3–5, 6–8, and 9–12) to include performance indicators, performance objectives, and examples of scenarios that illustrate these implementations. A significant development in the area of technology education, the NETS must be communicated to all school personnel with technology education responsibilities, in addition to parents and students who need to understand that instruction in these

areas is to be woven into existing curricula in order to be effective. Copies of the NETS can be ordered or downloaded through *ISTE* (http://www.iste.org/standards/index.html).

5. In addition to national technology and state standards, there are professional curriculum standards that have been approved by professional organizations. For example, if you are an English teacher, your national association is the National Council of Teachers of English (NTCE [http://www.ncte.org/]). Examples of other national associations include:

- *National Council for the Social Studies* (http://www.ncss.org/)
- *National Council of Teachers of Mathematics* (http://www.nctm.org/)
- *National Science Teachers Association* (http://www.nsta.org/)

Be sure to review your national professional standards, as you are reviewing your technology standards. For help with the actual integration of these standards with your curriculum, seek assistance from your colleagues or administrators. Professional literature, such as *A Guide to Integrating Technology Standards into the Curriculum* (Churma 1999), is helpful for actual samples of lesson plans that incorporate the standards.

Technologists will also need to make students aware of the ergonomics of technology settings if technology-related injuries are to be avoided. Simple instructions, such as do not lean against the mouse to avoid wrist strain, might help students and teachers avoid repetitive injuries.

As part of the professional responsibilities, the educational technologist must provide leadership, in practice and policy, for teaching students and teachers about the ethical use of technology. For example, students, of any age, that are interested in music know that it is possible to download songs, known as MP3 files. Many college and university technology departments are grappling with this issue as their network traffic is being slowed down by students that are collecting songs to burn onto their own CDs. Some students are also loading these files onto Web pages, which is easier for copyright and school agents to track. As a result, the question for the educational technologist becomes whether to filter the sites that offer illegal files, such as these.

Many educators will argue that students do not need to have their sites filtered, but that the students need to learn to evaluate information for themselves. Although this is an arguable position, the reality remains that many educators do not have the choice in certain institutions. If the choice is to filter the sites, you will have to be on your toes! Everyone has heard about the termination of the Napster site, but there are other sites that were reported to be more difficult to shut down. Some of these sites are Gnutella networks that operate off of multiple computers, as opposed to a single server (*Edupage*, 2 September 2001).

## *Learning Possibility*

To see what the fuss over MP3 is about, check out the *MP3Bot Search Engine* (http://www.informatch.com/mediabot/) and listen to a file. Can you think of a constructive, educational use for this site? Remember, some MP3 files are legal and accessible and are there for your use in creating interactive distance learning opportunities for your students.

## *Teaching Possibility*

Provide students with the experience of evaluating Web sites. Using an informational site, such as *The Good, the Bad and the Ugly or, Why It's a Good Idea to Evaluate Web Sources* (http://lib.nmsu.edu/instruction/eval.html), can provide group practice and background on the evaluation of sites. Next, allow students to evaluate some sites preselected by you. After the evaluation, work with students to compare findings. Listen carefully to how the students perceive the Web sites. Next, explain to students why the Web site is, or isn't, preferred. Help them to understand which type of site you want them to use for assignments and for searching. Explain your reasons so that they can apply these criteria as they are evaluating other Web sites.

---

Most educational technologists will only be asked to focus on technology operations, but some may also be asked to seek or monitor funding. The Federal Communications Commission's (FCC) Universal Service Fund (E-rate) offers telecommunications services subsidies, ranging from 20 percent to 90 percent (based on location and economic levels of the institutions), to public schools and libraries throughout the country. Applications that describe the services and projected costs for which the subsidies are requested must be submitted through the district or state, or directly to the *Universal Service Administrative Company* (formerly the Schools and Libraries Corporation) (http://www.universalservice.org/).

Always reaching to provide high-quality services economically, the educational technologist may be faced with questions about how to provide home services reasonably. Although it would not be a responsibility to advise personnel on purchases, the educational technologist will want to keep informed of the consumer developments, such as WebTV services or *iBrow* (http://www.boundless.com/ibrow/), that provide online-only connections. The technologist will find that these Internet options have shown varying acceptance in the home market. At the time this book went to press, some of these companies offered free school access. However, caveat emptor certainly applies! By the time connection fees, monthly fees, and taxes are paid, it is often more cost effective to purchase a computer and pay for monthly Internet service through a provider than to accept a free piece of equipment. The educational technologist will be sure to actually compute and compare yearlong, out-of-pocket costs of all technologies to answer "Are you really saving money by foregoing that computer?"

## Providing Software Support

Software selection should, of course, precede decisions on providing software support, but selection decisions are not always made at the school level. If you do make some selection decisions at the school level, approach these decisions through a team effort. Include your media specialist who is well trained in the selection of media, the classroom teacher who will be implementing the software, a few students who will be using the software, and a parent or other objective viewer who can point out elements that the others might overlook. When selecting software for the distance learning classroom, keep in mind that the element of motivation is important when making decisions on how the product is used (Bork 2000). For example, how does your product motivate students? How does it encourage students to respond and how does it respond to the students? How does the product keep the learning process active?

The technologist will need several resources to recommend to teachers who are involved in the software selection process. The ERIC Digest, *Seven Steps to Responsible Software Selection* (http://www.ed.gov/databases/ERIC_Digests/ed382157.html), will direct teachers to additional sources, such as Web sites and listservs that pertain to the selection process. This ERIC Digest includes a description of the steps in the selection process, including the following:

1. Analyze needs.

2. Specify requirements.

3. Identify promising software.

4. Read relevant reviews.

5. Preview software.

6. Make recommendations.

7. Get post-use feedback.

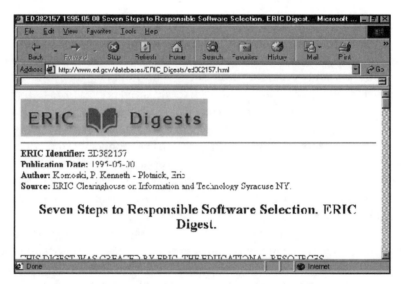

**Seven Steps to Responsible Software Selection** Web site:
**http://www.ed.gov/databases/ERIC_Digests/ed382157.html**

Be sure to also review the *Regional Alliance Schools Network* (http://ra.terc.edu) (Connecticut, Maine, Massachusetts, New Hampshire, New York, Rhode Island, and Vermont), a Web site that indexes teacher-produced reviews of software (http://ra.terc.edu/SoftwareEval/SoftwareEvalHome.cfm). The Southern Regional Educational Board offers *EvaluTech* (http://www.evalutech.sreb.org/), a searchable database of software. Another collection of review information, based on nominations of software by teachers in Florida, is the *Florida Educational Software Catalog* (http://www.itrc.ucf.edu/doecat). A benefit of the *Florida Educational Software Catalog* is that the software is keyed to multiple intelligences. For Florida teachers who want to use software that directly relates to state curriculum standards, the catalog also includes the identification of the Sunshine State Standards that each software package addresses, along with state bid prices for each product.

The educational technologist will help support teachers and parents in distance learning activities by offering software review sites. Some of these review sites might include:

1. *PEP: Parents, Educators, Publishers* (http://microweb.com/pepsite/)

2.  *SuperKids Educational Software Review* (http://www.superkids.com/aweb/pages/reviews /reviews.shtml)

3.  *TechLEARNING Product Guide* (http://www.schemazoo.net/jaguar/tmag_i/)

Next, keep in mind that references to high-quality Web sites of updated information will be useful for those who are starting out with online services. A few of these sources come to mind:

1.  *Blue Web'n Update* (http://www.kn.pacbell.com/wired/bluewebn) has provided quality resources consistently since 1995. With a keen sense of what teachers, media specialists, and technologists need to support learning, *Blue Web'n* is definitely a resource to explore.

2.  *Internet Resources Newsletter* (http://www.hw.ac.uk/libWWW/irn/irn.html), issued monthly since October 1994 through the Heriot-Watt University Library (Edinburgh, Scotland), notes high-quality, international sites.

3.  *The Scout Report* (http://wwwscout.cs.wisc.edu/report/sr/current/index.html) notes new Web sites useful to educators. Issued weekly since April 1994, it is one of the more senior online resources. Information is both reliable and targeted to the educator.

Due to their experiences with a variety of software packages and their abilities to quickly evaluate and learn new software applications, the educational technologist is ever aware of the problems that software design can bring to the classroom. Some experts note how the poor design of some software packages will have later impact on the learning experience, whether at school or home, because the software is too complex and the design itself does not allow a process to check errors (*Educom Review* 1999, 36). With the added incentive to get software products on the market as quickly as possible, many stages of the design process are overlooked.

Another trend that technologists will be monitoring is offering software applications online through Web access and through application service providers, rather than providing the applications off of the in-house server. For distance learning activities that often require the student and teacher to participate from a variety of locations, this is an ideal way to provide just-in-time software delivery and software support that are compatible with the resources that your school already uses. Will this trend also offer potential savings through a leased software arrangement? Monitor these software delivery changes through your listserv messages, professional meetings and readings, and Web sites.

## Providing Technical Support

The educational technologist would be wise to develop an arsenal of directional resources for students and teachers who wish to learn independently. For example, development of Web pages is a common activity in many schools, but the in-house expertise can be spotty. Through texts or online materials, tutorials are helpful for getting would-be Web page developers started (Tennant 1998).

Many online resources are available to the teacher who wants to create a Web page. First, direct teachers *to John December's Web Development* page (http://www.december.com/web/develop.html) for planning and development ideas to consider before posting a Web page online. For advanced users, such as the educational technologist, remember that there is a plethora of sites, such as the *Free Webmaster Tools* (http://www.free-webmaster-tools.com/). Some of these sites have more advertising than others, but many sites, such as this one, provide short, easy-to-understand articles for the beginner, such as *The Psychology of Color and Internet Marketing* (Renovato n.d.).

While you are on the task of developing Web materials, be sure that you help students and teachers monitor the quality of Web pages, based on their accessibility for users with disabilities. Federal mandates for accessible Web design include the Americans with Disabilities Act (ADA), Public Law 102-569, Section 508, the Assistive Technology Act of 1998, and the Telecommunications Act (Sprague 1999).

## *Learning Possibility*

Ask students and teachers to evaluate sites for users with disabilities. Access *Bobby* (http://www.cast.org/bobby/) at the Center for Applied Special Technology for guidelines, as well as an evaluation of your school's Web site. Is your school's site accessible? What are the pros and cons of your site? What could be done to enhance its accessibility? Are other teachers and administrators aware of how your Web site needs to be enhanced?

Beyond the scope of Web development, many technologists are being called upon to work with teachers in the actual design of courses. If so, it is important to determine whether you will function in the role of instructional designer or technical developer. Generally, it is safe to assume that in a PreK–12 school the teacher, or content expert, will function as the instructional designer and will make decisions on the content, pedagogy, instructional design, and preparation of content. The technologist may assist as the technical developer, offering suggestions on the technical aspects of development that address software, the interface, and the formative evaluation of the instruction (Meyen, Tangen, and Lian 1999). Especially with the increasing use of online teaching systems, such as BlackBoard, Embanet, or WebCT, agreement on who will do which part of the development will increase efficiency of the development, not to mention saving quite a few ruffled professional feathers.

Regarding the issue of instructional design, is there support for instructional design at the district level? Does a graduate of an academic program in instructional design provide this support? Are courses being developed based on basic principles of instructional design? These are questions that will be addressed with the increasing number of distance learning courses. Awareness of the instructional design process will help to ensure the quality of the design of distance learning courses. For example, the designers provide a needs assessment for the course, the linking of instruction to curriculum standards, and formative and summative evaluations of the instruction that is designed (Foshay 2001).

For online information and tools, *The Virtual Internet Guide* continues to provide up-to-date sources that keeps the technologist informed (http://www.virtualfreesites.com/internet.html), as does *FREEPCTECH* (http://freepctech.com), which focuses on helping PC users through e-mail. You will start adding your favorite sources as suggestions to your faculty and administrators. Think about organizing these sources online to help everyone access them quickly.

## Educational and Professional Sources for the Educational Technologist

Plentiful sources exist that provide updated information on evaluating technology by specifications, along with recommendations for purchasing. Some of the sources are available as complimentary copy in paper and online format (*Mobile Computing* [http://www.mobilecomputing.com/]), while others are available in online copy only. Admittedly, some of these free magazines tend to be printed infomercials; however, they do provide basic information that can be passed to other instructors for free.

Before purchasing distance learning technology components, be sure to corroborate the specifications with another printed source, vendor source, or district purchasing agent. It never hurts to get a second opinion—but it can hurt if you don't!

For the educational technologist who never benefited from a degree in technology, online learning opportunities are available. Whether for a certificate or degree, institutions such as SREB and the Western Governors University, a cooperative effort among multiple states and institutions, offer set prices. Standardized testing and portfolio development are used to encourage high levels of performance, while providing students a way of blending work and experience into the process. More information on these networking and technology programs is available online (http://www.wgu.edu/wgu/smartcatalog/search_prog.asp). Be sure to evaluate the institution and its accreditation status to prevent wasting time and money with a fraudulent institution. Check with the accrediting body for your region about the accreditation status of the institution before you sign up to take your first course. Just because an institution has an impressive Web site doesn't mean it also has an impressive curriculum (*Edupage*, 3 January 2001).

## Learning Possibility

If you are working with high school students, be sure that they are familiar with the concept of accreditation. You may be teaching in an accredited school, and students need to know that this means that the school and staff have undergone an intensive review and have been found to offer a quality program. Teach students how to review the accreditation status of colleges before they apply. For example, if you live in New York, your regional accreditation body is the *Middle States Commission on Higher Education* (http://www .msache.org/).

An educational technologist has to be savvy about time management. One of the smartest ways of using time is to be sure to read publications that are comprehensive and current. Technologists that follow listservs, such as EdTech, usually find themselves connected to a resource that is responsive and timely. Another online source that is chock full of technology-related information is *eSchool News Online* (http://www.eschoolnews.org). One of the more long-lived online publications that consistently offer Web news that is readily usable in the classroom is *Blue Web'n* (http://www.kn.pacbell.com/wired/bluewebn). Not only does *Blue Web'n* offer a subscription service, it also indexes Web tutorials, activities, projects, unit plans, lesson plans, and references by subject and grade. High quality of recommended sites is assured by evaluation with a rubric (http://www.kn.pacbell.com/wired/bluewebn/rubric.html) that helps the evaluator to check for "format, content, and learner process" (Hyman 1998, 34). More rubrics for evaluating Web sites are online at *Evaluation Rubrics for Websites* (Loogootee Community Schools, Loogootee, Indiana) and (http://www.siec.k12.in.us/~west/online/eval.htm).

## Learning Possibility

Do you need to purchase software or other technology item and you just don't have the time to pore through a variety of catalogs? Try the *Google Catalog Search* (http://catalogs.google.com/). Just enter the name of a software package or other item, such as "Photoshop," and let this catalog search engine locate the online companies that offer the products you desire. Compare features and prices of the products.

By regularly scanning information on technology news, grants, and conferences that includes reports of national events, the technologist will be in a position to provide positive direction for the school's distance learning activities. Conferences to be considered include:

1. *Association for Educational Communications and Technology (AECT)* (http://www.aect.org)

2. *Conference on Distance Teaching and Learning* (http://www.uwex.edu/disted/conference/) (Although this conference has a college/university focus, there are some aspects that apply to the PreK–12 environment.)

3. *Florida Educational Technology Conference (FETC)* (http://www.fetc.org) (Even non-Florida educators can benefit from this low-cost conference that offers hundreds of sessions and vendor booths. One of the largest U.S. conferences for PreK–graduate students and educators, FETC is more than twenty years old! To extend conference activities throughout the year, read *FETConnections*, an online publication [http://www.fetc.org/fetcon/index.html], that provides articles on topics such as copyright, multimedia development, and technology in the classroom.)

4. *National Educational Computing Conference (NECC)* (http://www.neccsite.org/) (Does your schedule conflict with a conference? Even if you cannot attend a conference in real time, many conferences offer Web pages with searchable conference proceedings, copies of which are available either online or on CD-ROM. For other conferences related to technology and distance learning, search the *ERIC Calendar of Education-Related Conferences* [http://webprod.aspensys.com/education/ericconf/eric_cal/introduction.asp] for current offerings for you, other teachers, and administrators.)

# Section B. By the School Library Media Specialist

The role of the school library media specialist has undergone an incredible transition since the introduction of the personal computer into the PreK–12 school curriculum during the 1980s. Today, the school library media specialist works wonders by identifying great quantities of materials that are appropriate to subject areas at all grade levels. School library media specialists are professionally trained to collaborate with teachers to plan and develop quality learning activities, gathering multiple subject sources from sites in, and out of, your school. In fact, the school library media specialist may be the information specialist or curriculum expert in your school.

Because of the many areas that affect instruction through the school library media center, models of information literacy instruction have been developed that include the *Big6 Model* (http://big6.com), the Kuhthau Information Seeking Process Model, the Stripling/Pitts Research Process (Young 1999, 32), and the Handy 5 Model (Grover et al. 1999). Although some elements of similarity exist between the models, the Handy 5 Model includes a process evaluation that occurs between the teacher, the school library media specialist, and the student, which focuses on how well the student understood the process of solving the problem.

## Teaching Possibility

Ask your students to select their future jobs. What are the computing/technology skills that they will need to do this job today? Will these skills change for the future? What are the skills that will remain the same? List these skills with your students.

Many of you may have seen references to the terms "information literacy" and "information skills," in the context of how students must be "information literate" and skilled in locating information. Along with the recent revisions of national and state standards to reflect the integration of technology in the curriculum, such as the "Information Literacy Standards for Student Learning" from *Information Power: Building Partnerships for Learning* (AASL and AECT 1998), more media specialists have focused on teaching these skills in the media center, not as skills taught in isolation, but as skills taught within the context of subject matter curriculum. Focus on these information skills, in view of the curriculum, is critical to the success of today's student and the success of the distance learner (Spitzer, Eisenberg, and Lowe 1999).

## *Learning Possibility*

Go to the *American Association of School Librarians* (*AASL*) Web site (http://www.ala.org/aasl/ip_implementation.html) or *Learning Through the Library* (http://www.ala.org/aasl/learning) to locate other resources on information literacy. Review the *American Library Association*'s definition of "information literacy" (http://www.ala.org/acrl/nili/ilit1st.html). Are your students informationally literate? How can you address these literacy needs in your classroom? Can you target applications of specific interactive distance learning technologies that can help you meet these literacy needs?

Another source of regularly published online articles on information literacy and information skills (e.g., *Evaluating Information: An Information Literacy Challenge* [Fitzgerald 1999] [http://www.ala.org/aasl/SLMR/vol2/evaluating.html]) is *School Library Media Research* (http://www.ala.org/aasl/SLMR).

## *Teaching Possibility*

Ask your students to search for a future home to purchase, and have them base the decision on where to locate on the quality of the area's education system. Students can access *Money Magazine's Places Rated* information (http://pathfinder.com/money/bestplaces/) and search on the indicators "teacher:pupil ratio" and "spending per pupil." (This is located under "Detailed Search.")

In the absence of an educational technologist, the school library media specialist may be the school's support member who will assist with development and technical support of distance learning activities. In the spirit of *Information Power: Building Partnerships for Learning* (AASL and AECT 1998), the school library media specialist will be instrumental in helping the teacher to:

1. Plan the distance learning activity.

2. Schedule the activity.

3. Search for media to support the learning.

4. Provide additional materials through purchasing or interlibrary loan.

5.  Support and supplement teaching activities.

6.  Monitor technical aspects of the distance learning.

7.  Evaluate and revise the activity.

Due to the initial costs of development, support, and equipment or connection costs, it is especially important for the school library media specialist to be involved with the development of the distance learning activity. Let's assume that the distance learning modality has already been selected and that the distance participants have been identified, to be sure that all teachers and support personnel are involved in this planning process.

1.  Who will plan the activity?

    - Teachers
    - School library media specialists
    - Paraprofessionals
    - Students
    - Administrators
    - District personnel

2.  How will the planning take place?

    - Same or compatible time zones
        - In person
        - Online chat
        - By telephone (audiobridge)
        - By compressed video
        - Through teleconferencing or videoconferencing
    - Incompatible time or day zones
        - E-mail
        - Recorded audiocassette/CD or videocassette/DVD
        - Traditional correspondence

It is important to develop an understanding of the project. This can be accomplished by jointly developing a lesson plan with the teacher. As a team, the media specialist and the teacher should answer these questions:

1.  Who are the learners? Gather as much background information as possible so that you can accommodate as many learning abilities and styles as possible. If you are unfamiliar with the group, ask a guidance counselor or student's previous teacher for input. Remember that even though all students may not be perfectly suited for the type of learning presentation, it is important to guide students in learning how to use as many distance learning modalities as possible. Try to determine:

    - Age range
    - Grade levels
    - Ability levels
    - Reading-level range
    - Experience with distance learning

2.  What are the goals for the learning? Is the distance learning activity designed to provide appreciation, content, practice, or review? Is this an initial lesson or a follow-up lesson? Can you succinctly describe the learning activity and the desired outcome? Can you communicate your goal(s) in one or two sentences?

3.  What are the curriculum standards that will be addressed? Most districts require teachers to address the state's curriculum standards in lesson plans or other curriculum planning documents. Do you know how to locate these standards for your state?

Most districts and states have curriculum standards that apply to all subject areas, e.g., Florida uses the *Sunshine State Standards* (http://www.firn.edu/doe), Missouri has its *"Show Me" Content Standards* (http://www.dese.state.mo.us), Oklahoma follows the *Priority Academic Student Skills* (http://www.sde.state.ok.us/), New Mexico uses the *Content Standards and Benchmarks* (http://www.sde.state.nm.us/), Wyoming follows its *State Standards* (http://www.k12.wy.us/NCA/standards/), etc.

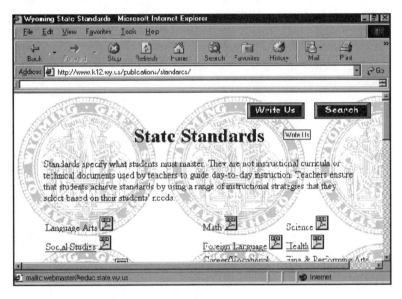

**Wyoming State Standards** Web site:
**http://www.k12.wy.us/NCA/standards/**

## *Learning Possibility*

Did you know that there are national education standards? You can view these at *Education World* (http://www.education-world.com/standards /national/index.shtml). This same site indexes state standards by subject area. Take a few seconds to link to your state's technology standards. (Note: Some states have not yet adopted technology standards.) If you are interested in comparing your state standards to those of another state, access *Achieve's Standards Database* (http://www.achieve.org/achieve.nsf/StandardsDatabase ?OpenForm) and do a side-by-side comparison of state standards, selected by subject criteria.

4. Develop your learning objectives. Be realistic when developing your objectives. Remember that it is better to fully accomplish one or two objectives than to try to achieve more than the students can accomplish during the given lesson, module, or unit. By developing specific learning objectives, you will answer:

- Who are your learners? (Be specific: Fifth-grade social studies students, twelfth-grade ceramics students, beginning teachers, etc.)

- What will your learners do as a result of the learning? (Be specific: "The learner will state the names of three rivers in Brazil," or "The learner will demonstrate the steps of creating a coiled pot," or "The learner will compose three learning objectives for each class lesson taught," etc.)

- What are the materials involved in this activity? For a distance learning activity, note the materials that will be used and how they are transmitted to the student.

- To what extent will this learning be demonstrated? In order to evaluate the learning, the teacher will decide the degree to which the learner must demonstrate the activity. The demonstration could be measured in terms of completeness, quality, or time. (Descriptions could include limitations, such as "with 100 percent accuracy," "with technical accuracy," "within ten minutes," etc.)

- What is the distance teaching method that will best support the learning objectives, and how does this activity complement local resources?

- Discuss costs and alternatives for the distance learning activity.

- What are the media that will be needed to facilitate the activity? (Many materials are now Web based, but you may need to purchase physical copies of disks, DVDs, etc. A good resource that will lead you to vendors is *The Librarian's Yellow Pages* [http://www.librariansyellowpages.com/]. This free resource, in print or online, is categorized by media and subject.)

- Will the activity be textbook based? Many districts are emphasizing resource-based learning, where the student takes a lead in identifying and using a variety of sources (print, nonprint, and online) to complete a research task. Emphasizing the process of learning how to learn, resource-based learning allows the teacher and school library media specialist to support this process. Literature provides recent readings on resource-based learning (Thomas 1999).

- Will students be involved in research activities to support the distance learning activity? Who will be involved in the activity? Distance learning requires many players, so be sure to plan ahead and understand who will be present, along with their roles. If you are unable to accomplish what you need at the school level, who are the district personnel that can help? How will you organize all of the details of a distance learning activity? Be sure to designate a specific place and system that helps you to compile information for each distance learning course or activity that you facilitate.

- What are the specific activities that will take place? List the exact steps that will take place to support your learning objectives.

- Technical activities

    Who will get the distance learning area ready to be used?

    Who will prepare equipment and make necessary connections?

    Who will gather materials and place them in the learning area?

    Who will monitor connection time or equipment use?

- Teaching activities

    Who will introduce the activity and participants?

    Who will present or demonstrate?

Who will monitor learning and behavior?

Who will summarize the activity and review the learning?

Who will close the activity?

Be prepared! List everything that will be needed, down to the last piece of chalk! Plastic bins with sealing tops can be used to store books, audiovisual materials, and supplies until they are used. The administrator may allocate specific funds for distance learning materials, through the media center, so that the media specialist can provide portable bins with generic materials for different types of distance learning that will take place in the media center, e.g., a videoconferencing teaching bin including manuals for equipment, tape, chalk, colored markers, overhead transparencies, etc.; a teleconferencing bin including a list of conference times and numbers, a plain telephone for call-ins, notepads, pens, etc.; or a Web course bin with lists of chat times, software manuals, a copy of the course map, etc.

What is the expected time frame for the activity? Remember that distance participants will probably be following a different time schedule. Therefore, the activity time will probably be set by compromising with other teachers. (Who will take care of letting other teachers know that students may have to leave class early or that they will return late, due to the scheduling of a distance learning activity?)

As a recommendation for consistency, use your school or district's set lesson plan format. If you do not have a set format, search for examples online. Working with your distance learning development team, tailor the format to the needs of your school.

Ideally, the school library media specialist has been involved in the distance learning activity planning process from the beginning. By this point, the teachers have completely developed the lesson plan to be followed, getting input from the media specialist on the media and technologies that will be used.

## Scheduling the Distance Learning Activity

Scheduling is critical to the distance learning activity and to the continuing support of the school library media center program. Initially, when distance learning is new, the school environment will be very supportive and accommodating. Your school library media center program may allow the entire center to be scheduled for the distance learning activity. However, some centers will continue to have other classes and students in attendance at the same time. How will all of these activities be coordinated, especially if the school library media specialist also has to provide technical support for the distance learning activity?

First, determine whether the media center or media specialist will be directly involved in the activity. If the answer is yes, here are a few ideas to help with scheduling:

1. Note the specific dates and times of the distance learning activity. Adjust, in advance, for time zone differences.

2. Advertise the upcoming activity and time through announcements, e-mail, newsletters, or posted signs, so that students, teachers, and administrators know the schedule.

3. Discuss the upcoming activities with the media center personnel. Get input on how the activity will affect the center operations.

4. Ask who will need access to the media center or media center personnel during the time that the distance learning activity is scheduled. Schedule a conference with these people to determine if there is a conflict or if their activities can be rescheduled.

5. If scheduled classes will continue, meet with those teachers to plan and design activities that students can complete without the media specialist, under the supervision of the teachers.

6.  Discuss with paraprofessionals how they will be helping students with materials circulation and selection, in addition to supporting requests from teachers. Include paraprofessionals in planning meetings.

7.  After plans have been made, communicate the schedule and service changes to administrators and other teachers.

## Searching for Media to Support the Learning

Once the schedule of the media specialist has been cleared, it is time to identify and organize materials that will support the distance learning. Based on the planning activities with the distance learning partners, the media specialist can begin to consider materials in different categories, such as:

*   Development materials for teachers.

*   Demonstration materials for teachers.

*   Materials for students.

Because you now know the content that will be taught, ask teachers if they need materials for development. Determine what they already have and the types of information they need. Identify background materials. These may come in the form of content books, journals, methods textbooks, and Web pages.

The books may be in-house or available through local schools, public libraries, university libraries, or state libraries. Search for these titles through networked or online catalogs. Popular content magazine articles and professional journal articles may be borrowed directly or through interlibrary loan. Also, copies of articles may be faxed (or e-faxed), e-mailed, or mailed to you. You will be searching for these articles through networked, online, or local periodical databases.

If you are gathering development materials outside of your school, you may need to contact the librarians or media specialists at other sites and arrange to meet with them and gather materials there. You might learn that you need to purchase development materials, especially if your collection is deficient in some of the content areas. Be sure that you have names of vendors who can supply materials quickly.

Keep records of names, telephone numbers, and e-mail addresses of the librarians and media specialists who help you gather materials. You will want to thank them, provide help to them in the future, and be able to contact them when you need materials again.

### *Online Files*

Online teaching professional material is abundant in the form of digests, lesson plans, professional organization material, and archival records. For example, if a teacher is coordinating a distance learning experience with another teacher in the state, encourage online development through e-mail by helping your teacher search for materials through the Educational Resources Information Center (ERIC). If the teacher is unable to locate adequate information, e-mail *AskERIC* (askeric@askeric.org) and request that the researchers help you find hard-to-locate information. (ERIC Digests are produced by the ERIC clearinghouses, one of which is the *ERIC Clearinghouse on Information and Technology* [http://ericit.org/ericdigests.shtml]. All ERIC Digests produced by all clearinghouses are located at http://www.ed.gov/databases/ERIC_Digests/index/index.html. (*Distance Education Guides* can be located in ERIC at http://askeric.org/cgi-bin/res.cgi/Educational_Technology/Distance_Education.) A recent digest, *Competencies for Online Teaching* (http://www.ericit.org/digests/EDO-IR-2001-09.shtml), suggests that specific online training is needed for online teachers and that certification for online teachers should also be a consideration (Spector and de la Teja 2001).

ERIC also has links to databases and archives of lesson plans and listserv communications. If you are unable to find a document that has already been prepared, you can look through the listserv archives to see if your topic has been discussed. If it has, e-mail the people who were involved in the listserv message for information. Some listserv groups, such as LM_NET, post HIT messages, which are compilations of answers to previously asked questions. Be sure to search your listserv for HIT messages or search for a FAQ (Frequently Asked Questions) file to see if your question has already been answered.

The use of the Internet as a research source has allowed instruction to address different levels of research. For example, for basic research, students can use a preselected source that you identify for them. For advanced research, students can use multiple sites that you identify, or use search engines to select sources that they will analyze for appropriateness to the topic. For original research, students can learn to use online communication tools for surveys and cooperative experiments (Barron and Ivers 1996). Students also need to learn to distinguish between categories of sources, whether communications (listserv, news group) or research (documents, database files, electronic journals, Web sites), for quality of content, based on factors such as whether the resources are edited, moderated, reviewed, and referred.

An interesting development in the world of Web search engines was the movement toward a more human-generated focus, as a combination of human- and software-developed indexes, as opposed to the formerly software-generated indexes. The reason for this change was that the human-selected sites were more useful and relevant, based on their selection by those familiar with the content (Weise 2000). However, the technology relating to searching continues to develop. One of the well-received search engines today is *Google* (http://www.google.com), with its claim to fame being that it searches over a billion Web pages in less than a second, using a system called PageRank. PageRank looks for Web pages that are linked by other Web pages. The more times a Web page is linked, the higher the ranking that page has on the Google system (McGarvey 2000). Keeping pace with search engine developments is important in understanding the logic behind the sites that are returned for your searches.

## *Learning Possibility*

Link to *Google* (http://www.google.com) and observe the clean interface. Try this Google feature: "I'm Feeling Lucky." This link takes you directly into the first Web page identified through your search. (You don't go through a selection process!) When I tried this feature, I keyed in "distance learning" + "PreK–12." Try this search yourself, and see where you are led!

Beyond the instruction on searches, terms and techniques to use, and the process of evaluating the sources returned in the search, make sure students are aware of the distracters that go with search engines. For example, pop-up boxes, banners, and advertisements are common on general search engines. One way to deal with these distracters is to work with students on search tools that include no advertising. However, a more beneficial strategy to use with older students is teaching them how to manage and evaluate these distracters. For example, let students know that some engines rank sites according to use, and some rank sites according to advertising money spent to list the sites higher in the search. Explain to students that these practices can be questionable; therefore, they need to be on the lookout to protect themselves as consumers (*Edupage*, 17 July 2001).

Additionally, the school library media specialist needs to remember that distance learning technologies are not limited to classroom teachers. For example, when working on search engines, students and teachers can benefit from online classes, such as those offered through *ICONnect* (http://www.ala.org /ICONN/index.html). If students get stuck in their searches, they can submit questions through *KidsConnect* (http://www.ala.org/ICONN/kidsconn.html). After you have introduced students to this learning site and demonstrated how to register for the course, students can work through the activities at the pace you have scheduled and submit assignments that you design.

When helping teachers to develop distance learning courses, offer to locate online information about the professional organization that may relate to either the teaching activity or the content area. For example, if you are working with another teacher to present fractals, be sure to contact the *National Council for Teachers of Mathematics* (http://www.nctm.org), as well as the *Community Learning Network Fractals Theme Page* (http://www.cln.org/themes/fractals.html).

What if your topic has not been discussed within your area and you can't find literature or a Web site? Help your teacher to locate a listserv or Usenet news group that discusses the topic. There are hundreds of groups that discuss educational topics. Use *Lizst* (http://www.lizst.com) or Diane Kovacs's *The Directory of Scholarly and Professional E-Conferences* (http://www.kovacs.com/directory/), two of several listserv databases to aid your search. If your topic has not been discussed within the chosen group, or addressed in a FAQ file, post a question and ask others for assistance.

While the teacher is checking out listservs, the media specialist can contact school library media online groups. To date, I have never seen a topic posted on LM_NET that did not receive some kind of response from other media specialists. For example, if your high school agriculture teacher is working with the topic of monocot plants, a posting to LM_NET for agricultural reference materials will probably result in several resource citations.

## *Community Content Experts*

A great way to enliven distance learning activities is to involve community content experts (e.g., speakers, folklore interpreters, living history resources, government officials). If both the sender and receiver do this, students get double the exposure to experts. Imagine a presentation (desktop video, videoconferencing) where students in California and Florida learn about their area's respective dangers—earthquakes and hurricanes. During the presentation, government representatives can provide historical information on the events, along with a discussion of how students and families can protect themselves in the event of an emergency. Can you think of a follow-up research project that students can conduct on these topics?

Begin to identify people who would be interested in working with students. The potential for cross-cultural learning can be right under your nose. Learning activities that teach students about food or seasons can be coordinated into the experience. Students can videotape these activities, and the videotape can be mailed to the other group prior to the distance learning activity. Audiotapes of local school library media specialists reading favorite regional stories can be shared prior to a distance learning activity about folklore. Where else can you search for materials for your topic?

- Search catalogs for content books or professional books from the school's collection.

- Search district or state catalogs for books that are unavailable in the local school.

- Check with local universities or public libraries for book titles.

- Search periodical databases for professional journal articles on methodology or content.

- Search periodical databases for content articles from popular magazines.

# Online Searching

Whether for students or teachers, a major function of the school library media specialist is teaching skills for locating online resources. The skills and strategies needed for online searching are finding their way into the media center daily.

## *Learning Possibility*

Ask teachers to access the *Freeality Internet Search* (http://www.freeality.com) as a gateway to a multiplicity of search engines. Discuss how they can explain to their students the need for the many search engines, noting the economic issues of search engines, such as requiring advertising dollars, listing companies in rank order by the amount paid to the search engines, the type of audience desired in comparison to the type of sites listed, etc. Review the strengths of the different search engine formats with the teachers as you demonstrate elementary search engines, such as *Ask Jeeves* (http://www.aj .com) or *Yahooligans* (http://www.yahooligans.com), then work through *DogPile* (http://www.dogpile.com) and *Yahoo* (http://www.yahoo.com) for middle school students, and then teach students to use *AltaVista* (http://www .altavista.com), *Infoseek* (http://www.infoseek.com), or *Hotbot* (http://www .hotbot.com) at the high school levels. Let the teachers experience the progression of search engine interfaces and features. If teachers can experience the different search interfaces, noting the similarities between the search processes, they will be more confident teaching their students that the different search engines are multiple tools—just as encyclopedias are multiple tools for locating information.

Are you or your students interested in contributing to an Internet directory, which is somewhat similar to those search engines that are really indexes? If so, the *Open Directory Project* (http://dmoz.org /about.html) offers the opportunity to become part of the open source movement of "Netizens." Students should appreciate the effort that it takes to meaningfully categorize links.

---

## *Learning Possibility*

When students have mastered the use of single search engines, consider challenging them to use the *Colossus Search Engine* (http://www.search enginecolossus.com), a collection of international search engines. Social studies students, who need to be aware that views of world events often differ in other countries based on perspectives, would benefit from this site. Ask students to identify and select a current event, e.g., civil unrest or military engagement. Student can search for news, in English, through a variety of international search engines and then read the news reports carefully to compare different viewpoints of the same event. When using *Colossus*, demonstrate to students the number of search engines that exist for U.S. sources. (Try the *About* search engine [http://www.about.com/] to look for guides on a variety of subjects.)

---

A good introductory file on the differences in search engines can be found at Terry Gray's *How to Search the Web: A Guide to Search Tools* (http://daphne.palomar.edu/TGSEARCH/). Though other search engines are available today, this link provides a simple discussion of the basics. *The Internet Search Tool Quick Reference Guide* (http://www.itrc.ucf.edu/iqr/) offers a good visual for helping beginners to conceptualize the different ways of using search engines. At *Bare Bones 101* (http://www.sc.edu/beaufort /library/bones.html), in addition to finding introductory materials on search engines, you will also find information on evaluating Web sites and specific help on a variety of search engines in current use.

Beyond teaching teachers how to search, introduce them to search services for educators, such as *AskERIC* (http://ericir.syr.edu/About/index.shtml) or *SERVE* (*SouthEastern Regional Vision for Education*) (http://www.serve.org) or its branch, *SEIR-TEC* (*SouthEast and Islands* [Puerto Rico and the Virgin Islands] *Regional Technology in Education Consortium*) (http://www.seirtec.org). Each of these sites provides access to information on lesson plans, online resources, and educational technology. If teachers become more proficient using the information at these three sites, their time spent in your training sessions would be well worth it. AskERIC also offers an information referral service, useful to both the teacher and the busy media specialist, that can be used just by sending the question to askeric@askeric.org. While you're at it, you might want to take technologists to *MyTech Support* (http://mytechsupport.ca/) or *Experts Exchange* (http://www.experts-exchange.com) where they can find answers to technology problems.

## *Learning Possibility*

Have you ever had a reference question that you couldn't answer? Most media specialists experience this, but there is a helpful source—the media specialist's reference trick, STUMPERS-L, a listserv with an archive (http:// domin.dom.edu/depts/gslis/stumpers) that is aimed at answering only the toughest reference questions. In addition to STUMPERS-L, there are media specialists worldwide who are helpful in sharing ideas, resources, and answers with other media specialists. If you haven't already, be sure to visit the searchable LM_NET (Library Media Network) archive, available through the ERIC Web site (http://askeric.org/plweb-cgi/fastweb?searchform+listservs).

## Evaluation of Web Sites

Because they are well trained in the selection process, school library media specialists are the in-house experts on evaluating Web sites. Students and teachers, who are increasingly depending on Web resources as documentation, need to know how to find the information diamonds! Evaluation resources and information continue to be published, but to get you started, review these sources:

- *Evaluating Web Sites* was developed by Debra Gniewek and Megan Fritz and includes evaluation activities. (http://www.crsd.org/webcontent/5_9_2001_15_26_18/webeval.htm)

- *Kathy Schrock's Guide for Educators: Critical Evaluation Information* houses multiple links to other evaluative resources. (http://school.discovery.com/schrockguide/eval.html)

- *Thinking Critically About World Wide Web Resources* is maintained by Esther Grassian of the UCLA College Library. (http://www.library.ucla.edu/libraries/college/help/critical/index.htm)

Beyond teaching students and teachers to search online and evaluate information, the school library media specialist has an opportunity to teach students how to organize their Web materials and links. For example, how do you want students to save links that they will be using at school? Will students have the opportunity to bookmark sites on your networks, using shared computers? Or would you like students to save their personal bookmarks at a bookmark site, such as *Bookmarksplus.com* (http://www.bookmarksplus .com)? For students and teachers who use multiple machines, this free service is a potential tool. Before registering students, it would be a good idea to thoroughly read this site's privacy policy and discuss it with your administrator. It wouldn't hurt to discuss this with parents also, or request a signed permission slip before encouraging students to list their bookmarks there. If there are objections to this or similar services, you can teach students how to develop a personal Web page of links to their sites.

Hopefully, the school library media specialist will see the need for providing media center policies and information on the Web. Some of your students may be truly distant, yet they will need services. How will you provide these services to students? Will you publicize your office telephone number? Will you accept reference requests through e-mail? Will you provide online training information on topics such as using the online public access catalog (OPAC) through Web resources? Will you provide this training through video presentations?

All media specialists are familiar with the frustrations of interlibrary loan lags, but these delays are not conducive to good online support. Will you provide students with online access to articles, such as through *Electronic Library* (http://ask.elibrary.com/)? Do you think that your district will provide a subscription to this type of service for all distance learning students in your district so that individual media centers will not have to subscribe?

Some refer to online library information as the virtual library, which includes access to local information, the OPAC, online periodicals and other databases, links to other online libraries and resources, and e-mail capabilities (Blake 1996). (Have you tried using actual "virtual libraries," such as the *Virtual Reference Desk* [http://vrd.org/about.shtml], *The Virtual Reference Desk Learning Center* (*for Kids*) [http:// askvrd.org/vrd/], the *Santa Monica Public Library* [http://www.smpl.org] [Go to the "Ask a Librarian" link {http://www.247ref.org}], the *Internet Public Library* [http://www.ipl.org], or *AskEric* [http://www .askeric.org]?) Concepts relating to the use of the virtual library's information must also be taught to students so that they can learn that selection impacts the content of materials (Weisburg and Toor 1996).

Although many of us believe that it will be years before the printed word goes out of use, the possibility remains that today's student will be reading tomorrow's assignment online. What can the media specialist do to help students begin to work with both printed and electronic formats? Leading students to examples of online documents, and demonstrating the use of the e-book viewers, would be a proactive step. Ultimately, the reader will determine the publishers' move in this area, but we can provide information on the advantages and disadvantages of both formats.

Other online services, such as *Yahoo! Briefcase* (http://briefcase.yahoo.com), are available so that students and teachers can easily transport files from home to school for use. A benefit of transferring files through your Web server is that you can provide for a higher level of file security through your network. This can also help to relieve storage burdens on a temporary basis. A drawback of this type of service is that you have no control of files stored at off-site locations, and there is a risk that the site owner might go out of business suddenly without providing you with warning time for retrieving your files.

Because school library media specialists are often asked to provide distance learning support, they seldom are the requesters of support. Nevertheless, for the media specialist who is searching for information on how to further develop the media center to support distance learning, the *Libraries of the Future Bibliography* (Gurstelle 1999) is highly recommended for its compilation of Web sites that provide current information and direction to professional statements of practice.

Media specialists will want to think about organizing a distance learning Web presence for the media center and school, in addition to their other Web resources. A wonderful way to communicate overall school activities, or special areas of instruction, the media specialist can take a leadership role in providing links to parents that help them support the school's activities.

## Learning Possibility

Access a school's Web site. An example of an interesting site that provided information by grade level is *Holly Hill Elementary School* (http://schools .volusia.K12.fl.us/hollyhille). How is your school's Web site organized? Is it easy to navigate? Can parents easily find contact information for teachers?

Do not forget that while school library media specialists are busy teaching everyone else about locating resources and using technology, they could probably use some refresher training themselves. Some states, such as Florida, have offered free online training through state universities. Check with your district development office or state institutions to see if you have similar opportunities available. These courses, offered cooperatively, are likely to change from term to term, year to year.

In your role as media specialist, you may be asked to help teachers locate lesson plans. Though there are several sites that are very well organized and can be located online through search engines under the topic lesson plans, don't overlook less obvious sources that are available through library vendors such as *Follett Software Company* (http://www.pathwaysmodel.com/resources/thematic-units). The thematic units on this site are useful because they demonstrate the importance of developing full units, in addition to single lesson plans.

# *Section C. By the Administrator*

Administrators want to help students and teachers succeed. The best way administrators can be supportive of distance learning activities is by being visible, involved, and genuinely interested in distance learning activities. Most administrators feel that visiting the classroom is a luxury, between handling discipline problems and telephone calls. It is true that discipline and routine telephone calls take a lot of time, but is it possible that those issues can be handled at the end of the day, or by another personnel member, to free up the administrator's time for getting involved with classroom and distance learning? The most critical business issue of a school day, the education of the students, can only be monitored at certain times. Students who see that the administrator is interested in what is going on in the classroom might be motivated to participate more actively in learning activities. As well, teachers who know that the principal is visiting classes are more likely to stay on task and engaged with their students. The helpful monitoring of learning, as part of the educational quality assurance and accountability processes, can, more than any one single factor, encourage all learners to stay on task. Remember, if you are the principal, you are the principal teacher. It is up to you to set the educational pace, whether through distance or traditional learning.

Management of distance learning is really no different from the normal school day management, with the exception of the need to monitor a few more details. Distance learning teachers need in-service training, development time, and planning time, as do traditional teachers. Distance learning teachers must apply national curriculum standards to the instruction, as should traditional teachers. Distance teaching can be enhanced through team teaching, as can traditional teaching. Distance learning students need orientation and counseling, as do traditional students. Evaluation is critical to the distance learning program, just as it is to the traditional learning program. Distance learning requires careful planning, selection of equipment and materials, and curriculum design—and guess what? So does traditional learning! As a result, many of the areas that the administrator is currently directing also apply to distance learning. Communication, cooperation, and coordination among all participants will encourage distance learning success (Sorenson 1997).

One of the first questions that must be answered, regarding support for distance learning, is who will direct teachers to get involved? Will the administrator make suggestions for distance learning courses? Will there be a lead teacher that facilitates and promotes distance learning? Better yet, can the administrator gather a team of interested faculty, parents, and students that will work together to identify the distance learning needs and possibilities for the school?

After the distance learning team has been identified, the administrator, or designee, should investigate if there are other schools in the district that are involved in distance learning. Can your designee or distance learning team meet with representatives of other schools or the district to find out about the distance learning solutions that have been found in their schools? Can you request this information from a district contact to share with your faculty or distance learning team? Are there other distance learning projects that you identify, through readings or online sources, that can help solve learning problems for your school? Have you seen presentations on distance learning at conferences that offer suggestions for your school?

Perhaps there is a local resource in the form of a college or university faculty member or administrator that knows of distance learning applications that can boost your curriculum. If you cannot find someone experienced with distance learning, maybe a college or university faculty member can direct you to another source.

One way to gather ideas for developing a distance learning plan for your school is by supporting interested teachers who are willing to attend conferences or workshops, in person or online, to find out more about distance learning. Work with your school library media specialist to identify journal articles and online resources that would provide direction on distance learning materials. This research can possibly lead you to an outside professional who is experienced in the distance learning field and who can provide project, funding, or vendor information to get you started with this course delivery format.

After you have worked with your staff to identify distance learning solutions, make sure that you are involved with the implementation. Encourage the teachers and students with lots of positive enthusiasm as they get started with the distance learning activities. Show interest by participating and observing the learning sessions. Promote these activities through announcements, school newsletters, Web sites, and parent-teacher meetings. Let your supervisor know that you are exploring distance learning solutions for a variety of content areas and that you are supporting faculty members to help get your distance learning program on the move.

Do as much as possible to remove roadblocks to distance learning. Help with scheduling by asking cafeteria servers to accommodate students who may have to change lunch schedules one day a week. Make sure that connections (whether online, satellite, or telephone) are in working order by testing them frequently, or by designating someone to test them. Try to plan for incidentals, such as extra postage, videotapes, or other supplies that might be needed by distance learning teachers. Speak with or e-mail the administrators at the other schools to communicate your pleasure at being able to cooperate or collaborate with their teachers and students. Ask if there are any problems that the two of you need to solve and how these problems can be avoided in the future. Decide how you will work together to resolve schedule conflicts, grade disputes, and discipline problems.

How will you measure your success? Keep anecdotal records and data, whenever possible. Record distance learning activities with a digital camera and incorporate the pictures in a PowerPoint presentation for teachers and parents. Interview students and parents and ask how they liked their distance learning activities. What would they change to improve the experience?

Once the initial planning and implementation is in place, the administrator can expand on distance learning activities. How? By thinking of other school populations that might benefit from a change in pace. Throughout a busy day, with tremendous demands for support and encouragement of all school populations, the administrator is often called upon to work miracles. Rather than viewing distance learning initiatives as another task to perform, the resourceful administrator needs to start looking at ways that technology can support and boost school achievement. For example, most schools have a segment of students that has been targeted as at risk. Many of these at-risk students really suffer from boredom, disappointment, and a lack of positive reinforcement in school (Stephens 1997, p. 4). Interactive distance learning technologies, though not the total solution, offer a starting point for working with at-risk students. Why should a principal work with a new technology to help students, when nothing else seems to work? It is because nothing else seems to work that the principal has few, if any, alternatives. Encouraging teachers of at-risk students to try new teaching models is an opportunity to renew programs that are not currently working.

Another leadership role for the administrator that supports distance learning is directing policy for students and teachers and their "technology classroom behavior." With these new learning environments, it is difficult to anticipate what will happen next. Colleges and universities have found, as communicated through an article title, "On Line, Ways to Misbehave Can Outpace College Rules" (McCollum 1999). And how do these students misbehave? They may be plagiarizing assignments (*Edupage*, 16 May 2001), inappropriately "sharing" homework, or they may be contributing to the reported millions of spam messages that are sent (*Edupage*, 7 May 2001). Of course, we realize that as technology continues to be used in creative ways, it is likewise being applied to develop solutions. For instance, software has been developed to catch students who are cheating on their assignments in computer programming classes (Wingfield 2002). For this computer programming example, part of the logic of the software is the tracking of punctuation and spacing. Continue to look for these types of software applications for teaching.

Related to improper online student behavior, however, most of the areas of concern (such as copyright, use of hardware and software, and e-mail) are already addressed in school board policy. Even though you are well aware of these policies, take the time to inform your staff, students, and parents of these policies. Ask for input on the policies. Do they need to be revised to reflect changes in the technology? Next, ask yourself how you are implementing these policies that relate to distance learning in your school. Are your rules too restrictive or too lenient? Do they allow for fair use by all students? Do your rules promote learning or do they impose restraints? Would it be possible for you to appoint a committee of teachers, staff, administrators, students, and parents to review these school policies and rules each year? Ask the committee how to best communicate this information schoolwide, in a positive way. Suggestions might include creating posters, brochures, or an in-house television program that spells out the rules in terms that students understand. As part of teaching computer and online ethics, explain why these rules are necessary. Simply sending a handout home to the parent is not sufficient. If you want the policies and rules to be meaningful, address them in the classroom or lab where they will be applied.

Does your school have a Web site that offers information to parents? Do you include this Web address in your school's telephone message so parents can access school information after school hours? Does your Web site allow parents to submit questions to school personnel?

To further increase communications with parents, through Web materials, guide your parents to quality resources. For example, suggest *Getting Ready for College Early* (http://ed.gov/pubs /GettingReadyCollegeEarly/) for middle school parents or *Preparing Your Child for College* (http://www .ed.gov/pubs/Prepare) for high school parents, both from the U.S. Department of Education. While you are at the U.S. Department of Education's home page, take a minute to read *Fathers' and Mothers' Involvement in Their Children's Schools by Family Type and Resident Status* (http://nces.ed.gov/pubs2001 /quarterly/summer/q2-5.asp). Search for other NCES publications online. If you would like to order these publications for distribution at a parent-teacher meeting, they are free and in English and Spanish. Call 1-800-USA-LEARN or 1-877-4ED-PUBS to order. (While you are speaking with the operator, ask if there are other recent resources, posters, or videotapes that you can use in promoting your school's learning.)

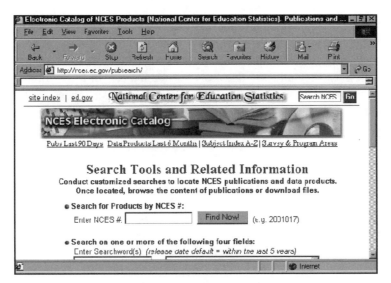

*Search Tools and Related Information at Center for Education Statistics* Web site: http://nces.ed.gov/pubsearch/

## *Learning Possibility*

Has one teacher too many come to your office this week to complain about a leaking ceiling or cracked plaster? If it is true that misery loves company, you will probably find some in the *Condition of America's Public School Facilities: 1999* (http://nces.ed.gov/pubs2000/2000032.pdf). Want to do something about it? Look to see if your district can qualify for special construction money or other grants at the National Clearinghouse for Educational Facilities (http://www.edfacilities.org). Also located at the U.S. Department of Education's home page is a link to *Grants and Contracts* (http://www.ed.gov/topics/topics .jsp?&top=Grants+%26+Contracts). Can you partner with administrators at other schools in your feeder pattern to develop meaningful distance learning projects that can qualify for federal grants?

---

The school administrator often needs support for his or her own busy day of activities. An example of a resource that can help the administrator is *iPing* (http://www.iping.com), a type of personal reminder sent to you, by you, by phone. When can you use a service, such as iPing? Have you ever missed an important district meeting with the superintendent or a meeting with parents? By setting up this reminder service, you have another assistant to help you remember activities during your busy day. However, beyond the use of technology for your personal support, by modeling the use of *iPing* you are sending a message to your faculty that you are trying to use new technologies to improve your services to the school. Being alert to new developments, such as the Wireless Application Protocol (WAP) that can support the delivery of information through wireless services and networks, demonstrates to your staff that you are searching for solutions that will help them as they try to heighten the level of instruction in the areas of technology and telecommunications for their students.

If you are an administrator who has still not found the time to promote, or is anxious about, online activities, know that online productivity tools tailored to the PreK–12 administrator are available. The principal who often feels isolated in the position can find sources, whether through the Web, e-mail, Usenet news group, or listserv, to support personal and staff development. For example, if a principal needs input on scheduling, material support, or collaborative planning and teaching from an administrator's point of view, a listserv can provide support. Listserv and e-mail activities are very much a part of the administrator's day. What kind of information will you receive through this listserv? Administrators share ideas, references to the literature, Web links, and research. For example, in a survey posted to the K–12ADMIN listserv, responding administrators reported that "they spent 50 percent of their administrative Internet time using e-mail" (Lemon 1997, p. 93).

## *Learning Possibility*

Log on and sign on to the K–12ADMIN listserv by sending an e-mail message to listserv@listserv.syr.edu. (Do not include a message in the Subject or Re: box of your e-mail headers. In the message, key "subscribe K–12ADMIN Your Name".)

Monitor the listserv activities for a while, before you post messages, just to get familiar with the current discussions and themes. Be aware of the quantity and quality of the responses you view. Do these messages support your professional interests? Remember, with any news group or listserv, if you do not wish your comments or requests to be viewed by all you can always contact the participants off the list by sending e-mail directly to the person instead of to the listserv.

For more listserv opportunities for administrators (or faculty) or to search another index of discussion groups, read *E-Mail Discussion Groups/Newsletters* (http://everythingemail.net/email_discussion.html) for a simple description of listserv software, commands, and names of lists. Try one of the lists, such as *TileNet* (http://tile.net). Click on the link to "lists" and either key in the word "education" or click on the letter "e." If this brings you too many examples, revise your search and look for a particular aspect of education.

As the building-level executive, school administrators have tremendous influence on future distance learning activities simply through their understanding that today's flexible and adaptable infrastructure can make or break tomorrow's distance learning possibilities. How? Just think of recent construction or renovation projects in your school. Something as simple and mundane as room layout, numbers and spacing of electrical outlets, and telephone or cable locations can either expand or limit how rooms are used. Facilities planning for data, voice, and video connections and space and layout design require considerable research and thought if flexibility and adaptability of classrooms to provide accommodations for distance learning are your goals. *From Now On* (http://www.fno.org/fnoindex.html#Technology), an online journal that includes information on technology planning, will provide support and ideas on how to implement planning.

Some administrators have not had the training to be able to understand where their schools stand in terms of technology. Resources are available in the literature to provide an overview of distance learning and the role of the administrator in managing the technologies (Barker 1992). Fortunately, administrators can assess their schools through an online questionnaire, the *Interactive School Technology and Readiness (STaR) Chart* (http://www.ceoforum.org/reports.cfm?RID=3), designed to provide schools with a starting point on how they rank for several areas, including hardware, connectivity, software, professional development opportunities, and the integration and use of technology. Take this questionnaire to get a baseline understanding of how your school ranks in terms of technology. If nothing else, you will gain knowledge of available resources just by having to answer the questions. Beyond this assessment tool, the *CEO Forum* (http://www.ceoforum.org/reports.cfm) offers reports that assess teacher preparation and professional development relating to PreK–12 schools. By following these sources, you will also develop a better understanding of how you can monitor and guide teacher preparation in your school. The *EducatorsNet* (http://www.educatorsnet.com/) is a great source for the administrator who needs to keep everyone up-to-date on educational issues, such as distance learning.

If you are in the early stages of designing distance learning opportunities for your school, you will certainly benefit from a how-to-do-it type of title, such as *Classrooms for Distance Teaching & Learning: A Blueprint* (Hegarty, Phelan, and Kilbride 1998). Based on a development project during which five distance learning classrooms were developed in Belgium, Finland, France, Ireland, and Italy, this title focuses on the actual steps that are involved in creating an interactive classroom, from consideration of the teaching activity and teaching style to the type of lighting and furniture that are required. A critical feature for distance learning—testing—is addressed in this publication. Another feature, rarely glimpsed in other distance learning titles, is a section on "How to Use the Classroom." Yes, this would need to be adapted to your specific distance learning room, but this section is a great starting point for thinking about just how to teach your teachers to use your facilities. How often do we assume that the instructors will know automatically how to use the equipment and how to adapt traditional teaching methods to distance teaching methods? Your media specialist can work with you to provide training assistance to faculty.

An early manual, *Managing Distance Education Courses* (Houdek 1990), is organized into chapters on recruitment, orientation, supporting the course development process, supporting teaching at a distance, and evaluation. This manual can be very useful to the administrator who is looking for direction on how to provide support for in-house distance learning activities.

You may already have access to a very thorough discussion of distance learning in the form of online coursework in one of your copies of the *School Administrator* (Russo 2001, 6–48). This in-depth article addresses elements important to principals, beginning with an overall summary of why you would care to use online learning in your district, developing an approach to implement distance learning (begin with planning!), funding, course content, and evaluation of courses. Additional sources are referenced that will be useful, from an administrator's point of view.

The administrator, more than any one school-based employee, has the potential of making educational strides within the school by decreasing the lack of technology, popularly referred to as the "Digital Divide" (http://www.ntia.doc.gov/ntiahome/digitaldivide/). How you develop teams within your school community will determine your level of success with technology and distance learning. How these teams implement meaningful distance learning curricula will determine your students' levels of success.

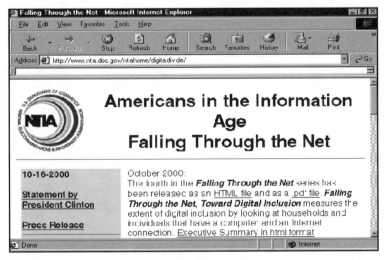

**Falling Through the Net (National Telecommunications and Information Administration) Web site: http://www.ntia.doc.gov/ntiahome/digitaldivide/**

# Section D. By Other School Personnel

Whole school support improves the environment for interactive distance learning opportunities. Examples for support of collaborative learning include working with guidance counselors to provide seminars on preparations for standardized testing or college entrance applications. Support can also be given by asking paraprofessionals to function as facilitators for compressed video courses. The importance of the facilitator and the contribution that the facilitator makes to the quality of the learning experience must be stressed (Moore, Burton, and Dodl 1997).

A public school group that should not be overlooked is that of the adult education classes that are offered evenings in the public school facility. The adult education administrators and instructors can partner with the day school staff members to offer distance learning instruction and support in computer applications and online courses, in addition to providing computer lab space for adult distance learners to take their courses. When thinking of the costs to set up labs, we want to make as much use of the equipment as possible. Community businesses that are interested in partnering with public schools might be more positive about participating during evening hours. Trumbull County, Ohio, developed the *Trumbull County Community Network (TCCN)* (http://www.trumbull.k12.oh.us/events/TCCNStakhldrep.pdf) that involved school, business, college, and community partners in a successful, multiyear project that continues to support distance learning for K–12 and postsecondary students (Watson 2001).

Many of your school staff members have multiple talents and skills that they can demonstrate in some distance learning courses. With some encouragement, most will be enthusiastic guest speakers in class. Staff members can also function as observers, assistants with materials distribution, and leaders for group sessions. The key to encouraging staff involvement is communicating your distance learning goals and including staff members in the planning process.

# Section E. By District Personnel

Assuming that there are district personnel that are responsible for distance learning activities, the first question is: Are all schools within the district connected to each other for video, voice, and data services (Yow 1996)? How are these schools connected to the other regional or state networks and the Internet? Electronic networks within the district will promote the sharing of existing resources and encourage interactive learning activities. If the answer to this first question is yes, who is communicating to other schools the possibilities for distance learning? How are teachers and administrators encouraged to share learning opportunities between schools? Are funds available to purchase support materials for these learning activities? Are district policies in place that support these learning activities? If a student and a distance learning teacher have a disagreement over class behavior or content, how is a conference arranged if they are located at different schools?

District personnel may not have been identified for the purpose of coordinating distance learning activities. If not, who will identify the district personnel member who most closely fills this function? Would it be more efficient to designate a district team to advise and coordinate distance learning within the district?

Professional, state, and national organizations distribute a mass of publications, documents, and opportunities for grant writing for district learning opportunities. To become involved in these activities, find out where this information is being funneled. In addition, if a distance learning person has not been designated for your district, the person that is currently filling this role may be very appreciative of your interests and may even ask you to help assume some of the duties of fact-finding and participation relating to distance education and grant writing.

If a district personnel member has been identified as the lead person for distance learning, find out about the reports or publications being distributed by this office. Invite this lead person to speak to your faculty or parent-teacher organization to describe the district's position on distance learning and the goals that have been set. Communicate that your school wants to get involved in interactive distance learning opportunities and would be glad to be the test site for new technologies.

The function of in-service education is generally a district responsibility, with districts starting to develop and schedule training in distance learning formats. Because teachers are generally in classrooms during the day, there are challenges in scheduling these training sessions in order to be effective. If you are part of this staff development function, some experiences with telecourses indicate that training for K–12 teachers is more successful if it occurs in the winter and is scheduled in the early evening (Cambre, Erdman, and Hall 1996, 41). Teachers must have already had training sessions for the modality itself. For example, if the training will be using the Internet, offer basic Internet sessions in advance.

If you are at the district level, do not assume that participants will know to seek out this training independently. You may send flyers to the individual schools, but often information does not get into the correct hands. Think of multiple ways to communicate your training opportunities.

During the training, encourage peer teachers to communicate directly with each other and to work cooperatively to produce distance learning materials as they are learning more about the technology itself. Adult learners appreciate working with their peers, especially after they have been working with PreK–12 students all day. This peer support often ensures a positive experience and promotes the kind of sharing of ideas that is needed to encourage distance learning.

Usually the district in-service training for distance learning modalities will be in the form of several workshops offered during a term, but some districts may decide to implement a large-scale training initiative. Such was the case for teachers in Indianapolis, where 3,000 teachers were trained in a year and a half by district personnel (Bohnenkamp and McMahon 2001). This training centered on integrating technology into the curriculum and was offered online with the help of the Indiana University School of Education and its Oncourse software through its *Cyberlab* (http://www.cyberlab.iupui.edu/). For this district, the training of administrators to use technology was the next planned implementation.

In 1997, South Dakota began a statewide project to train teachers to use technology at its *Technology for Teaching and Learning (TTL) Academy* (http://www.sdttl.com/) (Schopp and Rothernel 2001), a twenty-day residential training session hosted by universities and a technical institution. Training objectives were based on the ISTE NETS (National Educational Technology Standards). Though more than 30 percent of the teacher workforce in South Dakota had been trained as of that time, future academies were planned on a nonresidential basis through videoconferencing. DTL (Distance Training and Learning) was also offered to South Dakota teachers who wished to offer distance learning courses through videoconferencing (Gosmire and Vondruska 2001). A number of the DTL graduates have already offered distance learning courses, using videoconferencing. Through this delivery, which often paired teachers in different school districts, teachers learned that different school calendars or classroom management practices could hamper the coordination of delivery of distance learning courses. What was the solution? These issues were resolved by the development of consortia among some districts that promoted common calendars or policies.

For many educators, the most important contribution that a district can make to the distance learning classroom is the development of useful policies. When developing these policies, ask:

What are the federal or state laws that relate to the policy?

Have any national or state agencies already developed policies that may cover this situation?

What is the local policy already in place that might apply to this issue?

Does this policy effectively capture what is happening in the distance learning classroom? Do you have direct input from distance learning teachers on implementing this policy?

Are forms that apply to policies consistent with the policy? For example, if you are developing a parent release form on an Acceptable Use Policy (AUP), does the terminology of the policy agree with the form that you are asking the parent to sign?

Can your policy be enforced, and who will be responsible for this at the local school level or at the district level?

Are district contact offices and addresses listed on your policy?

Where is your policy posted?

Providing information about schools to the public is crucial at all levels. An example of good communication at the local level is the *Los Angeles School District's Home Page* (http://www.lausd.k12 .ca.us/) that includes a listing of school profiles and information on attendance and staffing.

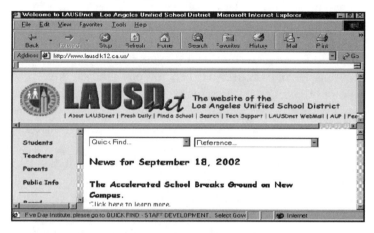

**Los Angeles School District's Home Page Web site:**
**http://www.lausd.k12.ca.us/**

A listing of school profiles at the state level is the *Florida School Indicators Report* (http://info .doe.state.fl.us/fsir/), which provides data for intra- and interdistrict comparisons. Another state resource is provided by the U.S. Department of Education in the form of the *District Locator* (http://nces.ed.gov /ccd/districtsearch/). This resource helps you search for the location and general information on districts nationwide. *Just for Kids* (http://www.just4kids.org) also offers data for comparison of schools. The national equivalent for postsecondary schools is *COOL* (*College Opportunities On-Line*) (http://www.nces.ed .gov/ipeds/cool/Search.asp), provided by the National Center for Education Statistics.

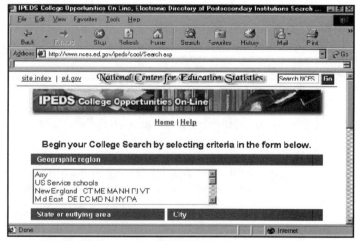

**COOL (College Opportunities On-Line) Web site:**
**http://www.nces.ed.gov/ipeds/cool/Search.asp**

To view an online comparison of schools supported by the housing industry look at *The School Report* (http://www.homefair.com/homefair/usr/nsrs/home.html).

Another significant contribution that district personnel can make to support distance learning is providing leadership in developing a purchasing plan that allows for regular equipment upgrades and replacements. The distance learning activities that are possible with Webcasts, for example, are just not possible with outdated hardware. Although it is unlikely that many PreK–12 districts will begin a regular cycle for replacement of equipment, like Indiana University (*Edupage*, 1 January 2000), where about 5,000 computers were replaced every three years, it is possible that a plan of perpetual purchasing can be developed so that, for example, all elementary machines are replaced one year, and all middle school machines are replaced during the next year. If you are aghast to think of the costs for replacing equipment every three years, let's think instead of how much you are spending to repair your equipment on your current purchasing plan.

District support can mean so much to a successful distance learning plan. By providing leadership in the areas of setting policy, training, purchasing, and servicing equipment, the district can help to make the distance learning classroom efficient and productive. Do not forget that the evaluation of this planning and coordinating function, along with the evaluation of other groups and task forces that contribute to setting the district's focus, will determine how you will continue future distance learning directions (Chamberlain 2000).

# Section F. By State Personnel

Most states have been represented in distance learning for several years. As early as 1992, a listing showed that forty-nine states were involved in K–12 distance learning delivery through a variety of formats, including television broadcasting, satellite, microwave, and video (Heffernan-Cabrera and Ayala 1992). In many states, personnel have been identified to coordinate the distance education function. As the distance learning process continues to be refined and defined, personnel changes and department changes, at the state level, will occur. However, knowing your state contacts, and contacts in neighboring or similar states, will help you to explore more distance learning options. Also, many of these state staff members provide in-service training opportunities at state, regional, and national meetings and workshops. They will be happy to share the resources and successes that they have had with you and your school.

State personnel have also been involved with the piloting and evaluation of distance learning activities. States, such as Alaska, through its Public Broadcasting Commission (1995), have evaluated the cost-benefit of services for video programs. A Star Schools grant that was used to implement two-way interactive video connections, along with training and support, to more than 100 schools was evaluated by the Iowa Distance Education Alliance (Maushak and Manternach 1997). Minnesota (1990) evaluated two-way interactive television systems for delivery to K–12 students in schools without sufficient enrollments to justify the offering of courses. The Southwest Educational Development Lab, serving Arkansas, Louisiana, Mississippi, New Mexico, Oklahoma, and Texas, evaluated distance learning technologies for applications in these states (Hudson and Boyd 1984). Michigan (1990) offered its schools a curriculum framework for foreign-language study that addressed the use of computer-assisted instruction, video, and interactive video for distance learning. Two state initiatives that emphasize convenience to the working adult have occurred in Kentucky and Missouri. Kentucky offers virtual adult education (http://www.kyvae.org/), and Missouri has piloted an online general education diploma (G.E.D.) (*Edupage*, 20 December 2000).

Many states, including New Jersey, responded to the Federal Telecommunications Act of 1996, which provided for universal access to resources through distance learning and the Internet (Peretz 1997). The financial impact of this legislation has been significant for schools and libraries that would have otherwise been limited in their online services.

The use of videoconferencing to provide multimedia mathematics instruction in the home was proposed for New York and cities in other urban areas, focusing on the need to develop statewide public and private partnerships (1994). North Carolina piloted and evaluated distance learning courses as early as 1986, with the goal of encouraging teachers to use interactive video programs for delivery. Issues of low-wealth schools and equity were evaluated by the Ohio Office of Education Oversight (1996), which suggested that cost effectiveness, in view of student outcomes, be regularly reviewed. The impact of state policy and limited finances was evaluated for rural Vermont schools that could benefit from distance learning technologies, showing that strong policy, along with creative financial strategies, are needed to maintain high standards (Carlson 1994). The role of states in the evaluation of policy and projects has been strong at the reporting level.

The classroom teacher is encouraged to find out about the state-level pilot programs and evaluations that have taken place, or are in process, to explore the possibility of either building on existing partnerships for distance learning or modeling some of the successful implementation designs that have already received state support. Reviews of the literature and state department of education Web page searches will provide contact information that will lead you to those that will provide assistance and direction.

The membership of the American Technical Education Association provides professional leadership through the support of presentations and discussions on how to design future instruction. For example, at its thirty-fifth National Conference (1998), the membership heard, in response to theories that the PreK–12 institutions will not be able to meet the challenge of a new information age. They also learned how the state of Tennessee was working "to refocus programs and funding in collaboration with state policymakers, economic developers, local school systems, and federally funded job training contractors to create a seamless system providing lifelong learning opportunities for K-80 [lifelong learners]" (Henderson, Curda, and Curda 1999). Among the features that are suggested for this seamless system are learner-centered instruction that can be delivered at the desktop, quick response to industry demands, and open entrance and exit enrollment, so that the competition for the same traditional learners will cease and the development of instruction for the nontraditional learner will increase. Does your state have a plan for reaching a similar goal of educating and training its workforce? The *National Association of State Boards of Education* (*NASBE*) offers a Web index (http://www.nasbe.org/Site_Map.html) that directs you to state education profiles, state departments of education links, and information on state education governance.

## Learning Possibility

Did you know that the *Hawaii Department of Education* (http://doe.k12.hi.us/) has 251 schools, with a 18:1 student/teacher ratio, and an average teacher salary of $36,598? This information was retrieved at the *National Association of State Boards of Education* (*NASBE*) Web site (accessed 4 January 2002) (http://www.nasbe.org/Educational_Issues/State_Stats/hawaii.htm). Access the NASBE state education agencies page (http://www.nasbe.org/SEA_Links /SEA_Links.html) to find out how your state compares. Is this information that you can use for comparing your district to other districts?

Demonstrating how cooperation between institutions and states improves educational access and economics, the Southern Regional Education Board (SREB), a coalition that has crossed regional accrediting associations since 1948 in Alabama, Arkansas, Delaware, Florida, Georgia, Kentucky, Louisiana, Maryland, Mississippi, North Carolina, Oklahoma, South Carolina, Tennessee, Texas, Virginia, and West Virginia, also supports the Southern Regional Electronic Campus. When working with various agencies of separate states, like SREB, policy issues must be addressed in order to move forward to the development and implementation stages (Jones 1994). Promoting this cooperation between independent and state postsecondary institutions, the *Electronic Campus* (http://www.electroniccampus.org/) of the SREB facilitates access at the associate, bachelor, and graduate levels. Students enroll in an institution, at which they can also apply for financial aid and register for courses at the Electronic Campus. Courses are taken electronically through the Internet. Combinations of courses, through distance and traditional learning, are allowed, but students have to check with advisors at their institutions to guarantee the transfer and acceptance of credits. Institutions participating in the Electronic Campus agree to follow the *Principles of Good Practice* (http://www.electroniccampus.org/student/srecinfo/publications /principles.asp) that address resources, curriculum, and institutional support.

State policy leadership helps to bridge interinstitutional cooperation between levels, such as secondary schools and community colleges. Because issues, such as dual enrollment in a distance learning setting, can affect secondary and postsecondary institutions, state policy that addresses quality assurance is needed to integrate distance learning into existing community colleges (Kovel-Jarboe 1997). Examples of the successful use of technology between cooperating K–12 schools and community college institutions have shown that these combinations of delivery at different levels are particularly important and beneficial to rural areas (Spears and Tatroe 1997).

States, such as Florida, Georgia, Maryland, and Ohio, have seen the need to provide educational leadership in the form of seamless systems that bridge levels for the PreK–20 student. Because of the many existing gaps in policy and coordination in some states, the seamless model can be very effective when distance learning solutions are explored for working and homebound adults (Boswell 2000). School districts, community colleges, and universities, whether independent or public, have the opportunity to bring a willingness to ease the transitional roadblocks that are currently between institutions by dovetailing curriculum and developing common policies, standards, and measures of learning outcomes for students that take courses through distance learning.

In addition to offering leadership by bringing institutions of different levels together, states can also offer leadership by providing meaningful statements of policy and position. For example, the state of Connecticut offers a *Position Statement on Educational Technology* (http://www.state.ct.us/sdeboard /tech.pdf) that provides direction to teachers and local districts. Further, the *Connecticut Statewide Educational Technology Plan* provides a statement of philosophy on technology in education, as well as information on distance learning. Documents such as these help districts and schools take action as they develop and implement their technology and distance learning plans.

In the world of a schoolteacher, nothing encourages communication with state personnel more than a toll-free number or a Web address. Teachers are very limited in their telephone contact, by both time and restricted use of long-distance services. It is imperative that teachers are able to contact your distance learning office with ease. Promote this contact in publications and at conferences to project your office as a clearinghouse of information on distance learning in your state.

Addressing the need to train its teachers in technology, Michigan offers free online courses on Web activities at *Teach for Tomorrow* (http://tft.merit.edu/). Facilitators for these courses are given free training that helps them guide teachers in their areas. Further partnering of state, university, community college, and K–12 schools in Michigan has resulted in the collection of "best practices" lesson plans for technology at *Best Practices of Technology Integration in Michigan* site (http://www.bestpractices.cc/) (Hoffman and Thompson 2000). Though listing developments at the postsecondary level, EDUCAUSE's *Effective Practices and Solutions* (http://www.educause.edu/ep/) is a good source for contemporary distance learning ideas.

State policies on distance learning and related technologies provide the direction that is needed by districts and local schools to plan. Keep in mind that these policies and master plans change and evolve. The state of California, for example, documented planning for technology in 1992 with its *Master Plan for Education Technology* (http://www.cde.ca.gov/edtech/mplan/) and in 2002 provided districts with *Education Technology Planning: A Guide for District Schools* (http://www.cde.ca.gov/ctl/edtechplan.pdf).

Throughout the United States, there is evidence that states are crossing institutional barriers and creating partnerships so that they can better serve their students. To continue these and future technology and distance learning developments, state departments of education must maintain a high level of communication with the individual teachers and principals of schools that are leading distance learning developments.

## Section G. By Federal Personnel

Though not as specific as state levels in terms of implementation, federal sources that provide overall mission statements and directives are available. The U.S. Department of Education sponsors some policy initiatives and development that are available through the Educational Resources Information Center (ERIC) and its *Clearinghouse on Information and Technology* (http://www.ericit.org). The *Clearinghouse on Information and Technology* offers a wealth of full-text documents and links on Educational Technology and Library Science. Be sure to look at a listing of all *ERIC Clearinghouses* (http://eric.ed.gov) to begin generating ideas on how these resources can help you.

One of the most noted ways that federal personnel have provided support for distance learning has been through the facilitation of grants. With a total $135 million grant for teacher training in technology, federal grants have varied in capacity building, implementation, catalyst, and length of support, from one to three years (Ganley 1999). Though these grants are awarded to colleges and universities, the funding is intended to support these postsecondary institutions as they assist with the development and technology training in school districts. Through grant funding, the U.S. Department of Education encourages postsecondary institutions to provide leadership for consortia that include PreK–12, state agencies, and nonprofit groups. These programs address different aspects of technology, such as school and library access through E-rate and distance learning through the Star Schools Program (Roberts 2000).

Federal offices, such as the Office of Educational Research and Improvement have evaluated the use of distance learning for rural school delivery (Batey and Cowell 1986). Findings showed that distance learning could increase the quality of instruction and offerings of content.

The U.S. Department of Education provides a newsletter, *Community Update* (http://www.ed.gov/offices/OIIA/communityupdate/archives.html), that is free to the public, in both print and electronic format. The newsletter commonly addresses topics of national concern to education and lists pamphlets, books, videotapes, and posters that are free to schools, teachers, and parents. In a recent issue (November/December 2001) is a description of President Bush's *Leave No Child Behind* plan and its four "pillars" that include: increase accountability for school performance, focus on what works, reduce bureaucracy and increase flexibility, and empower parents. This plan is further communicated at its Web page (http://www.ed.gov/offices/OESE/esea/). Request copies by e-mail (edpubs@inet.ed.gov) or by telephone (1-877-4ED-PUBS). Publications can also be downloaded.

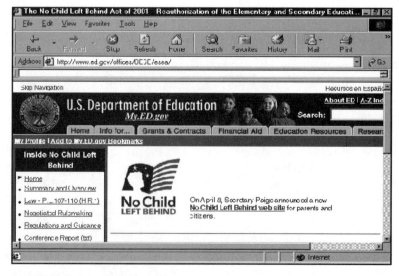

*No Child Left Behind* Web site:
**http://www.ed.gov/offices/OESE/esea/**

The *Community Update* regularly reports distance learning successes throughout the country, such as the Sabine Parish School System in Louisiana, which used a variety of grants, including federal grants, to network its district (Ashby 2001). The district used InTech to train its teachers to infuse technology into the curriculum, and LEADTech to train its principals to support the technology. Students and teachers have learned to be comfortable enough with the new learning and teaching styles. Other reports of the federal government's support of distance education using technologies are online (http://www.ed.gov/Technology), including reports of the Learning Anytime Anywhere Partnerships (LAAP).

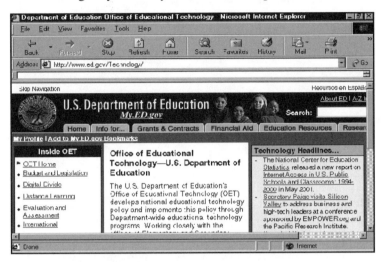

*Office of Educational Technology* (U.S. Department of
Education) Web site: http://www.ed.gov/Technology/

By modeling interactive distance learning activities itself, the U.S. Department of Education has been holding a series of satellite town meetings and programs that offer a discussion on topics of education. You can also participate in the town meeting through Webcasts, which are also archived online. Information on the meetings is online (http://ed.gov/inits/stm/) or call 1-800-USA-LEARN or 1-877-4ED-PUBS.

Federal personnel that work with funding opportunities usually provide contact information to key state and district personnel. As understandable as this is, given that there are many people who wish information, federal personnel are also helpful when they provide direct contact for teachers. One example of the direct contact is through the toll-free number for the U.S. Department of Education (1-800-USA-LEARN or 1-877-4ED-PUBS). A source of free materials and reports, live operators and information specialists will help you with your informational needs. Don't hesitate to ask about the latest publications, posters, and videotapes that are available.

In addition to the assistance and leadership provided, the federal government is also involved with the legal aspects of online communication and education. Beyond the better-known areas of filtering and child protection that can impact citizens at school or at home, federal legislatures and courts impact our computer behavior. Rulings have been made on the legality of searches of campus computers (*Edupage*, 13 July 2001) on the basis that it is reasonable to expect the records (or files) to be public. In terms of distance learning, would it be reasonable to expect that a student's course-related files are also public, even when they are housed on a privately owned computer? How far will the distance learning community extend, and how far will the legalities of searching extend? There is, of course, no way of anticipating how these questions will be answered next year, in five years, or even in ten years. As with most issues relating to distance learning, rulings will continue to develop. However, the safe computing guidelines should direct us in our learning activities.

# Section H. By Parents

Even after you have identified all of the professional documents and organizations that are available to you on distance learning, you have yet to explore one of your most varied and supportive groups—parents! Because Corporate America is so dependent upon technology today, many parents have a personal computer on the work or home desktop. This job-computer connection naturally promotes roles that a parent can assume in interactive distance learning activities, such as:

- co-instructor,

- demonstrator,

- facilitator,

- guest speaker,

- participant, or

- volunteer.

Parental involvement is crucial to the learning success of students. Before using interactive distance education learning activities, meet with parents to discuss the type of instruction you are planning. Explain how they can support what you are doing by being alert to distance learning possibilities. Invite them to communicate with you through e-mail. Ask them if they are available to volunteer to help with Web navigating, to participate in an online chat session, or if they would be willing to mentor a student on an assignment via e-mail. Encourage parents to become involved with their student's at-home distance learning activities by showing interest and asking to view readings, assignments, projects, and simulations. Active parenting and monitoring may help to stem some of the negative activities that students are doing. After all, as has been ruled in one Illinois court, parents are liable for illegal use of the Internet by their children and can be sued (*Edupage*, 11 December 2000). Awareness of negative behaviors and consequences may encourage more parents to pay attention to their children's Internet use.

Should parents encourage their children to use computers? Yes. Why? Not only do computers appeal to the fun part of all learning, but they are also required in almost every work aspect in the United States today. Parent encouragement can certainly help to get students accustomed to using applications and productivity programs and going online to research information to use to learn or solve some of life's problems. Teaching children that research can apply to all aspects of life, from finding a car adapter for a portable computer to buying tickets to go see Grandma, is critical to developing information literacy.

How do you encourage parents to help their children with technology? Whatever the type of technology that the parent wants the child to use, it is best for the parent to purchase it and start working with it themselves (Aycock 1991). This sounds simple, doesn't it? We already know that modeling works to promote student reading, so it is logical that parental modeling of technology use will do the same. A recent study of 500 children from ages nine to seventeen showed that 63 percent prefer being online to watching television, and 55 percent enjoyed being online more than being on the telephone (*Edupage*, 15 November 1999).

In preparation to helping students become successful distance learners, parents may ask you for a recommendation on the type of computer to purchase. You may consider making it your policy to never offer purchasing advice, because in the event that something goes wrong with the computer, you could be the blamed party. Instead, stay aware of resources that offer purchasing guides, such as *Buying a Computer* (Federal Consumer Information Catalog) (http://www.pueblo.gsa.gov/cic_text/misc/buy-computer/buycomp .htm) or *Computer Shopper* (http://zdnet.com/computershopper/). Be ready to direct parents to some of these purchasing resources, as an alternative to offering specific suggestions.

## *Learning Possibility*

To capitalize on the interest that students have for computers, access *KidSpace* at the *Internet Public Library* (http://www.ipl.org/cgi-bin/youth /youth.out.pl?sub=fun9800), which has a collection of sites that are good for parents and teachers to use with students. These sites include general ideas for art, craft, holiday, and recipe fun.

Parents who are new to distance learning may have questions about the safety of their children in online distance learning classrooms. The need for technology-related security has received a great deal of attention in the press, both in relation to the safety of hardware and files on the system and, more importantly, related to the safety of minors. Many public libraries and schools have addressed this former issue of security by using computer security fire walls, restricting users to software-controlled environments that limit user abilities, and having stringent user clearances. Many public schools think that they have answered this problem through Acceptable Use Policies.

Before starting a discussion of what is stated in an Acceptable Use Policy, often referred to as an AUP, know that there is a great deal of disagreement within the education profession, and in courts, on standards of acceptable computing practice and the monitoring of students, staff, and other users of computing equipment. In some cases, this disagreement has related to claims of infringing upon intellectual freedom and the freedom of expression, even though the right of the staff to monitor student expression has already been awarded through a U.S. Supreme Court ruling (*Hazelwood School District v. Kuhlmeier* [1988]) permitting high schools to censor student newspapers. This ruling was recently extended to college yearbooks in *Kincaid v. Gibson* (1999). Regardless of your sense of right or wrong related to this broad area, it would be wise to assume that you are working in a system where student and even faculty access to distributed information systems that support distance learning is considered a privilege and not an academic right. However, knowing this, you should be able to work within the framework of any AUP to structure a positive distance learning experience, for both your students and yourself.

Having introduced some of the issues that relate to AUPs, what are the elements that are included in most examples of these policies? As with any policy, the well-written AUP begins with an introduction to the policy, a description of the school and population for which the policy was designed, and a statement on how the policy will be followed and enforced. Next, three major sections are included in the AUP:

1. Inappropriate behaviors

2. Social mores and sensibilities

3. System/software usage

A section on inappropriate behaviors is important to both student and instructor because this is where limits are defined. What is acceptable for you to do on the computer system? What is unacceptable? The limits of behavior, as provided in the AUP, strike at the heart of ethical behavior in the computing world and offer an opportunity to teach students what responsible behavior is, as applied to computing. Some examples of acceptable (and unacceptable) behavior include:

1. Using organizational online resources to conduct research for educational purposes. *It is not acceptable to use organizational online resources to conduct personal research. For*

*example, unless you teach in an economic or financially related field, it is not acceptable for you to track your favorite stock or retirement fund each day.*

2. Using existing software on the network for educational purposes. *It is not acceptable to download software for a school network if this use for an organization violates the copyright law or if the agreement states that software will not be downloaded onto the network.*

3. Using organizational online resources to send someone a brief message, if asking for information that is directly related to your teaching duties. *It is not acceptable to e-mail your family members each day through a Hotmail account so that your school network operators cannot easily track your activities.*

4. Using organizational online resources to subscribe to and participate in chatroom activities, listservs, and news groups when these activities support the school's functions. *It is not acceptable to participate in chatrooms, listservs, and news groups for personal interests not related to school activities.*

5. Using organizational online resources to view materials and make copies that fall under the "Fair Use Guidelines" of the Copyright Act. *It is not acceptable to assume that if you can access, copy, import, or otherwise capture an item, element, symbol, or file, then it must be reasonable to use it without gaining permission of the copyright owner.*

## Learning Possibility

You have finally found the perfect Web site to use in your lesson. However, you know there is a risk that by the time you locate the site, the computer will have locked up and the students will lose interest. The solution? Use a program such as Web Whacker to copy the files and load them on your server for offline viewing. Question: Is loading these files onto your server considered acceptable use of the computing files? Why or why not?

---

6. Observing "safe data" behavior to protect the files and network of the institution. *It is not acceptable to expose networks and files to risk because you choose not to use virus scanners.*

7. Using your own account for all activities. *It is unacceptable to use another person's account, even if that person gives you the password to access the account. Why? This is an issue of permissions and monitoring. If another person has access to an account, that person may choose to act irresponsibly online. If the person is using someone else's account, it then appears as though the owner of the account is the one who is behaving irresponsibly. Why take the risk of being blamed for irresponsible behavior and losing your computing privileges?*

8. Managing and monitoring your own files. *It is not acceptable to move or destroy files that are resident on the computer and necessary to operate equipment and networks. Ask the educational technologist or media specialist how often it is necessary to recopy and replace files due to mischievous behavior? Assume that the computer used for distance learning technologies is akin to a classroom. Don't we want to teach students to treat computers with the same respect that they would use if they were in the teacher's physical classroom? Respect for property is demanded in the distance learning classroom.*

9.  Participating maturely and responsibly. *It is not acceptable to use inappropriate language, annoy, stalk, or threaten anyone in any way online. All learners have the right to feel just as safe behind the computer as they feel in the security of their own homes or classrooms.*

10. Abiding by all lab and computing rules as agreed upon by the school community. *Is it wise to give students the chance to observe a teacher who purposely violates computing rules, when the teacher could, instead, demonstrate positive and ethical computing behavior that, ultimately, benefits all users?*

## Learning Possibility

Locate the AUP for your school, district, and state. Are the student policies any different from the teacher versions? Are the policies restricted to behaviors while on campus, during schooltime, or do they cover all activities that may occur with the account issued by the district, regardless of time or place?

———————————

The mores and sensibilities related to computing are mostly an issue of civil behavior, and not legally prescribed behavior, although the violation of these could have legal consequences. For example, let's say that you are a social studies teacher, and you are taking your students on an online field trip. You give your students a Web address, and either you or the students mix up a "dot" (.) gov with a "dot" (.) com. The result is that the students still get a HIT off of the address, but, unfortunately, the student is directed to a pornographic site, without your even knowing that happened. The responsible student that has received instruction in the sometimes unpredictable world of online resources will know to correct the keying of the online resource and will retry accessing the site. How could an AUP protect the student and the teacher in this case?

Another issue relating to mores and sensibilities is that of proper netiquette. Users have caused themselves many more problems with their own keystrokes than you can imagine. Oftentimes these problems are unintentional and, more likely than not, related to a lack of attention to detail. Ask any user what his pet peeve is when online, and you will get many responses. Most experienced online users will agree that the lack of courtesy with e-mail messages is a true aggravation. Examples? The lack of courtesy is shown when:

1.  The e-mail sender uses no greeting and no closing, as though the sender expects you to remember that PINK48623@anyhost.com means a particular student's mother.

2.  The e-mail sender offers no context to the previous message as a follow-up.

3.  The e-mail sender "shouts" by placing everything in capital letters.

4.  The e-mail sender uses the same header over and over and does not begin a new message when the subject changes.

5.  The e-mail message is written with the expectation that the receiver will respond with an immediate reply.

6.  The e-mail message header includes multiple addressees in the "to" and "cc" list.

7.  The e-mail sender incorporates a cutesy signature file that requires a lot of storage.

8.  The e-mail message includes attached files that do not have descriptive filenames.

9.  The e-mail sender forwards FYI files that the sender finds interesting but that are of no interest to you.

10. The e-mail sender forwards mail from other people without their permission.

Often, because they themselves may have not had the opportunity to participate in any learning activities that involved technology, parents may be skeptical of the distance learning process and related technology. Try suggesting support materials to parents that they can use to learn about the distance learning process. For example, *The Distance Learner's Guide* (Connick 1999) offers a nontechnical description of the nuts and bolts of distance learning that includes discussions from choosing the program, how to decide if distance learning is appropriate for the learner, how to choose a distance education provider, and improving performance. Sections, such as "Learning to Learn," provide realistic and practical suggestions that will encourage parents to work with the students.

Parents can also read *CyberSavvy: The Direct Marketing Association's Guide to Online Basics, Behavior and Privacy on the Internet* (http://www.cybersavvy.org/). A feature of this document, which can be used as a guide for family Internet activities, is its Family Pledge that facilitates a discussion of what family members should do when, for example, they receive a "scary or threatening e-mail message." By opening the lines of communication in a low-key way, parents can speak to their daughters and sons about what concerns them about online activities. *GetNetWise* (http://www.getnetwise.org/) has a learning and growth focus, but this site also provides parents with information on online privacy and safety. As you develop your distance learning program, you will probably want to develop your own guide for parents and students. Be sure to keep notes about what to include in your guide as you offer distance learning courses.

## *Learning Possibility*

Did you think that cookies were only something that added inches to your waistline? Or that Web bugs were something like spiders? Cookies and Web bugs are software-directed information collectors for Web sites. For more on cookies, look at Netscape's description of how it uses this device for online information collection (http://home.netscape.com/legal_notices/). *The Internet Privacy Coalition* (http://www.privacy.org/ipc/) and the *Privacy Rights Clearinghouse* (http://www.privacyrights.org/) are good sources to check with future questions on Web privacy. In addition to including some more advice on privacy, the Awards page of *Interesting Places to Go* (http://places.to/Browse/awards.html) offers thousands of "safe" sites that parents can visit with their children.

Beyond safety issues, parents can use technology to monitor school information. Encourage your parents to go to their district's Web site to see what is available. For example, Palm Beach County, Florida, schools has a *Public Affairs* Web site (http://www.palmbeach.k12.fl.us/PublicAffairs/) that includes a *Parent Links* page. The *Parent Connection* (http://www.ccsd.net/parent/index.phtml) includes information that affects all Clark County (Nevada) families with school-age children, such as school lunches, testing schedules, the school calendar, and graduation requirements. Be sure to check your local school district's Web site to see what is being provided to parents in your area.

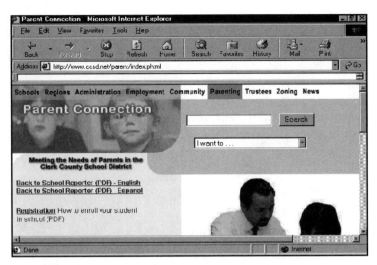

***Parent Connection*** **(Clark County, Nevada) Web site:**
**http://www.ccsd.net/parent/index.phtml**

In addition to monitoring local school activities, the technology exists for parents to use the Web to verify that their children are in attendance at school. Schools can easily post a copy of the absentee report for parents to see. Parents can also monitor the progress of their children within the school curriculum through quarterly grades and notes sent by the teacher. Imagine the convenience of reminding parents to send permission slips and supply money with a short e-mail message. Further, imagine the appreciation of the parent who receives a quick e-mail response from the teacher in answer to a question about the student's grades.

Beyond local school boards, state and federal departments of education have provided many print and Web resources intended to inform parents of current initiatives. For example, the U.S. Department of Education and the *Partnership for Family Involvement in Education* (http://pfie.ed.gov/) want to build upon existing partnerships to encourage students to stay involved in school, from preschool through college. The partnership supports activities nationwide and works to get participation from religious groups and volunteer organizations in addition to parents and schools. By the way, be sure to recall that the U.S. Department of Education has a toll-free number (1-800-USA-LEARN or 1-877-4ED-PUBS) where you can request publications on your topic of concern. Many of these printed documents that describe current initiatives, reference sources, and financial information can also be accessed through the department's Web site, a few of which include America Reads Challenge, Digest of Education Statistics, Direct Loans, Disabilities Education (IDEA), Nation's Report Card (NAEP), and Financial Aid for Students. Under Technology, there is information on the Digital Divide, technology conferences, Internet safety, and free resources for technology.

There are many resources to which you will want to direct parents. For PreK parents, there is *Building Your Baby's Brain: A Parent's Guide to the First Five Years* (http://www.ed.gov/offices/OERI /ECI/publications.html), *Helping Your Preschool Child* (http://www.ed.gov/pubs/parents/preschool/index.html), or *Learning Partners: A Guide to Educational Activities for Families* (http://www.ed.gov/pubs/parents /LearnPtnrs/index.html). *Summer Home Learning Recipes* (http://www.ed.gov/pubs/Recipes) will provide elementary parents with ideas on what to do during extended vacations to keep their children learning. Other free items can be found at *Federal Resources for Educational Excellence* (http://www.ed.gov/free).

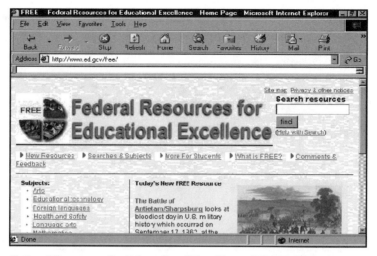

***Federal Resources for Educational Excellence (FREE)* Web site:
http://www.ed.gov/free/**

Some of these titles have accompanying videotapes available, so be sure to ask for them. And lest we forget a topic closely related to interactive distance learning technologies, do not pass up a copy of the *Parents Guide to the Internet* (http://www.ed.gov/pubs/parents/internet).

Do not forget that some parents will look to the school for guidance on reading for parents. Knowing some quality resources to recommend to parents, such as *Parenting Matters* (http://www.lifematters.com /parentn.html) or the *Minneapolis Star Tribune's* link to education (http://www.startribune.com/stories /1592/), will demonstrate your interest in involving them in their child's success.

Homeschooling parents will also have an interest in resources that you can suggest. For those parents who are aware of the need to align their curriculum with the National Science Education Standards, you can recommend *The Science Activities Manual* (http://www.utm.edu/departments/ed/cece/SAMK8.shtml). (Additional science resources can be found in the ERIC Digest, *Science in the Home School* [Lorson 1999]. *Let's Do Science!* (http://www.ed.gov/pubs/parents/LearnPtnrs/science.html) is another example of the publications for parents at the U.S. Department of Education's site (http://www.ed.gov/pubs/parents/) that includes other subject areas, such as writing, social studies, etc.

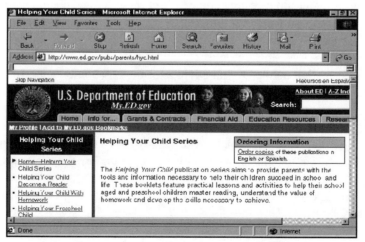

**U.S. Department of Education's *Helping Your Child Services*
Web site: http://www.ed.gov/pubs/parents/hyc.html**

# *Conclusion*

Because the model of distance learning includes more participants than any learning model practiced in the history of education, their roles demand coordination and cooperation if the distance learning model is to be successful. For many, regardless of level (whether local, district, state, regional, or federal), the coordination may provide a new facet to roles where planning and decision making were not vertically coordinated. Elements as simple as school calendars or equipment specifications now need to be coordinated so that varying levels of participants can coordinate activities. Coordinating at each level will require groups that had previously functioned in isolation to support the distance learning by promoting a sense of team effort that will facilitate distance learning. This team effort can result in great savings of time, energy, and effort that can be better spent on issues of curriculum development and coordination. An increasing number of alliances, consortia agreements, and professional networking can buoy the efforts of distance learning to levels of great accomplishment.

How can these efforts begin? Get involved with the existing distance learning groups in your school, district, county, or state. Find out how your groups can coordinate and participate with national efforts. Work within your professional organizations to further communicate these efforts and to link with existing successes. More likely than not, you will find that other institutions and organizations are looking for direction and leadership. The cooperation and partnership with other organizations will help your district to build meaningful alliances of support that will foster achievement, collaboration, and excellence in the field of distance learning.

Don't forget that the business community, which has representatives in many of the areas mentioned so far, has a great interest in our students becoming successful as independent distance learners. As many of us saw during the successful Net Days, parents and business partners were able to jointly put many schools online in a single day. Creative uses of resources can help move us closer to our goals of increased access to technology and distance learning opportunities.

Have we continued to build on the Net Day success? Is it possible that many of the technical support members of businesses are willing to support teachers by answering simple technical questions during the day that would otherwise go unanswered (Kelly 2000)? When businesses have computers that are ready to be discarded, can they just call their local schools and offer to install the machine on the network? Granted that this is already occurring in many districts, the bureaucracy of many school districts discourages this level of assistance. What can you do today to encourage a more cooperative effort? Who are the business, community college, or university contacts that would be willing to assist, for free, with answering questions or offering training sessions on in-service days?

Distance learning offers the opportunity to connect students of all ages, from preschool to postsecondary, from all locations, whether rural or international. Using distance learning technologies can bring students (present, past, and future) and educators into the classroom in ways that we are only beginning to explore. But as we all know, "access is not enough in the schools" (Tapscott 1998, 262). Beyond setting up and wiring computers, teachers must receive time, training, and support to help them implement distance learning activities. The levels of instruction are now only limited by our support of the curriculum and faculties that are making advances. Are you imagining the possibilities?

# *References*

"Alan Kay on Software Design, the Future of Programming & the Art of Learning." *Educom Review* 34, no. 2 (1999): 34–40.

American Association of School Librarians and Association for Educational Communications and Technology. *Information Power: Building Partnerships for Learning*. Chicago: American Library Association, 1998.

"Apple No Longer the Champion in Education," 23 March 2001, *Edupage* (owner-edupage@listserv.educause.edu) (http://www.educause.edu/pub/edupage/edupage.html).

"Are Parents Legally Responsible for Children's Internet Use?," 11 December 2000, *Edupage* (owner-edupage @listserv.educause.edu) (http://www.educause.edu/pub/edupage/edupage.html).

Ashby, Nicole. "Just a Click Away: Technology Connects a Rural Louisiana School District to the Rest of the World." *Community Update*, no. 87 (May 2001): 4–5.

Aycock, Heidi E. H. "How to Start Your Child with Computers." *Kids and Computers* 13, no. 12 (1991): S4 (2).

Barker, Bruce O. *The Distance Education Handbook: An Administrator's Guide for Rural and Remote Schools.* Charleston, WV: ERIC Clearinghouse on Rural Education and Small Schools, 1992. ERIC ED 340 547.

Barron, Ann, and Karen Ivers. *An Internet Research Model* (Proceedings of the Annual National Educational Computing Conference, 11–13 June 1996, Minneapolis, MN). ERIC ED 398 880.

Batey, Anne, and Richard N. Cowell. *Distance Education: An Overview.* Washington, DC: Office of Educational Research and Improvement, 1986. ERIC ED 278 519.

Blake, Virgil L. P. "The Virtual Library Impacts the School Library Media Center: A Bibliographic Essay." In *The Virtual School Library: Gateway to the Information Superhighway*, edited by Carol Collier Kuhlthau. Englewood, CO: Libraries Unlimited, 1996.

Bohnenkamp, Julie, and Jeff McMahon. "Community of Learners, Information, Communication and Knowledge." *T.H.E. Journal* 28, no. 11 (2001): 20–24.

Bork, Alfred. "Learning Technology." *EDUCAUSE Review* 35, no. 1 (2000): 74–81.

Boswell, Katherine. "Building Bridges or Barriers? Public Policies That Facilitate or Impede Linkages Between Community Colleges and Local School Districts." *New Directions for Community Colleges*, no. 111 (2000): 3–15.

"Buried Under a Mountain of Spam," 07 May 2001, *Edupage* (owner-edupage@listserv.educause.edu) (http://www.educause.edu/pub/edupage/edupage.html).

Cambre, Marjorie A., Barbara Erdman, and Leslie Hall. "The Challenge of Distance Education." *Journal of Staff Development* 17, no. 1 (1996): 38–41.

Carlson, Robert V. *A Case Study of the Impact of a State-Level Policy Designed to Improve Rural Schools in the State of Vermont.* Charleston, WV: Appalachia Educational Lab, 1994. ERIC ED 368 531.

Chamberlain, Shelley. "A Tec Coordinator's Road Map for the Information Highway." In *The Digital Classroom: How Technology Is Changing the Way We Teach and Learn*, edited by David T. Gordon. Cambridge, MA: Harvard Education Letter, 2000.

"Children Choose Web Surfing Over Channel Surfing," 15 November 1999, *Edupage* (owner-edupage@listserv .educause.edu) (http://www.educause.edu/pub/edupage/edupage.html).

Churma, Michelle. *A Guide to Integrating Technology Standards into the Curriculum.* Upper Saddle River, NJ: Merrill, 1999.

Connick, George P. *The Distance Learner's Guide.* Upper Saddle River, NJ: Prentice-Hall, 1999.

*Distance Education for All Ages in Minnesota: The K–12 Systems Perspective.* St. Paul, MN: Minnesota State Department of Education, 1990. ERIC ED 330 319.

"Female Freshmen Doubt Tech Skills," 22 January 2001, *Edupage* (owner-edupage@listserv.educause.edu) (http://www.educause.edu/pub/edupage/edupage.html).

"Firms Selling Bogus Degrees Increase on the Net," 3 January 2001, *Edupage* (owner-edupage@listserv.educause .edu) (http://www.educause.edu/pub/edupage/edupage.html).

Foshay, Wellesley R. "Can Instructional Design Deliver on the Promise of the Web?" *The Quarterly Review of Distance Education* 2, no. 1 (2001): 19–34.

Ganley, Susan. "Education Department Awards $135-Million to Support Technology in the Classroom." *The Chronicle of Higher Education*, 26 August 1999. (http://chronicle.com/daily/99/08/99082603n.htm) (26 August 1999).

Gosmire, Doreen, and Judy Vondruska. "Distance Teaching and Learning Academy." *TechTrends* 45, no. 3 (2001): 31–34.

Grover, Robert, et al. "Planning and Assessing Learning Across the Curriculum." *Knowledge Quest* 28, no. 1 (1999): 10–16.

Gurstelle, Carol R. *Libraries of the Future Bibliography*. St. Paul, MN: Metronet, 1999. (http://www.metronet.lib.mn.us/forlibs.cfm?id=176) (8 January 2000).

Heffernan-Cabrera, Patricia, and Celia C. Ayala. "From There to There with K–12 Distance Learning." In *Guide to Teleconferencing and Distance Learning*, edited by Patrick S. Portway and Carla Lane. Livermore, CA: Applied Business Telecommunications, 1992.

Hegarty, Michael, Anne Phelan, and Lisa Kilbride. *Classrooms for Distance Teaching & Learning: A Blueprint*. Dublin, Ireland: Audio Visual Centre, University College, 1998.

Hoffman, Ellen, and Ginny Thompson. "Putting the Research to Work." *TechTrends* 44, no. 2 (2000): 20–23.

Houdek, Elizabeth. *Managing Distance Education Courses* (The Guide Series in Continuing Education). Urbana-Champaign, IL: Office of Continuing Education and Public Services, University of Illinois, 1990.

Hudson, Heather E., and Charles H. Boyd. *Distance Learning: A Review for Educators*, 1984. ERIC 246 872.

Hyman, Linda Woods. "A Web Site as a Reference Resource: A Case Study of Blue Web'n." *Knowledge Quest* 27, no. 2 (1998): 33–35.

"Indiana University to Replace Computers Every Three Years," 1 January 2000, *Edupage* (owner-edupage@listserv.educause.edu) (http://www.educause.edu/pub/edupage/edupage.html).

"Internet Search Engines Suspected of Deception," 17 July 2001, *Edupage* (owner-edupage@listserv.educause.edu) (http://www.educause.edu/pub/edupage/edupage.html).

Jones, Sue. *Educational Technology: K–12 Planning and Investments in the SREB States*. Atlanta, GA: Southern Regional Education Board, 1994.

Kelly, Karen. "Partnerships: Making the Connection." In *The Digital Classroom*, edited by David T. Gordon. Cambridge, MA: Harvard Education Letter, 2000.

Komoski, P. Kenneth, and Eric Plotnick. "Seven Steps to Responsible Software Selection." *ERIC Digest*. Syracuse, NY: ERIC Clearinghouse on Information and Technology, Syracuse University, 1995. ERIC ED 382 157. (http://www.ed.gov/databases/ERIC_Digests/ed382157.html) (5 March 2000).

Kovel-Jarboe, Patricia. "From the Margin to the Mainstream: State-Level Policy and Planning for Distance Education." In *Building a Working Policy for Distance Education* (New Directions for Community Colleges, no. 99), edited by Connie L. Dillon and Rosa Cintron. San Francisco, CA: Jossey-Bass, 1997.

"Leaving No Child Behind." *Community Update* 93 (November/December 2001): 4–8.

Lederman, Tim. "Local Area Networks for K–12 Schools." *ERIC Digest*. Syracuse, NY: ERIC Clearinghouse on Information and Technology, Syracuse University, 1995. ERIC ED 389 277. (http://www.ed.gov/databases/ERIC_Digests/ed389277.html) (20 February 2000).

Lorson, Mark. "Science in the Home School." *ERIC Digest*. Columbus, OH: ERIC Clearinghouse for Science, Mathematics, and Environmental Education, 1999. ERIC ED 432 456. (http://www.ed.gov/databases/ERIC_Digests/ed432456.html) (20 January 2002).

Maushak, Nancy J., and Lynn Manternach. *Iowa Distance Education Alliance: Evaluation Report, July 1996–September 1997*. Ames, IA: College of Education, Iowa State University of Science and Technology, 1997. ERIC ED 416 818.

McCollum, Kelley. "On Line, Ways to Misbehave Can Outpace College Rules." *The Chronicle of Higher Education* 6, no. 4 (17 September 1999): A35–36.

McGarvey, Robert. "Search Us, Says Google." *Technology Review* 103, no. 6 (2000): 108–13.

Meyen, Edward L., Paul Tangen, and Cindy H. T. Lian. "Developing Online Instruction: Partnership Between Instructors and Technical Developers." *Journal of Special Education Technology* 14, no. 1 (1999): 18–31.

*Michigan Essential Goals and Objectives for Foreign Language Education (K–12)*. Lansing, MI: Michigan State Board of Education, 1990. ERIC ED 344 471.

Milken Exchange and the International Society for Technology in Education. "Will Teachers Be Prepared to Teach in a Digital Age?: A National Survey on Information Technology in Teacher Education." Santa Monica, CA: Milken Exchange on Education Technology, 1999. (http://www.mff.org/publications/publications.taf?page=154) (4 January 2001).

"Missouri Gets Good Grades for Online GED Preparation Program," 20 December 2000, *Edupage* (owner-edupage @listserv.educause.edu) (http://www.educause.edu/pub/edupage/edupage.html).

Moore, D. Michael, John K. Burton, and Norman R. Dodl. "The Role of Facilitators in Virginia's Electronic Classroom Project." In *K–12 Distance Education: Learning, Instruction, and Teacher Training*, edited by Michael G. Moore and Margaret A. Koble. University Park, PA: American Center for the Study of Distance Education, College of Education, Pennsylvania State University, 1997.

Moore, John. "Connecting the Schools: Another Phase of South Dakota's Plan." *TechTrends* 45, no. 3 (2001): 22–25.

"More E-Mail Users Take Spammers to Court," 14 January 2002, *Edupage* (owner-edupage@listserv.educause .edu) (http://www.educause.edu/pub/edupage/edupage.html).

"Next Napsters Wait in the Wings," 9 February 2001, *Edupage* (owner-edupage@listserv.educause.edu) (http://www .educause.edu/pub/edupage/edupage.html).

O'Sullivan, Lisa C. "Education Software." *AskERIC InfoGuide, 1996*. (http://askeric.org/Old_Askeric/InfoGuides /alpha_list/Education_Software-5.96.html) (4 January 2002).

"Palm Hopes Infrared Stations Expand Audience for PDAs," 7 July 2001, *Edupage* (owner-edupage@listserv .educause.edu) (http://www.educause.edu/pub/edupage/edupage.html).

Pease, Edward C. "A Purple Yearbook and Free Speech on Campuses." *The Chronicle of Higher Education*, 19 November 1999. (http://chronicle.com/weekly/sitesearch.htm) (6 January 2001).

Renovato, Pam. *The Psychology of Color and Internet Marketing*, n.d. (http:www.free-webmaster-tools.com /choosing-web-site-colors.htm).

"Report Urges Change in Male-Dominated Culture of Computer," 12 April 2000, *Edupage* (owner-edupage @listserv.educause.edu) (http://www.educause.edu/pub/edupage/edupage.html).

Roberts, Linda G. "Federal Programs to Increase Children's Access to Educational Technology." *The Future of Children: Children and Computer Technology* 10, no. 2 (2000): 181–85. (*The Future of Children* is online [http://www .futureofchildren.org], and full-image issues of the publication are available at no charge.)

Russo, Alexander. "Online Coursework." *School Administrator* 58, no. 9 (2001): 6–48.

"Rutgers Study Confirms That Web Makes Cheating Easier," 16 May 2001, *Edupage* (owner-edupage@listserv .educause.edu) (http://www.educause.edu/pub/edupage/edupage.html).

"Satellite Interconnection and Distance Delivery in Alaska: Toward the 21st Century." *Summary and Recommendations of the Satellite Interconnection Project Under the Direction of the Telecommunications Information Council*. Juneau, AK: Alaska Public Broadcasting Commission, 1995. ERIC ED 383 280.

Schopp, Melody, and Marlene Rothernel. "TTL: South Dakota Technology for Teaching and Learning Academy." *TechTrends* 45, no. 3 (2001): 26–29.

Sorenson, Chris. "Distance Education: Operational Issues." In *Encyclopedia of Distance Education Research in Iowa*, 2d ed., edited by Beth Kumar, Nancy J. Maushak, Michael Simonson, and Kristen Egeland Wright. Ames, IA: Teacher Education Alliance of the Iowa Distance Education Alliance, Iowa's Star Schools Program, 1997.

Spears, Suzanna, and Randy L. Tatroe. "Seamless Education Through Distance Learning: State Policy Initiatives for Community College/K–12 Partnerships." In *Building a Working Policy for Distance Education* (New Directions for Community Colleges, no. 99), edited by Connie L. Dillon and Rosa Cintron. San Francisco, CA: Jossey-Bass, 1997.

Spector, J. Michael, and Illeana de la Teja. "Competencies for Online Teaching." *ERIC Digest* EDO-IR-2001-09. Syracuse, NY: ERIC Clearinghouse on Information and Technology, Syracuse University, 2001. (http:www.ericit.org /digests/EDO-IR-2001-09.shtml) (21 January 2002).

Spitzer, Kathleen L., Michael B. Eisenberg, and Carrie A. Lowe. *Information Literacy: Essential Skills for the Information Age*. Syracuse, NY: ERIC Clearinghouse on Information and Technology, Syracuse University, 1999.

Sprague, Carolyn Ann. "Accessible Web Design." *ERIC Digest* EDO-IR-1999-09. Syracuse, NY: ERIC Clearinghouse on Information and Technology, Syracuse University, 1999. (http://www.ericit.org/digests/EDO-IR-1999-09.shtml) (4 January 2002).

Stephens, Gene. *Youth at Risk: Saving the World's Most Precious Resource*. Bethesda, MD: World Future Society, 1997.

Tapscott, Don. *Growing Up Digital: The Rise of the Net Generation*. New York: McGraw-Hill, 1998.

Teacher Preparation Star Chart: A Self-Assessment Tool for Colleges of Education—Preparing a New Generation of Teachers. CEO Forum on Education and Technology, 2000. (http://www.ceoforum.org) (8 March 2000).

"Teachers' Feelings of Preparedness." *Indicator of the Month*. Washington, DC: U.S. Department of Education, National Center for Education Statistics (NCES 2000-003), 1999. (http://www.nces.ed.gov/pubsearch/pubsinfo.asp?pubid =2000003) (16 February 2000).

Tennant, Roy. *Practical HTML: A Self-Paced Tutorial*. Berkeley, CA: Library Solutions Press, 1998.

Thomas, Margie Klink. "Resource-Based Learning." *Knowledge Quest* 27, no. 4 (1999): 26–30.

Universal Access to Learner-Directed Education Through Telecommunications: Developing the Electronic Superhighway as an Avenue for Community Learning. Albany, NY: State University of New York, Research Foundation, 1994. ERIC ED 375 810.

*Using Computers in Teaching: Telecourse Guide. A Pilot Project in Distance Learning by Satellite*. Raleigh, NC: North Carolina State Department of Public Instruction, 1986. ERIC ED 273 268.

Watson, Ruth. "The Trumbull County Community Network Project." *T.H.E. Journal* 28, no. 10 (2001): 18–26.

Weisburg, Hilda K., and Ruth Toor. "The Information Curriculum: Teaching Concepts for the Virtual Library Environment." In *The Virtual School Library: Gateway to the Information Superhighway*, edited by Carol Collier Kuhlthau. Englewood, CO: Libraries Unlimited, 1996.

Weise, Elizabeth. "Search Sites Brush Up on People Skills," 24 January 2000, *USA Today*. (http://www.usatoday.com /life/cyber/tech/review/crg841.htm) (26 February 2000).

Wingfield, Kyle. "Ga. Tech Develops Cheating Detector," 16 January 2002, *Excite News*. (http://apnews.excite.com/ article/20020116/D7H2PSIG1.html) (17 January 2002).

Young, Terrence E. "The Big Three Information Literacy Models." *Knowledge Quest* 27, no. 3 (1999): 32–35.

Yow, Donna. "Children First." *Internet World* 7, no. 4 (1996): 92–93.

# Chapter 7

# Evaluation of Interactive Distance Learning Activities

Evaluation of learning occurs throughout the school curriculum. As a result, all teachers should have experience with developing paper-and-pencil tests and other evaluative instruments. These more traditional forms of evaluation will not be the focus of this section. In our increasing efforts to meet a wide variety of learning styles and incorporate many learning modalities, we need to keep an open mind to changing the way that we evaluate interactive distance learning (Sanders and Morrison-Shetlar 2001). In order to consider this potential need for change, let's review the benefits of using interactive distance learning technologies (Chapter 2) so that we can justify building up the educational infrastructure to support distance learning modalities. Interactive distance learning:

- increases student interest in the day-to-day classroom activities.

- expands contact with students and teachers outside the campus-based school.

- offers limitless learning opportunities that are not confined to the normal seven-and-a-half-hour school day.

- actively engages teachers with curriculum development.

- keeps teachers up-to-date with educational trends.

- helps teachers to keep students on task.

- provides professional and personal development for teachers.

- is a source of pride for administrators.

- encourages administrators to spend more time on curriculum development and budgeting.

- allows administrators to increase the number of courses offered.

- allows paraprofessionals and staff members opportunities to support the learning process.

- helps to increase parent involvement.

- benefits citizen-taxpayers by keeping schools on task.

- provides citizen-taxpayers with opportunities to learn about distance learning technologies.

- provides citizen-taxpayers with a well-prepared, entry-level workforce.

With these benefits in mind, let us focus on the goals of the distance learning activities. With most learning activities, goals should provide a broad sense of what the student should be able to do with the new knowledge, skills, and attitudes gained. Based on the premise that all school activities should funnel into the desire for students to assume their roles in a democratic society upon graduation, distance learning activities merely offer additional modalities for student learning by expanding learning beyond the four walls of the traditional classroom. Thus, the goals of distance learning are the same as the goals for traditional instruction, but the teacher now has the tools and opportunities to implement new teaching strategies and modalities.

Before we continue this discussion, let's agree that many of our current teaching modalities have enjoyed success for years. The purpose of this handbook is not to discourage any teacher from using tried-and-true methods, but to encourage all teachers to take advantage of the many benefits gained by implementing distance learning technologies in their classrooms and current curricula.

This chapter discusses how to determine benefits of learning outcomes (Section A), how to establish grades (Section B), and how to determine material and personnel costs for budget justifications and projections (Section C). As you review these sections, note how these issues apply directly to your classroom and school situation. As you think about evaluations, consider how the practice of evaluation is being distributed through technology. For example, today students can go to *TeacherReviews.com* (http://teacherreviews.com/) and post and read reviews of college-level courses and teachers. The day may soon be here, however, when primary and secondary students have the same opportunity to voice their ideas about teachers and their learning experiences. With face-to-face learning, a principal can edit, and even shut down, a school newspaper, but what can a principal do if students post a nonsanctioned Web site that is managed independently of school equipment and resources? How do you think you would handle a situation where a minor-aged student posted defamatory online remarks about you, the teacher? If a Web site, such as this, is owned and posted by students anonymously, will you have any recourse to a potentially libelous posting?

# Section A. Determining the Quality of Materials

Though you already know this well, it bears repeating that good teaching requires the testing, or piloting, of materials. Distance learning requires this type of evaluation more so than other teaching modalities, due to the sometimes-absent instructor. If the instructor is not present to clarify questions or provide direction, students will waste time and become frustrated. Formative evaluation principles would urge you to test your materials to ensure the following:

1. Availability of required materials

2. Clarity of content

3. Specificity and logic of directions

4. Accuracy of Web links (if used)

5. Lack of conflict in content, deadlines, etc.

6. Variety of learning approaches

7. Evaluative tools used

Time spent verifying areas, such as these, will result in reduced panic among students. Additionally, formative evaluation allows you to test a variety of teaching techniques for effectiveness before your students come to class (Holmberg 1995).

# Section B. Determining Benefits of Distance Learning Technologies to Learning Outcomes

Consider this: A well-focused teacher who wants to create the best learning experience for students, but who is also aware of the increasing societal importance of standardized test scores and, in many cases, the linkage of these test scores to salary/raises and state rankings, should still be focused on the student's total experience in the classroom. With this in mind, how will distance learning modalities enhance (not replace) the traditional teaching/learning experience?

Teachers often develop learning activities that focus on content appreciation, presentation, practice, and review. Of course, these are not only the categories of activities used in classrooms, but these categories also follow the purpose of much of the structured teaching today and should be easily recognized by any experienced teacher or administrator, regardless of their experiences with distance learning technologies. "Evaluations based solely on participant reaction or numerical counts do not attack the central question of whether learning has taken place" (Hall and Nania 1997, 373). We know that this type of evaluation is often the easiest or most convenient, but it does not produce sufficient data to make decisions about the student's level of learning. Would you ever consider asking final exam essay questions, such as "How did you like this course?" or "How did you feel about your assignments?" This is not to say that this type of question does not have its value, rather it is just that this is not the question you want to ask to assess if your students learned the content. Likewise with distance learning, in view of the investments being made in the delivery and support of these technologies, we must research whether these investments are positively impacting learning. Otherwise, it will be difficult for administrators and legislators to justify programs and purchases, such as laptops, for students without seeing evidence of increases in student learning (*Edupage*, 15 September 2000, and 4 December 2000). With distance learning funding estimated to be $7 billion by 2003, this justification is critical (*Edupage*, 16 February 2001).

Can we truly evaluate the impact on distance learning with the measures that are commonly used today? Teachers that were involved with the measurement of student performance in the Star Schools Program in Iowa reported that student achievement was not indicated on their standardized tests and that the improvements were in the areas of assignment quality and the use of higher-order thinking skills (Maushak and Chen 2000, 224). The need to evaluate the learning modality for the type of critical thinking skill that it promotes becomes increasingly apparent as we realize that distance learning must provide opportunities for students to respond in ways that encourage constructive and collaborative learning (Jonassen 2000).

## Interactive Distance Learning Activities for Appreciation

Some of you may remember the days when field trips and auditorium programs that emphasized art and music skills were part of the learning experiences that broadened perspectives and provided the venue for teaching in contexts that promoted positive social behaviors, cultural appreciation, and active learning. Societal changes and school structures do not support many of the field trips or other activities that you might remember as brightening the school term. Most teachers want to include learning activities that are designed to provide appreciation, or exposure or awareness, of a topic, but because of the drive of school districts nationwide to increase test scores, these enrichment activities are decreasing. True, we can usually make good arguments that, indirectly, activities for appreciation will eventually benefit learning outcomes, but most educators recognize that these benefits are very general and difficult to measure. In the meantime, parents, building-level administrators, and school board members are using standardized test scores to put increased pressure on teachers to focus merely on cognitively oriented activities that translate into higher test scores. Many educators argue against stripping the curriculum of all cultural and behavioral activities, in favor of only teaching to the test. As you are designing interactive distance learning activities, keep in mind that you can creatively incorporate and relate these areas into your curriculum, but within the framework of time on task and performance on test scores.

## Learning Possibility

Look at your state's department of education Web page. Do you find a link to any report that compares student achievement on test scores by individual schools by county (district, township, or borough)? For example, the state of Florida offers the *Florida School Indicators Report* (http://info.doe .state.fl.us/fsir/) that profiles each public school by categories (e.g., number of students, number of students on free or reduced lunch, students with disabilities, gifted, Limited English Proficient, average class size, number of suspensions, absences, scores on state standardized tests, number of teachers with master's degrees or higher, average number of years teaching, composition of staff [by instructional, administrative, support], per pupil expenditure, and school operating costs per student). The state of New Jersey offers its *NJ School Report Card* (http://www.state.nj.us/njded/reportcard/index .html) with similar data. If this information is available for your state, how will you use it to compare learning outcomes in your district or in other districts? What are the characteristics of the schools that have the highest and lowest standardized test scores?

There is no doubt that this category of learning for appreciation is often neglected, yet it is a very important part of what is enriching for students and, as a result, has tremendous potential for lifelong learning. Without appreciation activities, where do students learn to sing, dance, develop artistic talents, run, work and socialize with peers, sit attentively during an assembly program, or memorize lines for a school pageant? We often hear from textbook-bound teachers that there simply is not enough time to cover all of the materials that need to be covered for the test.

## Learning Possibility

List as many opportunities as you have in your classroom for appreciation activities that can be keyed to your curriculum. Search for audio, online, or video materials that will support these activities. What would the distance learning equivalents be for these appreciation activities?

Fortunately, interactive distance learning activities help us to bridge some of these important gaps in the curriculum that have been unattainable, yet how are we measuring these benefits and outcomes? To ensure that learning is occurring and also to justify the activity, first determine how to tie in the appreciation activity with existing course content. No activity should occur in isolation. After all, this was the argument that, in many cases, caused the appreciation activities to be diminished in the first place.

## *Learning Possibility*

Imagine that you are teaching your students about the history of computers and you want the students to look at actual examples of computing machinery. There are many online sites that provide interactive activities and online galleries, such as *The Computer History Museum* (http://www.computerhistory.org) or the *Obsolete Computer Museum* (http://www.obsoletecomputermuseum .org/). Students can view pictures, displays, and even participate in some interactive activities that are designed to provide background on computing history. Because you, the teacher, have visited these sites in advance and have decided exactly what will be the focus of the activity, you will have a "museum plan" that directs the student to exact links and asks for responses to questions that you will ask. For example, you can direct your students to the *Computer Museum of America* (http://www.computer-museum.org) where they can look at the 1973 IBM Speakers Bureau Slide Show and find at Slide 112 a picture of the ENIAC. On the activities list, your question to the students might be "What does ENIAC stand for?" or "Who submitted the plan of design for the ENIAC?" or "Who were the first programmers for the ENIAC?"

Provide self-guidance as well as direction for students for time on task and evaluation by using printed directions or activities lists and a grading rubric. A good grading rubric communicates to students that they will be evaluated by specific criteria. These criteria should be objective based and reflect the level of importance of the criterion to the activity or assignment.

## *Learning Possibility*

We've all experienced the frustration of receiving grades on assignments and not understanding why we received the grade we did. By creating a rubric, you can help your students understand that having their work evaluated and receiving grades can be more predictable. A rubric is a list of the criteria against which the students are being graded, along with a possible range of points for each criterion. You can get online help with developing rubrics at *Rubistar* (http://rubistar.4teachers.org/). Rubrics are waiting for you in a variety of categories (science, research and writing, math skills). These existing rubrics can be revised and printed for use with your students.

If you ask students to search for items on a WebQuest or participate in a chat project, they will review and complete their assignments, focusing on the areas of importance as you have outlined in their activities sheet and grading rubric. If you create a few of these worksheets and rubrics each year, you will acquire a collection of rubrics in a few years. Even better, try meeting with a like-minded distance learning teacher who wishes to cocreate and share the activity sheets and rubrics. Remember, because of the conveniences of distance learning, this peer does not have to be local.

# Interactive Distance Learning Activities for Content Presentation

When designed for content presentation, interactive distance learning activities should be specifically keyed to the lesson's goals and objectives. For content presentation, think of how to evaluate the activity as it benefits learning outcomes. Just as you know how to determine if students have learned content in a lecture-based or group learning experience, you will have to determine if students learn content in an interactive distance learning activity.

Options for this type of assessment could include evaluations that are paper based (book report, research paper, written report, test, worksheet), oral (individual questions, live or through a lab situation), a student presentation (audiotaped, broadcasted on closed-circuit network, live, videotaped), or a demonstration or interpretation (creating a bulletin board, game, model, a video reenactment, designing a multimedia presentation or Web page, developing a time line, drawing a picture, chart, or tessellation). Remember, as you set your objectives for the learning activity, include criteria that measure the degree to which the student must demonstrate the learning.

## *Teaching Possibility*

Imagine that you are teaching fourth-grade math students to recognize geometric patterns. To demonstrate that a star shape is interconnected triangles (and to also tie this activity into American history and the development of the American flag), you might take the students to the *Betsy Ross* home page (http://www.ushistory.org/betsy/) where they can learn to make perfect five-point stars with one cut of the scissors. This activity combines math and social studies, while presenting students with a hands-on learning opportunity. As students work to follow directions, the teacher can also introduce elements of cause and effect. After completing the star, the students have to "deconstruct" it by cutting the points off. What will be the shape of the "center" of the star that is left? Students answering this question correctly can receive full credit for participation in the activity.

Let us reflect on this learning possibility and its relation to distance learning activities. Assuming that you have convenient Internet access in your classroom or in the media center, this learning possibility made it possible for you to present a fourth-grade lesson on the recognition of geometric patterns with a concurrent lesson on American History. This activity used an age-appropriate manipulative (paper and blunt scissors) that should have also reinforced spatial and critical thinking. Thus said, would it have been possible to present this lesson without the support of a distance learning technology? The answer is yes. Perhaps you have a traditional workbook that includes this activity, or perhaps you knew that the five-point star is included in many encyclopedia articles on Betsy Ross. However, distance learning modalities, in this case as a curricular resource for the teacher, greatly facilitate the development of a fun activity that may not be known by all teachers. With this activity, the student will show and tell the teacher which patterns, when combined, form to make the star. The student believes that this is just a fun activity, without realizing that evaluation is part of the teacher's goal.

Evaluation of learning outcomes is an area that we need to continue to address at the PreK–12 level. In addition to the studies cited in the Thomas Russell bibliography that collectively show no significant difference among distance learning modalities, studies continue to show that the no significant difference extends to outcomes based on learning styles of some student characteristics of a group of business educators (Truell 2001). Dominguez and Ridley (2001) found no significant differences between online and traditional course preparation for students who were going to continue a university program of study. At the PreK–12 level, a study of students participating in the WEB Project that assessed student performance for multiple years found a relationship between metacognition and motivation and metacognition and inquiry (Sherry et al. 2001). For additional action research related to this project, visit the *Action Research* page (http://www.webproject.org/action.html) at the *WEB Project* (http://www.webproject.org/home.html).

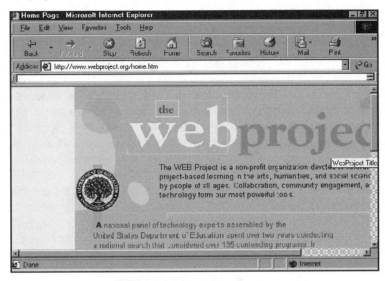

*WEB Project* **Web site: http://www.webproject.org/home.html**

For additional information, monitor the literature to look for additional evidence that distance learning promotes metacognition and increases student performance. Until then, think about how to help teachers conduct meaningful research while facilitating distance learning.

Studies conducted with postsecondary students suggest that distance learning students were more positive about their distance learning experiences than their face-to-face peers (Digilio 1998; Hogan 1997; Jones 1999; Klesius, Homan, and Thompson 1997; McCollum 1997; Yellen 1997–1998). However, the literature does not yet reflect enough studies that compare distance student benefits and attitudes to face-to-face students. If you are beginning distance learning projects, this is an area that you will want to begin studying, after you have developed your distance learning delivery techniques.

Just as a personal challenge, try to think of as many content presentation areas as possible for which you would like to have at least one distance learning tie-in. Share this list with your colleagues, media specialists, and educational technologists and ask them to be on the lookout for resources that would support each presentation area. You will be surprised how quickly your collection of distance learning activities will accumulate.

## Interactive Distance Learning Activities for Practice

Again, assuming that you will be focused on a lesson's goals and objectives, practice activities will be evaluated as they benefit learning outcomes. Practice activities that go along with interactive distance learning can be varied. In most American school systems today, we continue to conduct paper-based activities. Whether desired or not, based on your school and district directives, it may be a good transition for students and teachers new to the distant learning modalities to demonstrate their practice activities by using paper activities, such as scavenger hunts, fill-in-the-blank forms, and guided question activities. Do not forget that it is important to vary the modes of response to help students practice demonstrating their multiple intelligences. For example, ask students to recite the practice, illustrate the practice, demonstrate their practice, or develop their own product that demonstrates their practice. Remember, one of the driving forces for incorporating distance learning activities into the educational process is to help students and teachers learn in new and different ways.

## Learning Possibility

There is no doubt that students have a need for practice when learning multiplication tables in the third grade. Did you know that we base many of our mechanical learning tools for multiplication on "Napier's Bones"? You can view a demonstration of how Napier's Bones are applied to multiplication tables (http://www.cee.hw.ac.uk/~greg/calculators/napier/demo.html). How could you use *Napier's Bones in Various Bases* (http://cut-the-knot.com /blue/Napier.shtml) and ice-cream sticks to encourage students to create their own study guides for the tens or twelves tables? For other interactive math activities, be sure to link to *Interactive Mathematics Miscellany and Puzzles* (http://cut-the-knot.com/content.html) and (http://cut-the-knot.com /Curriculum /index.html).

Students can also benefit from using distance learning activities when the teacher agrees to create audiotapes (CDs) or videotapes (Webcasts) that offer oral dictation or practice for repetition of content, orally or written. For example, a Latin teacher can audiotape or videotape the vocabulary lessons for each section of the text. At the end of each day, when perhaps there is too much time to be used as free time and not enough time to begin a new activity, the teacher can play a tape that guides students through practice of spelling words, providing definitions of words or providing words for definitions. Many parents would be happy to provide blank tapes or CDs for duplication so that students could bring their own tapes home for practice each day. Online practice activities could also be created by using audio or video clips in Web pages. (Did you know that instruction in Latin is being revived in the United Kingdom with online assignments and multimedia used for language practice and instruction in Roman culture [*Edupage*, 17 January 2001]?)

Evaluation of practice activities implies a code of ethics on the part of the learner. Of course for younger students, you could ask parents to verify practice of the activity through their signature on a practice log. Wouldn't this be a great way to communicate to parents what their students will be practicing, along with involving them in their students' practice?

## Learning Possibility

Many young students (and adults) have problems with spatial skills required for using the mouse. For older students and adults, you probably already recommend playing electronic solitaire (you will find solitaire in Windows, under Start/Programs/Accessories/Games; please check with your principal or district policy first to make sure that the use of this game is acceptable for your school or community) or aviator. (Do you know how to find an "Easter egg" through the Excel spreadsheet program? For directions to the Excel "Easter Egg," go to the *Easter Egg Archive* [http://www.eeggs.com].) Younger students can practice "mousing" skills with an online puzzle at Random House's Web site (http://www.randomhouse.com/seussville/games /greeneggs). When the students are able to complete the puzzle in less than two minutes, you know that they are successful "mousers." Or students can practice with the *Lorax's Save the Trees* game (http://www.randomhouse .com/seussville/games/lorax). Students catch ten seeds in a basket, and then they get to plant the seeds.

## Interactive Distance Learning Activities for Review

Just as you evaluate for appreciation, content presentation, and practice, you will also evaluate review activities. Was the content learned? How will students be able to demonstrate that they have learned the content? In the past, students presented plays and pageants, demonstrating what was learned in the classroom. Most weeks, they had also looked forward to participating in spelling bees. Today, we can revive and refine that tradition in electronic ways. For the former example, students can videotape classroom plays and pageants and share their performances with sister classrooms, allowing the other class the opportunity to share, along with critiquing the performance. The performing students benefit from having other students involved in a formative evaluation of the performance before going onstage. For the latter example, students can arrange their own private spelling bee practice by downloading software that approximates the experience.

### *Learning Possibility*

*My Spelling Bee* (http://members.aol.com/Myspellbee/) allows users to tailor the program to their current needs through adding their own spelling words to the list. (Warning: Prior to downloading any software, be sure to verify local policy and procedures. Does your local network allow downloading? Which software programs do you use to check for viruses prior to downloading?)

## *Section C. Establishing Grades*

If we are willing to vary the learning modalities and teaching styles in our classroom, we need to be able to vary the evaluation styles. For example, if you are interested in developing portfolios, distance learning activities offer all kinds of possibilities to vary the evaluation process in ways that expand student and teacher portfolios. However, be sure that the product is keyed to the learning goals and objectives and that it does actually evaluate the learning. Remember that PreK–12 students will experience a wide variety of evaluative activities during their school experiences. Unfortunately, in more cases than not, these evaluative activities are not as learner-focused as they could be. Why should evaluation be learner-focused? Many educators believe that the evaluation should be a learning activity as much as it is a diagnostic tool. The process of evaluation can affect the student positively by encouraging analysis, practice, repetition, reinforcement, and synthesis of the content. How do you evaluate your students? How have *you* been evaluated? Just about all of us have had the experience of receiving a graded paper with a summative grade posted at the top of the first page. What does the grade mean, if it is not accompanied by appropriate descriptions? How do these two evaluation comments differ?

Comment 1: Good job, Gail. Your grade is B.

Comment 2: Good job, Gail. Your grade is B. You have identified ten Internet sites that apply to the history of computing. You have also summarized each site so that the reader knows if it would be productive to access the site. Did you forget to include your introduction and conclusion in the paper? (In addition to reviewing the content of your paper, please be sure to proofread carefully. I am going to e-mail you some practice exercises that will help you review spelling, punctuation, and capitalization rules.) Please see the electronic comments I have inserted throughout your file. (Hover over the highlighted areas so that a pop-up box appears. I have also recorded several comments for you to listen to with your headset.) Keep up the good work!

Obviously, whether included in distance learning or not, the evaluated activity should provide as much information as possible. Full and specific feedback will help the student who needs and wants as much information on his or her performance as possible. In the example above, the student, a distance learner, receives far more specific feedback in Comment 2 than in Comment 1. If you are a distance learner yourself, which comment would help you improve upon your next assignment, if your teacher were not physically present in your class?

Agreeing that specific and complete evaluation is desirable, and if instruction is increasingly based on a distance learning modality, how will you modify your evaluative activities for your students?

## Scenario

Imagine that you are a social studies teacher that has used e-mail, a chatroom, Web boards, and online databases in the presentation of a one-week theme on the ecology of the Amazon rain forest and its impact on the American economy. Your students have been fully engaged and the teaching/learning activity was positive for all. Not only was the activity fun for you, the instructor, but it was also obvious that your students entered class enthusiastically each day that you worked on rain forest activities. You have experienced a great deal of self-satisfaction about your work to incorporate distance learning technologies in a meaningful way for your students. Now you are wondering how to conclude this activity with an evaluation.

---

Think of the enjoyment that students have experienced during the past week. Doesn't it make sense that the evaluation of student learning should likewise be an enjoyable and meaningful learning experience? You will probably agree that using a paper-and-pencil multiple-choice test to evaluate the distance learning rain forest experience will not enhance this experience. Make your evaluations meaningful and consistent with the other elements of the learning process. How? Think about using the same medium for evaluation as you used for instruction. For example, for this scenario, you could develop a grading rubric that lists the elements that will be evaluated in a multimedia presentation produced by the students, either singly or as small groups, that projects the impact of the rain forests on medical care in the United States. Because the rubric will indicate the emphasis of your evaluation, students can use it as they are developing their multimedia presentations, guaranteeing that the content and quality will be addressed as you, the teacher, have determined. Appropriately, the students will be applying the knowledge they have gained through their study of the Amazon rain forest.

If you are thinking that deciding how to evaluate your instruction in a more up-to-date method is a difficult task, you have something in common with the educator who is beginning to work with distance learning activities. Perhaps you remember the concept of test reliability and test validity from your days in an educational course, such as Educational Foundations 101. Although some of your colleagues may not have had, or taken, the opportunity to even think about evaluative alternatives, you are proactively considering this issue as you spend time reading this handbook.

## *Learning Possibility*

In case you do not have grade book software in your school, you can find online directions for creating a grade book using Microsoft Excel at the Microsoft Web site (http://www.microsoft.com/education/default.asp?ID= ManagingGrades) (Managing Grades with Excel 2002). The method used to locate this source demonstrates that a distance learning modality can be used to locate instructions on how to use a local applications package. Even though you are not working directly in a distance mode, you can use distance learning modalities to support your teaching actions. (If you are a technology trainer, you can use this tutorial, along with the provided PowerPoint presentation.)

Before leaving this section, a discussion of portfolios is appropriate. We should recognize that portfolios are receiving a great amount of attention in the profession. As always, be sure to evaluate any process through the literature before implementing it in the classroom. *Portfolio Assessment* (Albert 1996) (http://askeric.org/Old_Askeric/InfoGuides/alpha_list/Portfolio_Assessment-5.96.html), an AskERIC InfoGuide, provides examples and a wealth of background information on portfolios. An ERIC Digest, "Electronic Portfolios: A New Idea in Assessment" (Lankes 1995) (http://www.ed.gov/databases/ERIC_Digests/ed390377 .html), is also available through the ERIC Database. As you are considering the use of the portfolio, be sure to understand that portfolio development requires a full understanding of the purpose of the portfolio. By creating a grading rubric, you are setting the criteria that will be used to evaluate the portfolio that will also guide the student in creating the portfolio. Together, the portfolio and rubric will serve as important tools that document the prior learning. In addition, thought should be given to who will be evaluating the portfolios and where the contents will be stored.

- Will your portfolios be paper based?

- Will your portfolios be electronic?

- How long will the contents be saved and by whom?

- Will they require scanning and inputting?

- Who will take care of the electronic management of the portfolios, and at what cost?

- Will your portfolio be the sole basis for grading? If so, what will you do to establish estimates of reliability and validity for the portfolio evaluation process?

A full discussion of the portfolio process points out that portfolios can have a variety of applications (Martin 1999, 83). These include:

1. Accountability (student work combined with teacher records)

2. Admission

3. Developmental (developed for personal, as opposed to evaluative, use)

4. Educational (student progress)

5. Electronic

6. Employment

7. Learning

8. Proficiency (student competence)

9. Showcase

10. Teacher

11. Working or collection

Just as students and teachers would tailor résumés to support particular job objectives, portfolio format and content can vary due to purpose. Questions to keep in mind as you are developing the portfolio are "What does this portfolio item demonstrate?" and "How does this portfolio item contribute to the overall purpose of the portfolio?"

Beyond classroom use, it is quite possible that you will be creating a portfolio sometime in your own career for purposes of documentation and evaluation of professional activities. If you are applying for national teacher certification (*National Board for Professional Teaching Standards* [http://www.nbpts.org/]), you will become well aware of the portfolio development process where you collect samples of your classroom materials, student work, and videotapes of classroom presentations to document your classroom interactions with students and reflect on how these samples help to demonstrate your effectiveness in the classroom.

In addition, some teachers collect materials for portfolios to take to job interviews, or to share during in-service presentations. However, just as you will need to develop an appreciation of this process by taking ownership, organizing, evaluating, reflecting, and preserving evidence of your professional and educational development, you will also need to instill this appreciation in your students. Without the recognition that the portfolio process itself is more than just saving bits and pieces of work in a folder, there is little benefit from this process.

# Section D. Determining Material and Personnel Costs for Budget Justification and Projections

Many educators and legislators realize that the continuing costs of technology in education have not been justified in terms of increased demonstrated student learning outcomes. The days of limited opportunities for student participation in the area of distance learning are over. Never before have we had as much potential for reaching out from our classrooms. In a time of five-cents-per-minute long-distance telephone calls, whether through the teacher's own cellular telephone or a classroom telephone, we are connected. Classrooms are being equipped with high-speed Internet connections, students are going home to computer workstations complete with cable modems that provide nearly unlimited bandwidth, and, as measured by Moore's Law, computing power doubles faster than ever. However, although we have what would appear to be unlimited opportunities, we do not have unlimited budgets, and we must ask what is the cost of this nearly unlimited distance learning infrastructure.

For years, we have enjoyed the luxury of working in a profession, education, that has not always placed a direct return on investment (ROI) dollar value on our teaching activities. However, if we wish to request funds to allow us to continue, or increase, our distance learning opportunities, we must be able to demonstrate that the costs of distance learning are reasonable. The Annenberg Foundation is a group that has focused on the costs of learning related to distance education. At its *Research and Evaluation* Web site (http://www.learner.org/edtech/rscheval/), you can find *The Flashlight: Phase I Report*, one of the first attempts to apply cost analyses to a large number of public schools. As evidenced through the program named *Flashlight: Tools, Methods, Strategies of Evaluation*, researchers realize that instructors need support with the development of evaluation studies, questions, and research designs. One of the activities of the Flashlight Project has been to develop actual questions and cost analysis processes that the educator can use to survey, interview, and further study the use of technology in education.

Distance education has been evaluated with multiple models, such as market research, institutional planning, educational psychology, and quality assessment (Calder 1995). Whether the purpose of the evaluation is to market, plan, provide information on the learner, or self-evaluate, the goal of evaluation is to gather information on the delivery of education. A form of research that is popular with educators today is action research—research that addresses problems and seeks solutions. Following the action research model, you will first state the problem and then you will begin to consider the data that will be collected. You will decide to whom the data will be reported and, finally, how to institute the solutions that were suggested through your collection of data. The action research model has been shown to incorporate technology in the gathering of data as well as with the problem-solving strategies (Woolls and Loertscher 1999).

The following action research guidelines have been provided by Dr. Thomas MacFarland (Senior Research Associate, Office of Research and Planning, Nova Southeastern University, Fort Lauderdale, Florida).

## *Action Research: Survey Guidelines*

To improve evaluation practices in the PreK–12 classroom and to satisfy the request by administrators and parents to show evidence that students are learning, many teachers engage in some type of survey research activity. This section will bring to your attention a few points to consider so that the surveys you create for classroom evaluations are focused and of high quality.

### STEP 1

When you consider creating a survey, determine your audience. Your audience may be your class population, or your audience may be a sample of students or parents. If you decide to use a sample, determine if the sample is representative of the population:

1. The population consists of all individuals who could reasonably be asked to participate in the survey.

2. The invited sample consists of all individuals who were asked to complete the survey.

3. The responding sample consists of all individuals who returned a usable survey.

#### *Population and Sample*

Consider the population (all potential respondents) and the sample (the respondents who are actually asked to participate in the survey). Ideally, the sample should represent a manageable number of subjects (like a class of students or all of the parents of one class of students) and it should be representative of the population. When you select a sample, be sure to decide how you will track the members of the sample to differentiate between the invited sample (those who are asked to respond) and the responding sample (those who actually respond to the survey).

### STEP 2

Prepare a survey that includes:

1. A header with the (a) name of the school and (b) name of the survey

2. A statement of the purpose of the survey

3. Instructions for survey completion

4. Questions asking for background information of the individuals

5. Questions focusing directly on the purpose of the survey

6. Directions for processing and returning the survey

### Survey Preparation

A brief survey that is well prepared and concise will receive more attention and result in a higher response rate than a long, confusing survey. As a general guide, do not send out a survey that is more than two sides of a single page, unless you have very unique needs and require an abundance of information.

As the survey is prepared, place an identifying header at the top of the first page that includes the name of school and the name of the survey:

## Charles Babbage Middle School

### Survey of Home-Based Technology Use

Immediately after the survey header, include a "Purpose of This Survey" statement. This statement should be simple and it should explain why participants should participate in this activity:

**Purpose of This Survey:** Charles Babbage Middle School wants students to use technology in a variety of distance learning initiatives. As part of a plan to develop good support services for distance learners, we need to know if students have personal computers, fax machines, and other forms of technology available to them at home or other places away from school. This survey has been developed to help gather information from parents about the availability of technology to students to help us develop plans to explore distance learning opportunities for all students at Charles Babbage Middle School.

---

Place directions on how to complete the survey immediately after the purpose statement. These directions should be simple. Do not assume that they are self-evident. Even if the survey has a cover letter, also include these instructions on the survey because cover letters are often misplaced by the time the participants actually complete the survey.

Immediately after the purpose statement and instructions for survey completion, include any background information requests that you plan to use. For example, do you plan to differentiate survey results between families that have a Macintosh PC (iMac) and a Windows-based PC? Do you plan to differentiate survey results between students in one grade level and students in another grade level? A sample follows:

What type of personal computer(s) do you have at home? Please mark all choices that apply:

_____ Macintosh

_____ Windows-based

_____ Other

What is the grade level for your child(ren) at Charles Babbage Middle School? Please mark all choices that apply:

_____ 6th grade

_____ 7th grade

_____ 8th grade

---

*Guidelines continue on page 244.*

Do not ask for any more background information than you plan to use. Too many questions may keep participants from responding to your survey and, in turn, reduce overall percentage completion rates. Ideally, you want to have more than a 50 percent response rate, so make it easy for participants to respond.

The next section includes the survey statements. These statements are very hard to construct and they take a great deal of planning and review by a broad group of teachers, administrators, and potential respondents. Things to consider:

- The purpose statement should offer guidance so that extraneous and off-topic statements are eliminated.

- Often a survey of excessive length will have a lower return rate than a survey that is more focused and of reasonable length.

What type of rating scale do you plan to use for the survey: 1 = Strongly Disagree to 5 = Strongly Agree, or will Yes/No responses meet your information needs? The following sample statements present the same concept, but using two different rating scales:

### Sample Statement 1

Our family has an adequate amount of technology at home to support our child(ren) at Charles Babbage Middle School (mark one selection only from the following scale):

_____ 1 Strongly Disagree

_____ 2 Disagree

_____ 3 Neither Agree nor Disagree

_____ 4 Agree

_____ 5 Strongly Agree

### Sample Statement 2

Our family has an adequate amount of technology at home to support our child(ren) at Charles Babbage Middle School (mark one selection only from the following scale):

_____ 1 Yes

_____ 2 No

———————————

Whichever scale you plan to use, be sure to review the statements so that their wording matches the scale. Also, avoid compound statements in your survey statements since they ask the participant to consider two topics, but they only allow one potential response.

The survey should end with processing and return directions. Be sure to provide a specific date (deadline), contact address, and contact person for survey return, and identify the person who prepared the survey and the date the survey was prepared. A sample on how to prepare this processing and return information follows:

Please use either the enclosed envelope or ask your child(ren) to return this survey to:

Charles Babbage Middle School
123 Main Street
Anytown, Florida 33429
Attention: Ms. Smith, Technology Coordinator
Surveys should be returned by October 1, 2003
Prepared by the Technology Office, September 2003

---

If you use the postal service to distribute the survey, provide invited respondents with a self-addressed and postage-paid envelope for survey return, and provide additional postage directions for processing returns through international mail, if your survey is far-reaching.

## STEP 3

Prepare a summary that describes how you analyzed and presented the data with the:

1. Use of a spreadsheet or specialized statistical analysis software

2. Presentation of results in the form of tables

3. Presentation of results in the form of graphs

### Data Analysis and Presentation

After the surveys are returned, how do you plan to tabulate the data? In most cases, a simple spreadsheet (Excel or Lotus 1-2-3) that reports frequency distribution and measures of central tendency (median, mode, mean, and standard deviation) should be sufficient. If you plan to attempt any type of statistical analysis, the spreadsheet could possibly be converted to a Minitab or SPSS data file.

References for data analysis and presentation include the following:

Data analysis tutorials (http://www.nyx.net/~tmacfarl/STAT_TUT/stat_tut.ssi)

Minitab Statistical Analysis Software (including access to a free thirty-day trial download of the complete software package) (http://www.minitab.com/products/13/demo/index.htm)

SPSS Statistical Analysis Software (http://www.spss.com/)

Finally, how do you plan to report survey results? In most cases, a simple presentation in the form of a table is adequate. Or, you may find it best to present outcomes in the form of tables and graphs. Review the literature for examples of tables and graphs and hints on how they are constructed. Fortunately, most software packages are quite user-friendly as they support the creation of easy-to-read tables and graphs.

*Guidelines continue on page 246.*

## *Action Research—Comparing Differences Between Groups*

To improve practices in the PreK–12 classroom and to provide evidence to administrators and parents that students are learning, many teachers conduct research projects that compare differences between groups to determine if there is a significant difference in behaviors. Here are a few points to consider so that your research activities are focused and of high quality.

### STEP 1

Determine the nature of the data you plan to collect. Data can be viewed as being either parametric (measured) or nonparametric (counted). Data can also be viewed as being nominal (named), ordinal (placed in order), interval (equal intervals between scores), or ratio (data with a true zero value, which allows percentage comparisons).

### STEP 2

Prepare a meaningful methodology that supports comparison(s) between groups, providing detail on the following parts of the project:

1. Who

2. What

3. When

4. Where

5. Why

6. How

Statistically analyze the data. In most cases, you will use one of the following statistical tests to compare diffrerences between groups:

1. Chi-Square

2. T-Test

3. Correlation (Pearson's Test and/or Spearman's Test)

4. Analysis of Variance (ANOVA)

5. Regression and Model Building

Prepare an interpretation of the statistical outcomes in the form of:

1. Tables

2. Graphs

3. Selected Levels of Probability

## DATA

Data can take many forms. As a classroom teacher, you may need to know if there are gender differences in technology skills, with the variable gender defined as B = Boys and G = Girls. Or, you may instead need to know if there is an association between test scores from a state-administered standardized test and attendance.

Data can be viewed in many ways. One way to view data is to differentiate between parametric data and nonparametric data. Parametric data are measured data. A combined SAT score of 1250 is a measured datum in that you have a reasonable expectation that someone with this score did better on the test than someone who had a combined SAT score of 925. Nonparametric data are counted data. For example, how many boys do you have in your class? This type of counting activity, based on gender in this case, yields a nonparametric datum.

Another way to view data is to create categories that are organized on the way data are quantified. It is generally agreed that there are four types, or levels, of data measurement:

1.  Nominal measurement. Nominal data are counted (or named) and are conveniently placed into predefined categories. Consider the number of males and females in a sample. Assuming that each subject can only be either male or female at any one time, the number of male subjects is a nominal datum.

2.  Ordinal measurement. Ordinal data are ranked data. As such, ordinal data allow greater inference than data associated with the nominal scale. Consider how family income is typically reported when viewing student records. Only rarely would you know the exact dollar amount of a student's family income. Instead, you typically know family income in terms of its place on a range of family incomes:

    $19,999 or less

    $20,000 to $29,999

    $30,000 to $39,999

    $40,000 to $49,999

    $50,000 or more

    This range is placed in order, thus the term "ordinal measurement."

3.  Interval measurement. Interval data are measured in equal intervals. Consider test scores on a 100-point test. The difference between a score of 89 and 90 is supposed to equal the difference between a score of 45 and 46. This scale represents equal intervals between data and they provide a level of precision that was not found with nominal data and ordinal data.

4.  Ratio measurement. Ratio data are like interval data, but ratio data also have two other very important characteristics: (A) Ratio data have a true zero and (B) Ratio data are real numbers and they can be subjected to standard mathematical procedures (e.g., addition, subtraction, multiplication, division). Because of this characteristic, ratio data can be expressed in "ratio" form. With ratio data, you can assume that fifty is truly twice the measure of twenty-five.

*Action Research continue on page 248.*

## METHODOLOGY

The planning and implementation of methodology for an action research project is often viewed as the most important part of the activity. The methodology should be written in narrative form, and it should explain in detail the following:

1. **Who.** Everyone involved with the action research activity must be identified. Be sure to describe how participants (e.g., researchers, subjects) were selected. Rarely does PreK–12 action research allow the luxury of random selection. Instead, you typically work with the students in your class only. If that is the case, be sure to describe who the participants were and how they were assigned to the activity.

2. **What.** Every score and measurement must be provided. Data are often presented in table format, or appended to the final report if the data file is too large.

3. **When.** Exact dates and times are essential for full identification of methodology. Regarding expected detail, the term (Fall Semester 2003) is acceptable, but the dates (2 October 2003 to 18 December 2003) would be more descriptive and meaningful.

4. **Where.** Within policy limitations, be as descriptive as possible in terms of setting. The term Charles Babbage Middle School; Anytown, Florida, is ideal, but local policy may limit you instead to use the broad descriptor, a middle school in southeastern Florida. What is most important here is to know if the location was in a real school setting or in a nonschool setting.

5. **Why.** Procedures must be justified and based upon sound principles of practice, but they must also be realistic. Perhaps in the perfect world, you would have the luxury of random assignment for students in your action research project. The reality, however, is that this practice is not possible under most circumstances.

6. **How.** The general sequence of actions should be so clear that a peer should be able to replicate the project.

## STATISTICAL ANALYSIS

Most action research in the PreK–12 classroom will be organized as a One Group Pretest/Posttest Design and the selected statistical analysis technique is based on the level of measurement associated with this project. In this type of design:

1. The researcher has an intact group (i.e., a class of thirty-two students).

2. The group is given a pretest assessment, to provide baseline measurement.

3. The group is then exposed to a treatment condition.

4. After a predetermined period of time, the group is then given a posttest assessment, to determine change (gain or loss) in scores or whatever measurement was previously assessed.

5. The data are then subjected to the most appropriate statistical test.

Imagine that you are an English teacher and that you have a group of ninth-grade students who are currently studying the play *Romeo and Juliet*. You decide to introduce distance learning activities into your presentations and students are encouraged to use resources on the Internet for a research paper about the play. You administer a pretest on Internet search strategies before class presentations and the same test is given to students six weeks later, after they have completed their research papers.

Using this scenario, the statistical test that you would use clearly depends on the level of measurement from the pretest-posttest instrument. If the data are nominal (counted), then you would typically use the Chi-square test. If the data are, instead, interval (measured in equal intervals), you would typically use a t-Test.

Common statistical tests used in PreK–12 action research are included in leading software packages and include the following:

1. Chi-Square

2. T-Test

3. Correlation (Pearson's Test and/or Spearman's Test)

4. Analysis of Variance (ANOVA)

5. Regression and Model Building

## PRESENTATION OF RESULTS

After data are obtained and statistical tests are completed, results are prepared, usually in the form of tables and graphs. Consider the following table and graph, based on pretest and posttest scores for boys and girls in a class of twenty-six students. Although the software generates a great deal of information, the basic organization of this scenario is:

1. Seven boys passed the pretest.

2. Five boys failed the pretest.

3. Six girls passed the pretest.

4. Eight girls failed the pretest.

5. The calculated Pearson Chi-Square test yields a probability value of .431. If you accept .05 as the selected probability level (as is the case in most PreK–12 research), the Chi-square results for this test provide evidence that there is no difference between boys and girls on pretest results. (The calculated probability value of .431 is *not* less than or equal to .05; therefore, there is no difference between the two groups, i.e., boys and girls, on pretest results.)

*Action Research continue on page 250.*

The following tables (properly referred to as contingency tables) are typical of the type of output generated by leading software packages.

### Crosstabulation

**Gender * Pretest Crosstabulation**
Count

| | | Pretest | | Total |
|---|---|---|---|---|
| | | Pass | Fail | |
| Gender | Boy | 7 | 5 | 12 |
| | Girl | 6 | 8 | 14 |
| Total | | 13 | 13 | 26 |

**Chi-Square Tests**

| | Value | df | Asymp. Sig. (2-sided) | Exact Sig. (2-sided) | Exact Sig. (1-sided) |
|---|---|---|---|---|---|
| Pearson Chi-Square | .619(b) | 1 | .431 | | |

Cost reviews have already shown that interactive distance learning technologies provide cost savings in adult student time (Fletcher 1994), but how else should savings be determined?

- By level of participant (student, teacher, technologist, administrator)?

- By function (planning, evaluating, supporting)?

- By cost of materials (personnel, hardware, software, connection charges)?

You can determine:

- Costs per student, in comparison with other delivery methods,

- Costs per student at different thresholds, i.e., are the costs per method the same, regardless of the number of students?,

- Overall cost of delivery method, including direct and indirect costs,

- Out-of-pocket costs for student, by delivery method, or

- Curriculum development costs.

How can you develop a plan to measure the costs? First, do you know the cost of offering a traditional course? You probably know what your district receives per student funding. You also know teacher costs. But do you know the overall administrative costs of your school? Or, do you know the overall operating expenses (principal, guidance, library, cafeteria, nurse, etc.)? How much does it cost for transportation of a student to and from your school?

In studying the costs of distance learning, what are the additional costs? One postsecondary model was identified for determining costs of distance learning, as well as prices charged, at a state-supported institution (Taylor, Parker, and Tebeaux 2001). These costs also included administrative costs. For public-supported institutions, you may be limited by board rule or legislation as to how much you can charge a student in your district, which may vary from what you are allowed to charge out-of-district and out-of-state students. Another model did not include administrative costs and only included direct costs (Karelis 1999). This model shows that costs do not continue to increase, even though enrollments increase. Then the question becomes, at what enrollment point do distance learning course costs equate to face-to-face costs? If grant money is used to develop the course, how will funds for future revisions be provided? Is it desirable to reduce, or share, development costs by offering the instruction to a variety of students in many districts? Or is it desirable to reduce development costs by purchasing packaged curriculum and delivery systems? Isn't this what we already do, in a sense, when we purchase reading curricula? These funding and cost options are being considered throughout the educational world, at all instructional levels. Caution must be taken to consider the instructional goals and objectives before allowing the cost models to drive the decisions. At what cost do we decide to continue original course development that is personalized for small groups of students? Conversely, what will be the price of delivering a packaged curriculum to large groups of students? The following questions should be asked in relation to costs of distance learning:

1. Can you take the overall costs and divide them by course? Or by enrollment?

2. Are there other fees that students have to pay?

3. What are the facility costs?

4. What are the equipment costs?

5. Are there special supply costs?

6. What are the book costs?

7. Are there other material fees?

8. Are there delivery costs (e.g., videoconferencing or Internet fees)?

9. What are the instructional support costs?

10. Are there telephone costs?

11. What are the special equipment outlay costs (per subject/per student)?

12. Will there be travel costs for faculty?

13. What are the faculty development costs?

Here is a question to consider: How does your school district charge students from other districts who want to take your distance learning courses? For help with answering these questions, explore the *Teaching with Independent Learning Technologies (TILT) Programme* (http://www.elec.gla.ac.uk/TILT /TILT.html). This project, based at the University of Glasgow in Scotland, promoted the idea that teaching and learning with technology is more productive. TILT was organized into six groups and described the different focuses of each group, including applying instructional technology to teaching, evaluating learning and cost, and organizing dissemination. What can we gain from the TILT Programme reports?

Whether you look at purchase orders or spreadsheets, the distance educator must consider the costs of:

1. Connection

2. Equipment

3. Hardware

4. Materials (printed)

5. Networking infrastructure

6. Software

7. Training

Of these, which cost is the greatest? Chances are that training costs will far exceed capital outlay costs. Not only does the training cost include direct costs, but it must also include costs of substitute teachers if the classroom teacher is attending daytime sessions.

The literature does not indicate an overabundance of formulas for cost accounting for distance learning. One simple formula is offered by Rumble (1992):

$$\textbf{TC} = \textbf{F} + \textbf{VS}$$
where $\textbf{TC}$ = Total Cost
$\textbf{F}$ = Fixed Cost
$\textbf{V}$ = Variable Cost (includes teacher salaries, curriculum costs)
$\textbf{S}$ = Number of students

This formula assumes that fixed costs do not vary, based on student numbers. Another formula (Chang et al. 1983, 136) is used to determine cost per student per hour (CSH). This formula takes into account:

1. The cost of *developing* instructional materials (Consider the hourly rates of personnel producing copy and any overhead costs. Can you estimate the price of developing a printed page? An electronic page? A Web page? A videotape? Are you including the price of supplies, clip art, etc.?)

2. The cost of *distributing* instructional materials to the users (Consider duplication costs in terms of personnel, supplies, and overhead costs.)

3. The cost of presenting the instructional materials to the users (Consider the costs of media, subscription fees, connection fees, supplies, and personnel.)

Therefore, CSH equals:

1. Costs of development of the instructional materials/average number of students per lifetime of the materials (companies are spending 30 percent of the training budget for e-Learning [Foshay 2001, 20]) plus

2. Costs of distribution/average number of students per distribution plus

3. Presentation costs/average number of students per presentation.

Can you apply this formula to a distance learning course in your school? Remember that you need to know the cost of a traditional course in your school to make comparisons.

PreK–12 educators are becoming more accustomed to justifying expenses, due to overall accountability and changes in school decision-making structures. Even though this higher level of justification is required, many schools are not aware of how hidden costs, such as utilities and service contracts, are figured into budgets. Return on investment (ROI) is a type of cost-benefit analysis that expresses costs saved for a particular institution. How can you apply ROI? For a more thorough discussion of methods used to estimate and evaluate costs of interactive distance learning technologies, consult Chapter 8, "The Cost of Distance Learning," in *Distance Learning: On the Design of an Open University* (Chang et al. 1983). Only through comparisons for your particular situation can you determine if distance education is more cost effective than face-to-face teaching, as suggested in the literature (Brent 2001; Cukier 1997).

Although most evaluative models should apply to distance learning, assuming that distance learning is no different from traditional learning, there is confusion over whether one format is more cost effective than the other. Perhaps this could possibly be due to personal preferences of those discussing the cost effectiveness, because they are concerned that if they show that distance learning has a greater delivery cost, the course could be put back in a traditional delivery model and vice versa. Concern over program change, due to either perceived or uncommunicated costs, is an educational reality. Also, keep in mind that the element of cost is only a part of the overall evaluation of distance learning.

At this point, we should address the purpose of the evaluation. What do we want to find out, as a result of the evaluation? If you agree that the purpose of distance learning is to support the mission, goals, and objectives of the school, then we should ask "How does distance learning support the mission, goals, and objectives of the school?" Therefore, evaluative questions (Calder 1994) could focus on how we monitor:

1. Progress toward the mission, goals, and objectives of the school

2. Teaching practices and support

3. Student learning

4. Student services and support

Hawkes (1996, 28) provides an evaluation model that addresses the role of both technology and teaching through:

1. Technical criteria of equipment requirements, specifications, and performance.

2. Instructional criteria of interactivity, integrative capacity, learner control, learner/instructor attitudes, and learner achievement.

3. Organizational criteria that describe daily distance learning use and the support and training required within the school setting.

4. Ethical criteria, e.g., how the distance learning technologies are used for all students.

Hawkes suggests multiple evaluative methods that can be applied to distance learning, such as participant observation, interviews, focus groups, document review (in-house records and plans), participant logs or journals, portfolios (of teachers and students), expert review, and case study. Validation can occur in the form of surveys, standardized tests, and experiments.

## Learning Possibility

Did you know that there is an organization (external agency), recognized by the American Council on Education (ACE), that reviews distance learning programs for secondary and postsecondary (through the master's level) institutions? It is the *Distance Education and Training Council* (*DETC*) (http://www.detc.org). Link to the *Useful Resources* (http://www.detc.org/content/usefulResources.html) or *Free Publications* (http://www.detc.org/content /freePublications.html) (*Is Distance Education for You?* [http://www.detc.org/downloads/IsDistanceEducationforYou.pdf]) to review many distance education links.

## Learning Possibility

*ACE* (http://www.acenet.edu/) also provides the *Distance Learning Evaluation Guide* (1996) as a criteria checklist to use for the evaluation of courses and programs. Addressing the categories of (1) learning design, (2) learning objectives and outcomes, (3) learning materials, (4) technology, (5) learner support, (6) organizational commitment, and (7) subject, the guide is easy to use and apply, regardless of the level of instruction. However, don't confuse ease of use with lack of depth, because the questions are pointed and thought provoking, e.g., under the category of learning materials (reading level), a question is "Is the reading level of instructional materials keyed to the reading competence of the average participant?" Before you jump to answer this question, further ask:

How would you describe the "average participant" in your program?

Do you know what the reading level is of the average participant?

How did you locate this information? By guess? By standardized test?

How have you evaluated your reading materials? By guess? By using a reading formula? (If you don't know how to use a reading formula, chances are that some other teachers in your school do not either. Because this information is critical to the learning process, request an in-service training program on using reading formulas to evaluate learning materials.)

---

## *Learning Possibility*

An online survey, *Barriers to Distance Education Survey* (posted by Zane L. Berge) (http://cgi.umbc.edu/cgi-bin/dharley/misc/barrier_survey.pl), a well-respected distance educator, assesses sixty-four possible "barriers," beginning with "accreditation issues" and ending with "inability to adequately monitor the identity of the DL (distance learning) participants/students." Completing and submitting this survey would fulfill quite a few distance learning needs for you.

If you have never seriously considered the many issues that could be barriers (or learning opportunities) for distance learning, completion of this survey would give you the chance to seriously consider these items for your school. Why not note some of these perceived barriers to share with your administrator?

Providing data to the profession is a responsibility we all share. Knowing that the results of this data will be well used should be a reward in itself! (Look for future publications by Dr. Berge that describe this survey.)

---

Consider this scenario: You have taken a position in a middle school as a technology coordinator that oversees two learning labs of forty computers each, along with seventy-five classrooms, each with school network and online access. In an attempt to standardize on one electronic mail package, the school's technology committee is considering Microsoft Outlook, Netscape Communicator, and *Star Office* (http://www.sun.com/products/staroffice/). Can you determine the financial impact of this decision?

| Cost Comparison of E-Mail/Browser Packages | | | |
|---|---|---|---|
| **Costs Using** | **Microsoft Outlook** | **Netscape Communicator** | **Star Office** |
| Additional hardware | | | |
| Enhanced networking infrastructure | | | |
| Software purchases for 155 computers | | | |
| Training costs for 75 classroom teachers | | | |
| Training costs for 2,200 students | | | |

As you found when completing this comparison, Star Office is available at a low cost and is used by many schools. Can you locate other freeware or shareware programs that can substitute for costlier office productivity software?

When estimating the costs of a software package conversion, you will also wish to include the costs required to convert archived files or messages from one format to the new format. Do not assume that all file formatting will transfer neatly from one software package to another. Also, do not forget that you need to determine not only the time on task to reformat and make file corrections, but you will also need to make some allowance for the work that will not be done while you are making the corrections. Though difficult to calculate, this cost is often overlooked. For example, if you are asking a paraprofessional to make corrections in a twenty-page manual, how will you compensate for not getting the telephone answered or not having in-class help with a reading group while the corrections to the manual are being completed?

Are your distance learning activities designed to provide appreciation, content, practice, or review? If evaluation is to be goal directed, then, in many cases, the evaluation activity for distance learning could be based on these four teaching purposes: appreciation, content, practice, and review. Remember that even NASA has to determine the cost per pound of launching payloads. Doesn't it make sense that you will be asked to provide similar quantification for your classroom activities?

For hardware, networking, and software costs, in many cases, these components are already being brought into PreK–12 schools, regardless of the desire of teachers to use distance learning modalities in the classroom. When considering the technologies available for instruction, first take an inventory of the existing equipment and software that can be evaluated for distance learning purposes.

Industry relies on reports of companies, such as the Gartner Group, to provide estimates of technology costs when they cannot be provided in house. The total ownership cost (TOC), based on a variety of variables depending on who is conducting the study, should include categories for:

1. Installing software

2. Performing upgrades

3. Installing, configuring, and tuning new servers

4. Adjusting existing servers and networks

5. Total replacement costs

Estimates, per user, depending on the study, range from $5,000 to $12,000. For PreK–12 schools, this is a rather wide range. To provide more meaningful data, the school would be wise to look at more specific numbers for an academic year (Sheehan 1998), for example:

1. Purchase costs (include hardware, peripherals, software, lab furniture, and subscriptions)

2. Support costs (include salaries of technicians and telephone support charges)

3. Expected life span of the materials

The following worksheet is a starting point for collecting data for estimating the total cost of ownership of hardware and software to support interactive distance learning activities.

| Hardware/Software Inventory Worksheet | | | |
|---|---|---|---|
| **Item** | **Manufacturer** | **Model** | **Number** |
| Server (designate the number of users) | | | |
| Desktop computer | | | |
| Laptop/notebook computer | | | |
| Hard drive (external) | | | |
| CD-ROM drive | | | |
| CD-ROM writer | | | |
| Monitor–15" | | | |
| Monitor–17" | | | |
| Monitor–21" | | | |
| Speaker | | | |
| Sound card | | | |
| Video card | | | |
| Modem | | | |
| Backup drive | | | |
| Storage media (CD-ROM, diskette) | | | |
| Fax | | | |
| Other peripherals | | | |
| Operating system license | | | |
| Operating system upgrade | | | |
| E-mail package | | | |
| Office productivity software | | | |
| Other software | | | |
| Laser printer | | | |
| Color printer | | | |
| Scanner | | | |
| Personal data assistant (PDA) | | | |
| Videoconferencing workstation | | | |
| Interactive whiteboard | | | |
| Distance learning software license | | | |

## *Learning Possibility*

Many districts simply are finding the cost of networking software to be too great. If this is the case in your district, and you are feeling adventurous, you can try to use *Linux* (http://www.linux.com/), an open source networking system. A companion site that will probably be needed is the Linux documentation (http://linuxselfhelp.com/). If you decide to go the open source route, don't forget that *Star Office* (http://www.staroffice.com/), an applications suite, and *Opera* (http://www.opera.com/), a slimmed-down Internet browser, are available for you and your students to use at little or no additional charge, other than your time to download and configure the software. Don't forget to first find out if downloads are permitted for your school's network.

---

Support costs can vary, based on services offered (Leach and Smallen 1998). Not only could support costs include the obvious costs of salaries of technicians and telephone support charges, but they can also include an apportioned part of district help desk services and Web development and maintenance. For districts that are putting elements of interactive video or Web courses online, costs for this development would need to be included as well.

Let us estimate that if you purchased 100 computers, a server, and a networking system ($300,000) that you expect to last for three years, supported by one technician who is earning $50,000 annually, including benefits (remember to include three years of salary), your major expenses for three years might be:

$300,000 expenses + $150,000 (salary for three years) = $450,000

$450,000/100 computers = $4,500 per computer/port for three years or

$1,500 per computer/port per year

Assuming that these figures would be accurate, your Total Cost of Ownership (TCO) would be $1,500 per year. Total cost of ownership does not provide the complete picture of technology in the classroom. For example, think of the number of hours that one of these computers is used. If the computer is in a lab environment, used seven hours a day, five days a week, for fifty weeks a year (in the case of a year-round school), it could possibly be used for 1,750 hours a year (5,250 for three years). If you divide $1,500 (TCO for one year) by the number of hours per use in one year, 1,750, the result is $ .86 (rounded) per hour. Working with the scenario a bit further, let's multiply $ .86 by twenty students per lab hour and the result is about $17.14 for a class to be in the lab for an hour. (This formula does not include the capital cost of the space allocated for the lab, electricity, insurance, etc.) Does this amount sound reasonable for your school?

Various formulas exist for determining systems costs. Be careful when deciding on a formula to consider all costs, along with all factors. In our example above, for example, if the technician is not the person who monitors the lab, an additional salary may need to be calculated for three years. Additionally, if you are developing software, Web products, or other instructional materials, these costs must be calculated. Based on the information you calculate through an analysis like this, you need to go a few steps further to calculate the scale barrier. The scale barrier for our example would be the point at which the costs of the technology-supplemented classroom are less than the costs of the traditional classroom (Karelis 1999). Actual development costs need to be considered when determining the scale barrier.

Other elements to determine when analyzing costs of distance learning include:

What access is offered outside the classroom? Outside the school building? In portable classrooms? What are the charges related to the access?

What types of other supporting media/materials are available?

What are the human resources capable of using this machinery?

What are the policies and procedures related to distance learning (copyright and fair use) and related charges?

What is the cost of in-house personnel available to provide support for distance learning?

What is the cost of district personnel available to provide support for distance learning?

Are there other local district, regional, state, or national charges related to distance learning courses?

Some states or state universities provide teachers and students with free e-mail and online access. How should these costs be attributed to distance learning expenses?

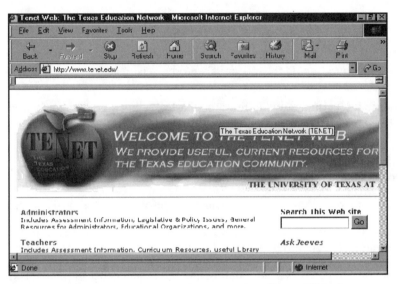

**The Texas Education Network at the University of Texas Web site:
http://www.tenet.edu/**

Distance learning teachers and administrators will be involved with the purchasing aspects of courses. Awareness of the practices, policies, and procedures required for the purchase of distance learning materials will alert you to the current levels of funding and economic purchases.

## *Learning Possibility*

It would be helpful to find listservs for guidance on how to get involved in the dollar cost of building a distance learning infrastructure. Go to *ERIC* (http://ericir.syr.edu/Virtual/Listserv_Archives/) and search the listserv titles. Select one of the listservs and search its archives for grant URLs.

If you would like to show a leadership role in distance learning in your school, get involved with the technology (or advisory) committee to support and help garner resources to support your school's activities. Participating on the curriculum committee will keep you current on opportunities to implement distance learning activities.

Many local businesses want to support their schools in financial ways. How are the schools in your area working with local businesses to obtain donated equipment, services, and software? Most districts have policy and procedure on donated materials, since old equipment that needs a great deal of maintenance does not especially help a school. Many local businesses support school efforts by giving additional purchase discounts.

If you are part of a school project for which initial software, hardware, and service costs are provided through grant support, be aware that your school will probably be required to pay all future costs. Therefore, consider how you will budget for this project once the grant support ends.

When investigating cost effects of distance learning, it might also be helpful to research:

- Absenteeism

- Parent satisfaction

- Student satisfaction (When asking questions relating to satisfaction, don't overlook asking how the course could have been taken otherwise.)

In addition, it is imperative to research the following student learning outcomes:

- Is there any noticeable decline or increase in behavioral referrals, i.e., disciplinary reports about students?

- Do distance learning students complete more assignments than face-to-face learners?

- Is there more student-teacher contact time before and after the distance learning experience?

- Can you correlate the technology budget to the use of distance learning technology? Can you correlate the technology budget to math or reading scores?

- Can you compare test grades before and after the teacher implements distance learning, using the same measures?

- Are final exam scores comparable?

- Have students improved their end-of-term grades after being involved in distance learning opportunities?

Statistical evaluations are important, but do not overlook how meaningful it is to share anecdotal records of student and teacher comments and testimonies about distance learning courses. Be sure to also note the comments that attest to the real-world limitations of distance learning. These will be important as you work to evaluate and improve the distance learning opportunities.

Keep track of your development time, in the same way that an attorney keeps a log of billable hours. This helps to place a value on distance learning from a teacher's perspective, separate from student learning outcomes. Because the initial development costs will probably be the greatest expenditure, you will want to spend your time developing a course that will be used more than once so that the costs can be distributed (Gaud 1999). Careful planning and developing will help to ensure that course quality is high and that reuse is likely.

Work with systems administrators to get a weekly report of Internet activity by class and by student if students are issued individual accounts. Find out the number of online connect hours to communicate how many students are on task, in addition to the cost of online activities. Assuming that many distance learning teachers maintain Web pages, be sure to run a counter on the class Web page to know how many times it is being used. Again, this provides a suggestion on the levels of student engagement with distance learning activities.

You may also need to be concerned with disposal costs of equipment, including computers and monitors. Many of the products used to create technology are toxic, so equipment cannot just be tossed into the garbage can. Equipment requires special handling and disposal by a company that has the resources and knowledge to dispose of it in an environmentally safe way. How can you avoid or reduce these disposal costs? You can try to refurbish or repurpose the technology and use it in another area (*Edupage*, 18 December 2000). There are several online sources for groups that are interested in donating and receiving recycled computers. Try to communicate with Usenet news groups such as *soc.org.nonprofit* or *k12.ed.tech* (look for more PreK–12 news groups at *Yahoo* [http://dir.yahoo.com/Education/K_12/Usenet/]).

What did the typical computer cost ten years ago? How would you compare these costs to the cost of a computer today? Compare the power of computers that are ten years old to today's computers. When you think about the changes, sometimes staggering, you must also think of the opportunities that are available to PreK–12 students and teachers today that were not available ten years ago, due to computing limitations. It was about ten years ago that we began multimedia developments. Prior, we did not have the luxuries of graphics, audio, or media. Even though there were distance learning opportunities ten years ago, it has been the development of computers that can now handle the memory capacity needed to deliver graphics, audio, and media online that has propelled the development of distance learning opportunities.

## *Learning Possibility*

Find a seasoned teacher in your local area who has used interactive distance learning technologies for at least one year. Ask about the costs of the distance learning activities for the year. Also, find out how much time it takes to learn a new technology, system, or opportunity for distance learning? How much time does it take to maintain currency with this technology? Are there any cost-benefits to using this technology? What is being saved in terms of time? In terms of dollars? How are those students benefiting from these activities? What are the improvements in student learning that the teacher has witnessed? Can this improvement be documented? What is your impression of how attuned this teacher is to all aspects of distance learning in that classroom?

---

Interview a principal with five or more teachers using distance learning, so that judgment is broad based and not an individual evaluation of specific members of the faculty. How does the principal support the distance learning? How are costs considered when working on budgets or giving permission for the implementation of distance learning activities in the schools? Because PreK–12 students are going to be largely campus based, do the principals have any view on how distance learning augments instruction, or do they merely see it as value-added?

In order to consider distance learning, administrators need assurance of:

1.  Future costs

2.  The geographic area of the school plant and students to be served

3.  Integration of proposed purchases with the current technology base

4.  User-friendliness

5.  Amount of capital outlay

6. Flexibility and upgrading of system

7. Costs of at-home support

8. Media center online resources

9. Human and family costs to engage in distance learning

# *Conclusion*

Because distance learning technologies have offered alternatives to the traditional classroom, we are beginning to reconsider how education operates. Once-established patterns are coming under question. Even the very nature of interaction, interactivity, is being questioned based on learning outcomes. There is evidence demonstrating that interactivity is not a requirement for learning (Mason 1994; Russell 1997). Your contribution to this element can be great if you will keep data that compares student achievement.

Ideally, education is education, whether it takes place through distance learning technologies or through traditional instructional methods. Therefore, some of the same issues will continue to be evaluated, such as class size (Johnson 1999), retention, grades, and student satisfaction and achievement (Martin and Rainey 1997). However, some issues mentioned in this chapter are unique to distance learning and warrant further study.

A few of the recommendations on how to accomplish studies in your interactive distance learning environment can be easily implemented. The body of literature on evaluating distance learning continues to grow. Evaluation models are being suggested, based on which models are appropriate to use for certain types of instruction. Certainly, the techniques to measure the effectiveness of using videoconferencing will vary from those used to assess performance using online tutorials or other technologies (Almstrum et al. 1996). As we continue to develop interactive distance learning technologies to use in classroom delivery, these assessment techniques will become more effective in helping us to make evaluative decisions about distance learning. Imagine the possibilities!

# *References*

Albert, Susan K. *Portfolio Assessment*, 2 May 1996, an AskERIC InfoGuide. (http://askeric.org/Old_Askeric /InfoGuides/alpha_list/Portfolio_Assessment-5.96.html) (4 January 2002).

Alstrum, Vicki L., Anders Berglund, Mary Granger, Joyce Currie Little, Diane M. Miller, Marian Petre, Paul Schragger, and Fred Springsteel. "Evaluation: Turning Technology from Toy to Tool: Report on the Working Group on Evaluation." Proceedings of the Annual Joint Conference on Integrating Technology into Computer Science Education, 2–6 June 1996, Barcelona, Spain.

Brent, Brian O. "Is Distance Education a Cost-Effective Alternative to Traditional Classroom Instruction?" *School Business Affairs* 67, no. 2 (2001): 33–39.

Calder, Judith. "Evaluation and Self-Improving Systems." In *Open and Distance Learning Today*. New York: Routledge, 1995.

———. *Programme Evaluation and Quality: A Comprehensive Guide to Setting Up an Evalaution System*. London: Kogan Page, 1994.

Chang, T. M., H. F. Crombag, K. D. J. M. van der Drift, and J. M. Moonen. "The Cost of Distance Learning." In *Distance Learning: On the Design of an Open University*. Boston: Kluwer-Nijhoff, 1983.

Cukier, Judith. "Cost-Benefit Analysis of Telelearning: Developing a Methodology Framework." *Distance Education* 18, no. 1 (1997): 138–52.

"Digital Diplomas," 16 February 2001, *Edupage* (owner-edupage@listserv.educause.edu) (http://www.educause.edu/pub/edupage/edupage.html).

Diglio, Ann. "Web-Based Instruction Adjusts to the Individual Needs of Adult Learners." *Journal of Instruction Delivery Systems* 12, no. 4 (1998): 26–28.

"Disposing of School Computers," 18 December 2000, *Edupage* (owner-edupage@listserv.educause.edu) (http://www.educause.edu/pub/edupage/edupage.html).

*Distance Learning Evaluation Guide*. Washington, DC: American Council on Education, 1996.

Dominguez, Paula Szulc, and Dennis R. Ridley. "Assessing Distance Education Courses and Discipline Differences in Their Effectiveness." *Journal of Instructional Psychology* 28, no. 1 (2001): 15–19.

"Ed-Tech Success Hard to Assess," 15 September 2000, *Edupage* (owner-edupage@listserv.educause.edu) (http://www.educause.edu/pub/edupage/edupage.html).

Fletcher, J. D. "Effectiveness and Cost of Distributed Instruction Technology." Proceedings, ED-Media 94—World Conference on Educational Multimedia and Hypermedia, 25–30 June 1994, Vancouver, BC, edited by Tom Boyle et al., 1996. ERIC ED 388 308.

Foshay, Wellesley R. "Can Instructional Design Deliver on the Promise of the Web?" *The Quarterly Review of Distance Education* 2, no. 1 (2001): 19–34.

Gaud, William S. "Assessing the Impact of Web Courses." *Syllabus* 13, no. 4 (1999): 49–50.

Hall, Michael L., and Sharon Nania. "Training Design and Evaluation: An Example from a Satellite Based Distance Learning Program." *Public Administration Quarterly* 21, no. 3 (1997): 370–85.

Hawkes, Mark L. "Evaluating School-Based Distance Education Programs: Some Thoughts About Methods." *NASSP Bulletin* 80, no. 582 (1996): 26–33.

Hogan, Robert. "Analysis of Student Success in Distance Learning Courses Compared to Traditional Courses." Paper presented at the Sixth Annual Conference on Multimedia in Education and Industry, 23–25 June 1997, Chattanooga, TN. ERIC ED 412 992.

Holmberg, Borje. *Theory and Practice of Distance Education*, 2d ed. New York: Routledge, 1995.

"Internet Latin Shows That It Isn't Stuck in the Past," 17 January 2001, *Edupage* (owner-edupage@listserv.educause.edu) (http://www.educause.edu/pub/edupage/edupage.html).

Johnson, Doug. "Will Small Class Sizes Improve Education?" *Knowledge Quest* 27, no. 3 (1999): 42–43.

Jonassen, David H. *Computers as Mindtools for Schools: Engaging Critical Thinking*. Upper Saddle River, NJ: Merrill, 2000.

Jones, Edward R. "A Comparison of an All Web-Based Class to a Traditional Class." Paper presented at the 10th Society for Information Technology and Teacher Education International Conference, 28 February–4 March 1999, San Antonio, TX. ERIC ED 432 286.

Karelis, Charles. "Education Technology and Cost Control: Four Models." *Syllabus* 12, no. 6 (1999): 20–28.

Klesius, Janell P., Susan Homan, and Theron Thompson. "Distance Education Compared to Traditional Instruction: The Students' View." *International Journal of Instructional Media* 24, no. 3 (1997): 207–20.

Lankes, Anna Maria D. "Electronic Portfolios: A New Idea in Assessment." *ERIC Digest*. Syracuse, NY: ERIC Clearinghouse on Information and Technology, 1995. ERIC ED 390 377. (http://www.ericit.org/digests/EDO-IR-1995-09.shtml) (4 January 2002).

"Laptops Pose New Challenge on Campus," 4 December 2000, *Edupage* (owner-edupage@listserv.educause.edu) (http://www.educause.edu/pub/edupage/edupage.html).

Leach, Karen, and David Smallen. "What Do Information Technology Support Services Really Cost?" *CAUSE/EFFECT* 21, no. 2 (1998): 38–45.

Martin, Elaine D., and Larry Rainey. "Student Achievement and Attitude in a Satellite-Delivered High School Science Course." In *K–12 Distance Education: Learning, Instruction, and Teacher Training*, edited by Michael G. Moore and Margaret A. Koble. University Park, PA: American Center for the Study of Distance Education, College of Education, Pennsylvania State University, 1997.

Mason, Robin. *Using Communications Media in Open and Flexible Learning*. London: Kogan Page, 1994.

Maushak, Nancy J., and Kuo-Tsai Chen. "Learners and the Learning Environment: Impact of Technology Use in K–12 Schools in Iowa." *The Quarterly Review of Distance Education* 1, no. 3 (2000): 215–24.

McCollum, Kelly. "A Professor Divides His Class in Two to Test Value of On-Line Instruction." *Chronicle of Higher Education* 43, no. 24 (21 February 1997): A23.

Rumble, Greville. *The Management of Distance Learning Systems*. Paris: UNESCO, International Institute for Educational Planning, 1992.

Sanders, Diana W., and Alison I. Morrison-Shetlar. "Student Attitudes Toward Web-Enhanced Instruction in an Introductory Biology Course." *Journal of Research on Computing in Education* 33, no. 3 (2001): 251–62.

Sheehan, Mark. "Considering Thin Client Computing for Higher Education." *CAUSE/EFFECT* 21, no. 3 (1998): 7–10. (http://www.educause.edu/ir/library/html/cem9832.html) (25 February 1999).

Sherry, Lorraine, Shelley Billig, Daniel Jesse, and Deborah Watson-Acosta. "Assessing the Impact of Instructional Technology on Student Achievement." *T.H.E. Journal* 28, no. 7 (2001): 40–43.

Taylor, Thomas H., G. D. Parker II, and Elizabeth Tebeaux. "Confronting Cost and Pricing Issues in Distance Education." *Educause Quarterly* 24, no. 3 (2001): 16–23.

Truell, Allen D. "Student Attitudes Toward and Evaluation of Internet-Assisted Instruction." *Delta Pi Epsilon Journal* 43, no. 1 (2001): 40–49.

Woolls, Blanche, and David V. Loertscher. "Testing the Effect of the School Library Media Center in a Block Scheduling Environment." *Knowledge Quest* 28, no. 2 (1999): 16–25.

Yellen, Richard E. "Distant Learning Students: A Comparison with Traditional Studies." *Journal of Educational Technology Systems* 26, no. 3 (1997–1998): 215–24.

# Afterword

## *What have I affirmed through writing this book?*

1.  A book on interactive distance learning technologies cannot be finished. Every time I read a newspaper or journal or went online, I would have a new snippet of information to include in this handbook. Knowing when I was finished, as opposed to deciding when to stop, has often interfered with my compulsion to collect articles, URLs, and scraps of fascinating resources. Fortunately, staff members at Libraries Unlimited seem to be able to accommodate this type of behavior, and I appreciate their patience.

2.  Our students are going to grow up to be very confused spellers! Techno-spelling requires that we capitalize within the middle of a word, we use "marketing" spelling instead of "dictionary" spelling, and we spell words any way we like—which will probably please most students. To those of you who are valiantly trying to teach your students correct spelling formats, trudge on. To those of you who have any influence on techno-spelling or marketing spelling, have a heart for the teachers who are trying to teach their students standard spelling skills.

3.  Speaking of spelling, electronic spell checkers and grammar checkers still leave much room for improvement. Please forgive any errors that I have made.

4.  Another bit of assistance that we educators can provide to our PreK–12 colleagues who are using distance learning technologies relates to stability of URLs. We are all guilty of trying to organize a better Web page, but is renaming that directory really worth the loss of the link by potentially thousands of visitors? Until the technology has met the demands of the ever-changing URLs, please consider that you may be disrupting tomorrow's lesson in the classroom. If you must change the Web address, at least try to provide a forwarding message from the previous URL. And for those of you who influence networkers and Webmasters, convey to them how they contribute to electronic confusion each time they change servers and URLs. (Do you think we could have a URL change moratorium once a year?) This problem has been noted more than once in e-mail messages and conversations as something that discourages the use of distance learning technologies.

5.  Many teachers believe that they don't have the time to use distance learning technologies. Successful teachers have learned to incorporate existing distance learning resources into the classroom, one item at a time. Then, as they become more confident using these resources, they begin to create and share some of their own resources. We encourage these teachers to continue their efforts and applaud their willingness to take a step into unfamiliar teaching territory.

6. Money follows success. If you want to get started with distance learning technologies, incorporate what you can do with what you have. As you become more adept with using distance learning technologies, you will be recognized by your peer teachers, your administrators, your students' parents, but most importantly by your students. They will give you the help and encouragement you need to continue and to seek support through grants and special funding. Don't overlook corporate sources of funding and partnering (Krebs 1999). At the *Distance Learning Resource Network* Web site (http://www.dlrn.org/library/dl/funding.html), you can review funding sources (Lane 2000) that have been used in other states.

7. There is an incredible body of literature, information, and data, in both print and electronic formats, that has been compiled by educators—and much of it is free for the searching. These resources have been compiled by educators who care enough to compile, compose, critique, and edit them for use by all of us. We are truly indebted to these educators for taking the time to create and capture these materials. As Odasz (1999) observed after his experiences with teaching Internet skills to communities in Alaska, "Quantity and quality of relationships are increasing" and "Instead of the 'information age' we have the 'relationship age.' " (2) Our colleagues have proven this to be true in the many professional, online relationships that they are developing. Their willingness to share and communicate resources and experiences has certainly perpetuated the rapid growth and acceptance of distance learning.

If you think that you may one day wish to pursue courses in distance learning, look at programs offered through the *United States Distance Learning Association* (http://www.usdla.org/), which has provided a listing of institutions that offer degrees in distance learning for PreK–12 (http://www.usdla.org/html /resources/dllp.htm). Because you are now aware of so many distance learning resources, I think you will find your own distance learning education to be quite rewarding.

Good luck to those of you who realize that interactive distance learning technologies provide us with incredible teaching and learning possibilities to share with our colleagues and students.

# *References*

Krebs, Arlene. "Funding K–12 Curricula and Technology," October 1999, *Converge*. (http://www.convergemag .com/magazine/story.phtml?id=2530000000001202) (23 January 2002).

Lane, Carla. "Funding Sources and Methods for K–12 Distance Education," 2 August 2000, Distance Learning Resource Network. (http://www.dlrn.org/library/dl/funding.html) (29 January 2002).

Odasz, Frank. "On the Frontier of Online Learning, in Galena, Alaska." *Multimedia Schools* 6, no. 2 (1999): 42–45.

# Index

# About the Author

Jan Yates has served as a teacher or media specialist at the elementary, middle, secondary, undergraduate, and graduate levels since 1976. She has also worked as an administrator at a community college. She has degrees in English (B.A.), Library Science (M.S.), and Information Science (Ph.D.), all of which were earned while she was either a nontraditional or distance learning student. Jan currently serves as the program professor of Computer Science Education and Educational Media in the Graduate Teacher Education Program of the Fischler Graduate School of Education and Human Services at Nova Southeastern University in Fort Lauderdale, Florida.